Dublin

timeout.com/dublin

Published by Time Out Guides Ltd, a wholly owned subsidiary of Time Out Group Ltd.
Time Out and the Time Out logo are trademarks of Time Out Group Ltd.

© **Time Out Group Ltd 2009**
Previous editions 1998, 1999, 2002, 2004, 2007.

10 9 8 7 6 5 4 3 2 1

This edition first published in Great Britain in 2009 by Ebury Publishing
A Random House Group Company
20 Vauxhall Bridge Road, London SW1V 2SA

Random House UK Limited Reg. No. 954009

Random House Australia Pty Limited 20 Alfred Street, Milsons Point, Sydney, New South Wales 2061, Australia
Random House New Zealand Limited 18 Poland Road, Glenfield, Auckland 10, New Zealand
Random House South Africa (Pty) Limited Isle of Houghton, Corner Boundary Road & Carse O'Gowrie,
Houghton 2198, South Africa

Distributed in the US by Publishers Group West
Distributed in Canada by Publishers Group Canada

For further distribution details, see www.timeout.com

ISBN: 978-1-84670-099-6

A CIP catalogue record for this book is available from the British Library.

Printed and bound by Firmengruppe APPL, aprinta druck, Wemding, Germany.

The Random House Group Limited supports The Forest Stewardship Council (FSC), the leading international forest
certification organisation. All our titles that are printed on Greenpeace approved FSC certified paper carry the FSC
logo. Our paper procurement policy can be found at www.rbooks.co.uk/environment.

Time Out carbon-offsets all its flights with Trees for Cities (www.treesforcities.org).

Time Out Guides Limited
Universal House
251 Tottenham Court Road
London W1T 7AB
Tel + 44 (0)20 7813 3000
Fax + 44 (0)20 7813 6001
Email guides@timeout.com
www.timeout.com

Editorial

Editor Sam Le Quesne
Deputy Editor Claire Boobbyer
Listings Editor Sam Le Quesne
Proofreader Cathy Limb
Indexer Lesley McCave

Managing Director Peter Fiennes
Editorial Director Ruth Jarvis
Series Editor Will Fulford-Jones
Business Manager Dan Allen
Editorial Manager Holly Pick
Assistant Management Accountant Ija Krasnikova

Design

Art Director Scott Moore
Art Editor Pinelope Kourmouzoglou
Senior Designer Henry Elphick
Graphic Designers Gemma Doyle, Kei Ishimaru
Advertising Designer Jodi Sher

Picture Desk

Picture Editor Jael Marschner
Deputy Picture Editor Lynn Chambers
Picture Researcher Gemma Walters
Picture Desk Assistant Marzena Zoladz
Picture Librarian Christina Theisen

Advertising

Commercial Director Mark Phillips
Sales Manager (GB and Ireland) Alison Wallen
Advertising Sales Hot Sales Ltd, Dublin

Marketing

Marketing Manager Yvonne Poon
Sales & Marketing Director, North America Lisa Levinson
Senior Publishing Brand Manager Luthfa Begum
Marketing Designers Anthony Huggins, Nicola Wilson

Production

Group Production Director Mark Lamond
Production Manager Brendan McKeown
Production Controller Damian Bennett
Production Coordinator Julie Pallot

Time Out Group

Chairman Tony Elliott
Group General Manager/Director Nichola Coulthard
Time Out Communications Ltd MD David Pepper
Time Out International Ltd MD Cathy Runciman
Group IT Director Simon Chappell
Head of Marketing Catherine Demajo

Contributors

Introduction Sam Le Quesne. **History** Claire Boobbyer, Sam Le Quesne. **Dublin Today** Bridget Hourican. **Architecture** Claire Boobbyer, Emma Cullinan. **Literary Dublin** Claire Boobbyer, Sam Le Quesne. **Where to Stay** Sam Le Quesne. **Sightseeing** Sam Le Quesne. **Restaurants** Sam Le Quesne. **Cafés** Sam Le Quesne. **Pubs & Bars** Eoin Butler. **Shops & Services** Sam Le Quesne. **Festivals & Events** Claire Boobbyer (*Chapter and verse* Sam Le Quesne). **Children** Sam Le Quesne. **Film** Sam Le Quesne. **Galleries** Sam Le Quesne. **Gay & Lesbian** Brian Finnegan. **Music** Eoin Butler (*A high price to pay* Mark O'Connell). **Nightlife** Eoin Butler (*Indie reign* Tanya Sweeney). **Sport & Fitness** Sam Le Quesne. **Theatre & Dance** Sam Le Quesne. **Trips Out of Town** Christi Daugherty, Liam Hourican. **Directory** Claire Boobbyer.

Maps john@jsgraphics.co.uk, except page 255, studio@graphics-it.com (Copyright Irish Rail) and page 256, the Railway Procurement Agency (www.rpa.ie).

Photography by Alys Tomlinson, except: page 14 akg-images/Erich Lessing; page 17 Getty Images; page 18 PA Archive/PA Photos; page 192 PA Photos, page 195 Ros Kavanagh.

The following images were provided by the featured establishments/artists: pages 29, 41, 154, 155, 158, 169, 185.

The Editor would like to thank Deirdre Geraghty, Aine Kavanagh and all contributors to previous editions of *Time Out Dublin*, whose work forms the basis for parts of this book.

Contents

Introduction 6

In Context 11

History 12
Dublin Today 22
Architecture 25
Literature 29

Where to Stay 35

Where to Stay 36

Sightseeing 53

Introduction 54
Trinity College & Around 57
Temple Bar & the Cathedrals 61
St Stephen's Green & Around 69
O'Connell Street & Around 78
The North Quays & Around 83
Docklands 87
The Liberties & Kilmainham 91
Dublin Bay & the Coast 95

Eat, Drink, Shop 99

Restaurants 100
Cafés & Coffee Shops 117
Pubs & Bars 123
Shops & Services 138

Arts & Entertainment 153

Festivals & Events 154
Children 159
Film 163
Galleries 167
Gay & Lesbian 171
Music 176
Nightlife 186
Sport & Fitness 191
Theatre & Dance 195

Trips Out of Town 199

Getting Started 200
Newgrange & the Boyne Valley 201
The Wicklow Mountains 207
Kilkenny & Around 213

Directory 219

Getting Around 220
Resources A-Z 226
Further Reference 237
Index 239
Advertisers' Index 244

Maps 245

Ireland 246
Dublin Environs 247
Dublin Overview 248
Dublin City 250
Central Dublin 252
Street Index 253
DART & Rail 255
Luas 256

Introduction

Dublin is a city that everyone raves about. Displaced locals get all misty-eyed about the pubs, the craic, the hilarious, friendly people they left behind; recently returned visitors wax lyrical on everything from the architecture to the seafood; tourist brochures conjure visions of a Celtic utopia where historic, cobbled streets always lead to a pint of Guinness and a traditional sing-song, where adorable shops and top-class restaurants are to be found on every corner. But, while much of that is in fact true, don't be surprised if you still find yourself feeling a little disappointed by what you find. The fact of the matter is that nowhere, not even the mythical 'fair city' of Ireland, can live up to that much hype. Dublin is no theme park to oirishness, nor is it some quaint provincial backwater where every second person is bubbling over with blarney and bonhomie. It is a modern, hard-working, affluent centre of commerce and industry; it is a cultural capital; it is home to some of Europe's most accomplished artists and academics. It is a city that deserves to be taken seriously. And, for those who do, it is a richly rewarding, fascinating place.

Of course, as is true of any great city, Dublin can be pretty much whatever you want it to be. Visitors who want to spend their days on the trail of the past will find beautifully preserved mansions and castles, meticulously curated museums, magnificent churches and cathedrals, and streets, parks and docksides steeped in the events of yesteryear. But if you'd rather sample the very latest flavours from today's top chefs or dance through the night to the sound of this week's white label releases, you can do that too. Simply put, Ireland's capital city is prepared to meet its visitors more than halfway, but only those who can be bothered to make an effort. Dublin does not wear its charms on its sleeve, you'll need to dig a bit to find something more lasting than the tourist schtick and the themed pubs and restaurants that line the sightseeing trails.

So make a detour down that side street, spend a few hours trailing through the parks and gardens, take your time in the museums, talk to people in the pubs, watch a hurling match, ride the DART out of town to Howth, Dalkey and Malahide, catch a play, or just sit on the Liffey boardwalk and let it all pass you by. Whatever you decide to do, you can rest assured that at least one of the clichés about this city really is true: Dublin genuinely does have something for everyone.

ABOUT TIME OUT CITY GUIDES

This is the sixth edition of *Time Out Dublin*, one of an expanding series of more than 50 guides produced by the people behind the successful listings magazines in London, New York, Chicago, Sydney and many more cities around the world. Our guides are all written and updated by local experts who have striven to provide you with all the most up-to-date information you'll need to explore Dublin, whether you're a local or a first-time visitor.

THE LOWDOWN ON THE LISTINGS

We have tried to make this book as useful as possible. Addresses, telephone numbers, websites, transport information, opening times, admission prices and credit card details have all been included in the listings, as have details of other selected services and facilities. However, owners and managers can change their arrangements at any time. Before you go out of your way, we strongly advise you

o call and check the opening times and other particulars. While every effort has been made to ensure the accuracy of the information contained in this guide, the publishers cannot accept responsibility for any errors it may contain.

PRICES AND PAYMENT

Our listings detail which of the four major credit cards – American Express (AmEx), Diners Club (DC), MasterCard (MC) and Visa (V) – are accepted by individual venues. Many businesses will also accept other cards, such as Maestro and Carte Blanche, as well as travellers' cheques issued by a major financial institution.

The prices we've supplied should be treated as guidelines, not gospel. Fluctuating exchange rates and inflation can cause charges, particularly in shops and restaurants, to change rapidly. If prices vary wildly from those we've quoted, ask whether there's a

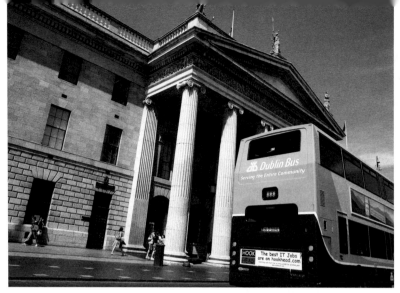

good reason, then please email to let us know. We aim to give the best and most up-to-date advice, and we always want to know if you've been badly treated or overcharged.

THE LIE OF THE LAND

To make both book and city easier to navigate, we've divided Dublin into areas, assigning each one its own section in the Sightseeing part of the book. These are: Trinity College & Around, Temple Bar & the Cathedrals, St Stephen's Green & Around, O' Connell Street & Around, The North Quays & Around, Docklands, The Liberties & Kilmainham, Dublin Bay & the Coast. These area designations have also been used in addresses throughout the guide, and are illustrated on the overview map on pages 248-9.

For all addresses given in the book, we've included details of the nearest public transport option(s) and a reference to the series of fully indexed colour maps at the back of this guide, which start on page 246. The locations of hotels (❶), restaurants (❶), bars (❶) and cafés (❶) have been pinpointed on these maps; the section also includes two transport maps (see pages 255-256) and a street index (page 253).

Advertisers

We would like to stress that no establishment has been included in this guide because it has advertised in any of our publications and no payment of any kind has influenced any review. The opinions given in this book are those of Time Out writers and are entirely independent.

TELEPHONE NUMBERS

The city code for Dublin is 01 (drop the 0 if dialling from outside Dublin). All phone numbers listed in this guide take this code unless stated. Mobile phones do not require the 01 prefix. We've identified premium-rate and mobile numbers, which will incur extra calling costs.

The country code for Ireland is 353. To dial numbers as given in this book from abroad, use your country's exit code (00 in the UK, 011 in the US) or the + symbol (on many mobile phones), followed by the country code, followed by the number as listed. For more on phones, including information on free and premium-rate numbers, see page 233.

ESSENTIAL INFORMATION

For all the practical information you might need for visiting the city, including customs and immigration information, disabled access, emergency telephone numbers, the lowdown on the local transport network and a list of useful websites, turn to the Directory at the back of this guide. It starts on page 220.

LET US KNOW WHAT YOU THINK

We hope you enjoy *Time Out Dublin*, and we'd like to know what you think of it. We welcome tips for places that you consider we should include in future editions, and take notice of your criticism of our choices. You can email us at guides@timeout.com.

> There is an online version of this guide, along with guides to more than 50 other international cities, at **www.timeout.com**.

In Context

History	**12**
Dublin Today	**22**
Architecture	**25**
Literature	**29**

Features

The house that Swift built	17
The rising tide	21
Change is abroad	23
The best Buildings	26
The importance of being Dublin	33

The Shaw Birthplace. *See p30.*

History

From Gaels and Vikings to asylum seekers, anti-corruption campaigners and Europhobes.

There is no conveniently straightforward answer to the question of how old Dublin is. Historians are forever deliberating over where to draw the line between seasonal, nomadic settlement and thriving village – from whence to trace Ireland's first and largest city. In 1988 the powers that be made the questionable decision to mark the city's thousandth anniversary, counting from the first imposition of taxes in Dublin, but the area around the city is known to have been inhabited in one form or another since around 8,000 BC. The Gaels, who arrived sometime around the first century AD, are believed to have come up with the name 'Dubhlinn' (meaning 'the black pool', probably referring to a tidal pool in the estuary of the now-subterranean River Poddle). The city's modern Irish name, Baile çtha Cliath, is derived from 'Ath Cliath' ('the ford of the hurdles'), believed to have been the name of an occasional Celtic settlement some 400 years earlier.

FIRST FOOTINGS

After the arrival in the early fifth century of the Welsh missionary Maewyn Succat, Dublin became the centre of one of the earliest Christian orthodoxies in Europe. Something of a golden age of Christianity followed, producing some of the finest religious art in the world, including the Ardagh Chalice, the *Book of Durrow* and, perhaps most famously, the *Book of Kells* (*see p58*).

By 841, Norwegian Vikings had established a permanent urban settlement in the area and were using Dublin as a base from which to plunder surrounding regions. Enriched Dublin became a powerful stronghold, and the first permanent dwellings were constructed near what is now Temple Bar.

Viking Dublin came under regular attack from the Irish after 936, particularly by Brian Borœ and Mael Sechnaill, the last great High Kings of Ireland. It would be Borœ who at last defeated them on Good Friday 1014.

Kilmainham Gaol.
See p18 and p94.

THE ENGLISH ARRIVE

The English stepped firmly into the Irish fray in 1166, after the King of Leinster (which included Dublin) was deposed by a neighbouring king. He turned to Henry II, King of England, for help. In return he offered to make Leinster subject to Henry's overlordship. As an added incentive, he promised his eldest daughter to whoever led the invasion.

And so it was that an expeditionary force, led by the Earl of Pembroke, Richard de Clare (better known as Strongbow), set sail in August 1170 to seize Dublin. The deposed king was restored, and Strongbow remained in Dublin as governor. The following year, Henry II proclaimed Dublin to be under his control, thus cementing a political sphere of influence that was to remain for almost 1,000 years.

TUDOR RULE

In many respects, Dublin was a medieval town like any other. It certainly suffered from the same insidious problems, mostly related to chronic overcrowding. With a population of 5,000 crammed inside the city walls, both disease and fire were hazards. Other threats included open sewers, filthy drinking water and, worst of all, starvation. In 1295 food shortages were so severe that it was said that the poor were driven to eat the criminals on the gallows. During the famine of 1317 gruesome rumours spread that mothers had resorted to eating their own babies. While that's almost

certainly apocryphal, the horrors of the Black Death certainly were not. By 1348 the city's population had mushroomed to nearly 35,000, but the epidemic would claim a third of them.

As Dublin grew and stumbled, the rest of Ireland was living under tribal kingdoms, largely beyond English control. The area under direct English rule extended only 48 kilometres (30 miles) from Dundalk to the Wicklow Hills, an area known even now as 'the Pale'. This boundary gave rise to the expression 'beyond the pale', meaning something that is uncontrollable or unacceptable.

It was not until the Tudor period (1485-1603) that English power was consolidated across Ireland. When Henry VIII split England from the Roman Catholic Church in 1531, he took the opportunity to seize Church land in Ireland, redistributing it among his supporters, both English and Irish. It took him no great leap of imagination from proclaiming himself head of an Anglicised Irish Church to fully fledged King of Ireland.

When Henry's youngest daughter, Elizabeth, became queen (after a brief period of Catholic restoration under his eldest, Mary), she launched a campaign to civilise Ireland, 'for the reformation', as she put it, 'of this barbarous people'.

During this time, Catholic Dubliners were constantly persecuted. Acts of Parliament in 1536 and 1539 dissolved the city's monasteries, forever altering the urban landscape. In 1558, the Bacall Iosa (a wooden staff said to have been bequeathed to the city by St Patrick) was ritually burned, and the following year all relics and icons were removed from the city's churches. In 1560 the English proclaimed Ireland an Anglican country, and Protestants took over the Catholic churches, leaving the dispossessed Catholics to worship in cellars.

The closure of the monasteries would have a disastrous result on the city's economy and social order. The knock-on effects of unemployment and the curtailing of Catholic charitable funds all but cancelled out initiatives to clean the city and improve the living conditions of its poorest inhabitants. In 1575 another outbreak of Black Death claimed a further third of the population.

CROMWELL

By the mid 1600s Dublin was pronounced to be overwhelmingly Protestant, widening the gulf between the Anglicised capital and the rest of Ireland. Outside the city, discontent grew among the oppressed Catholic majority. Civil unrest was rife.

By 1649, though, the English civil war was over. Oliver Cromwell, (*photo right*) now head of the fledgling new republic, was obsessed by the idea that, if it were not brought to heel, Ireland could be used to mount an invasion of England. And so it was that on 15 August of that year Cromwell landed an army of 12,000 in Dublin and (after a short pause in which he commandeered St Patrick's Cathedral as a stable) proceeded to Drogheda. What followed was to be remembered as one of the most shameful acts of English – indeed, of any nation's – military history, an act of such irrepressible wickedness that the shadow it cast over Anglo-Irish relations has never fully healed. Over 3,000 Irish soldiers were murdered on a single night in Drogheda – most had already surrendered and some were burned alive while taking refuge in a church. Another bloody day in Wexford saw the deaths of 2,000 people, including hundreds of civilians. Slowly but inexorably, the country was, in fact, 'brought to heel'. Land amounting to nearly 23,166 square miles (60,000 square kilometres) was seized from Catholic landowners and redistributed among Cromwell's Protestant supporters. That act alone would help keep the country tied to England for centuries.

RENAISSANCE

After the restoration removed the Cromwells from the picture, the Duke of Ormond was appointed Lord Deputy of Ireland and, at the end of the 17th century, the city again began to change rapidly. Narrow medieval streets were

Marauding **Oliver Cromwell**.

rebuilt in the wide, neoclassical style that had become popular in Paris and Amsterdam, and squares and parks were created. This is when Temple Bar was developed; Marsh's Library was built in 1702, and Trinity College library was started in 1712.

The Earl of Drogheda, Henry Moore, purchased land north of the river on which he built Henry Street and its environs. Banker Luke Gardiner set out Henrietta Street, a prime aristocratic quarter north of the river, and later Gardiner Street, which was overseen by architect James Gandon. Indeed, Dublin without the iconic influence of Gandon would be, in many ways, an unrecognisable place; he also designed Beresford Place, Custom House, the Kings Inns and the Four Courts. The new Parliament House was opened in 1731, and, 20 years later, building began on the new façade of Trinity College, the largest piece of collegiate architecture in Europe.

As the aesthetic influence of the Enlightenment merged with the city's growing wealth, Dublin entered something of a cultural golden age in the 1770s. For the upper classes at least, it was a belle époque, and many took great advantage of their new-found status. During this time Dublin was second only to London in terms of music, theatre and publishing. George Frideric Handel lived on Abbey Street in 1741-42; indeed, the debut performance of his *Messiah* was held just around the corner in Fishamble Street. At the same time, playwrights Richard Sheridan, Oliver Goldsmith and William Congreve all lived and worked in Dublin, as did philosopher and politician Edmund Burke, satirist Jonathan Swift (*see p17* **The house that Swift built**) and the founder of the *Spectator* magazine, Richard Steele.

'Spirit of Swift, spirit of Molyneux, your genius has prevailed! Ireland is now a nation!'
Henry Grattan

However, the glamorous façade hid an underbelly of growing dissent. The crushing defeat of King James II at the Battle of the Boyne in 1690 forever ended the hopes of Catholic England. The newly installed Protestant monarch, William of Orange, passed laws that didn't exactly outlaw Roman Catholicism, but that made life very difficult for those who practised it. Catholics were forbidden to hold any office of state, stand for Parliament, join the armed forces or practise law. Most crucially, they could neither vote nor buy any land. It is no big surprise, given all of that, that by the latter half of the 18th century, barely five per cent of the land in Ireland was in Catholic hands. Disenfranchised Catholics migrated from the countryside, and Dublin found itself with a Catholic majority. Into the city's thriving intellectual scene came rich new seams of dissent. All the ingredients were there to make Dublin a hotbed for radical political thinking. And for radical political activities as well.

In an all-too-familiar pattern, sectarian animosity turned into violence. Gangs like the Liberty Boys (mostly Protestant tailors' apprentices) slugged it out daily on the streets with the Ormond Boys (mostly Catholic butchers' assistants). On one particularly violent occasion, a gang of victorious Liberty Boys left their rivals hanging by their jaws from their own meat hooks.

REBELS WITH A CAUSE
In 1782, after months of negotiation, the reformist politician Henry Grattan won legislative independence from the English Privy Council, which had been required to approve all laws passed in Ireland since the time of Henry VII. An excited crowd gathered outside the parliament building on 16 April to hear Grattan proclaim, 'Spirit of Swift, spirit of Molyneux, your genius has prevailed! Ireland is now a nation!' Some, though not all, of the anti-Catholic legislation was repealed, most notably the restriction on Catholics being allowed to practise law (although the ban on holding public office remained). Grattan became something of a hero, but he was certainly no revolutionary. He did not believe in full independence from England. Indeed, one of the first acts of his new parliament was to approve the sending of 20,000 Irish sailors to assist the English navy.

When, in 1798, a fleet of French troops arrived to assist a Catholic uprising in County Kilkenny, the English government got jittery. Two years later, when Dubliner Wolfe Tone orchestrated his own, pan-sectarian rebellion of 'United Irishmen' London became convinced that it had cut Ireland too much slack. When another French fleet attempted to land at Lough Swilly, the reprisals were brutal. As many as 10,000 rebels were executed or deported. With all of this rebellion in the air, Grattan's parliament lacked the teeth to save itself from being abolished by the Act of Union in 1801, which reimposed direct rule from London.

The effect on Dublin was crushing. Much of the former ruling class left, and they took their wealth with them. The city was left without effective representation. A storm was gathering over the country, and the results would be devastating.

In 1803, after an abortive rebellion led by 25-year-old Dubliner Robert Emmet (*photo p16*), the British once more became concerned about French support for the Irish nationalist cause. Emmet's botched rebellion was a sad saga – in strategic terms at least, a complete failure – but the romantic mythology to which he contributed was a more powerful gift to the nationalist cause than anything he achieved in his short and tragic revolutionary career. The most influential nationalist movement of the 19th century appreciated the value of mythology only too well, and it was that, rather than any strategic success, that would make the Fenians vital players in the struggle for an independent Ireland.

The devastating potato famine of 1846-51, and England's slow and disinterested response to it, galvanised support for the independence movement, and the next 15 years saw the growth and spread of the Fenians, first in Dublin, then among the burgeoning Irish-American community in the US (many of whom had fled to America to escape the famine and anti-Catholic oppression). Fenian newspapers were printed on both sides of the Atlantic, and although the group made attempts at armed rebellion, their exploitation of the media was far more successful than their relatively modest paramilitary activities. Much of the Fenian's initial activity amounted to little more than publicity stunts, exercises in what would now be termed 'public relations', albeit audacious ones (nobody can seriously have expected success when, in 1866, they tried to invade Canada with an army of 800 men). No, the Fenians tapped into something much more potent, something immeasurably more significant to the nationalist cause than the symbolic occupation of a public building, or the assassination of British dignitaries. By far the most powerful weapon in their arsenal was Ireland's burgeoning sense of national identity, a celebration of its history, language and culture; the very stuff, in short, of what it meant to be Irish.

THE EASTER UPRISING

By the turn of the 20th century, the end of direct rule from London seemed closer than ever. The Home Rule Bill received its third reading in the British Parliament, and looked all but certain to become law within months. However, a vociferous loyalist movement had emerged among the Protestant majority in the north. At a meeting in Belfast Town Hall, half a million men and women signed a covenant to

Robert Emmet, rebel with a cause. *See p15.*

resist Home Rule – many signed with their own blood. Senior political figures demanded the exclusion of six counties from any independent Irish state – Derry, Antrim, Tyrone, Down, Armagh and Fermanagh – known collectively as Ulster. The passage of the bill was slowed, and the outbreak of World War I the following year kicked the issue into the long grass.

Nearly 200,000 Irish men volunteered for service with the British army in World War I, some hoping that their loyalty would win concessions after what everybody thought would be a relatively short conflict. With the prospect of Home Rule suspended – at least for the time being – a split occurred in the independence movement. Some, such as John Redmond, the leader of the Irish Parliamentary Party, believed that no further action should be taken while Britain was at war. Others, though, saw the chaos and confusion of war as perfect cover from which to strike a decisive blow for the nationalist cause.

A group of men from the Irish Volunteers and the Irish Republican Brotherhood planned a rebellion to occur in Dublin on Easter Sunday 1916. Plans for the rebellion were beset with problems from the start. A shipment of 20,000 rifles was seized en route from Germany, and Roger Casement, a former British diplomat and prominent member of the Irish Volunteers, was arrested. When the ostensible leader of the Volunteers, Eoin MacNeill, found that he had not been kept fully informed about plans for the rebellion, he petulantly took out a newspaper advertisement announcing that the Sunday 'manoeuvres' had been postponed for 24 hours.

The fact that they must have known how remote was their chance of success serves to highlight the magnitude of what the rebels were about to attempt – men like trade unionist James Connolly, schoolteacher Patrick Pearse, barman Sean MacDermott must have known that martyrdom was the most they could hope for. Others took part out of fervour, swept along by the romantic appeal of such a hopeless gesture of defiance. Still, it would be wrong to assume that, when Patrick Pearse read out the proclamation of independence on the steps of the General Post Office building on that Easter Monday morning, he did so with the full weight of public opinion on his side. Some Dubliners found the actions of the Easter rebels treacherous, especially as many of the city's sons were at that moment fighting in Flanders. In any case, five strategic sites were seized that morning and occupied by the rebels – the Four Courts, St Stephen's Green, Liberty Hall, Jacob's Biscuit Factory and Boland's Flour Mill. Disorder ensued, and 5,000 soldiers were sent from London to assist the police. After almost a

The house that Swift built

had been in his blood from birth and he had maintained an interest in religion from his early days. Born to Anglo-Irish protestant parents, Swift was ordained into the Church of Ireland in 1695 and later appointed Saint Patrick's Cathedral Dean in 1713, a post he held until his death in 1745. It was in the course of this posting that he nurtured an interest in the fate of ill-fated Dubliners; he donated funds for the building of an Alms house for incapacitated elderly women.

Before he died Swift searched for the site of the new hospital for the mentally ill and it stands today on the plot he chose. In 1746, St Patrick's Hospital, was granted a Royal Charter. It was built between 1749-56 by architect George Semple and its architectural plans were modelled on the second Bethlem Hospital in London. St Patrick's Hospital, James's Street, opened in 1757 and is one of the oldest continuously functioning psychiatric institutes in the world. Today, its wards are named after those who journeyed with him: Stella (Esther Johnson), his life-long companion, and the only other woman in his life, Vanessa (Esther Vanhomrigh). The day clinic at nearby St James's Hospital is also known as the Jonathan Swift Clinic.

The ghost of writer Jonathan Swift wafts around the wards of St Patrick's Hospital. Multiple phantom sightings of the Irish satirist have been reported in the last 250 years. This should come as no surprise to anyone who has wandered its corridors as Swift, in an outstandingly generous legacy, left his estate – made up of his book royalties – for the foundation of a psychiatric hospital in Dublin.

Swift's fortune on his death in 1745 amounted to £12,000 (€15,370) which, in today's figures, is closer to £2 million (€2,561, 672). Swift also wrote a management plan drawing on ideas developed from his posting as governor of the Bedlam Hospital (Bethlem Royal Hospital) in London. During his tenure, Swift was dismayed at the way mentally ill patients were put on display for the entertainment of fee-paying spectators.

Swift had also developed an empathy with those on the margins of society while Dean of St Patrick's Cathedral. Matters of the church

Ironically, Swift himself was declared mentally ill three years before he died by a lunacy commission. Today, it is understood he suffered from Menière's disease, a condition of the inner ear affecting balance and hearing.

In the satirical lyrical language for which Swift was so famous, he wrote:
"He left the little wealth he had
To build a house for fools and mad;
Showing in one satiric touch
No nation needed it so much."

week of fighting, the rebels were beaten into submission and the city centre lay in ruins. Horrified by the bloodshed, Pearse surrendered the following Sunday evening, and was later executed in Kilmainham Gaol (*photo p12-13*). In all, 77 death sentences were issued. Last to be killed was James Connolly, who, unable to stand because of a broken ankle, was shot sitting down.

THE CONFLICT INTENSIFIES

Anti-British feeling, subdued by the onset of war, was inflamed by the list of those executed or imprisoned after the rebellion. Meanwhile, a power vacuum was left at the heart of the nationalist cause, and it was to be filled by two men whose names have become synonymous with the fight for independence. Éamon De Valera was an Irish-American maths teacher who led the garrison at Boland's Mill, while Michael Collins was a West Cork man and former English émigré, who returned home to help the Irish Republican Brotherhood. In 1918 De Valera's new party, Sinn Féin, won 75 per cent of Irish seats in the British general election, but the new MPs convened not in London, but in Dublin, at the Dáil Éireann (the Irish Parliament), where they once again declared Ireland a republic. While De Valera went to rally support in America, Collins concentrated on his work as head of the military wing of the Irish Volunteers (later to become the Irish Republican Army, or IRA). The long, bloody war for Irish independence was now well under way.

The conflict reached its nadir when, on 21 November 1920, Michael Collins ordered 14 undercover British operatives to be executed in their beds. In retaliation, British troops opened fire on a crowd of football spectators at Croke Park in Dublin, killing 12 people. Later the same day, two senior IRA men and a Sinn Féin supporter (an innocent one, as it happened) were executed at Dublin Castle. Collins came out of hiding to lay a wreath at their funeral. The tit-for-tat cycle continued for another eight months, until a truce was declared on 9 July 1921. A delegation led by Collins travelled to London, where they met with representatives of the British government, including Lloyd George (then prime minister) and Winston Churchill. Negotiations culminated on 6 December with the signing of the Anglo-Irish Treaty, after which Collins is said to have remarked that he had signed his own death warrant.

The treaty conferred dominion status on 26 counties, known collectively as the Irish Free State. The remaining six (all largely Protestant) Ulster counties refused to join, thereby partitioning Ireland along geographical, political and religious lines. Dominion status

Afghan asylum seekers in St Patrick's Cathedral in 2006. *See p21.*

brought limited independence for the so-called Free State, with important elements of British authority enshrined in the constitution. King George V remained head of state in Ireland, represented by a governor general (as in Canada, Australia and New Zealand). A requirement that members of the Dáil swear allegiance to the British Crown was almost as contentious an issue as the partition.

Supporters of the treaty, led by Michael Collins and Arthur Griffith, argued that it offered the best terms available and should be seen as a start. But the opponents, led by Eamon De Valera, would accept nothing less than full independence. De Valera disassociated himself from the treaty, and Sinn Fein was divided. The treaty was ratified by just seven votes. Even the withdrawal of British troops from the capital for the first time in eight centuries, or the handing over of Dublin Castle to the provisional government, did not quell the rising tide of Republican anger.

The flashpoint came in April 1922, when anti-treaty forces clashed with Free State troops at the Four Courts area of Dublin. Fighting also broke out at the General Post Office on O'Connell Street, and the battle lasted for eight days until De Valera's supporters were forced to surrender. The fledgling government passed emergency legislation that allowed the army to shoot armed Republicans on sight; 77 people were executed and 13,000 imprisoned in seven months, with many more on hunger strikes. In Ulster, the death toll for the first half of 1922 was 264 people. The Civil War rolled on for a year, characterised by a vicious, bloody cycle of aggression and reprisal, until De Valera suspended his anti-treaty efforts in 1923.

Whether Collins was right – that a fully united Irish Republic could be achieved by peaceful means – is something we shall never know. His death at the hands of an IRA hit man in August 1922 ensured that it would be De Valera's more callous brand of political conviction that would define Irish politics until the British finally caved in to the inevitability of an Irish Republic a decade and a half later. But the road was far from smooth, the route a long way from consensus. The deep wounds inflicted by civil war on a people already scarred by oppression, privation and battle are all too evident even today in those six awkward little counties to the north. Perhaps Collins' vision of the road from Free State to republic was altogether too optimistic – romantic, even – and the depth of division meant that civil war was, indeed, simply inevitable.

Years later, though, even De Valera conceded that not accepting the treaty had been a mistake. In any case, the blood price was dear.

Eight decades on, the shadow of the gun has still not been removed from Irish politics.

The aftermath of civil war dominated the political scene for the rest of the decade. In 1926 De Valera split from the Republicans to form Fianna Fail ('Warriors of Ireland'). He became a passionate critic of what he saw as the Free State's betrayal of the Irish people, and in the election of 1927 his party won as many seats as the government. Fianna Fail members refused en masse to take the oath of allegiance, and were for a time disallowed from taking their seats. The election of 1932 returned a Fianna Fail victory, thanks in part to the 'help' of the IRA, which indulged in a judicious touch of ballot rigging and voter intimidation in support of De Valera. (He felt little in the way of obligation, however; when the organisation refused to disarm a few years later, he was the one who declared it illegal.)

BUILDING THE REPUBLIC

In the subsequent years, the streets of Dublin became relatively free from violence for the first time in decades (with a few notable exceptions), and the capital experienced something of a cultural renaissance. The Four Courts and O'Connell Street were rebuilt; the city gained a clutch of new theatres, fashionable shops and coffee houses (most famously, Bewley's on Grafton Street) and Ireland's first radio station started broadcasting from a small office on Little Denmark Street in 1926.

The Fianna Fail government lasted for 17 years, during which time the gap between Britain and Ireland widened as never before. The enforced oath of allegiance was scrapped, Roman Catholicism was officially prioritised as the majority religion and in 1937 the name of the Free State was formally changed to Éire. However, the general perception that De Valera's government was more interested in abstract Republican ideals, rather than immediate issues such as social welfare, would eventually cost them dearly. Fianna Fail was ousted by a coalition of Fine Gael ('Tribe of the Gaels') and Sean MacBride's Clann na Poblachta ('Republican Party') in 1948. A year later, Ireland – still minus the six counties – was at last declared a Republic.

THE DARK BEFORE DAWN

Although Ireland remained neutral throughout World War II, this did not by any means make it immune to the austerity of the times. Rationing of basic items including clothes, fuel and food ended in 1949, but for a variety of reasons Ireland saw little of the economic boom that lifted Europe over the next 50 years. Industrial output fell significantly and wage controls were introduced, while shortages continued to force up the price of basic goods. All of these factors, combined with extremely high unemployment, contributed to a surge in economic migration, particularly to Britain, with an average of 40,000 people a year leaving Ireland by the early 1950s.

There was no small irony in the fact that the post-war depression that hit so hard was caused by a conflict Ireland had resolutely avoided being part of. But the country had nobody to blame but itself for the self-inflicted cultural oppression that followed, as the government used strict censorship laws to ban works by, among others, Brendan Behan, Austin Clarke, Edna O'Brien, George Bernard Shaw and Samuel Beckett, as well as an occasionally baffling list of international authors, from Marcel Proust, Jean-Paul Sartre and Sigmund Freud to Noel Coward, Dylan Thomas, Ernest Hemingway, John Steinbeck, Tennessee Williams and even Apuleius, the second-century philosopher. Meanwhile, tensions between the Church, the government and the population were intensified when pressure from the Catholic Church forced the government to abandon plans for a progressive programme of pre- and post-natal healthcare legislation that was, by all accounts, desperately needed at the time.

'It's too early to tell if the Celtic Tiger has turned to Celtic Tabby.'

Things began to change in the 1950s, when an ambitious programme of grants and tax breaks attracted a new wave of foreign investment. When Sean Lemass took over as president, he became Ireland's first true economic manager; his expansionist policies led away from an agrarian economy as the country took its first steps to competing in the world market. In 1973 Ireland joined the European Economic Community.

In Dublin, in a kind of celebratory demolition derby, monuments erected by the British during the occupation were destroyed by the IRA – most symbolic among them, Nelson's Pillar on O'Connell Street, a replica of London's Nelson's Column.

By the early 1970s, though, the violence became more serious, with the resumption of sectarian strife in Northern Ireland reopening old political and religious wounds. After the notorious Bloody Sunday killings in January 1972, a crowd of up to 30,000 protestors laid siege to the British Embassy in Dublin for three days before burning it down.

CHURCH AND STATE

In 1983 the so-called pro-life movement launched a vociferous campaign to have the constitution amended to include a ban on abortion (despite the fact that such a ban already existed in Irish law). Enthusiastically backed by the Catholic Church, the referendum passed. Campaigning on both sides rumbled on until 1992, when the issue again hit the headlines with the infamous 'X Case', in which a 14-year-old Dublin girl was raped, became pregnant, but was restrained from travelling to England for an abortion. An impassioned public debate ensued, heightened when the girl herself declared that she would commit suicide unless the decision was overturned. Eventually, the Supreme Court ruled that not only was it legal for her to travel, but that under those circumstances it was not unconstitutional for her to have an abortion performed in Ireland.

For many, the ultimate sign of the changing times came when divorce was finally legalised after a referendum in 1995. Although the result was close enough to keep it mired in the courts for another couple of years (the final count had a margin of victory of just half a per cent), the passage of a law that would have been unthinkable a generation earlier told of the immense change happening in the country.

When a series of well-publicised scandals rocked the Irish religious establishment in the 1990s (a damaging rap sheet of embezzlement and child abuse), it seemed that the days of the all-powerful Church in Ireland were numbered.

THE HERE AND NOW

The 1990s may have been a period of great social upheaval, but they were also a time of unprecedented economic prosperity, and Dublin reaped the rewards. Investment soared and unemployment plummeted. Expats returned in droves. Those were heady days – 'Celtic Tiger' became as familiar a buzzword as 'dot-com', and Ireland's burgeoning high-tech industries were what gave the tiger its sharpest teeth.

Prosperity, however, did not come without a price. In Dublin, crime went up, threatening the city's traditionally easygoing reputation. In 1996 journalist Veronica Guerin was murdered while investigating organised crime in the capital, and her death shocked the nation. (In May 2008, Patrick Holland, the man named in a Special Criminal Court trial in 1997 as the person police believe killed the reporter, was jailed for eight years by a London court following a conviction for a 2007 kidnap and ransom plot. Holland has not been convicted of Guerin's murder.) Affluent Dublin became an attractive destination for economic migrants, especially Romanians and Nigerians, and fresh tensions began to bubble up.

At the end of the 20th century, the tiger began to falter. The EU, which had lavished money on the country, shifted its attention, and funds, to Eastern Europe, and could yet come calling on Dublin with its palm out, asking for returns on its investment. It's too early to tell if the Celtic Tiger has turned to Celtic Tabby. Ireland has weathered the global economic downturn better than most European economies, but the pinch has been felt: growth is down, unemployment up, and the adoption of the euro keeps prices artificially high.

Social and political tensions in Dublin society persist (*see below* **The rising tide**), but such problems are no longer confined to the internecine disputes of the Irish people. In May 2006, an estimated 41 Afghan asylum seekers occupied St Patrick's Cathedral for several days, threatening to starve to death unless they were granted leave to remain. Their claim, that a return to Afghanistan would be tantamount to a death sentence, struck a familiar chord, echoing the rhetoric of similar protests around the world. (*Photo p18*). When police finally cleared St

Patrick's, bearing waif-like figures on stretchers and with no satisfactory conclusion reached, Dubliners were left with precious few answers and a feeling of growing unease.

In May 2008 taoiseach Bertie Ahern resigned after 11 years as prime minister; he also resigned as leader of Fianna Fáil. His successor, in both posts, is Brian Cowen. The decision to resign came a day after Ahern launched a court challenge in an attempt to limit the role of a public inquiry, known as the Mahon Tribunal (www.planningtribunal.ie), investigating planning corruption during the 1990s. Questions regarding the involvement of Ahern's personal finances have been asked.

In June 2008 the Irish voted in a referendum on the Lisbon Treaty, which is aimed at increasing the efficiency of the machinery of European Union bureaucracy and promoting greater transparency in EU functions. The Irish rejected the treaty which has put the kibosh on plans to ratify it. Under EU rules all 27 member states must ratify all treaties for them to be written into law.

The rising tide

The riot of O'Connell Street on 25 February 2006 was an unexpected event for everyone, including the so-called 'knackers' that many Dubliners cite as the instigators behind it. The events of that Saturday afternoon were not so much a clash between Republicans and Unionists as perhaps the first real rebellion against the Celtic Tiger's growth: for an afternoon, the city's disenfranchised took back the capital, whose recent wealth has seemingly passed them by.

A Unionist march was planned in memory of the victims of Republican violence and was to pass in front of O'Connell Street's General Post Office, a bastion landmark of Irish Republicanism. Sinn Féin leaders, viewing the march as deliberate provocation, had issued a stay-away order to all party members. It seemed, then, that any protest to the march would be unlikely (anarchists are generally not drawn into the North-South division, and the smaller Republican splinter groups, who may have been up for a ruck, arguably do not have the organisation to mobilise it). So when a thousand rioters descended on the city's largest boulevard, with little regard for the usual rules of engagement at a protest, An Garda Síochána were clearly overwhelmed. What the state had not accounted for was the animosity of

the 'bar-stool Republicanism' from some of the harder inner-city neighbourhoods, which viewed the state's allowance for such a march to take place on their turf as one final betrayal too many. It was also an opportunity for many to have a pop at the Establishment who, as they see it, has only taken an interest in poorer neighbourhoods during the country's huge growth of the last decade when opportunities for 'regentrification' have occurred, and prices on formerly state-subsidised houses can be bumped up.

What started off with a couple of hundred insurgents in the first wave of protests on O'Connell Street steadily grew in numbers as more and more friends were called in for the action. As the troubles spread over the river into the more salubrious south-side shopping streets, looters began to chance their luck in some of the city's high-street stores, in the knowledge that police back-up was unlikely to arrive for some time. In fact, police officers were so stretched that containment and general crowd control around the city were proving hopelessly unattainable; at one point, bystanders could view a trail of torched cars alongside Trinity College on Nassau Street, to the left, and the surreal prospect of usual Saturday shoppers lining Grafton Street to the right.

Worrying about the limping tiger?

Dublin Today

Tiger, tiger, burning out.

If this is your first visit to Dublin in a number of years, you'll notice some changes, subtle and not so subtle: fewer cranes on the skyline, more sales signs in shops and the luxury department stores no longer crammed to overflow with salon-ed blondes fighting over embossed handbags. And, then you open the property section of the paper, and desperation hits you between the eyes…

Ireland, like the US and the rest of Europe, is heading towards recession – the difference being that Ireland has never experienced a recession before. It has, of course, been in a bad way – in the 1980s it was known as the 'sick man of Europe' – but that wasn't a recession, it was the status quo. Recession implies a boom to recede from, and the only real boom of the 20th century was the Celtic Tiger, 1994-2006 RIP.

Just as the Tiger presented Dublin with a new set of circumstances, so does the recession. Are Dubliners better prepared than other Europeans to meet the recession because they're used to roughing it? Or are they worse off because they can't face a return to scrimping and saving? Right through the Tiger years, sniffy commentators, both national and foreign, derided the garish nouveau riche lifestyles.

Did the Irish get spoiled in the years of plenty? Are they going to emigrate their way out of this recession in time-honoured fashion?

It's safer not to predict. The recession is only kicking in (and is still denied by some, though anyone trying to sell their house has the truer picture); things may crash spectacularly, or slide gracefully. No one can say how Dublin will fare. But the city has some idea of which bits of the Tiger's legacy will go and which will stick. The flash new cars, the second homes, the designer labels, the holidays abroad, the high-end restaurants – these are already on the wane. If unemployment continues to rise – 5.7 per cent in June 2008 – we may even see a falling off of guestworkers from Poland and Lithuania. But that pre-Tiger city of exclusively white, Catholic churchgoers; of invariably execrable coffee (but invariably excellent tea); of supermarket shelves given over to dairy, beef, Cadbury's and pork; of epic quests for the holy grail of olive oil; of Leeson Street nightclubs serving only wine; of state monopolies on telecoms and air travel … all those characteristics that made Dublin unique among Europe's capitals, and frequently made it infuriating, are gone forever. There's no return. Recession, not retreat.

The Dublin you visit today bears the marks of the recent boom. It is multicultural with large groups of Polish, Lithuanian, Nigerian and Chinese. You can buy olive oil in corner shops, sushi in supermarkets and unpronounceable spices in specialist shops; the coffee is hit-and-miss but since much of it is served from multinational chains, you can't complain it's worse than home. You can drink beer, whiskey, alcopops or whatever you fancy in nightclubs until 2.30am. You can choose your air-carrier and you won't pay much. The white, Roman Catholic natives have become 'sacrament Catholics' – they enter church for christenings, first communions, weddings and funerals, and not every Sunday.

So much for the changes (which have now become features), what about continuity? What survived the Tiger and is surviving the recession? Well, the political system for one. Ireland behaves like a one-party state, going through the motions of democracy. In fact, the Tiger only strengthened the dominant party, Fianna Fáil's hand. The first parliament of independent Ireland met in 1922; Fianna Fáil has been in power 58 of the ensuing 86 years, and has not lost an election in 21 years! Since 1989 Fianna Fáil's been in coalition, but as it's by far the dominant coalition partner (currently 78 seats to Labour's 20), this hardly dents the party's ascendancy. It managed, during the boom years, to present itself as the only party capable of driving the economy, and now it

Change is abroad

After ten years of steady immigration, Dubliners have finally got over exclaiming at foreigners and strange languages on their streets, and are adopting something of the nonchalance of other Europeans towards a multicultural capital.

Until 1995 the population was almost exclusively Irish Roman Catholic; the only visible foreigners being the Spanish teenagers who arrived every summer to learn English. But, ten years later, ten per cent of the population was non-Irish born, rising to 17 per cent in Dublin. That's one in six, and you sense it immediately in the streets where you'll hear Polish, Russian, Chinese, Yoruba and most other European languages.

The effect is palpable, although inevitably more in some areas than others. Multi-ethnicity has little impacted the leafy suburbs, but take a side street off O'Connell Street and the shop signs are in Polish or Russian, and the wares are gherkins and Zubrowka. Continue on up to Parnell Street and you're into Chinatown, with your pick of Chinese restaurants. Wander round the formerly Jewish district of the South Circular Road and you'll see a mosque.

Thursday's *Evening Standard* has a Polish supplement. Arambe theatre group puts on Irish plays with African actors. And, ironically, immigration has revived the churches.

The big question, now that the recession has arrived, is will the immigrants stay? Or are they *gastarbeiters* who will move onto the next booming economy? Already there are signs of a falling-off of Polish and Lithuanian workers – they were mostly young, single, frequently

worked in the construction industry, and never intended to stay permanently.

Other communities, particularly non-EU, seem more settled. However, Irish citizenship is not easy to come by, especially since 2004 when the right to citizenship through birth was rescinded. Many of the immigrants currently in residence are not naturalised; some are parents of Irish children but this does not safeguard them from deportation.

Aside from the obvious symbols of restaurants, shops and theatres, what mark have immigrants made and how assimilated are they? Politically, they scarcely figure – South African-born Moosajee Bhamjee became the first Muslim in parliament, where he sat between 1992-97, and former asylum seeker, Rotimi Adebari, is mayor of Portlaoise, but these are the rare examples of immigrants making their presence felt politically. This is unsurprising. According to the pattern of the rest of Europe, it takes a generation for immigrants to 'buy into' their countries of residence. There is little to suggest that Ireland will be any different. On the contrary, although Ireland is famed for its friendliness, this is an insular and self-obsessed island. The Irish still tend to think of nationality as in the blood; despite lipservice to the 'new Irish', they do not yet regard their immigrants as Irish, and are not therefore intensely interested in them. This will change. The most interesting development will come when a second generation immigrant writer contributes to the great Irish literary tradition. The Irish are awaiting their Hanif Kureishi and Zadie Smith to change their vernacular.

presents itself as the only party capable of riding the recession. And the people are buying it. Everyone bitches about Fianna Fáil but come election day everyone votes for them, despite the allegations of cronyism and corruption that constantly bedevil the party and which led to popular leader, Bertie Ahern, resigning in April 2008.

The Irish parliament, the Dáil, fails to reflect the changes in society. No immigrant sits in the current Dáil, and almost 20 per cent of members, including the leaders of the two main parties, are the children of previous members. There are only 23 women, giving Ireland one of the worst figures of female representation in Europe (just 14 per cent). So, politically, Ireland, for all its olive oil, sushi and Korean restaurants, doesn't look much different to the 1930s and '40s, when the Dáil was made up of middle-aged Catholic men, who regarded their seats as their birthrights, and Fianna Fáil was the only party on the landscape.

What else has survived the Tiger? The weather of course, and the drinking, which the Irish complain is a stereotype, but every survey shows the Irish are the biggest binge drinkers in Europe and the figure went up, not down, during the Tiger years. Ireland's reaction to new opportunities wasn't to stop playing and start working, it was to work hard, and play harder with the proceeds, which means the country's reputation as carousers never suffered, though its health did. 'Ireland has her madness, and her weather still', as WH Auden wrote 70 years ago. The high prices are another invariable feature. People complain they came in with the Tiger, but actually Ireland has always been expensive (because it's an under-populated, insular island, and it doesn't check what the neighbours are charging). The constantly derided transport system is a further ubiquity – bus corridors and the Luas tramlines have improved things, but plans for a much-needed metro look like being shelved.

What do the changes and the continuity mean for the visitor? Well, if you're looking for casual work, you may find it a bit, but not much, harder to come by. If you're here on holidays, you won't be fazed. Dublin, even at the height of the boom, wasn't London, New York or Paris. Nobody came to shop or eat in fancy restaurants – the choice was always limited, standards were liable to slip, and prices were high. People come to Dublin for the sea, the scenery, the culture, and the craic – that untranslatable Gaelic word, which is an oxymoron, meaning something like 'frenzied, laid-back fun'. The famed scenery began to be encroached on during the boom – including plans for a motorway through the Hill of Tara,

which is going ahead despite international outcry – so, in this respect, the recession means respite. The boom certainly added a new dimension to the craic – more ethnicity, more festivals, more varied places to eat, and some great regeneration along the docks, Smithfield and O'Connell Street. But it also generated a busier populace, with less time to sit back and shoot the breeze (hence the rise in binge drinking – cramming into two hours what used to be drunk in five). Conversation, a cornerstone of craic, suffered badly – it was all property, property, property. So, if the recession means fewer Michelin-starred restaurants, at least Dubliners are guaranteed a return to witty, property-free conversation.

What about culture? It's a cliché that art thrives during recessions; but that depends on the art. To put it simplistically, film-makers, pop singers, TV shows and zeitgeist novelists – those who go global and whom the money backs – do better in a boom, while poetry, theatre, trad/rock/blues and the radical chic emerge in recessions. However, the cliché stands for Ireland because our reputation as a cultural mecca rests on the famished arts: poetry (Yeats, Kavanagh, Heaney), theatre (Synge, O'Casey, Beckett, Friel), trad/rock/blues (The Chieftains, Rory Gallagher, Thin Lizzy), and the radical chic (Joyce, Beckett, Flann O'Brien). The Irish cultural genius was always a response to hard times, not to a golden age. The Tiger produced boy bands, chick lit and a few fine films. But the number of trad sessions in Dublin pubs went down, because of the incursion of piped music, and there were fewer venues for new bands than in the 1970s when U2 rocked the Baggot Inn. So the downturn may see Dubliners returning to what they do best – black humour in the teeth of despair and plaintive lyrics falling like rain.

This is a transition time and transition times are fun. One of the best periods ever to be in Dublin was during the early '90s, just before the boom kicked off. Nightclubs and art spaces were opening and closing all over the city. Walking along Thomas Street today you sense something like that happening now. Then there was an air of expectation, now it's more an air of challenge or contrivance, but the creative spirit is abroad. The biggest challenge is this: if things get bad, will it be fight or flight? The Irish are the most mobile of Europeans, with strong communities worldwide, and a long, long tradition of emigrating their way out of desperate periods. But now we have an immigrant population of our own. If the reversal of emigration turns out to be permanent and not just for Christmas, then the Tiger will have generated a true revolution.

Custom House.

Architecture

Architectural aspirations.

The word Georgian is very nearly synonymous with Dublin, and the Georgian era was a period of mercurial advancement for the city – at least in architectural terms. Most of the city's memorable buildings were constructed during the reigns of kings George I to IV (from 1714 to 1830), when Ireland was in the fold of the British Empire. Elegant Georgian buildings line the wide streets in the south inner city as well as pockets north of the river Liffey, creating a cityscape that is more than the sum of its parts.

Recent times have been less glorious. An economic slump during much of the 20th century led to a bleak period in Irish architecture, with few notable buildings. Exceptions include: the International-style **Busáras**, designed in 1953 by Michael Scott, with its glazed façade that echoes Le Corbusier's Maison Suisse and Cité de Refuge in Paris; and the beautiful **Guinness Storehouse**, built in 1904 as a homage to the urban elegance of the Chicago School. During the 1960s and '70s, many Georgian buildings were knocked down to make way for office blocks. The longest Georgian terrace in Dublin, Fitzwilliam Street, was severed in the 1970s

when a chunk was knocked out to make way for offices. The demolition caused an outcry, and was a turning point in the preservation of period buildings. When the building boom began in the mid 1990s, everything was in place to make the most of it: native architects, who had coped with the slump by working abroad, returned with knowledge gleaned at the drawing boards of the likes of Frank Lloyd Wright, Le Corbusier, Renzo Piano, Richard Rogers and Norman Foster. Ronnie Tallon even designed a bank building in Lower Baggot Street that resembles the façade (not the plan) of Mies van der Rohe's Seagram building in New York.

So although an awful lot of mean, dark apartment blocks and semi-detached housing remains, the last decade has seen a rise in the quality of architecture across the country. Architects such as O'Mahoney Pike are leading the way in the design of a new type of light-filled apartment. Good examples of their work

▶ For more on **Docklands architecture**, see pp87-90.

In Context

The Le Corbusier-esque **Berkeley Library**.

can be seen at Hanover Quay, draped in glass
'winter gardens', in Dublin's Docklands, and
the wedge-shaped apartments in a circular
Victorian gas storage facility (South Lotts
Road). Also in the Docklands are the beautiful
stepped-back Clarion Quay apartment
buildings, in timber, render and glass.

THE OLD AND THE NEW
Dublin's core is small and many interesting
buildings huddle near the centre, so it's easy
to undertake an architectural tour on foot.

To the west of the city centre is the former
medieval area, and if you search around in
Christ Church Cathedral (*see p66*) and

 Buildings

The best

For audacious white modern architecture
Trinity College engineering building
extension. *See p27.*

For exciting eco-architecture
Green Building. *See p28.*

For 18th-century neo-classicism
Custom House (*see p26*) and City Hall
(*see p62*).

For Georgian grandeur
Merrion Square. *See p29.*

For renaissance architecture
chq building. *See p28 and p140.*

St Patrick's Cathedral (*see p68*) you'll
discover bits of medieval structure that were
retained when the cathedrals were substantially
rebuilt in the late 1800s. These include Christ
Church's 12th-century Romanesque doorway
on the end of its southern transept, and the
early 15th-century tower of St Patrick's.
From Essex Street in Temple Bar you can
gaze down on to the old city wall and the
outline of Isolde's Tower.

Substantial neo-classical buildings, dating
from the 18th and early 19th centuries, face
the River Liffey and areas just to the south of it.
The architects behind these projects included
Edward Lovett Pearce, Richard Cassels,
William Chambers, James Gandon and
Thomas Cooley, all of whom played vital roles
in the history of Irish architecture. They came
from well-connected families, and many had
either taken the grand tour to France and Italy
themselves, or were under the influence of
those who had. Pearse, who was related to Sir
John Vanburgh (designer of Blenheim Palace
and Castle Howard in England), toured Italy,
and his love of Palladian architecture is evident
in the design of the granite **Bank of Ireland**
building (College Green), dressed in ionic
columns made of Portland stone. It was later
extended by Gandon.

Sir William Chambers' **Casino** garden
building for the Marino Estate, in north Dublin,
resembles Andrea Palladio's 1571 Villa Rotunda
in Vicenza, Italy. His protégé, James Gandon,
took the style with him when he went on to
design the **Four Courts** (Inns Quay), a granite
building with Portland stone trimmings
overlooking the Liffey, and the monumental
yet neatly scaled **Custom House** (Custom
House Quay), modelled after Chambers'
Somerset House in London and built in 1791.
(*Photo p25*). (Look across from the Custom
House to see the ill-considered, pyramid-topped
recent office building that has been dubbed
'canary dwarf'.) Gandon gained the Four
Courts commission on the death of the
original architect, Thomas Cooley. Cooley had
already designed another neo-classical gem,
the Exchange (now **City Hall**) on Cork Hill.

Richard Cassels also took up the reins
when his mentor Pearse died. He continued
the Palladian theme, albeit using classical
adornment in a more subtle way, when he
designed a huge town house for the Earl of
Kildare, on Kildare Street. **Leinster House**,
as it is known, is now the seat of parliament.
It's flanked by the neo-classical **National
Library** and **National Museum** (both
designed by two Thomas Deanes, a father-and-
son team, in the late 19th century), creating a
grand classical courtyard marred somewhat

by the car park in its midst. The new glass pavilion, through which you enter the courtyard, is a finely detailed structure by Bucholz McEvoy Architects, one of the city's most gifted young practices.

The other side of the parliament building faces **Merrion Square**, one of Dublin's finest Georgian squares. Others include nearby **Fitzwilliam Square** and **Mountjoy Square** on Dublin's northside, which has suffered from deprivation, but whose innate beauty has seen it through to recent restoration.

Merrion Square is a Dublin architectural highlight. On its north side, at No.8, are the offices and bookshop of the **Royal Institute of the Architects of Ireland**. A large town house on the west side, at No.45, is home to the **Irish Architectural Archive**; the fittings for its exhibition room came from the Royal Institute of British Architects' Heinz Gallery in London. To the east is the **National Gallery**, which has been given a new wing by Scottish architects Benson + Forsyth. Its cathedral-like entrance is a cavernous, suitably monumental prelude to a trip round the gallery itself. A bookshop and café flank the wide staircase that leads you to the art; high above, visitors cross a thin bridge from one gallery to the next.

From the entrance of the new wing you can head down Nassau Street past the walls of **Trinity College**, above which towers the Ussher Library, designed in 1999. A walk around Trinity is an architectural treat, as the university has commissioned some of the best architects over the centuries: people like Cassels (Printing House, 1734), Chambers (exam hall, 1785; chapel, 1798), and Dean and Woodward (museum, 1857).

A recent extension to the **Mechanical and Manufacturing engineering building**, an angular composition of white elements by Grafton Architects, picked up the latest in a trophy cabinet full of architectural awards won by Trinity college buildings. The **Ussher Library**, which has a vast void at its centre overlooked by scarily low-walled balconies, sits next to the Le Corbusier-esque **Berkeley Library**.

Another compact architectural tour can be conducted in Temple Bar. Many of the new structures in the area were knitted into existing buildings (stand-alone, wow-factor buildings are a rarity in Dublin), and are of a pared-down style, but they revolutionised the acceptance of modern architecture in Ireland. Check out **Meeting House Square**, with its **Gallery of Photography** in reflecting Portland stone, and the red-brick, zinc-punctuated **National Photographic Archive**, with its low curved-arch entrance. On the west side of Meeting House Square is the Gaiety School of Acting, and to the east is the rear of the **Ark Children's Cultural Centre**. At the heart of the latter is a band of metal strips, framed by green copper, that opens up to create a canopy over a stage, for outdoor performances.

On nearby Eustace Street is the **Irish Film Centre**, converted from a mix of old buildings.

City Hall extension. *See p28*.

You walk through to the auditorium and the internal, glass-topped courtyard (with café, bookshop and curved box office) down a passageway floored with blue-lit glass paving slabs that resemble strips of celluloid.

Off Eustace Street is Curved Street, flanked by the **Art House** and the **Temple Bar Music Centre**. Both are white buildings with vast, metal-framed and mullioned windows in the industrial Modernist style that permeates many of the 'new' Temple Bar buildings. Don't miss the overtly Modernist **Temple Bar Gallery and Studios** and the **Black Church Print Gallery**; the design of the latter's window divides were inspired by a compositor's typeface holder.

> **'The striped concrete office block, which stands on one central leg, broke through the low-rise skyline in a brutalist fashion like none other in Ireland.'**

Those shiny solar panels and wind turbines you can see on the roof of apartments in Crow Street belong to the **Green Building**. Its witty and experimental design – balconies are made from old bicycle frames and one door has discarded piping and other metal scraps behind a perspex screen – makes for a pleasingly human feel. Get a view of the internal atrium (which provides passive-stack ventilation) by going into the urbanely urban furniture shop, **Haus**, on the ground floor.

You can enter the Temple Bar quarter in a number of ways, and one of the most dramatic is beneath the 1975 **Central Bank** building by Sam Stephenson, which caused a row over its height when it was built: the striped concrete office block, which stands on one central leg, broke through the low-rise skyline in a brutalist fashion like none other in Ireland.

North of the River Liffey, you'll see Ian Ritchie's landmark 394ft (120m) **Spire**, which was put up in O'Connell Street in 2003. It replaced Nelson's Column, blown up in 1966 by the IRA. The needle-shaped Spire, made of a rolled stainless steel sheet, was designed to be free of any political or nationalistic symbols, its metal surface intended to let people fix their own significance on it.

East of the city are the **Irish National War Memorial Gardens** in Phoenix Park. Designed by architect Sir Edwin Lutyens and built between 1933 and 1939 they commemorate the fallen Irish soldiers of World War I.

THE NEW AND THE NEWEST

On the other side of Temple Bar is the Liffey, with its clutch of new bridges. The **Ha'penny Bridge**, built in 1816, has long been a postcard favourite. In 2000, it got a new neighbour in the form of the **Millennium Footbridge**. With its bronzed aluminium handrail, the design of this sleek steel bridge echoes its arched neighbour, but has a much gentler, more buggy-friendly curve. Another recently completed footbridge, this time in the Docklands, has a steel deck held by two upturned 'claws', giving the neatly scaled bridge a nice dynamic. Upriver, to the west, is Santiago Calatrava's sculptural road bridge the **James Joyce Bridge**, which has the beauty of form shared by his bridges worldwide, though it's way out of scale for the relatively narrow Liffey. Caltrava's **Samuel Beckett Bridge** in the Docklands, due for completion in 2009, looks set to be a much better fit. Also look out for the manta ray form of **Spencer Dock Bridge** under construction over the Royal Canal. Watch that space.

The **chq**, a former industrial tobacco warehouse by John Rennie underwent a €40 million redevelopment in 2007 and now houses shops and restaurants. (*See p140*). It also won the 2008 Best Restoration Project at the Royal Institute of the Architects of Ireland Awards.

In the civic architecture arena **Dublin City Council's office building** next to City Hall on Palace Street opened in mid 2008.

Looking ahead, Daniel Libeskind will complete a Docklands project in 2010, when the finishing touches are scheduled to be added to his angular, tilted **Grand Canal Theatre**, sliced with geometric openings (in addition, he is designing three offices on the site). This will overlook a square, by US landscape designer Martha Schwartz, that will extend out over the water at Hanover Quay. The **Grand Canal Dock Development** will also see a futuristic luxury hotel open. The hotel, to be run by Monogram, is designed by Portuguese architect Manuel Aires Mateus.

Kevin Roche's €400 million **Convention Centre** for Spencer Dock on the Liffey is due to open in 2010. Ireland's National Theatre, the **Abbey**, is slated to get a new home at George's Dock following the results of an international design competition and the **U2 Tower**, to be built by Fosters + Partners by 2011, will boast a sky-high viewing platform amid its facilities.

Meanwhile, watch the media space for the controversial planning decision that will allow Bono and The Edge to demolish the hotel they own, the **Clarence**, and replace it with a white futuristic Fosters + Partners edifice known as the Skycatcher or, more disparagingly by its opponents, as a flying saucer. (*See p41*).

Yeats exhibition at the
National Library. *See p31.*

Literary Dublin

A portrait of the artists.

Since the 17th century Dublin has produced writers who have perplexed, outraged and enchanted readers around the world. From the savage indignation of **Jonathan Swift** to the political ambiguity of **Brendan Behan** and the weird complexities and scatological humour of **James Joyce**, Dublin's literary luminaries have always been subversive. It seems as if each generation produces a great writer with a rebellious streak a mile wide and a desire to push society's boundaries. And so they have.

JONATHAN SWIFT

Few would argue that the era of modern Irish writing began when Jonathan Swift (1667-1745) first put angry pen to paper. Still unchallenged as the capital's most irritated misanthrope, Swift lived in England for many years before becoming Dean of **St Patrick's Cathedral** in 1714. Much of his work was published anonymously at the time. Given his brazen scorn of British attitudes to Ireland this was understandable. His fiercely satirical works include *A Tale of a Tub*, in which he bemoans the madness of a writing career. The book's sardonic style shocked England, but they

hadn't seen anything yet – his political writing would be much more controversial.

In 1725 the English government decided to impose a debased copper coinage on Ireland. Some people, particularly the coins' manufacturers, stood to make huge profits. Writing under the name of JB Drapier, Swift heaped scorn on the proposal, asking, 'Were not the people of Ireland born as free as those of England? How have they forfeited their freedom? Are they not subjects of the same King? Am I a freeman in England, and do I become a slave in six hours crossing the channel?'

He later heaped insult upon injury in one publication after another, most famously in *Gulliver's Travels*, and most outrageously in *A Modest Proposal*, in which he advocates eating Irish babies as a solution to the country's famine. He took his scorn to his grave – he now lies in St Patrick's Cathedral next to Stella, his longtime companion, where his epitaph reads, 'Here is laid the body of Jonathan Swift, Doctor of Divinity, Dean of this Cathedral Church, where fierce indignation can no longer rend the heart. Go, traveller, and imitate if you can this earnest and dedicated champion of liberty.'

The **Shaw Birthplace** marked by a commemorative plaque. *See p77.*

OSCAR WILDE

No trawl around Dublin's literary past would be complete without mention of one Oscar Fingal O'Flahertie Wills Wilde (1854-1900), even though this great wit and dramatist spent most of his creative life in London. Born at **21 Westland Row**, Wilde was educated at **Trinity College**, where he studied classics from 1871-74. Here, at Trinity, he won the Berkeley Gold Medal for Greek and became a protégé of the classicist and wit Sir John Pentland Mahaffy. After studying at Magdalen College, Oxford, Wilde embarked on a diverse and brilliant literary career, in which he dabbled as a novelist, poet and, bizarrely enough, editor of Woman's World magazine (1887-89). His brilliantly comic plays are still regularly performed: *Lady Windermere's Fan* (1892), *An Ideal Husband* (1895) and *The Importance of Being Earnest* (1895) are probably the best known.

Wilde's devastating wit helped him conquer London, in part because he was regularly quoted in the British press, charming the world with phrases like: 'If you are not too long, I will wait here for you all my life' and 'Men always want to be a woman's first love. Women have a more subtle instinct: What they like is to be a man's last romance'. But his popularity was to be his undoing, and in 1895 he was prosecuted for homosexuality: *The Ballad of Reading Gaol* (1898) and *De Profundis* (1905) are painful records of his time in prison. Bankrupt and disgraced, he died in Paris in 1900, reminding himself, 'We are all in the gutter, but some of us are looking at the stars.'

GEORGE BERNARD SHAW

Another Irish upstart in London was the playwright and polemicist, George Bernard Shaw (1856-1950). Born in Dublin at **33 Synge Street** (now a museum, *see p77*), Shaw left for London in 1876. Success proved elusive initially, however, and his first five novels were all rejected by publishers.

He would ultimately write 50 plays, usually with themes of politics, class struggle, gender politics and nationalism. Among the most successful of his works are *John Bull's Other Island* (1904), exploring Anglo-Irish relations, *Man and Superman* (1903), *Saint Joan* (1924) and, of course, *Pygmalion* (1913), which eventually morphed into *My Fair Lady*. Shaw, who once wrote, 'Life is no brief candle to me. It is a sort of splendid torch which I have got a hold of for the moment, and I want to make it burn as brightly as possible before handing it on to future generations', was awarded the Nobel Prize for Literature in 1925 – he accepted the prize itself but declined the money that should have come with it.

Despite his self-imposed exile and his occasional complaints, Shaw never lost his fondness for his homeland and upon his death he left a third of his royalties to the **Irish National Gallery**, where his statue now stands.

WB YEATS

The late 19th century was a time of great political agitation in Ireland. The emergence of an indigenous, nationalist literature was a project spearheaded by the writer and critic George Russell (AE), Lady Gregory and Ireland's greatest poet, William Butler Yeats

(1865-1939). Born at **5 Sandymount Avenue** (in the south-east of the city), Yeats spent much of his childhood in Sligo and London. His father, JB Yeats, and brother Jack were both painters of note. He co-founded the Abbey Theatre in 1904 with Lady Gregory, so many of his early plays were performed there, including *The Countess Cathleen* (1892) and *Cathleen ni Houlihan* (1902), in which his great love Maud Gonne played lead.

'Are changed, changed utterly: a terrible beauty is born.' WB Yeats

It was in verse, however, that Yeats truly excelled. The poem 'Easter 1916', his response to the Easter Rising, was one of the most profound things written about that day:
'MacDonagh and MacBride
And Connolly and Pearse
Now and in time to be,
Wherever green is worn,
Are changed, changed utterly:
A terrible beauty is born.'
Having dabbled in mysticism and eastern philosophies, much of Yeats' later poetry is even darker in tone, and *Sailing to Byzantium*, *The Second Coming* and *The Circus Animals Desertion* are all undoubted masterpieces.

Yeats became a senator of the Irish Free State in 1922. The following year, he was awarded the Nobel Prize for Literature. Having been financially dependent on the patronage of others for much of his life, legend has it that Yeats, upon learning from the Lord Mayor of Dublin that he was to be a Nobel Laureate, interrupted the Mayor's speech to demand, 'Yes, yes, just tell me what it's worth!' Yeats died in France in 1939; as had been his request, his body was later reinterred in Sligo. The National Library on Kildare Street has a permanent Yeats exhibition (*photo p29*).

JM SYNGE
Playwright John Millington Synge (1871-1909) was born to an old clerical family in the suburb of Rathfarnham, although it was his family holidays in County Wicklow that gave him a first taste of the country life he later depicted so vividly in his plays. After studies at Trinity College, he spent several years idling in Paris before visiting the Aran Islands in 1898; the islands and the language of the Irish peasantry were to have a long-lasting effect on him.

Upon his return to Dublin, he joined in the tempestuous politics at the Abbey Theatre. His early plays – *Riders to the Sea*, set on the Aran

Islands, and *The Well of the Saints* – were performed there, and were so well received that he joined with Yeats and Lady Gregory as a director of the theatre. He wrote to a friend that Yeats looked after the stars while he saw to everything else. But he would not be famous for looking after things, but for wonderful artistic chaos. When Synge's masterpiece – *The Playboy of the Western World* – was performed there in 1907, the mayhem that ensued became known as the 'Playboy Riots'. The audience was outraged as the play depicted the protagonist killing his father; they were then infuriated further by the use of the slang word 'shift' for women's underwear.

Sadly, Synge had little time to enjoy his success, and just two years later he died of Hodgkin's disease. He now lies in **Mount Jerome cemetery** in the southern suburb of Harold's Cross.

JAMES JOYCE
Not all of the city's literati were wild about the Irish literary revival, of course. In fact, Dublin's supreme literary chronicler, James Joyce (1882-1941), was deeply suspicious of the movement, rejecting the romanticisation of peasantry in favour of a vastly more sophisticated aesthetic system. Born in **Rathgar**, Joyce was educated at **University College**, on **St Stephen's Green**.

From the beginning of his writing career, Joyce struggled against what he saw as the city's old-fashioned, intractable conservatism. He was only 22 when he decided he'd had enough of it. After a short stay in **Sandycove** (his home there is now a museum, *see p98*), Joyce left Dublin in 1904 with his lifelong companion Nora Barnacle. The day before he left, he wrote a heated article for a local broadsheet denouncing the Irish literary revival as introverted. He loved Dublin until he died, but he would never live here again.

His travels took him to Paris and Trieste, in Italy, where he eked out a living teaching English. During this period he wrote poetry, collected as *Chamber Music* in 1907, and short prose sketches or 'epiphanies', some of which appear in his early aborted novel *Stephen Hero*. The first of his prose books to appear was *Dubliners*. Although the book was completed in 1907, it was not published until 1914, as to Joyce's undying fury, nobody in Ireland would touch it. The book – which gorgeously explored a number of negative themes of death, disease and entrapment, all on the streets of Dublin – was too dark for Joyce's publisher, George Roberts, and the two fought over its contents for years as the book languished, unpublished and unread. On Joyce's final visit to Dublin in 1912, Roberts destroyed the entire first edition in a rage. Joyce left the country the next day and never returned. The book was ultimately published in London to great critical acclaim.

Dubliners was followed in 1916 by the autobiographical novel *A Portrait of the Artist as a Young Man*, which charted Joyce's difficult decision to abandon Ireland and Roman Catholicism for the 'silence, exile and cunning' of his artistic vocation.

In 1920 he went to Paris for a week and stayed for 20 years. It was there, in 1922, that he finally completed his masterpiece, *Ulysses*, first begun in 1914. The complex novel traces what happens on 16 June 1904 (the date on which Joyce met his wife Nora) to Stephen Dedalus, a Dublin student, and Leopold Bloom, a Jewish advertising canvasser. Loosely following the structure of Homer's *Odyssey*, the novel's many incredibly complicated experimental literary devices soon brought Joyce international critical fame, but at the same time its frank descriptions of sexual fantasy and bodily functions courted controversy; the book was officially banned in many countries, including the US, for decades. While *Ulysses'* setting is intrinsically Dublin (Joyce surely had a map of the city in his head), its obscurity was deliberate. He wrote to a friend that he had written so many 'puzzles' into it that it would take scholars 100 years to figure them all out, and he was not far wrong in that.

Having finished with the daylight world in *Ulysses*, Joyce plunged into the world of dreams in his last novel, *Finnegans Wake* (1939), which took him 17 years to write and which was, he liked to say, an attempt to dramatise 'the history of the world'. The incredibly complex novel is 'set' in the Mullingar Inn, Chapelizod, and takes place in the dreams and dream-language of a publican named Humphrey Chimpden Earwicker and those of his wife and children Anna Livia Plurabelle, Shaun the Post, Shem the Penman and Issy. Its structure is circular – the last sentence is unfinished (it ends with the words 'along the'), and then connects with the first words of the first chapter ('riverrun'). This is in line with the novel's theme of resurrection and eternal recurrence. It remains a uniquely daunting book, but also a rewarding one. Joyce fled to Zurich to escape the German occupation of France, and he died there in 1941.

SAMUEL BECKETT

Like the other famed writers before him, Dublin's third Nobel laureate, Samuel Beckett (1906-89), spent much of his life outside of Ireland. After attending **Trinity College**, Beckett lived in Paris, and went so far as to write in French in order to disassociate himself from the English literary tradition. While in Paris in the late '20s, he became a friend of Joyce, who dictated some of *Finnegans Wake* to him. Unlike Joyce, though, Beckett came back from his self-imposed exile and wrote a bitter collection of stories, *More Pricks Than Kicks* (1934), in a garret in **Clare Street**. It seems as though he was still bitter in 1938 when he wrote the story *Murphy*, in which a character assaults the buttocks of the statue of national hero Cúchulainn in the **General Post Office**. (Careful observers will notice that the statue does not, in fact, possess buttocks.)

'To get enough to eat was regarded as an achievement. To get drunk was a victory.' Brendan Behan

Beckett returned to Paris in 1937, and then spent much of World War II on the run from the Gestapo in the South of France. After the war, the man who once said, 'I have my faults, but changing my tune is not one of them', produced the clutch of tartly worded, gloomy but funny masterpieces that would bring him international fame, including his most famous play *Waiting for Godot* (1955), characterised by its spare dialogue, stark setting and powerful, symbolic portrayal of the human condition. Later works, such as *Endgame* (1958) and *Happy Days* (1961), concentrate even further on language with minimal action.

Dublin never completely disappeared from Beckett's work, however, with **Dún Laoghaire pier, Dalkey Island** and **Foxrock railway station** all recognisable in works like *Malone Dies* (1958) and the monologue *Krapp's Last Tape* (1959). Beckett was awarded the Nobel Prize for Literature in 1969, but chose not to accept it in person. With the characteristic modesty of a man who remained obsessively private all his life, Beckett gave away most of the 375,000 kroner cash that came with the award; he subsidised friends and artists in Paris, and made a substantial donation to his alma mater, **Trinity College**.

BRENDAN BEHAN

Playwright, bon vivant, drunkard and general hellraiser, Brendan Behan (1923-64) grew up on **Russell Street**. His father was a house painter who had been imprisoned as a Republican towards the end of the Civil War, and so Behan grew up steeped in the lore and history of that struggle. At 14 he was already a member of Fianna Éireann, the youth organisation of the IRA, and when the IRA launched a bombing campaign in England in 1939, Behan was trained in explosives and sent abroad, but he was arrested the day he arrived in Liverpool.

He was subsequently sentenced to three years' borstal (juvenile) detention. He spent two years in a borstal in Suffolk, where he passed much of his time reading in its excellent library. After his release, Behan returned to Dublin, where he was arrested again in 1942 for shooting at a detective during an IRA parade. This time he was sentenced to 14 years in prison. Again, he used his time behind bars to educate himself, studying the Irish language and literature, and soon his descriptions of his borstal life were being published in *The Bell*.

Clearly born under a lucky star, he was released in 1946 as part of a general amnesty. He moved to Paris for a time, but returned to Dublin in 1950, where he cultivated a reputation as one of the city's more rambunctious figures; he was particularly associated with the kind of Dublin Algonquin Roundtable that developed at **McDaid's Pub** (*see p123*).

In 1954 his play *The Quare Fellow* (about a condemned man awaiting execution) went into production at a tiny theatre in Dublin. It was well received, and two years later a production of the play at Joan Littlewood's theatre in London brought Behan the fame he'd always wanted – particularly after a notorious drunken interview on BBC television. From then on, Behan was an international celebrity, and he never hesitated to play the role of the drunken Irishman.

Behan's second play, *An Giall* (The Hostage, 1958), was commissioned by Gael Linn, the Irish-language organisation. Behan later translated the play into English, and Joan Littlewood's production had successful runs in London and New York. Still, most agree that Behan's autobiographical novel *Borstal Boy* (1958) was his best work. Its first chapters are extraordinarily evocative. By the time it was published, however, he was suffering from both alcoholism and diabetes.

His problems were so severe that he simply could not write (it was said that he couldn't hold a pen for shaking), so his publishers suggested that, instead of writing, he should dictate into a tape recorder. This resulted in *Brendan Behan's*

The importance of being Dublin

What is it about Dublin that inspires her writers? Two of its novelists, who have adopted the Irish capital as their home, talk to *Time Out* about the city's role as their literary muse and offer up tips to aspiring writers.

John Banville, Man Booker prize winner for his novel *The Sea*, explained that the allure of the city is the idiosyncracies of her people. 'Certainly Dubliners, and the Irish in general, are the People of the Word. We love to talk, and love to hear ourselves talking, and will say anything, no matter how cruel, for the sake of a witticism. When a politician or a churchman is caught committing some enormity, what fascinates us is not so much the sin, but the account the sinner gives of himself. In this city, if you tell a good enough story, you can get away with anything.'

For Colm Tóibín, who has also been inspired by hotter, continental Spain, it is the appeal of the city's Georgian architecture and the certainty of the temperate northern hemisphere weather.

'I love the Dublin winter, it's reliable, it's cold and it's dark by half four. Between October and April it's a very good time to finish a book. It's a lovely time because you know exactly how the days go, there's no variation. It's never absolutely freezing like, say, New York.'

Tóibín, in deference to the city's unique literary cachet, pays homage. 'Dublin has a really significant tradition that you can choose to forget about or think about. I love the National Library, where there is an original *Ulysses*...If you walk down out of the National Library, you can see the pub where Barnacle worked, or Clare Street where the Becketts have a business. The city has a lot of literary echoes that other cities don't have'.

Working in a café with your laptop perched on your knee sipping on organic coffee from Central America isn't the way to create a literary masterpiece for a disciplined writer. Both Banville and Tóibín share the sentiment that home is where the hard work is done. Banville works from his apartment in the centre of town on the river.

'No real writer will be seen working in public, which puts Sartre and The Beaver in their places.' But, he proffers: 'Dunne & Crescenzi wine bar (*see p119*) is the perfect place to hide out with a book when the Muse is in one of her sulks.'

Tóibín tends to agree : 'I like the three galleries – the National, the Municipal and the Irish Museum of Modern Art for inspiration – but I mostly stay home.'

Island (1962), a collection of anecdotes and essays in which it appeared that he had moved away from the Republican extremism of his youth. The man who once described himself as 'a drinker with a writing problem' was, by then, spending most of his time in Los Angeles and New York, where he hung out with famous people, attended parties, became very drunk and fell down a lot, or was arrested, or ended up in the hospital.

After Behan's death in Dublin on 20 March 1964 (he once said that the only bad publicity was 'your own obituary'), an IRA honour guard escorted his coffin to **Glasnevin Cemetery**.

THE BEST OF THE REST

Elizabeth Bowen (1899-1973) spent her early years in Dublin before moving to London and becoming an air-raid warden. Among her novels is *The Last September* (1929), which tells the story of the decline of a great house in Ireland during the Civil War.

A canal bank statue off **Baggot Street** commemorates **Patrick Kavanagh** (1905-67), a native of Inniskeen, County Monaghan, who described his country childhood in *A Green Fool and Tarry Flynn* (1948). He moved to Dublin in the 1930s, where he wrote his long poem *The Great Hunger* (1942). However, he was never financially secure: he even started his own newspaper, *Kavanagh's Weekly*, but it didn't last for long. Many of his poems describe the Grand Canal where his statue now sits.

Brian O'Nolan (1911-66), aka Flann O'Brien or Myles na Gopaleen, was born in County Tyrone but brought up in Dublin, where he worked as a civil servant. *At Swim-Two-Birds* (1939) is a burlesque and multi-layered novel about a Dublin student writing a book. It won the praise of James Joyce and contains the poem 'A pint of plain is your only man', to be recited over a round of drinks in the Palace or any of the (numerous) other bars associated with O'Brien.

THE NEW GENERATION

While some prestigious Dublin-born writers, such as **Jennifer Johnston** (b.1930; *Shadows on Our Skin, The Ginger Woman*), **Colum McCann** (b. 1965; *This Side of Brightness, Dancer*) and the much-acclaimed **John McGahern** (b.1934; *Amongst Women, That They May Face The Rising Sun*) have chosen to make their home elsewhere, many Irish writers make Dublin a vibrant literary capital.

These include **Neil Jordan** (b.1950), best known as a film scriptwriter and director, but also a successful novelist (*Dream of a Beast, Sunrise with Sea Monster*), and John Banville (b.1945), one of Ireland's most important literary figures thanks to his highly acclaimed

philosophical novels such as *Dr Copernicus* (1976), *The Book of Evidence* (1987) and *Eclipse* (2000). His most recent success has been *The Sea*, his 2005 Man Booker Prize-winning novel about an elderly art historian revisiting his childhood following the death of his wife.

The respected author **Colm Tóibín** (b.1955) lives here, too; his novels include *The Blackwater Lightship* – which was shortlisted for the Booker Prize – and *The Master*. (*See also p33* **The importance of being Dublin**).

Women writers are increasingly making their voices heard, and notable among them are the poet **Eavan Boland** (b.1944), who explores issues of nationality and gender in the collections *New Territory* (1969), *The Journey* (1987) and *In a Time of Violence* (1994); the playwright **Marina Carr** (b.1965; *Portia Coughlan, By the Bog of Cats*), and the novelist **Anne Enright** (b.1962), whose quirky novels *What are You Like?* and *The Pleasure of Eliza Lynch* are now finding a wider audience. In 2007 Enright won the Man Booker prize for her fourth novel, *The Gathering*, that relates the reflections of a bereaved sister, Veronica, on the death of her alcoholic brother, Liam. The rich narrative charts her exploratory journey back through the trials and mores of her large dysfunctional family in an attempt to understand the cause of her brother's demise.

Probably the most successful Dublin writer of recent years, however, is **Roddy Doyle** (b.1958), who has managed to impress both the critics and the general public alike. He's best known for his Barrytown trilogy – *The Commitments, The Van* and *The Snapper* – where his colourful language, combined with an easy sense of humour and a crowd of realistic characters, brought life to Dublin's economically deprived suburbs. The 1993 Booker Prize went to his autobiographical novel *Paddy Clarke Ha Ha Ha*.

Like Doyle, in recent years many of the city's younger writers have moved away from a self-consciously introspective prose style, choosing to dramatise the physical and social changes in Dublin during the last two decades. **Keith Ridgway**'s (b.1965) novels *The Long Falling* and *The Parts* have won acclaim for their frank depiction of the city's subcultures.

Finally, and most recently, the novelist **Sean O'Reilly** (b.1969) has been creating quite a stir with his angry, raucous intellectual Dublin thriller *The Swing of Things*. His latest novel, *Watermark*, takes place in an unnamed Irish city and tells the story of a woman on the margins of urban society, examining classic and universal themes of love, sex and death.

Those who love the city's literary past are hoping this means its influence and heritage will continue to grow.

Where to Stay

Where to Stay	36
Features	
The best Hotels	37
With or without you	41
Top of the morning	51

Buswells Hotel. *See p41*.

Where to Stay

The boutique clique, happy hostellers, friends, families and suits: Dublin has rooms for them all.

Last chance to stay at the 19th-century **Clarence**. *See p39.*

The last few years have seen an increase in the number of ambitious hotel projects being launched in Dublin. Whether they are signalling the end of an era (as with the demolition of the **Clarence**, once Dublin's hippest hotel; *see p39*) or the beginning of a new one (witness the style offensive launched by the oh-so-trendy **Dylan**; *see p45*), one thing's for sure: the city's hotel industry is in rude health. The Docklands, in particular, will be getting more than its fair share of signature hotels, as big-name architects like Manuel Aires Mateus inject some glamour into the quaysides (*see p90*). But it's not all about five-star makeovers: as we go to press, plans are being submitted for a 'monastic, no star' hotel by Grafton Architects, in which polished concrete rooms will give budget accommodation a Le Corbusier spin.

Of course, just like anywhere, Dublin also has its fair share of duds. There are plenty of dank,

dark, hideous establishments, last decorated in 1981 with plaid curtains, floral carpets and the dirt of decades in the corners, and they all seem to charge €100 a night or more. But fear not: in the following pages, we've carefully weeded out the worst and provided a list of the best each area has to offer. You may have to be flexible – if you want a sea view but you haven't got much cash, consider staying in a guesthouse (some of them are wonderful and, for the money, better than anything you could expect from a large hotel). Similarly, if you want to stay in Temple Bar or around Dame Street, but you're a light sleeper, bring earplugs – those are noisy areas. It's also worth mentioning that only the most expensive hotels have air conditioning: bear this in mind if you plan to visit in the summer and you hate stuffy bedrooms.

Wherever you stay, you're likely to get sick of the standard Dublin breakfast of eggs, bacon and sausage – sometimes with white and black pudding – fairly quickly. The bigger the hotel, generally speaking, the more likely you are to face the hellish prospect of the breakfast buffet. Guesthouses inevitably provide the most innovative morning options.

WHAT'S WHERE

Unlike many other busy tourist towns, Dublin's hotels are not concentrated in any particular area of the city; it is possible, in other words, to stay in virtually any neighbourhood. Budget hotels tend to cluster just north of the river, but there are a few good ones south as well, while luxury just spreads out wherever it damn well pleases: the fabulous **Fitzwilliam** (*see p39*) perches on the edge of St Stephen's Green, the celeb fave **Morrison** (*see p48*) looks over the Liffey with cooler-than-thou hauteur. Downriver is the sleek **Clarion Dublin IFSC** (*see p49*), where business bods like to stay close to the office action; inland, the newly decked-out **Shelbourne** (*see p47*) and the gorgeous **Gresham** (*see p48*) keep the traditionalist flags flying. Meanwhile, hideaways like **Number 31** (*see p48*) are squirrelled away all over the place. And out in the suburbs, the big touristy **Fitzpatrick Castle Dublin** (*see p52*) and **Clontarf Castle Hotel** (*see p51*) make the most of Dublin Bay.

A WORD ABOUT THE LISTINGS

Rates listed here are given as general guidelines only, and you should always check with the hotel to see if prices have changed before you book a room; hotels can, and do, change their rates frequently. Rates can also vary depending on the day of the week, the month of the year or if any special events are on in the city.

Almost all of Dublin's hotels are now no-smoking throughout, so unless otherwise stated, assume this to be the case. Also, it's wise to check hotel websites for special offers, and always ask if any are available before you book. Many hotels will give lower rates for children if you book in advance. VAT is included, but be aware that at the upper end of the market, hotels may also add a 12 to 15 per cent service charge.

Around Trinity College

Deluxe

Westin

Westmoreland Street, Dublin 2 (645 1000/ www.thewestindublin.com). All cross-city buses. **Rates** €179-€489 double. **Credit** AmEx, DC, MC, V. **Map** p252 F3

The Westin's imposing 19th-century façade (the building was once a bank) suggests an interior of traditional grandeur and exclusivity, and happily, the reality does not disappoint. The elegant reception area is all marble columns and exquisite plasterwork; a hall of mirrors lines the Westmoreland Street entrance. Rooms are decorated in mahogany and neutral shades, with comfortable beds, soft linen and modern dataports; many have sweeping views of the city. The hotel's bar, the Mint (not to be confused with Mint, the much-discussed restaurant in Ranelagh; *see p116*), is located in the old vaults. Well worth a splurge.
Bar. Business centre. Concierge. Disabled-adapted rooms. Gym. Internet (free high-speed, wireless). Parking (€23/24hrs). Restaurant. Room service. TV: pay movies.

> ❶ Green numbers given in this chapter correspond to the location of each hotel or hostel as marked on the street maps. *See pp250-252.*

Top ten Hotels

For budget beds
Abigail's Hostel (*see p43*); **Avalon House** (*see p44*); **Isaac's Hostel** (*see p51*); **Kinlay House** (*see p44*; **Mount Eccles Court** (*see p49*); **Trinity College** (*see p39*).

For business
Brooks Hotel (*see p39*); **Buswells Hotel** (*see p41*); **Clarion Dublin IFSC** (*see p49*); **Conrad Hotel** (*see p45*); **Hilton Dublin** (*see p47*); **Shelbourne** (*see p47*); **Westbury Hotel** (*see p39*); **Westin** (*see left*).

For escaping the crowds
Clontarf Castle Hotel (*see p51*); **Marina House** (*see p52*); **Phoenix Park House** (*see p51*).

For families
Abode Apartments (*see p48*); **Clarion Dublin IFSC** (*see p49*); **Molesworth Court Suites** (*see p42*).

For glitz and glamour
Clarence (*see p39*); **Dylan** (*see p45*); **Fitzwilliam** (*see p39*); **Morgan** (*see p42*); **Morrison** (*see p48*).

For home comforts
Central Hotel (*see p43*); **Gresham** (*see p48*); **Harrington Hall** (*see p47*); **Merrion Hotel** (*see p45*); **Number 31** (*see p48*).

Expensive

Trinity Capital Hotel

Pearse Street, Dublin 2 (648 1000/www.capital-hotels.com). All cross-city buses/DART Pearse.
Rates €139-€159 double. **Credit** AmEx, DC, MC, V. **Map** p252 G3 ❷

Tucked in beside Dublin's fire station, the Capital attracts business and leisure travellers in equal numbers. The brightly painted rooms are enhanced by subtle art deco touches, but they're a bit on the small side; the decor makes some of them look like classy dorm rooms, and some of the bathrooms are tiny. Still, service is friendly, there's a handy restaurant and lobby lounge, and the nightclub and bar is a lively party spot. Trinity's sister hotel is on Grafton Street. *Bar. Disabled-adapted rooms. Internet (free high-speed, wireless). Parking (€10/24hrs). Restaurant. Room service. TV: pay movies.*

Budget

Trinity College

College Green, Dublin 2 (896 1177/www.tcd.ie). All cross-city buses/DART Pearse. **Rates** *per person* €60-€72. **Credit** MC, V. **Map** p252 F3 ❸

From mid June until the beginning of September, Trinity College provides its on-campus halls of residence as budget accommodation. The 16th-century university could hardly be more central, and there are the added bonuses of stone buildings, cobbled squares and lots of trees. There's a choice of single, twin or double rooms, as well as larger apartments (in Goldsmith Hall, right next door to the campus); not all the rooms are en suite, so make sure you specify what you're after when you book. A continental breakfast is included in the price of a room. *Bars (2). Parking (free, weekends only). Restaurant.*

Around Temple Bar

Deluxe

Clarence

6-8 Wellington Quay, Dublin 2 (407 0800/ www.theclarence.ie). All cross-city buses/ Luas Jervis. **Rates** €209-€349 double. **Credit** AmEx, DC, MC, V. **Map** p252 E3 ❹

If you are curious to see what the soon-to-be 'old Clarence' looks like, then this might be your last chance, as the building that has enshrined the U2 frontmen's hip hotel for the last 12 years is slated for demolition (*see p41* **With or without you**). But until then (no official date for the commencement of work had been set at the time of writing) it will be business as usual at this swish address. The large, sound-proofed guest rooms are elegantly decorated and luxuriously appointed (crisp sheets with four-digit thread-counts are topped by soft duvets; tiled bathrooms are filled with covetable bath products). If you can tear yourself away from the views of the Liffey from the big windows in your room, the Tea Room restaurant (*see p107*) and the Octagon Bar (*see p130*) downstairs are well worth your time and money. There's also a spa for pampering. *Bar. Concierge. Disabled-adapted room. Gym. Internet (free high-speed, wireless). Parking (€25/24hrs). Restaurant. Room service. Spa. TV: DVD.*

Fitzwilliam

St Stephen's Green West, Dublin 2 (478 7000/ www.fitzwilliamhotel.com). All cross-city buses/Luas St Stephen's Green. **Rates** €195-€255 double. **Credit** AmEx, MC, V. **Map** p251 F4 ❺

A very smart hotel overlooking St Stephen's Green (and with the benefit of an in-house Michelin-starred restaurant, Thornton's; *see p101*), the Fitzwilliam is undeniably posh, and yet it remains refreshingly free from the kind of snobbish attitude affected by some of the city's other blue-chip hotels. That's not to say it doesn't have plenty to show off about: effortlessly elegant guest rooms have all the trimmings, right down to fresh flowers and duck-down duvets, and bathrooms packed with lovely products and thick, fluffy towels. The pared-down glamour of the lobby and the helpful staff give you a sense of what's in store from the moment you walk in. And if food is your thing, Kevin Thornton's eponymous restaurant will blow your socks off, or else there's the more low-key Citron, beloved of well-manicured ladies on their way to or from the Temple Bar boutiques. *Bar. Concierge. Gym. Internet (free high-speed, wireless). Parking (€10/24hrs). Restaurants (2). Room service. TV: DVD.*

Westbury Hotel

Grafton Street, Dublin 2 (679 1122/www.jurys doyle.com). All cross-city buses/Luas St Stephen's Green. **Rates** €219-€435 double. **Credit** AmEx, DC, MC, V. **Map** p252 F4 ❻

After a €14 million refurbishment in 2008, this upmarket hotel is looking very swanky indeed. The understated style of its guest rooms and the myriad luxurious touches, such as the Acqua di Parma bathroom products) exudes wealth and sophistication, while its bright, spacious lobby is a discreetly grand place to stop for a drink (either in the high-rolling bar or in the café overlooking Grafton Street). Its central location makes the Westbury an ideal base for weekend visitors who want a hassle-free HQ for sights and shops, as well as a classy pit stop for lunching ladies and the city's *beau monde*. *Bar. Business centre. Concierge. Disabled-adapted rooms. Gym. Internet (free high-speed). Parking (€20/24hrs). Restaurants (2). Room service. TV: pay movies.*

Expensive

Brooks Hotel

59-62 Drury Street, Dublin 2 (670 4000/ www.brookshoteldublin.com). All cross-city buses/Luas St Stephen's Green. **Rates** €155-€215 double. **Credit** AmEx, MC, V. **Map** p252 E4 ❼

THE SHORTLIST
WHAT'S NEW | WHAT'S ON | WHAT'S BEST

- Pocket-sized guides
- What's on, month by month
- Full colour fold-out maps

The rather cramped guest rooms of this sophisticated hotel on Drury Street feature dark purple and muted gold colour schemes that will look lovely to some, tacky to others. But the elegant furnishings of the lobby will appeal to all tastes – and if the frenzy of busy Dublin pubs starts to wear you down, you can soothe your nerves in the exclusive ambience of the hotel's Jasmine Bar. This is afavourite of business travellers: expect a preponderance of suits.

Bar. Business centre. Concierge. Disabled-adapted room. Gym. Internet (free high-speed, wireless). Parking (€6.35/24hrs). Restaurant. Room service. TV: DVD.

Buswells Hotel

23-27 Molesworth Street, Dublin 2 (614 6500/ www.quinnhotels.com). Bus 10, 11, 13, 46A/ Luas St Stephen's Green/DART Pearse. **Rates** €288 double. **Credit** AmEx, DC, MC, V. **Map** p252 G4 ❽

This traditional hotel is saved from feeling stuffy or dated by a strong sense of class. The rooms are distributed across three Georgian buildings and exude charm, from their hefty Georgian windows to the views of the broad streets below. The fact that the hotel is divided into separate buildings gives it a slightly eccentric feel; finding your room could be a tough proposition after a night on the whiskey. But it's undeniably elegant, the rooms are big and

With or without you

It was Dublin's most talked-about hotel when home-grown rock stars Bono and the Edge unveiled it after a boutique-chic makeover back in 1996, and now the **Clarence** (*see p39)* is once more in the spotlight after an announcement in 2008 that the owners have received planning permission to make it bigger, better and altogether grander than it already is. Great news, then? Not entirely. Because, while the hotel's famous proprietors believe that the way forward is to demolish this 19th-century structure and allow the prestigious Foster + Partners to raise up a futuristic eight-storey edifice from its ashes, there are those who have their doubts. In fact, for architectural lobbyists like the Irish Georgian Society (IGS), it boils down to more than just doubts. It is a matter of right and wrong.

In an open letter to the *Irish Times*, the IGS stated its objections very clearly. It was 'extremely concerned' by the decision reached by An Bord Pleanála (the Irish body empowered to grant planning permission for new developments). Why, the Society demanded, had the board granted permission for the scheme when their own senior planning inspector had advised against doing so, citing 'the negative impact on the built heritage' as the principle reason? The letter went on to describe the plans for the new hotel as a 'second rate building by a first rate architect' and deplored the proposed demolition of the interiors of the neighbouring buildings, Dollard House and Nos.9-12 Wellington Quay, which it describes as 'protected structures'.

The owners of the Clarence disagree. 'With an exceptional design, the new Clarence will be an iconic building and will make a significant contribution to the life of our capital,' a spokesman said.

The media hype and the increased chatter in the city's blogosphere have created a heightened sense of anticipation towards the project. Pictures in the media may have earned the new Clarence the unofficial moniker of 'the flying saucer' but only time will tell whether it will improve or irredeemably scar the city's southern 'quayscape'. The only thing that is certain is that the project will go ahead, with or without the support of the people.

superbly decorated, and the place as a whole has a marvellous quirky spirit – in part because its location near the government buildings make its bar and restaurant hubs of political intrigue.

Bar. Business centre. Concierge. Disabled-adapted room. Internet (free high-speed, wireless). Gym. Parking (€2.80/hr day, free nights). Restaurant. Room service. TV.

Molesworth Court Suites

Schoolhouse Lane, Dublin 2 (676 4799/ www.molesworthcourt.ie). All cross city buses/ Luas St Stephen's Green. **Rates** €180-€420 suites. **Credit** AmEx, MC, V. **Map** p252 F4 ❾

On a quiet side street in the heart of the city, these excellent self-catering apartments make a good option for families or groups of friends. Each of the spacious apartments is fully self-contained, cosy and comfortable, with all bed linen provided. Some are attractively designed and, for the price, there seems little to complain about. Shops, restaurants and pubs are a short walk away.

Internet (free high-speed, wireless). Parking (free). TV: DVD.

Morgan

10 Fleet Street, Dublin 2 (679 3939/ www.themorgan.com). All cross-city buses. **Rates** €150-€250 double. **Credit** AmEx, MC, V. **Map** p252 F3 ❿

Designed to within an inch of its life, the Morgan is, first and foremost, a trendy hotel (the kind of place where one's lack of €500 trainers seems, somehow, to matter) but it is also a very comfortable and attractive spot in which to lay your head for a few nights. The spacious bedrooms are decked out in calming pale tones, with splashes of original Irish art, while the hotel's cocktail bar has tapas, a DJ and an occasional bongo player. On which note, be warned: rooms looking out on to Fleet Street can be noisy in the small hours; ask for a room at the back of the hotel or on one of the upper floors. The hotel also offers apartments with kitchens for extended stays.

Bar. Business centre. Concierge. Disabled-adapted rooms. Internet (free high-speed, wireless). Parking (€9/24hrs). Restaurant. Room service. TV: DVD.

Paramount

Parliament Street & Essex Street, Dublin 2 (417 9900/www.paramounthotel.ie). All cross-city buses. **Rates** €155-€350 double. **Credit** AmEx, MC, V. **Map** p252 E3 ⓫

You'd never guess it from sitting in the Turk's Head bar (*see p133*) on a Saturday night, but this hotel is something of a hidden gem. It's not a peaceful place – the aforementioned bar and nightclub packs in partiers most nights – but it looks quite good. The bedrooms are reminiscent of 1930s chic, done up in subtle tobacco tones, with leather headboards, dark wood furnishings and soft lighting. The spacious rooms are equally popular with raucous pleasure-seekers and low-key weekenders, but ask for rooms on the upper floors if you're not keen on earplugs. *Photo p44.*

Bar. Concierge. Disabled-adapted rooms. Internet (free high-speed). Room service. TV: pay movies.

Buswells Hotel. *See p41.*

Moderate

Central Hotel

1-5 Exchequer Street, Dublin 2 (679 7302/
www.centralhotel.ie). Bus 16, 16A. **Rates** €78-€89
double. **Credit** AmEx, MC, V. **Map** p252 E3 ⑫
This comfortable, 187-year-old hotel is unique in that
it's a prime piece of real estate (right off Dame Street
near Temple Bar) that the designers haven't yet got
their hands on. This, you can't help but think, is how
all hotels here used to look: floral fabrics and busy
carpet patterns everywhere, the furniture likely to
have battered edges – and a real sense of quirky independence. The spacious rooms are a bit tired (and
somebody renovate those bathrooms, please), but
they have wonderful architectural touches and big,
old sash windows. The cosy Library Bar is a haven
of civility with its leather armchairs, blazing fires,
wood panelling and books: it's the thinking
Dubliner's trendy hangout. The restaurant is attractive and particularly pleasant early in the morning,
when light streams through its huge windows.
Bars. Concierge. Internet (free high-speed, wireless).
Restaurant. Room service. TV.

Eliza Lodge

23-24 Wellington Quay, Dublin 2 (671 8044/
www.dublinlodge.com). All cross-city buses/Luas
Jervis. **Rates** €115-€230. **Credit** AmEx, MC, V.
Map p252 E3 ⑬
Don't be put off by the pokey little reception area at
this otherwise decent riverside hotel. Some people
may be disturbed by the incessant clatter and rumble of trucks down on the quays, but double glaz-
ing keeps it very much in the background, and
the sweeping views of the Liffey more than make
up for the pesky traffic. While the rooms won't feature on any television interior design programme,
they're big and bright, and the price is very good
for what you get.
Parking (€24/24hrs). Restaurant. TV.

Temple Bar Hotel

15-17 Fleet Street, Dublin 2 (677 3333/
www.towerhotelgroup.ie). All cross-city buses/
Luas Abbey Street. **Rates** €120-€220 double.
Credit AmEx, DC, MC, V. **Map** p252 F3 ⑭
Temple Bar has earned itself a raucous rep over the
last few years (the drunken stag parties, the sick-
splashed pavements) and it has to be said that this
hugely poular hotel is right in the thick of the action.
But if that doesn't put you off, then there is much to
be said for staying right in the centre of things – and,
despite its busy nightclub, the hotel does well to
maintain an air of civility. There's a grown-up reception area, comfortable (if plain) rooms and a team of
helpful, switched-on staff. Even so, if you're looking
for an oasis of serenity, or even a bit of peace and
quiet, this probably isn't the place for you.
Bars (2). Internet (free wireless). Parking
(€24/24hrs). Restaurant. Room service. TV.

Trinity Lodge

12 South Frederick Street, Dublin 2 (617 0900/
www.trinitylodge.com). All cross-city buses/Luas
St Stephen's Green. **Rates** €195-€250 double.
Credit AmEx, DC, MC, V. **Map** p252 F3 ⑮
Set in a nicely maintained Georgian property,
Trinity Lodge has a chic, laid-back style, with some
of its guest rooms featuring paintings by Irish artist
Graham Knuttel. Downstairs there's a pleasant
restaurant where you can expect high-quality nosh
of a morning (own-baked bread, freshly squeezed
orange juice and the like). In a second building
across the road, six more rooms have a more
contemporary feel but are equally well done. Staff
are friendly, and the place is well located for the
restaurants and bars of the city centre. Because the
building is listed, there's no lift.
Bar. Internet (free wireless). Parking (€2.50/hr/€6
overnight). Restaurant. Room service. TV.

Budget

Abigail's Hostel

7-9 Aston Quay, Dublin 2 (677 9300/
www.abigailshostel.com). **Rates** *per person*
€16-€58. **Credit** AmEx, MC, V. **Map** p252 F2 ⑯
The new kid on the budget block, Abigail's has a
refreshingly sunny approach to shoestring accommodation. Sure, you may find yourself wedged into
a room with seven other people (although, for a few
euros more you can bag a room of your own) but the
decor is modern and welcoming, and the common
areas are upbeat and smartly decked out. Even the

Where to Stay

The **Paramount**: a window into 1930s chic. *See p42.*

communal kitchen has a nice feel to it. All of the guest rooms are shared (save for a couple of coveted singles) with as many as eight and as few as two in the bunks – but it never gets rowdy and security is tight (CCTV cameras are trained on the entrance door – a comforting, rather than Orwellian, touch in the busy, hectic hub of Temple Bar).
Internet (free high-speed, wireless).

Ashfield House

19-20 d'Olier Street, Dublin 2 (679 7734/www.ash fieldhouse.ie). All cross-city buses. **Beds** *per person* €13-€58. **Credit** AmEx, MC, V. **Map** p252 F2
This brightly decorated, cheery hostel has basic but clean en suite rooms (two, four and six beds), and larger dorms. Facilities include a bureau de change and free luggage storage, as well as cosy dining areas, with pool table, television and internet access. Its security is highly rated.
Internet (free high-speed, wireless).

Avalon House

55 Aungier Street, Dublin 2 (475 0001/www.avalon-house.ie). Bus 16, 16A, 19, 22, 155. **Rates** *per person* €16-€39. **Credit** AmEx, MC, V. **Map** p251 E4
A firm favourite among Dublin's budget travellers, this pleasantly warm and cheery guesthouse occupies a lovely old red-brick building. Its pine floors, high ceilings and open fireplace make it a thoroughly pleasant place in which to relax. Rooms range from dorms to doubles, and all are immaculately clean. In fact, this place has all you really need: cheerful rooms in a safe location at a cheap price. And its most recent addition (a branch of the

excellent Bald Barista café just up the road; *see p118*) is perfect for charging up the system with a morning espresso and planning out the day.
Internet (free high-speed, wireless). Restaurant.

Four Courts

15-17 Merchants Quay, Dublin 8 (672 5839/www.fourcourtshostel.com). All cross city buses/Luas Four Courts. **Rates** *per person* €18-€36. **Credit** MC, V. **Map** p250 D3
Set in several pretty Georgian buildings overlooking the Liffey, this friendly hostel has all the basics, and a few charming details besides. Its setting at the edge of the river (opposite the eponymous Four Courts) is exceptional, and the guest rooms have big windows, polished wood floors, desks and other nice touches that make the plain, metal bunk beds slightly more bearable. It has 24-hour access, free continental breakfast, good security, laundry facilities, a games room, internet access and a place to park your car: in short, more than most hostels give you for the money.
Internet (free high-speed). Parking (€8/24hrs, €20 deposit). Restaurant.

Kinlay House

2-12 Lord Edward Street, Dublin 2 (679 6644/www.kinlaydublin.ie). All cross-city buses. **Rates** *per person* €24-€41. **Credit** AmEx, MC, V. **Map** p252 D3
This beautiful red brick building in one of Dublin's oldest neighbourhoods (just steps from Christ Church Cathedral; *see p66*) is a great setting for a hostel. It's quiet and leafy enough for a good night's kip but close enough to Temple Bar to be within post-pub crawl stumbling distance. There's a large

self-catering kitchen and dining room, a TV room and colourful meeting room. Dorms are small but clean, and the front desk is open around the clock. Toast and coffee are served each morning for breakfast until 9.30am.
Internet (free high-speed, wireless).

Around St Stephen's Green

Deluxe

Conrad Hotel
Earlsfort Terrace, Dublin 2 (602 8900/ www.conradhotels.com). Bus 10, 11, 13, 14, 15, 44, 46A, 47, 48, 86/Luas St Stephen's Green. **Rates** €189-€304 double. **Credit** AmEx, DC, MC, V. **Map** p251 F5 ㉑
The long-established Conrad, on a prominent site on the corner of St Stephen's Green, is a firm favourite among the suited, laptop-wielding types who've made Dublin the business hub that it is: expect fast internet connections, big desks and fax machines. Bedrooms are nicely done in neutral colours, with big windows, individual temperature controls for the air con and fabulous bathrooms. The gym is excellent, and reduced rates are available for the use of the nearby K Club golf course. The hotel pub might lack character, but local office workers still pack the place every night; and the Alex restaurant is a particularly sleek hotel diner for those with expense accounts.
Bars (2). Business centre. Concierge. Disabled-adapted room. Gym. Internet (free high-speed, wireless). Parking (€7.50/24hrs). Restaurants (2). Room service. TV: pay movies.

Dylan
Eastmoreland Place, Dublin 4 (660 3000/ www.dylan.ie). Bus 11,13, 16, 16A/Luas Charlemont. **Rates** €220-€395 double. **Credit** AmEx, DC, MC, V. **Map** p251 H5 ㉒
Cool enough to stay in the Dylan? You wish. This is the boutique hotel that everyone's talking about: from the oversized lanterns strewn around its entrance to the iPods in its immaculate guest rooms, every detail of this hotel has been carefully thought out. The guests who breeze in and out of the swish lobby and stylish cocktail bar (check out the funky zinc counter) are the kind of well-dressed hipsters who seem entirely at home among the sumptuously upholstered furniture, the yards of trendy wallpaper and the minimalism of the bright, white terrace. Guest rooms are a triumph of understated style blended with flashes of boldness (the bedheads, in particular, are stunning). Bathrooms are loaded with gorgeous Etro products, beds are clothed in Frette sheets, the in-room safes are laptop-compatible – you get the picture. This is serious luxury aimed at people who expect nothing less.
Bar. Concierge. Internet (free high-speed, wireless). Parking (€20/24hrs). Restaurant. Room service. TV: pay movies.

Merrion Hotel
Upper Merrion Street, Dublin 2 (603 0600/ www.merrionhotel.com). Bus 10, 13, 13A/DART Pearse. **Rates** €455-€595 double. **Credit** AmEx, DC, MC, V. **Map** p251 G4 ㉓
Housed inside four restored, listed Georgian houses, the Merrion doesn't shy away from a little frill here, a delicate striped couch there. No, this place is definitely in touch with its feminine side. Downstairs the

Where to Stay

The safe and secure **Abigail's**; a favourite with no-nonsense hostellers. *See p43.*

public spaces are dominated by quiet, girly drawing rooms where fires glow in hearths and you long for tea and scones, and – hey presto! – they're yours at the drop of a few euros. The impressive contemporary art on the walls is part of one of the country's largest private collections. Service is discreetly omnipresent, and the spacious rooms overlook either the government buildings or the hotel's 18th-century-inspired gardens of acacia and lilac. Pamper yourself in the Tethra Spa, stretch your credit card at the Michelin-starred Patrick Guilbaud restaurant (*see p108*) or dine at the somewhat cheaper and more atmospheric Cellar (*see p111*). *Photo p48-49*.
Bars (2). Concierge. Disabled-adapted rooms. Gym. Internet (free high-speed). Parking (€20/24hrs). Pool (indoor). Restaurants (2). Spa. Room service. TV: DVD/pay movies.

O'Callaghan Davenport Hotel

Merrion Square, Dublin 2 (607 3500/ www.ocallaghanhotels.com). DART Pearse/all cross-city buses. **Rates** €150-€315 double. **Credit** AmEx, DC, MC, V. **Map** p251 H4 ㉔

It may have made good use of the impressive 1863 façade of Merrion Hall, but most of the rest of the upmarket Davenport was built in the 1990s and, in a rather old-fashioned way, is utterly modern. The lobby is nice enough, as are the guest rooms (even if they won't conform to everyone's idea of chic interior design), and the location is suitably swanky. But, truth be told, there are better hotels in town for the price.
Bar. Business centre. Concierge. Disabled-adapted rooms. Gym. Internet (free high-speed, wireless). Parking (€10/24hrs). Restaurant. Room service. TV: pay movies.

Shelbourne Hotel

27 St Stephen's Green North, Dublin 2 (663 4500/ www.marriott.co.uk). Bus, 11, 14, 15. **Rates** €199-€359. **Credit** AmEx, DC, MC, V. **Map** p251 G4 ㉕

After having had more than €40 million lavished on it by its new owners (this 19th-century Dublin landmark is now a member of the Marriott empire), the Shelbourne is looking pretty damn good. It always was the doyenne of Dublin hotels (albeit in a slightly faded kind of way) but now this five-star is once again a major contender, with more than just the prestige of a long and eventful history to offer. From the candelabras in its echoing marble lobby to the Egyptian cotton sheets and sumptuous bathrooms on the floors above, the Shelbourne is all about good living. Of course, as is the usual story with the finer things in life, it ain't cheap, but at least you can see where the money is going: expensive products, fine fixtures and top-dollar amenities are on hand in all the guest rooms. The Horseshoe Bar is a great nook for a nightcap, while the Lord Mayor's is the place for afternoon teas. At the time of writing, work was underway on a fancy in-house spa.
Bar. Business centre. Concierge. Gym. Internet (free high-speed, wireless). Parking (€25/24hrs). Restaurant. Room service. TV: pay movies.

Expensive

Harrington Hall

69-70 Harcourt Street, Dublin 2 (475 3497/ www.harringtonhall.com). Buses 10, 11, 15A, 15B, 16, 16A, 20B, 62/Luas Harcourt. **Rates** €89-€179 doule. **Credit** AmEx, DC, MC, V. **Map** p251 F5 ㉘

This beautiful hotel occupies two adjoining houses close to St Stephen's Green. The property was once the home of Timothy Charles Harrington, former Lord Mayor of Dublin, who clearly had excellent architectural taste. The exquisite stuccoed ceilings have been retained, and there's much to praise here: the warmth, attentiveness and personal touch of the service, the beautifully appointed lobby and the spotless, simple but elegant bedrooms. Rooms at the rear look out across the Iveagh Gardens (*see p70*). This is one of Dublin's outstanding small hotels.
Disabled-adapted room. Internet (free high-speed, wireless). Parking (free). Room service. TV.

Hilton Dublin

Charlemont Place, Grand Canal, Dublin 2 (402 9988/www.hilton.co.uk/dublin). Bus 14, 15, 44, 48A/Luas Charlemont. **Rates** €195-€233 double. **Credit** AmEx, DC, MC, V. **Map** p251 F6 ㉗

The main selling point of this modern chain hotel is its tranquil setting overlooking the leafy banks of the Grand Canal, offering a view so bucolic you could forget you're right in the middle of the city. The bedrooms are decorated, as you might expect, in contemporary style (though you might not expect the fabrics to be quite so reliant on strange, checkerboard patterns), and they get lots of light. In honour of its core clientele, the Hilton has the full complement of business facilities: internet access, fax machines, impressive-looking phones, a boring bar. The restaurant overlooks the canal, which makes up a bit for its somewhat chain-hotel look.
Bar. Business centre. Concierge. Disabled: adapted rooms (5). Internet. Parking (€10/24hrs). Restaurant. Room service. TV: DVD/pay movies.

Moderate

Kilronan House

70 Adelaide Road, Dublin 2 (475 5266/ www.kilronanhouse.com). Bus 11,13, 16, 16A/Luas Harcourt. **Rates** €110-€170 double. **Credit** AmEx, MC, V. **Map** p251 F6 ㉘

It may look just like another B&B from its modest terraced façade but Kilronan House is an elegant and, above all, welcoming place that has been renovated with real class. The staff are never short on enthusiasm (and the massive, varied breakfasts served in the sunny front room will set you up for the day). Some of the guest rooms in the handsome Victorian building still have original period features and high ceilings; newer bedrooms do not (although they do have a bit more space). *Photo p50*.
Internet (free high-speed, wireless). Parking (free). Room service. TV.

Number 31

31 Leeson Close, Dublin 2 (676 5011/www.number 31.ie). Bus 10, 46A/Luas Charlemont. **Rates** €150-€320 double. **Credit** AmEx, DC, MC, V. **Map** p251 G5 ㉙

Set in one of the city's most fashionable locales, this unique guesthouse is a real find, combining modern design with an almost rural tranquillity. Most of the soothingly decorated bedrooms occupy a Georgian townhouse, although a few are in the beautifully designed modern mews building where delicious own-made breakfasts are served (*see p51* **Top of the morning**). Warm yourself in front of the peat fire in the sunken lounge or wander through the lush gardens for some green therapy.

Internet (free high-speed, wireless). Parking (free). TV.

Around O'Connell Street

Deluxe

Gresham Hotel

23 Upper O'Connell Street, Dublin 1 (874 6881/ www.gresham-hotels.com). Bus 11, 13/Luas Abbey Street. **Rates** €290-€600 double. **Credit** AmEx, MC, V. **Map** p251 F1 ㉚

A key part of Dublin's political and leisure history (it featured in the Easter Rising as a refuge and, later, as a hideout), the Gresham has been taking care of visitors for 200 years. The grand façade, vast lobby and charming bar are all elegant, but not overwhelmingly so; here it's all about comfort. A lengthy renovation has given this grande dame a badly needed upgrade, and all rooms now have luxurious fabrics in soothing tones, satellite televisions and all the usual four-star extras. The gargantuan, buzzy lobby bar is a popular local meeting place.

Bars (2). Concierge. Disabled-adapted room. Gym. Parking (€14/24hrs). Internet (free high-speed). Restaurants (2). Room service. TV: pay movies.

Morrison

Ormond Quay, Dublin 1 (887 2400/www.morrison hotel.ie). Bus 30, 90/Luas Jervis. **Rates** €165-€285 double. **Credit** AmEx, DC, MC, V. **Map** p252 E2 ㉛

With an interior designed by John Rocha and every fancy boutique touch from in-room iPod docks and (in the grander rooms) Macs with wireless keyboards to gorgeous bathrooms with aromatherapy toiletries and sunken baths, the Morrison lives up to its reputation for sophisticated luxury. It is ideally located across the river from Temple Bar (just a few steps away from the action but with a pleasingly sequestered feel). A lot of work has been done on the interior in recent years, and the results are stunning (the hotel has also expanded in size recently). The comfortable rooms plead to be enjoyed, with Egyptian-cotton bed linen and the sheer decadence of Portuguese limestone in the bathrooms. The two bars (especially the intimate Morrison Bar; *see p137*) and the Halo restaurant are, as you would expect, design-literate, good-quality operations. *Photo p52.*

Bars (2). Concierge. Disabled-adapted rooms. Internet (free high-speed, wireless). Parking (€14/24hrs). Restaurant. Room service. TV: pay movies.

Expensive

Cassidy's Hotel

Cavendish Row, Upper O'Connell Street, Dublin 1 (878 0555/www.cassidyshotel.com). All cross-city buses/Luas Abbey Street. **Rates** €89-€160 double. **Credit** AmEx, DC, MC, V. **Map** p251 F1 ㉒

The family-owned Cassidy's Hotel is across the street from the historic Gate Theatre, and within about ten minutes' walk of Temple Bar and Dame Street's hustle. The hotel is larger than it looks from the outside (there are more than 100 bedrooms in there, somehow), and has a handy restaurant and a cosy bar. Rooms are smallish and simple, but not cramped or uncomfortable. Rooms at the back are quieter, but those at the front have a better view. Charmingly, if you've forgotten to bring a good book, the front desk will lend you one.

Bar. Disabled-adapted rooms. Gym. Internet (free high-speed, wireless). Parking (free). Restaurant. Room service. TV.

Moderate

Abode Apartments

Quay Apartments, Eden Quay, Dublin 1 (814 7000/www.abodedublin.com). All cross-city buses/ Luas Abbey Street. **Rates** *per person* €93-€107. **Credit** AmEx, MC, V. **Map** p251 F2 ㉝

One in a string of locations around the city, these smart riverside apartments are a nice alternative to hotel accommodation (especially for longer stays or

Merrion Hotel. *See p45.*

for those with kids). Floor-to-ceilingwindows let in plenty of daylight and make the most of the views (these apartments are situated on the top two floors of a modern block) and the street-level video intercom provides the peace of mind that is sometimes missing in Dublin's self-catering sector. Kitchens are perfectly serviceable and the staff (who are contactable 24/7) are helpful and pleasant. Other locations include the very central Adelaide Square and the award-winning Wooden Building in Temple Bar. *Internet (free or €4/24hrs high-speed). Parking (€10/24hrs).TV.*

Hotel St George
7 Parnell Square, Dublin 1 (874 5611/ www.stgeorgehoteldublin.com). Bus 10, 11, 11A, 16, 16A, 19, 19A/Luas Abbey Street. **Rates** €129-€218 double. **Credit** MC, V. **Map** p251 F1 ③④
The public spaces of the Hotel St George are really quite grand, thanks to the many original architectural features that have been carefully preserved in this pretty Georgian building (think marble fireplaces, crystal chandeliers and huge antique mirrors). The smallish bedrooms are considerably simpler in design. The decor here is a bit basic (new curtains wouldn't go amiss, for example). Still, it's a quiet, pleasant place, and the bar and original 18th-century parlour add to its rather particular charm. *Bar. Internet (free wireless). Parking (free). TV.*

Budget

Mount Eccles Court
42 North Great Georges Street, Dublin 1 (873 0826/ www.eccleshostel.com) All cross-city buses/Luas Abbey Street. **Rates** *per person* €17-€36. **Credit** AmEx, MC, V. **Map** p251 F1 ③⑤

This lovely little hostel in a Georgian building on North Great Georges Street is a great option for those who find bigger facilities intimidating. Its ten bedrooms and ten dorms are secured with keycard locks and are neatly decorated with neutral walls and nice touches like potted plants. There's 24-hour access, bedding (including sheets), luggage lockers, internet access, bike storage, hot showers, and TV and music lounges. They also have apartments for rent, if there are a few of you and your purse strings stretch beyond dorm prices. *Internet (€1/hr high-speed).*

North Quays & Docklands

Expensive

Clarion Dublin IFSC
International Financial Services Centre, Dublin 1 (433 8800/www.clarionhotelifsc.com). All cross-city buses/DART Connolly. **Rates** €135-€180 double. **Credit** AmEx, DC, MC, V. **Map** p251 G2 ③⑥
Yes, it's a chain hotel, and big with business travellers; but don't be put off. This is an excellent hotel: great looking, well run, fabulous location, decent prices and lots of extras. The guest rooms are spacious with sweeping views of the River Liffey; they're done in soothing neutral colours, all cream and taupe; they feature Egyptian cotton duvets, large TVs, free broadband and even video-game consoles. The laid-back atmosphere in the stylish bar and restaurant is more relaxing than intimidating; those after something more energetic can try out the fully-equipped gym or the truly gorgeous heated indoor pool. As chain hotels go, it doesn't get much better than this.

Bars (2). Business centre. Concierge. Disabled-adapted rooms. Gym. Internet (free high-speed, wireless). Parking (€12/24hrs). Pool (indoor). Restaurant. Room service. Smoking rooms. TV: DVD/pay movies.

Moderate

Days Inn

95-98 Talbot Street, Dublin 1 (874 9202/ www.daysinntalbot.com). Bus 33, 41/Luas Abbey Street. **Rates** €99-€150 double. **Credit** AmEx, DC, MC, V. **Map** p251 F1 ⑰

Someone has been doing some thinking at the Days Inn, with the result that now, where the boring chain hotel decor once was, you'll find lots of brushed wood, chrome and neutral colours. Bedrooms in this four-storey hotel are a bit on the small side, but they're nice enough for resting between bouts of shopping on nearby O'Connell Street. However, the fact that the hotel's website touts a soft drinks machine among the 'amenities' is an indication of the kinds of extras you can expect here. (There's also an ice machine – now that's what we call class.)
Disabled-adapted room. Internet (free high-speed, wireless). Parking (free). TV.

Hotel Isaac's

Store Street, Dublin 1 (855 0067/www.isaacs.ie). All cross-city buses/Luas Busáras. **Rates** €99-€159 double. **Credit** AmEx, MC, V. **Map** p251 G2 ㊳

The first thing people tend to notice about Isaac's (apart from the fact that its neighbourhood is not the shiniest example of modern Dublin) is the impressive reception area, with its flamboyant lighting and mantelpieces. Bedrooms are a little less OTT, sadly; but, (comparitively) dull though they are, they have all you need. Isaac's is distinguished mostly by lovely touches like the verdant courtyard and the snug garden lounge. There's a small bar and an Italian restaurant downstairs for emergencies. But do make sure you take a cab home at night.
Bar. Disabled-adapted rooms. Internet (free wireless). Parking (€10/24hrs). Restaurant. Room service. Smoking rooms. TV.

Park Inn

Smithfield Village, Dublin 7 (817 3838/www.park inn.ie). Bus 25, 26, 37, 39, 67, 68, 69, 70/Luas Smithfield. **Rates** €99-€150 double. **Credit** AmEx, MC, V. **Map** p250 C2 ㊴

Part of the vast global hotel group Rezidor, the Park Inn deserves a mention if only for the fact that it manages to not betray what it actually is: a chain hotel. In every way, this characterful hotel is a welcome little slice of easy-living modernity among the historic buildings of charming Smithfield Village. Irish music is one of the hotel's themes – suites are named after Irish musicians, there are large murals in the spacious bar, and CDs on the stereos in most rooms. The bedrooms themselves are modern and bright – perhaps too much so, with splashes of vivid yellow and bright red, and glass-brick walls – but

Kilronan House. *See p47.*

Top of the morning

It's the most important meal of the day, and yet many hotels put little thought into what they are going to lay on for breakfast. Some city hotels, however, have put so much effort into the morning meal that it has become a major selling point, and the reason why guests come back, year after year, like bees to a honey pot. So breakfast-lovers, take note: these are some of the best Dublin has to offer.

Top of the list, surely, must be the spread at **Number 31** (*see p48*). In this elegant guesthouse, tucked away in a leafy residential mews, great things emerge from the kitchen. Breads, jams and marmalades are all made in-house, as is the muesli and granola (and the rhubarb compote, the stewed pears, the fresh fruit salad – the list goes on). And if that all sounds a bit girly, real men can start their days with full

Irish breakfasts, eggs Benedict, kippers, mushroom frittata and the rest.

Another decent breakfast menu can be found at **Kilronan House** (*see p47*), where legendary fry-ups have been cementing the arteries of hotel-guest relations for many years (there are also a good many healthier options for calorie-counters), while the budget hostel **Avalon House** (*see p44*) has been blessed with a branch of **Bald Barista** (*see p118*), which serves the finest coffee in town.

As you might expect, many of the larger hotels also lay on top-dollar buffets and breakfast menus, and self-caterers have a wide choice of excellent purveyors of pastries and coffees for their morning assembly line: the food hall at **Fallon & Byrne** (*see p151*) is the only option for DIY breakfast chefs; the unbeatable pâtisserie at **Léon** (*see p121*) can be relied on to produce the goods for you.

---

the overall emphasis is on comfort. The restaurant serves modern Irish food but there's more exciting fare to be had just a short walk across the river in Temple Bar.
Bar. Concierge. Disabled-adapted rooms. Internet (free wireless). Parking (€10/24hrs). Restaurant. Room service. TV.

Budget

Isaac's Hostel

2-5 Frenchman's Lane, Dublin 1 (855 6215/ www.isaacs.ie). All cross-city buses/DART Connolly/ Luas Busáras. **Rates** *Per person* €18-€40. **Credit** MC, V. **Map** p251 G2 ㊵

Near Busáras bus depot and Connolly Street train station, this is the aristocrat of Dublin's hostels. Isaac's takes the backpacker concept of humble frugality and turns it on its head. Calling itself 'Dublin's first VIP hostel', it has the usual mix of bunk beds, lockers and TV rooms, but adds a heady cocktail of extras like polished wood floors, a restaurant and an attractive (free) sauna. There's also internet access, a kitchen for guests to use, pool tables – and a friendly and relaxing atmosphere.
Internet (free wireless). Restaurant. Smoking rooms.

Phoenix Park House

38-39 Parkgate Street, Dublin 8 (677 2870/ www.dublinguesthouse.com). Bus 10, 15, 24, 25, 66, 67/Luas Heuston. **Rates** €89-€132 double. **Credit** AmEx, DC, MC, V. **Map** p250 A2 ㊶
On the edge of scenic Phoenix Park, this guesthouse has clean and well-appointed en suite rooms, with an emphasis on good value for money. Though

there's no restaurant, there are several good eateries nearby. Children are welcome, and there's plenty for them to do nearby (not least at the superb, kid-friendly Dublin Zoo; *see p86*).
Parking (€7/24hrs). Room service. TV.

Dublin Bay & the Coast

Deluxe

Clontarf Castle Hotel

Castle Avenue, Clontarf, Dublin 3 (833 2321/ www.clontarfcastle.ie). Bus 130/DART Clontarf Road. **Rates** €168-€400 double. **Credit** AmEx, DC, MC, V.
Now that it's had €10 million spent on it, Clontarf Castle is looking every inch the swanky modern hotel (except, of course, for the elements of the 12th-century structure that have been artfully integrated into the design). The original castle here was built in 1172 by Hugh de Lacy, Lord of Meath, and while there's not much left of that structure, what remains does give the hotel a unique atmosphere; particularly impressive is the vast reception area, with looming castle walls, grand piano and proud lion sculptures standing guard. Decadent blood-red fabrics cover the armchairs, and while there might be the odd suit of armour or faded tapestry dotted about the place, it's far from fusty, thanks to various striking modern touches (such as the new glass entrance, which accounted all on its own for a million of the refurb money). And pared-down decor, cast-iron bathtubs and mod cons aplenty ensure the guest rooms are suitably grand. Well-appointed

conference facilities mean that many of your fellow guests may be decked out in suits.

Bar. Business centre. Concierge. Disabled-adapted rooms. Gym. Internet (free high-speed). Parking (free). Restaurant. Room service. TV: pay movies.

Expensive

Fitzpatrick Castle Dublin

Killiney, Co. Dublin (230 5400/ www.fitzpatrickhotels.com). DART Dalkey. **Rates** €129-€220 double. **Credit** AmEx, DC, MC, V.

Standing nobly at the top of the hill overlooking the village of Dalkey, the Fitzpatrick is a regal-looking place that does indeed look like a castle. Actually, it's a crenellated manor house, but no less impressive for it: guest rooms are decked out in a kind of country chic (some with truly extraordinary sea views), and the rambling old lounge is a joy, filled with lots of sofas, pianos and working fireplaces. The elegant 20-metre indoor swimming pool is handy, and there's a decent basement restaurant, the Dungeon (naturally), and a more expensive formal restaurant upstairs for fine dining; the Library bar is lively and attractive with a wine and cocktail menu to please drinkers. Fitzpatrick also offers long-stay apartments.

Bar. Business centre. Concierge. Gym. Internet (free wireless). Parking (free). Pool (indoor). Restaurants (2). Room service. TV: pay movies.

Boutique luxury at the **Morrison**. *See p48.*

Portmarnock Hotel & Golf Links

Portmarnock, Co. Dublin (846 0611/www.port marnock.com). Bus 32, 42. **Rates** €139-€179 double. **Credit** AmEx, MC, V.

Justifiably renowned for its excellent golf course overlooking Portmarnock beach, this hotel's emphasis is firmly on conservative luxury. All the sumptuously decorated bedrooms have either a bay view or a view of the links, and you can dine at the excellent Osborne restaurant. The relaxing Jameson bar, with panelled walls and glowing fires, was truly designed for drinking whiskey. The hotel caters equally for business and pleasure, with understated but efficient service; if you're here for the golf, you can be sure your outings to one of the first courses developed in Ireland will be well organised. And if you are a golf widow, you should find plenty of compensations in the range of relaxing treatments and beautifying therapies – including full- and half-day packages – on offer at the in-house Oceana spa.

Bars (2). Business centre. Concierge. Gym. Internet (free wireless). Parking (free). Restaurant. Room service. Spa. TV.

Moderate

Deer Park Hotel & Golf Courses

Howth, Co. Dublin (832 2624/www.deerpark-hotel.ie). Bus 31A, 31B/DART Howth. **Rates** €100-€184 double. **Credit** AmEx, DC, MC, V.

Unquestionably the best thing about this hyper-modern hotel, perched above the sleepy fishing village of Howth, is its sweeping view of the rugged North Dublin coast. It's enduringly popular with golfers and rugby weekenders, and its location (some distance off the main road) makes it tranquil and relaxing. Rooms are spacious, and most enjoy grand sea vistas; there's a large indoor swimming pool with sauna and steam room, a spa, tennis cours, and the bar has a sizeable outdoor area. Howth (*see p95*) is a short walk away, and the hotel is conveniently close to the DART station. Needless to say, there are always a few special offers and packages aimed at golfers (and, for that matter, weekenders and families), so call or look online to find out what's on.

Bar. Disabled-adapted rooms. Gym. Internet (free wireless). Parking (free). Pool (indoor). Restaurant. Room service. Spa. TV.

Budget

Marina House

7 Dunleary Road, Dún Laoghaire (284 1524/ www.marinahouse.com). Bus 7, 46A/DART Monkstown. **Rates** *per person* from €19. **Credit** MC, V.

This popular hostel has dorms as well as one double and one twin room. Amenities include laundry facilities, a TV room and a kitchen open to guests. A cheap and pleasant way to get a little sea air.

Internet (free high-speed, wireless).

Where to Stay

Sightseeing

Introduction	54
Trinity College & Around	57
Temple Bar & the Cathedrals	61
St Stephen's Green & Around	69
O'Connell Street & Around	78
The North Quays & Around	83
Docklands	87
The Liberties & Kilmainham	91
Dublin Bay & the Coast	95

Features

The best Places to go	54
Pack it in	55
Walk: The holy trail	64
Walk: Out of sight	72
Small world	78
Through a glass darkly	92

National Museum of Ireland. *See p86.*

Introduction

Ways of seeing it.

For a city with such a significant reputation, Dublin is surprisingly diminutive in scale. The city centre comprises just a few manageably sized neighbourhoods, bisected by the Liffey, and you'll find that it's no distance at all from the top of **O'Connell Street** (on the north side of the river; *see p79*) to the peaceful **Grand Canal** (*see p90*) on the south side. By far the best way to set about exploring the place is on foot. In fact, if you've got a car, park it right now and try never to think of it again unless you're heading out of town – the traffic is too heavy and the town too small to make driving worthwhile. All you need is a good map, a bit of sunshine (not all that rare in these parts, despite the jokes) and a pair of comfortable shoes.

Despite its compact layout, Dublin manages to pack in a good deal of variety. There are historic buildings by the dozen, plenty of green spaces and quiet squares, and enough shops, bars and restaurants to gobble up your holiday allowance ten times over. It is a city with a strong sense of its past (it seems that every few steps brings you to another statue, another heritage plaque announcing the birth place of this playwright, the first home of that poet). And yet, an equal portion of its landscape has been consigned to the future, with a crop of modern structures and buildings contending with the Georgian terraces and the ancient bell towers – of these, O'Connell Street's **Spire** (*see p79*) is undoubtedly the most recognisable, while the many signature bridges that span the Liffey and the multi-million euro developments and regeneration projects from **Smithfield** (*see p84*) to **Docklands** (*see pp87-90*) are there to be discovered.

FINDING YOUR FEET

The main action is concentrated in and around the two most central neighbourhoods of **Temple Bar** (*see pp63-65*) and **St Stephen's Green** (*see pp69-71*). The former, a maze of tiny cobbled streets and busy thoroughfares, is home to the largest concentration of bars, restaurants, night spots and trendy shops. It is also home to the city's two major cathedrals, **St Patrick's** (*see p68*) and **Christ Church** (*see p66*). But somehow, it copes admirably well with its personality clash of holiness and consumerism, and while the idea of awe-inspiring monuments to Christianity and raucous parties of staggering

The best Places to go

For high art
Dublin Writers' Museum (*see p82*); **Hugh Lane Gallery** (*see p82*); **Irish Museum of Modern Art** (*see p93*); **National Gallery of Ireland** (*see p76*).

For history
Dublin Castle (*see p62*); **General Post Office** (*see p81*); **Kilmainham Gaol** (*see p94*); **National Museum of Archaeology & History** (*see p73*).

For the fun of it
Guinness Storehouse (*see p92*); **Imaginosity** (*see p159*); **Science Gallery** (*see p59*).

Lazy days in **Iveagh Gardens**. *See p70.*

stags existing side by side may have caused friction among the locals, it seems to go pretty much without a hitch as far as visitors are concerned. The rule of thumb is simple: if you want to raise hell, hit the pubs and clubs of Temple Bar after dark; if it's heaven you're interested in, stick to the cathedrals.

More sophisticated by far is the neighbouring St Stephen's Green and its clutch of excellent museums around Kildare Street (notably the **National Museum of Archaeology & History**; *see p73*) and the treasure trove of fine art that is the **National Gallery of Ireland** (*see p76*). And for consumer culture, this is also Dublin's ground zero, thanks to nearby Grafton Street with its shops, cafés and restaurants.

The other main shopping hub is O'Connell Street (and its tributary, the ever-busy Henry Street), which culminates in a spearhead

of excellent museums dotted around Parnell Square (most notably the **Hugh Lane Gallery**; *see p82*). To the west of here is the up-and-coming **Smithfield** (*see p84*) and, further still, the vast **Phoenix Park** (*see p86*) – also home to **Dublin Zoo** (*see p86*) – while just across the bridge to the south is the formidable campus of **Trinity College** (*see p57*), with its ancient claim to fame in pride of place in the **Old Library & Book of Kells** (*see p58*). And finally, to the east is the heady mix of past, present and future that is the city's **Docklands** (*see pp87-90*).

NEED TO KNOW

For information on using **Dublin Bus**, **Luas** and the **DART**, *see pp221-223*. For maps (including DART and Luas maps), *see pp255-256*. For tourist information, *see p235*.

Pack it in

72 hours in Dublin

On day one, acclimatise to the city with a wander around the lovely buildings, gardens and raucous playing fields of **Trinity College** (*see p57*). While you're there, get a rush of blood to the brain at the on-campus **Science Gallery** (*see p59*), before slipping off for a bite at the **Lemon Crêpe & Coffee Company** (*see p119*) or, for something much fancier, the **Town Bar and Grill** (*see p105*). Afterwards, head down to Dame Street to see the glorious lobby of **City Hall** (*see p62*), then make your way next door to **Dublin Castle** (*see p62*). Don't feel obliged to pay to get inside the building; instead, wander through the Upper Yard to the free Dubh Linn Gardens and the **Chester Beatty Library** (*see p62*).

On day two, take a walk down towards **St Stephen's Green** (*see pp69-77*), the business hub of the city. Eat at some of the fanciest restaurants in town (**Thornton's** is a good bet; *see p101*) and shop yourself silly on Grafton Street. Top it off with a night on the town in **Temple Bar** (*see pp124-133*).

On your final day, soak up some culture. Compare and contrast the splendours of **St Patrick's Cathedral** (*see p68*) and **Christ Church Cathedral** (*see p66*), before fuelling up on buns and oodles of tea at **Cake Café** (*see p122*). Next, head up O'Connell Street and lose yourself in the intricacies of Francis Bacon's studio inside the **Hugh Lane Gallery** (*see p82*). Round it off with an arty flick at the **Light House Cinema** (*see p164*).

A week in Dublin

Having done the above on your first few days, spread the net a bit wider with a day exploring the wilds of **Phoenix Park** (*see p86*) and **Dublin Zoo** (*see p86*). Then, after a well-deserved kip, wake up fresh for a tour of Kilmainham and the Liberties, starting at the **Guinness Storehouse** (*see p92*) and **Kilmainham Gaol** (*see p94*), and ending up with a dose of cutting-edge creation at the **Irish Museum of Modern Art** (*see p93*). The next day, drift back into town and linger on the **North Quays** (*see pp83-86*) and in **Temple Bar** (*see pp61-68*) – seek out the corner cafés and quirky shops. Lunch at **Gruel** (*see p103*) or **Fallon & Byrne** (*see p102*) and take part in the daily rituals of Dubliners. Try, too, to devote a day to **Docklands** (*see pp87-90*), the formerly atrophied limb of the city into which the life-blood of investment and bold design is now freely flowing.

Finally, having followed the advice above, you'll have had quite enough of city life, so rent a car and take a day trip to the glorious Wicklow Mountains to see the ancient monastery at **Glendalough** (*see p209*), or up to **Newgrange** (*see p201*) to take in the mysteries of its paleolithic burial mounds. If that sounds too energetic, hop on the DART to **Howth** (*see p95*) or **Dalkey** (*see p98*) for bracing sea walks followed by steaming plates of seafood at **Aqua** (*see p116*) or a pint in one of Dalkey's many lovely pubs.

Trinity College & Around

Where the students live and learn.

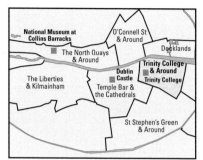

There's a great atmosphere surrounding the sprawling, leafy campus of Trinity College – a pleasant blend of lofty academia (thanks to the grand buildings and statuary) and the vibrant traffic of students who move about the place in noisy gaggles or occupy the tree-shaded perimeters of the green, immersed in study or (more likely) lazy summer afternoon chats. Although increasingly cluttered with new buildings to cater for a growing student population, the campus is still spacious and gracious, interspersed with elegant walks and gardens, luxuriating in its thesis that a proper education is a matter of more than books and exams. And its mix of old and new buildings, classical with 1970s brutalism and elegant contemporary, is one that works.

Trinity College

Map p251 & p252

Founded in 1592 by Queen Elizabeth I for the scions of the Anglo-Irish Ascendancy in order to protect them from malign popish influences abroad, the university succeeded in stemming the 16th-century brain drain, and drew the sons of notable families back from England and Europe. Past pupils include JM Synge, Bram Stoker, Jonathan Swift, Samuel Beckett and Oscar Wilde, as well as Edmund Burke – philosopher, statesman and a man who saw nothing contradictory in asserting Ireland's right to independence while insisting it remain part of the British Empire – and Oliver Goldsmith, poet and general wit, whose statue stands guard over the main College Green entrance.

Roman Catholics were uneasily catered for in an academic version of the old famine soup kitchens: those who changed their religion were welcome within Trinity's walls. By the time this decree was lifted, in the late 18th century, it was the Catholic hierarchy's turn to snub Trinity. Until 1970 all Catholics were banned by the Church from attending unless granted a special dispensation from the archbishop; one not lightly given. But this rather troubled history only makes Dubliners more affectionate towards an establishment prized for its aura of doddering academia and ivory-tower impracticality.

Despite the friendly way in which Trinity stands open to the bustle of the city, most of the buildings are still out of bounds to all but students and staff. As you enter Front Square you'll see Sir William Chambers' neo-classical **Chapel** and **Examination Hall**. The Chapel interior – elegant, with a stuccoed ceiling – looks rather like a mini Houses of Parliament, with two rows of pews facing each other rather than the altar. If you're lucky, you'll catch a wedding or choir practice, otherwise there is a sung Eucharist every Sunday at 10.45am and evensong on Thursdays at 5.15pm.

The extremely pretty **Campanile**, designed by Charles Lanyon, rises up directly opposite the main portico, framing beautiful, ancient maple trees. During the summer, **Campus Tours** (see p58) takes visitors around all the major on-campus sights.

The **Museum Building**, close by the **Old Library** (see p58) was inspired by John Ruskin's celebration of Venetian Gothic and designed by Benjamin Woodward and Thomas Deane in 1852. Its immediate success led to a commission for the two architects and the stonemasons (the O'Shea brothers from Cork) to create a similar building for Oxford University. The outside of the building can be walked around, and the imposing foyer can be visited – complete with its skeleton of an Irish elk – but the rest is for students and staff only.

Although the elevation from Nassau Street doesn't look like much, it is worth making a detour to check out the new **Ussher Library**, adjacent to the Arts Block, and the adjoining **Berkeley Library**, two fine examples of 1970s brutalism. You won't be allowed into the Ussher – even visiting students need a letter of introduction – but you can press your nose up against the window and catch a glimpse of the large atrium, which creates a lovely column-of-light effect. The Berkeley, on the other hand, does allow visitors (into its loos, at least – you'll need student ID or a letter of introduction to use the academic facilities). Outside the Berkeley is Pomodoro's *Sphere within a Sphere* (it's that deconstructed golden ball that looks a bit like a Dalek hatching out of an egg, in case you're in any doubt). The **Pavilion** (or 'Pav' to anyone who has ever set foot in the place), a drab enough building at the edge of the cricket pitch, comes into its own every summer by virtue of getting sun longer than almost anywhere else in the city. Gangs of students and former alumni mob the place, spilling out of the bar on to the steps and pitch. The **Douglas Hyde Gallery** (*see below*), in the Arts Block, exhibits intriguing international artists.

Campus Tours

Trinity College (896 1661/www.tcd.ie). All cross-city buses/Luas Abbey Street/St Stephen's Green. **Open** *May-Sept Tours* 10.15am, 10.55am, 11.35am, 12.15am, 12.55am, 1.35pm, 2.15pm, 2.55pm, 3.40pm Mon-Sat; 10.15am, 10.55am, 11.35am, 12.15am, 12.55am, 2.15pm, 2.55pm Sun. **Closed** Oct-Apr. **Admission** €5; €10 (incl Old Library & Book of Kells). **No credit cards. Map** p252 F3.
These informative (well OK, not always *that* informative, but invariably enthusiastic) student-led tours are a fun way to whisk around the historical and architectural highlights of the campus. The tours last for half an hour and depart from a desk at the Front Arch of the College.

Douglas Hyde Gallery

Trinity College (896 1116/www.douglashydegallery. com). All cross-city buses/Luas Abbey Street/ St Stephen's Green. **Open** 11am-6pm Mon-Wed, Fri; 11am-7pm Thur; 11am-4.45pm Sat. **Admission** free. **Map** p252 F3.
This neat modernist exhibition space could scarcely be more at odds with the fusty, old-world atmosphere that Trinity tends to project to the outside world. The gallery showcases the work of a wide variety of contemporary artists (recent shows have included exhibitions by Trisha Donnelly and Verne Dawson, with shows by such big names as Miroslav Tichy programmed for 2009). There are also occasional live music performances and art-house film screenings in the evening (check the website or ask at the gallery reception for details of upcoming events).

Old Library & Book of Kells

Trinity College (608 2308/www.tcd.ie/library). All cross-city buses/Luas Abbey Street/St Stephen's Green. **Open** *May-Sept* 9.30am-5pm Mon-Sat; 9.30am-4.30pm Sun. *Oct-Apr* 9.30am-5pm Mon-Sat; noon-4.30pm Sun. **Admission** €8; €7 reductions; €16 family; free under-12s. **Credit** AmEx, MC, V. **Map** p252 F3.

'Kelly's Book', as it still gets called occasionally, is Trinity's most famous artefact, but it suffers slightly from *Mona Lisa* syndrome: it's so endlessly reproduced that it seems underwhelming in real life. The remarkable craftwork and intricate design are highly impressive, but frankly not show-stopping. The book, designed around the ninth century, is an illuminated copy of the Gospels in Latin, lovingly created by early Christian monks; at any one time four pages are on display – two illustrated and two text – inside a bullet-proof glass case. Alongside is the *Book of Durrow*, an even earlier illuminated manuscript of the Gospels, made in about 675. It disappeared in the 16th century for a century, during which time it was used as a lucky charm by a farmer: he used to pour water on it to cure his cattle. Otherwise, you may be treated to the sight of the *Garland of Howth* (fragments of the Gospels in ornate Irish majuscule script), which was on display alongside the Book of Kells during our last visit.

There's also a multimedia exhibition to take you through the process of creating such texts – for die-hard bibliophiles only – but most people just come to gawp at the texts (if that: peering over a fellow tourist's shoulder is about as good as you can hope for). Still, each summer, an average of 3,000 people a day troop through the Old Library, designed by Thomas Burgh and built between 1712 and 1732. And, although the Long Room is just that, and can accommodate more even than are allowed in at any one time, the vaulted, echoing, dimly lit expanse is definitely best seen as empty as possible. This is the

Science Gallery.

city's most beautiful room: a perfect panelled chamber with rows of double-facing shelves holding about 200,000 lovingly bound old volumes, accessed by antique ladders and guarded by busts of literary giants (and, of course, by actual security guards). Running down the centre of the room is a spine of ten large, climate-controlled glass cases that are reserved for displays of particularly rare or ancient volumes.

Science Gallery

Trinity College, Pearse Street (896 4091/
www.sciencegallery.ie). All cross-city buses/Luas St
Stephen's Green. **Open** varies with programme.
Admission free. **Map** p251 G3.

The newest and most innovative museum to open its doors on Trinity campus, the Science Gallery takes a fresh, fun and lively look at the applications of science across a number of walks of life. There is virtually nothing that these guys are not into: whether it's commissioning exhibitions of techno-thread clothing (meaning clothing that responds, thinks, even grows on its own) or 2008's superb Lightwave exhibition (back again in 2009) to displays of robotic art (that is, robots that are built to create art) and the series of Raw debates on subjects as diverse as the future of biofuels and the efficacy of anti-depressants. Basically, the Science Gallery is a completely fascinating, laudable new venture, and anyone with even a passing interest in the appliance of science should go take a look. There is no permanent exhibition but there's usually something going on, so it's always worth dropping in (check the website of what's on

when). Even if it's just to sit down with an excellent cappuccino in the small on-site café and enjoy the light, white and, in all senses, bright surroundings.

Parliament & Bank

Map p251 & p252

Opposite Trinity's main gates, doubtless ready to receive the brightest of its graduates, are Edward Lovett Pearce's **Houses of Parliament**, now the HQ of the Bank of Ireland. This Palladian building was the seat of power from 1728 until, like turkeys calling for an early Christmas (and motivated by huge bribes and handouts), it voted its own dissolution in the 1800 Act of Union, allowing the country to be governed directly from London. Only the hushed and panelled **House of Lords** is still intact, although the former **House of Commons**, where the public now goes about its banking business, is a far more impressive room. Outside stands a statue of Henry Grattan, statesman, orator and the man who first – though prematurely – hailed the new Irish nation in 1782 with the words, 'I am now to address a free people'.

House of Lords

Bank of Ireland, 2 College Green (671 1488).
All cross-city buses. **Open** 10am-4pm Mon-Wed,
Fri; 10am-5pm Thur. *Guided tours* 10.30am,
11.30am, 1.45pm Tue. **Admission** free. **Map** p252 F3.

Sightseeing

Queen Of Tarts

"Queen of tarts 'must be' one of the treats experienced when you visit Dublin". New York Times.

Pastry Shop & Cafe

Cow's Lane, Temple Bar.
Tel: 01 6334681

Also
Dame Street, Dublin 2.
Tel: 01 6707499

www.queenoftarts.ie

Monday - Friday	7.30 am - 7 pm
Weekend	9 am - 7pm

Temple Bar & the Cathedrals

Earthly delights and holy sights.

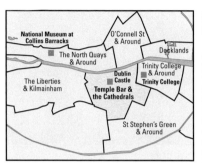

National Museum at Collins Barracks

O'Connell St & Around

The North Quays & Around

Docklands

Trinity College & Around

The Liberties & Kilmainham

Dublin Castle

Trinity College

Temple Bar & the Cathedrals

St Stephen's Green & Around

Temple Bar is the dynamo at the heart of Dublin, always at the frontline of new developments, whether it's a plan to enable the whole district as a free Wi-Fi area or whether it's a daring new architectural project (*see p41* **With or without you**), or simply the tireless evolution of new music venues, funky hotels, drinking dens and clubs. But there is another, contrasting side to the district's character. The city's two great cathedrals, and indeed much of its religious heritage (*see p64* **The holy trail**), also stand proudly within the boundaries of Temple Bar, only a short walk, and yet a world away, from the rowdy stags and hens and the hordes of wining and dining tourists. And it is, for the most part, a peaceful coexistence; more than that, in fact, it is thanks to this very dichotomy that Temple Bar is one of the most alluring (and undoubtedly the most visited) neighbourhood in Dublin.

Dame Street & around

Map p251 & p252

Dame Street may have the dimensions of a grand old colonial boulevard, but it is a far from pleasant place in which to stroll. Thundering traffic, smoky air and a general aura of frantic scurrying mean it is best used as a means to an end. Luckily, there are plenty of interesting side streets to duck into. These lead one into another, allowing you to re-emerge on to the main thoroughfare for points of interest, such

as the **Olympia Theatre** (*see p198*), with its pretty coloured-glass canopy and shabby Victorian bordello interior.

Further down towards Trinity College is the **Central Bank**. This rather overbearing building was highly controversial when it went up. Walking up towards Christ Church, opposite the Olympia, is **Dublin Castle** (*see p62*), tucked away down a spindly side street. The castle has a faintly hangdog air, as if unsure of its role. At least one thing's for sure: the Dubh Linn gardens round the back are usually a reliably peaceful retreat. There too is the magnificent **Chester Beatty Library** (*see p62*); if you only have time for one cultural pit stop while in Dublin, make it this one. Next to the castle entrance and facing down towards Grattan Bridge is **City Hall** (*see p62*), Dublin's best building. Originally the Royal Exchange, for years this was the HQ of Dublin Corporation, partitioned and subdivided into a rabbit warren for civil servants, its glories totally disguised.

After an extensive and expensive renovation programme, it was reopened in 2000 and now is a rarely used but always accessible city centre public resource.

Back down towards Trinity and opposite the Central Bank is **South Great George's Street**, nucleus of one of the city's better shopping, eating and bar areas. Note, too, the fine red-brick George's Street Arcade, a covered Victorian market full of stalls selling second-hand books, records, clothes, collectable stamps, postcards and, increasingly, deli and organic food. At the far end is the little pedestrianised fashion haven of Castle Market. Carry on up South Great George's Street on the opposite side of the road and, on the corner with Aungier Street, is the **Whitefriar Street Carmelite Church** (*see p63*), built on the site of an ancient 13th-century priory that was confiscated as part of the Dissolution of the Monasteries Act in 1539. The Carmelites returned three centuries later and set up shop in the current building, designed by George Papworth, although the present entrance, with its two-storey Italianate façade, was put up as recently as 1914.

Chester Beatty Library.

Further down South Great George's Street, you come to Wexford Street and Camden Street, an area with a lively mix of new cultures known for good Middle Eastern grocery shops and delis. If you're looking for huge vats of almond flour or sticky baklava, this is where to go.

Chester Beatty Library

Clock Tower Building, Dublin Castle, Dame Street (407 0750/www.cbl.ie). All cross-city buses/Luas Jervis/St Stephen's Green. **Open** *May-Sept* 10am-5pm Mon-Fri; 11am-5pm Sat; 1-5pm Sun. *Oct-Apr* 10am-5pm Tue-Fri; 11am-5pm Sat; 1-5pm Sun. *Guided tours* 1pm Wed; 3pm, 4pm Sun. **Admission** free; donations welcome. **Map** p252 E3.
Many of the finest works from Sir Alfred Chester Beatty's priceless art collection are housed in this purpose-built museum. An Irish-American mining magnate with a passion for the East, Chester Beatty settled here in the 1950s and bequeathed his life's collection to the Irish people in 1969. Manuscripts, icons, miniature paintings, early prints and objets d'art from Europe and the Far East take you through the differing traditions of belief and learning in the Western, Islamic and East Asian worlds. Beautiful Buddhas, intricate Chinese lanterns, delicate snuff boxes and Japanese woodcuts stand beside illuminated, ninth-century copies of the Koran and some of the earliest Christian scrolls. And if you tire of religious artefacts, a collection of illustrated 20th-century texts includes a storybook by Matisse and charming Parisian fashion plates from the 1920s. Upstairs is a Zen roof garden, while on the ground floor is the Silk Road café (*see p121*), serving good Middle Eastern-style food, and a carefully stocked museum shop offering postcards, wall hangings, cute toys and even some large furniture pieces.

City Hall

Dame Street (222 2204/www.dublincity.ie). All cross-city buses/Luas Jervis. **Open** 10am-5.15pm Mon-Sat; 2-5pm Sun. **Admission** €4; €2 reductions; €10 family. **Credit** MC, V. **Map** p252 E3.
When keeping pace with street life becomes all too much, and you need somewhere to catch your breath and reflect, City Hall has just the right kind of empty grandeur. Entering through the main Dame Street portico, you find yourself in Thomas Cooley's large domed atrium, complete with mosaic floor and sweeping staircases. Around the central space are frescoes by James Ward, showing scenes from the history of Dublin, such as the Battle of Clontarf, and four marble statues, one of which is Daniel O'Connell, taken in out of the rain from its original perch beside what is now the Central Bank. Carvings and stuccowork are equally lovely. In the basement is the Story of the Capital, an exhibition detailing the city's history of government, and a tiny café.

Dublin Castle

Dame Street (677 7129/www.dublincastle.ie). All cross-city buses/Luas Jervis/St Stephen's Green. **Open** (by guided tour only) 10am-4.45pm Mon-Fri; 2-4.45pm Sat, Sun. **Admission** €4.50; €2-€3.50 reductions. **No credit cards**. **Map** p252 E3.
Formerly the seat of British power in Ireland, and efficiently infiltrated by spies during the Michael Collins era, this isn't really a castle – no moat, no drawbridge to lower against invading hordes, no turrets from which to pour boiling oil – more a collection of 18th-century administrative buildings, albeit very fine ones, built on a medieval plan of two courtyards. A figure of Justice stands over the main entrance, dating from the time of British rule, and is something of a sardonic joke – she stands with her

back to the city, wears no blindfold and her scales tilt when filled with water. In 1922 this is where the last Lord Lieutenant of Ireland, FitzAlan, symbolically handed over the castle to Michael Collins, who kept him waiting seven minutes. When FitzAlan complained, Collins retorted, 'We've been waiting over 700 years, you can have the extra seven minutes.' The Castle's current role is to provide venues for grand diplomatic or state functions, and occasional artistic performances, such as concert recitals. The interior, including beautiful State Rooms, is operated on a pay-per-view basis, but you can wander freely around the exterior.

Whitefriar Street Carmelite Church

Whitefriar Street, off Aungier Street (475 8821/ www.carmelites.ie). Bus 16, 16A, 19, 19A, 83, 122/Luas St Stephen's Green. **Open** 7.30am-6pm Mon, Wed-Fri; 7.30am-9pm Tue; 8.30am-7pm Sat; 7.30am-7pm Sun. **Admission** free. **Map** p251 E4.
The altar of this Byzantine-looking church is said to contain the relics of St Valentine, donated by Pope Gregory XVI in 1835, and so has a busy season with couples around the big day in February. Another treasure of the church is *Our Lady of Dublin*, a beautiful medieval wooden statue of the Virgin Mary. The only example of such sculpture in Dublin, it was rescued long after the Reformation was thought to have destroyed all such pieces, and is believed to have been used as a pig trough during the intervening years. At the back of the building – turn right in the antechamber just before you get to the church proper – is a very pretty little secluded garden with neat lawns, rows of rose bushes and one little bench.

Temple Bar & around

Map p251 & p252

Temple Bar entered a seriously bad patch in the mid 1990s. Whether that bad patch is over yet is a moot point. Cheap flights from the UK turned it into a hot destination for rowdy stag and hen parties, and the after-dark character of the area became distinctly sleazy. Although a deliberate 'No Stags or Hens' policy by local businesses – hotels, hostels, pubs and restaurants – gradually succeeded in discouraging this kind of tourism, the area isn't out of the woods yet. These days, Temple Bar tends to feature prominently in media scare stories about teenage binge-drinking, and certainly it is still pretty unsavoury on weekend nights and exam result days. However, the good efforts of local businesses continue, and attempts to shed this louche character are beginning to pay off.

During the day and early evenings, however, this remains one of the city's most charming neighbourhoods. The pedestrianised 18th-century cobbled streets make it ideal territory for the touristic *flâneur*, with enough shops, galleries, bars, cafés and general architectural diversity to keep interest alive. Old streetscapes

are preserved alongside contemporary, often eco-friendly architectural projects – such as the glass-panelled Arthouse building on Curved Street, now home to the film-makers organisation Filmbase.

Begin at the Dame Street end with a stroll past the Central Bank plaza where, on a Saturday, teenage goths hang around, dressed like mini Marilyn Mansons. The **Irish Film Institute** (*see p164*), on Eustace Street, is an art-house cinema showing a good range of independent and European films (there's also a café that serves reasonable food). Behind the IFI is **Meeting House Square**, the heart of the area's cultural entertainment programme. Open-air film screenings – mainly of old classics – alternate with concerts, puppet shows, circus performers and dance events during the summer. Throughout the year, the Square is home to a hugely popular Saturday food market, which attracts faithful local foodie types and delighted visitors. Selling everything from organic chickens, vegetables and artisanal cheeses to olives, oysters and sushi, it is both a place for the weekly shopping and tapas-style grazing. Buskers playing traditional music add to the usually highly genial atmosphere. Come Sunday, the space gets transformed into a craft and urniture market, showcasing Irish and international pieces.

Our Lady of Dublin at **Carmelite Church**.

Sightseeing

A small second-hand book fair on **Temple Bar Square** every Saturday and Sunday is also worth a visit – you won't find first editions or rare manuscripts, but if you're looking for vintage paperback editions of favourite classics, your chances are high. Here, too, on Sundays you will find Speaker's Square, lasting from 2pm to 6pm. This is an opportunity for anyone with a grievance, grudge or passion to get it off their chest. All are welcome, and, as with London's Hyde Park equivalent, the ranting can be top class.

The **Gallery of Photography** (*see p168*), three purpose-built levels on Meeting House Square, has a permanent collection of modern Irish photography, regular exhibitions of contemporary local work and touring shows; downstairs is a great collection of photography books and arty postcards. The Gallery also runs photography and print techniques courses and rents darkroom space. Facing it across the square is the **National Photographic Archive** (*see p27*), full of excellent, often poignant photographic records of Irish life.

Walk: The holy trail

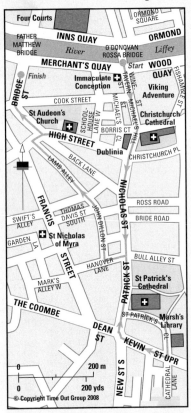

There are so many historic churches and cathedrals huddled together in this part of town that it seems a shame to simply drop in on them one at a time. A much better

idea by far is to strive for a higher plane of sightseeing, to free your soul from its earthy shackles and embark on a crusading tour of God's houses, great and small. In other words, why not walk round them all in the same day?

Start your spiritual journey on the southern side of the O'Donovan Rossa bridge, where you will find the **Church of the Immaculate Conception** (*see p67*) almost immediately opposite you. Have a quick look inside and then continue on your way around the corner to Winetavern Street. At the top of this street, as you pass this wonderful ivy-covered townhouses, you will be confronted by the spire of **Christ Church Cathedral** (*see p66*) and the low sweep of its immaculately tended green. You can spend hours or (as do many of the tour groups who come steaming through here) just a matter of minutes absorbing the wonder that is Christ Church. Try, though, to keep an eye on the details (for the scale of the interior can be overwhelming), such as the beautiful floor tiles (especially those in the baptistry) and the stonework (to which there are clear, illustrated guides at various information points inside the cathedral). Make time, too, to properly explore the crypt, which has more than its famously mummified cat and rat to offer – in particular, the glorious *Missale Romanum*, printed in Turin in 1925.

When you are ready to leave Christ Church, set off down the traffic-choked Nicholas Street towards **St Patrick's Cathedral** (*see p68*), a few minutes' walk down what is, truth be told, a rather uninspiring (some might even say ugly) road. As you near **St Patrick's Park** (*see p68*) and the cathedral itself, make a snack stop at **Bite of Life** (*see p118*), the bright little café that makes the corner with Bull Alley.

Around the corner, on Temple Bar itself, the **Original Print Gallery** (*see p168*) and **Temple Bar Gallery & Studios** (*see p168*) stand side by side. The Original Print Gallery specialises in limited-edition prints, and these increasingly come from the Black Church Print Studios upstairs, making this something of a success story for an area that has a designated role in the promotion of culture. The Temple Bar Gallery shows work that is innovative and – if not always appealing – usually local.

Duly fortified, continue on to the cathedral itself, whose interior serves both as a monument to devotional architecture and (more so than Christ Church) to Anglo-Irish life (stop to read the various monuments that commemorate celebrated figures of the Anglican Ascendancy).

Back in the fresh air, you have the choice of dallying at St Patrick's Green or paying a visit to the splendid **Marsh's Library** (*see p67*), or else pressing on with the route, which now loops back round towards the river via the quaint little John Dillon Street, a charming and altogether more peaceful alternative to the noise and fumes of Nicholas Street. Continue along this backwater of red-brick terraces (noting the diminutive dome of St Nicholas of Myra peeping out from behind the rooftops) until you reach the gates of the historic Iveagh Market (one of the philanthropic bequests of the Guinness family to the capital's slum-ridden neighbourhoods). Pause for a peek inside at the overgrown excavation site – at the time of writing, planning permission had been granted for the conversion of the market into a high-end food hall (there was even talk of an on-site micro brewery) with a boutique hotel sited at the rear. Watch this space.

After a short walk up Lamb Alley, you will emerge at Thomas Street West and see the time-worn medieval façade of **St Audoen's Church** (*see p68*) to your right, the last stop on your holy trail. If you still have the energy, join one of the church's excellent guided tours; if not, stop off for a well-earned pint at the **Brazen Head** (*see p125*), just around the corner on Bridge Street Lower, and ease yourself back into the world of Man.

Round the corner on Wellington Quay, enjoy the beautiful townhouse architecture of the **Clarence** hotel (*see p39*) while you still can – plans are underway to transform it into an altogether different, some would argue incongruous, building (*see p41* **With or without you**). Opposite the back entrance to the Clarence (on Essex Street), the **Project Arts Centre** (*see p168*) always had an eclectic and ambitious programme of theatre, comedy and art projects. However, the big blue building is not the most sympathetic of spaces, and audiences can still be elusive.

Crossing Parliament Street brings you to the Old City. Before entering it, look one way for **City Hall** (*see p62*), and the other, down on the Quays, facing Grattan Bridge, for the Sunlight Chambers. These hark back to the days when every Irish family had an industrial-sized bar of Sunlight soap beside the kitchen sink – 'the story of soap' is told in a delightful double bas-relief frieze that runs around the building. Further on is **Fishamble Street**, the oldest street in Dublin, where Handel's *Messiah* was first performed and where regular free open-air renditions of the piece are still staged.

Grafton Street
Map p251 & p252
The bawdiness of the Molly Malone statue, with her low-cut top, heaving bosom and barrow full of cockles and mussels (she's known locally as the 'tart with the cart'), is not continued throughout Grafton Street. In fact, because this is Dublin's shopping heartland (the entire street is given over to the pursuit of retail therapy), its most serious problem is that of overcrowding. Come Christmas, the swell of the crowd will propel you irresistibly through the doors of **Brown Thomas** (*see p139*), whether you want it or not. However, there are a few bright spots even for the retail-shy. **Bewley's Oriental Café** (*see p118*), halfway up on the right, narrowly escaped a dreadful fate in recent years when two of the city's brightest young entrepreneurs stepped in to prevent the lovely old 19th-century building from being sold.

Leading off Grafton Street in every direction are streets filled with pubs, cafés and restaurants. Worth a visit are the literary pubs: **Davy Byrne's** (*see p127*) on Duke Street for the Joyce aficionados, and **McDaid's** (*see p123*) on Harry Street for the Brendan Behan and Flann O'Brien fans. (And less bookish punters might like to know that opposite McDaid's is a statue of rock icon Phil Lynott, frontman of Thin Lizzy.) At the top of Grafton Street, opposite St Stephen's Green, is a permanent setting for a constantly changing sculpture.

Every six months – January and July – the sculpture is replaced by a new piece.

Tucked in behind Bewley's, is **St Teresa's Carmelite Church and Friary**, built towards the end of the 18th century and before Catholic emancipation in a deliberately discreet location. Improbably large and imposing inside, the church still does a good trade in city-centre worshippers. The tiny courtyard outside has a low-key, forgotten appeal. Opposite the courtyard is the back entrance to **Powerscourt Townhouse Centre** (*see p140*).

The Cathedrals & around

Map p250, p251 & p252

Here you will find the intersection point of Dublin's two historic Golden Ages: the medieval period, when Dublin was a significant stop-off on the great Viking trade routes that stretched from the Baltic to North Africa; and the 18th century, when Ireland's capital briefly flowered as the second city of what was at that time the burgeoning British Empire.

Memorials in both cathedrals to the large number of Irishmen who lost their lives fighting Britain's colonial wars, the French Huguenot presence in both **St Patrick's Cathedral** (*see p68*) and in **Marsh's Library** (*see right*), and the assortment of languages spoken in Dublin during the Middle Ages (colourfully recreated in the audio accompaniment to the **Dublinia** exhibition, *see right*) are all proof of something that many Dubliners seem unaware of: namely, that the city experienced both periods of great wealth and large influxes of foreign nationals long before the 1990s.

As you come round the top of Lord Edward Street, **Christ Church Cathedral** (*see below*) seems less impressive than you might expect, almost dwarfed by the surrounding buildings. The best way to approach it is from the river (*see p64* **The holy trail**). Just opposite the entrance to Christ Church is the **Lord Edward** pub (named after that dashing aristocrat-turned-rebel; *see p129*), with all the tattered but convivial charm of a real Dublin watering hole.

An enclosed elevated walkway crosses Winetavern Street and connects Christ Church to Dublinia. Looking west at the top of the hill, **St Audeon's Church** (*see p68*) stands over the last surviving Norman gateway to the city. Open just a few months of the year, St Audeon's boasts pleasingly simple medieval architecture that makes it well worth a visit. Looking south towards the Dublin Mountains, the spire of St Patrick's Cathedral rises in surprisingly close proximity to Christ Church.

Christ Church Cathedral

Christ Church Place (677 8099/www.cccdub.ie). Bus 49, 50, 54A, 56A, 65, 77, 77A, 78A, 123/Luas St Four Courts. **Open** *June-Aug* 9am-6pm daily. *Sept-May* 9.45am-5pm daily. **Admission** €6; €4 reductions. **Credit** *Shop* MC, V. **Map** p252 D3.
Catering to a minority religion in a country where even the majority religion has seriously fallen from favour in recent years, Christ Church, like St Patrick's, relies heavily on tourism and on the services of voluntary staff to pay for its upkeep (which, according to the cathedral's website, costs €2,500 per day). Dubliners chiefly know it as a place to hear the bells ring out on New Year's Eve (it boasts 'the largest full-circle ringing peal in the world') and for the beautiful choral evensongs (Wednesdays and Thursdays at 6pm, Saturdays at 5pm and Sundays, 3.30pm). The original Viking cathedral was put up circa 1030, but the existing Anglo-Norman building dates from the 1180s, with many subsequent restorations. Inside, it is handsome rather than spectacular; if any cathedral can be called cosy or compact, this is the one. Like so many other notable church buildings in Ireland, Christ Church suffered from some over-enthusiastic Victorian restoration, but the huge crypt that runs the full length of the cathedral dates from its first stone incarnation in the 1170s and goes some way to representing the medieval character of the place. Many kings and conquerors worshipped here, from the Norman mercenary Strongbow to the ill-fated James II, and his rival and successor to the throne of England, William of Orange. In 1871, the whiskey-maker Henry Roe funded a restoration so thorough it left him bankrupt, and purists enraged.

Temple Bar.

Keep an eye out for the heart-shaped iron box said to contain the heart of St Laurence O'Toole, and for 'the cat and the rat'. Their mummified remains were (supposedly) found in an organ pipe and were put on display in mid chase, like a single frame from a ghoulish Tex Avery animation; actually, they provide a welcome break from the austerity and pomp that characterise Christ Church. *See also p64* **The holy trail**.

Church of the Immaculate Conception

4 Merchants Quay (6771128). All cross-city buses/ Luas Four Courts. **Open** 9am-5pm daily. **Admission** free. **Map** p250 D3.

More commonly known as the Adam and Eve (reportedly because, back in the days of Penal Law, forbidden masses were secretly conducted in a pub of that name just around the corner on Winetavern Street), the Immaculate Conception is an interesting church. The site of a Fransiscan friary as far back as the mid 13th century, it was suppressed and abandoned in 1541 before being taken up again centuries later in various guises, ending with this final incarnation (begun in 1834 and completed in 1938). It's still an active part of the Irish Franciscans' operation and there is much going on here, but most visitors will be content to have a quick gander at the semi-baroque style interior and a wander around the kitsch giftshop. *See also p64* **The holy trail**.

Dublinia

Christ Church, St Michael's Hill (679 4611/ www.dublinia.ie). Bus 49, 50, 51B, 54A, 56A,

65, 77, 77A, 78A, 123/Luas Four Courts. **Open** *Apr-Sept* 10am-5pm daily (last admission 4.15pm). *Oct-Mar* 11am-4pm Mon-Fri (last admission 3.15pm); 10am-5pm Sat, Sun (last admission 3.15pm). **Admission** €6.25; €3.75-€5.25 reductions; €17 family. **Credit** MC, V. **Map** p252 D3.

The crudely interactive features of this exhibition on the world of medieval Dublin seem to date from a pre-digital age, but overall this exhibition is the best of its kind in the city. A scale model of medieval Dublin helps place the two cathedrals in their geographical context, while a reconstructed archaeological dig is probably most interesting for the newspaper clippings that accompany it – they chart the history of the noble but doomed protest to save the site of one of Viking Europe's most significant settlements at Wood Quay from destruction at the hands of Dublin Corporation. St Michael's Tower, although no match for the Gravity Bar in the Guinness Storehouse (*see p137*), provides a fine view of the heart of old Dublin.

Marsh's Library

St Patrick's Close (454 3511/www.marshlibrary.ie). Bus 49X, 50, 50X, 54A, 56A, 77X, 150/Luas St Stephen's Green. **Open** 10am-1pm, 2-5pm Mon, Wed-Fri; 10.30am-1pm Sat. **Admission** €2.50; €1.50 reductions. **No credit cards**. **Map** p251 D4.

This is the oldest public library in Ireland (and the only 18th-century building still used for its original purpose). Marsh's Library stands like a miniature working version of Trinity College's Long Room. It is located just past the entrance to St Patrick's (and

Dublinia.

in comparative solitude), and the slow, steady ticking of the clock in its main room adds to the old-world atmosphere. The mitres that stand on top of the bookcases, and the wire cages (where visitors were locked in with particularly precious books, lest they be tempted to borrow them) recall the library's founder, Archbishop Narcissus Marsh.

St Audeon's Church

High Street (677 0088). Bus 123/Luas Four Courts. **Open** Phone for details. **Admission** free. **Map** p250 D3.
Just changing to year-round opening at the time of writing, this medieval parish church is well worth a look (visitors can either browse the visitors centre on their own or else join up with one of the guided tours for a closer look inside). This church is still very much in use, so discretion is required.

St Patrick's Cathedral

St Patrick's Close (453 9472/www.stpatricks cathedral.ie). Bus 49X, 50, 50X, 54A, 56A, 77X, 150/Luas St Stephen's Green. **Open** *Mar-Oct* 9am-6pm Mon-Sat; 9-11am, 12.45-3pm, 4.15-6pm Sun. *Nov-Feb* 9am-6pm Mon-Fri; 9am-5pm Sat; 10-11am, 12.45-3pm Sun. **Admission** €5.50; €4.20 reductions; €15 family. **Credit** MC, V. **Map** p250 D4.
This, the largest church in Ireland, dates from the 13th century but was founded on a far older religious site associated with St Patrick and dating from the fifth century. As a memorial to Anglo-Irish life in

The holy green of **St Patrick's Park**.

Ireland, it tells a more interesting tale than Christ Church, and its many plaques and monuments commemorate various celebrated figures of the Anglican Ascendancy, from Richard Boyle (Earl of Cork and 'Father of Chemistry') and John Philpot Curran (who provided the legal defence for rebel leader Wolfe Tone and fathered Sarah Curran, fiancée of the later rebel leader Robert Emmet), to former presidents of Ireland such as Erskine Childers (whose father was executed during the Irish Civil War) and Douglas Hyde (father of the Irish language revival movement). The monuments also serve as a reminder of the generations of Irishmen who served, fought and lost their lives for the British Empire: not just on the fields of France in the two World Wars (a Roll of Honour here lists the names of the 50,000 Irishmen killed fighting in the British army in World War II), but also in such far-flung places as Sudan, Burma and Afghanistan throughout the 19th century. Most consist of wordy, typically sentimental Victorian eulogies, but some are touchingly compassionate, and seem to reflect the poignant mood cast by the shadow of the tattered regimental colours that still hang from the inside wall.

All that said, St Patrick's remains most famous for its association with the celebrated writer and satirist Jonathan Swift. Most of his best-known works were written while he was dean here from 1713 to 1745. Deeply cynical and yet touched by a sort of social conscience that seems at odds with his time, Swift's savage criticisms of the cronyism and ineptitude that marked England's colonial administration of its largest island neighbour were powerful enough to bring down governments; unfortunately for him, they made him many enemies in the process, and ensured that his own career would remain somewhat stunted. Swift advocated a humane approach to the treatment of the mentally ill, and he left a large sum of money after his death to found St Patrick's Hospital (*see also p17* **The house that Swift built**). Swift is buried here alongside his partner, friend and confidante, Stella. *See also p64* **The holy trail**.

St Patrick's Park

St Patrick's Close (453 9472/www.stpatricks cathedral.ie). Bus 49X, 50, 50X, 54A, 56A, 77X, 150/Luas St Stephen's Green. **Open** *Dec-Jan* 8am-4.30pm Mon-Fri; 10am-4.30pm Sat, Sun. *Feb, Nov* 8am-5pm Mon-Fri; 10am-5pm Sat, Sun. *Mar, Oct* 8am-6pm Mon-Fri; 10am-6pm Sat, Sun. *Apr, Sept* 8am-8pm Mon-Fri; 10am-8pm Sat, Sun. *May-Aug* 8am-9pm Mon-Fri; 10am-9pm Sat, Sun. **Admission** free. **Map** p250 D4.
A pleasant (and surprisingly large) green expanse adjoining the cathedral of the same name, this park is a popular place for local workers to come to eat their sarnies and for tourists to decompress after a tour of the holy delights next door. At the eastern edge of the park are several wall-mounted plaques commemorating the brightest stars in Ireland's literary firmament.

St Stephen's Green & Around

Great walks, green spaces, fine art and major museums.

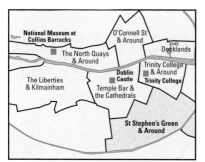

As is evident from the rows of stern grey Georgian townhouses that line up around its lush squares, St Stephen's Green and its environs was at one time a thriving residential neighbourhood. These days, however, few people can afford to live in this part of town, which has instead become the city's commercial hub where most of Dublin's major offices are to be found – alongside, of course, the highly regarded **National Gallery of Ireland** (*see p76*) and a clutch of museums headed up by the **National Museum of Archaeology & History** (*see p73*). It is a beautiful neighbourhood in which to lose yourself in a long, meandering walk – not just around the Green itself but among some of the lesser known parks and gardens (*see p72* **Out of sight**), and along the historic streets that lead down to the quiet waters of the Grand Canal. Many visitors see little beyond the confines of Merrion Square (a favourite pit stop of organised tours; it seems as if every famous 19th-century Dubliner lived here at one time or another) but why not stretch your legs a little further and take a walk along the canal, and up on to the Liffey?

St Stephen's Green

Map p251

After a morning spent pushing through swarms of shoppers, the wide expanse of **St Stephen's Green** comes as a blessed relief. This elegant, beautifully designed park – known simply as 'the Green' – was a common ground used for hangings and whippings until 1800. Today it opens out at the end of Grafton Street with tree-studded lawns, a languid pond with willows, island and stone bridge, a children's playground and formal gardens. It fills up on warm summer days, but seldom feels crowded. Entry once cost a guinea, but in 1877 Lord Arthur Guinness (in his second greatest legacy to the city) pushed through an Act of Parliament making it free – and funding the design that you see, more or less unchanged, today. Wander its paths to find the curious collection of stone circles and arguably the park's finest statue – George Moore's *WB Yeats*. In a city where statuary realism rules with an iron fist, Moore's work stands out for its expressionistic approach – not that this means much to local yoofs, who regularly cover it with graffiti.

Other public artworks sprinkled around the green are Henry Moore's gloomy bust of Joyce, and busts of the poet James Clarence Mangan and the revolutionary Countess Marcievicz. A statue of Protestant rebel Wolfe Tone stands defiantly on the south-western corner. In sharp contrast, the *Three Fates* – a gift from Germany in recognition of Irish aid in the years following World War II – slouch coolly atop a fountain at Leeson Street Gate. Also, outdoor art exhibitions are not uncommon, and there is usually live music at the bandstand in summer.

If you stroll around the Green's perimeter, you can take in the historical oddity that is the **Huguenot Cemetery** on the north-east corner, as well as the illustrious Shelbourne Hotel (*see p47*). Once the city's most exclusive hotel, the Shelbourne is still a byword for luxury. Take a rest in one of its bars – movers and shakers favour the tiny Horseshoe Bar – or have a cup of tea and a scone in its plush lobby.

The expansive green is guarded by elegant terraces of Georgian townhouses, although in recent years hotels and other newcomers have muscled in; chic shops are gaining a foothold on the Grafton Street corner. Otherwise, lovely old buildings line the streets in every direction. Yeats dismissed them as 'grey 18th-century

Leisure time in the city's hidden **Iveagh Gardens**.

houses', but the tourists who walk for miles to see them clearly think otherwise. Generally four storeys high, most have plain exteriors; owners expressed themselves in colourful doors and lavish door-knockers. Like well-bred aristocrats, these houses keep their extravagances well concealed: inside are spacious, beautifully proportioned rooms, sweeping staircases and ornate plasterwork. Two of the best examples of the style are on the southern side of the green in the two conjoined townhouses that make up **Newman House** (*see right*). The outside is plain, but the elaborate interior plasterwork was so risqué that it was covered up when the building was part of the Catholic University. Also part of the university was nearby **Newman University Church** (*see p71*); Gerard Manley Hopkins was professor of Classics here from 1884 to 1889, and James Joyce was a student from 1899 to 1902. Quotations from Hopkins are engraved in the church, though there's nothing from the anti-clerical Joyce; and yet, for all Joyce's contempt for the church and, in some measure, the university, a glance at the comments book shows that it's his association with the place that inspires most visitors. A room where Joyce attended classes has been lovingly restored.

Newman House backs on to the ethereally lovely 19th-century **Iveagh Gardens** (*see right*), laid out by Nenian Neven and created

in 1863. South of St Stephen's Green, meanwhile, the **National Concert Hall** (*see p185*) is a fine, imposing building, but one with several shortcomings – acoustic, in particular. On the western side of the Green rises the façade of the **Royal College of Surgeons**, elegant, imposing and still pockmarked with 1916 uprising bullet holes. Also on this terrace is the glass-domed **Stephen's Green Centre** (*see p140*).

Iveagh Gardens

Entrances to park: Hatch Street Upper; Clonmel Street, off Harcourt Street (no phone). All cross-city buses/Luas Harcourt. **Open** 10am-6pm Mon, Tue; 10am-7pm Wed, Fri; 10am-8pm Thur; 9am-6pm Sat; 11am-4pm Sun. **Admission** free. **Map** p251 F5. *See p72* **Walk: Out of sight**.

Newman House

85-86 St Stephen's Green South (716 7422). All cross-city buses/Luas St Stephen's Green. **Open** (tours only) *June-Aug* 2pm, 3pm, 4pm Tue-Fri. **Admission** €5; €4 reductions. **No credit cards. Map** p251 F5.
These conjoined townhouses on St Stephen's Green South, originally the Catholic University of Ireland and now owned by University College Dublin, are probably the finest example of 18th-century Georgian architecture in the city that are open to the public. Built in 1738 for Irish MP Hugh Montgomery, No.85 has a sombre façade that hides

a spacious, elegant interior. When it was bought by the Catholic University in 1865, its superb plasterwork was thought too smutty for young men, so the female nudes were covered up. Juno's curves are still hidden by a rough costume although other figures have been returned to their natural state. The house contains the famous Apollo Room, with lavish panels depicting Apollo and the Muses, and a magnificent saloon where allegories promoting prudent economy and government are framed by rococo shells and foliage. No.86 was begun in 1765 by Richard Whaley, father of notorious gambler Buck, and was later bought by the university. Head to the top of the house via the back stairs to see poet Gerard Manley Hopkins's spartan bedroom and study, which has been carefully preserved. Restoration work has improved the hall, stairs and landing at No.86.

Newman University Church

87A St Stephen's Green South (478 0616/ www.universitychurch.ie). All cross-city buses/ Luas St Stephens Green. **Open** 9am-5pm Mon-Fri; 9am-5.30pm Sat; 9.30am-4pm Sun. **Admission** free. **Map** p251 F5.

At one time, this church was UCD's answer to Trinity College. Now it's a favourite setting for society weddings, although its opulent, neo-Byzantine interior found little favour when it was completed in 1856. One of Dublin's most fashionable churches.

St Kevin's Park

Camden Row (no phone). All cross-city buses/Luas St Stephen's Green. **Open** *Dec, Jan* 8am-4.30pm; Mon-Fri; 10am-4.30pm Sat, Sun. *Feb, Nov* 8am-5pm Mon-Fri; 10am-5pm Sat, Sun. *Mar, Oct* 8am-6pm Mon-Fri; 10am-6pm Sat, Sun. *Apr, Sept* 8am-8pm Mon-Fri; 10am-8pm Sat, Sun. *May-Aug* 8am-9pm Mon-Fri; 10am-9pm Sat, Sun. **Admission** free. *See p72* **Walk: Out of sight**.

Kildare Street & around

Map p251 & p252

Pleasant side streets lead from the bustle of Grafton Street to Dawson Street and the **Mansion House**. This Queen Anne-style building has been the official residence of the Lord Mayor of Dublin since 1715. Neighbouring **St Anne's Church** is where Bram Stoker was married in 1878. The interior dates from 1720, and the loaves of bread left there are a reminder of an 18th-century bequest to the city's poor.

From Dawson Street, wander east along Molesworth Street towards Kildare Street and **Leinster House** (*see p72*), seat of the Dáil (Irish Parliament) since 1922. Leinster House is flanked by the equally serious grey façades of the **National Library of Ireland** (*see p73*) – first stop for researchers into family heritage – and the **National Museum of Archaeology & History** (*see p73*).

The Venetian-inspired red-brick building on the corner of Kildare and Nassau streets, once the Kildare Street Club for the gentlemen of the Ascendancy, now holds the **Heraldic Museum** (*see below*).

Heraldic Museum

Kildare Street (603 0200/www.nli.ie). All cross-city buses/Luas St Stephen's Green. **Open** 9.30am-8.30pm Mon-Wed; 9.30am-4.30pm Thur, Fri; 10.30am-12.30pm Sat. **Admission** free. **Map** p252 G4.

In 1886 George Moore said of the Kildare Street Club: 'It represents all that is respectable, that is to say, those who are gifted with that oyster-like capacity for understanding…that they should continue to get fat in the bed in which they were born.' The building is now divided between the Alliance Française and the Heraldic Museum (a dull display of objects showing armorial bearings, scarcely worth a visit now that the genealogy and family history section has been moved to the National Library). There is, however, an amusing frieze of monkeys playing billiards carved by the O'Shea brothers, who also did the stonework on Trinity's Museum Building, around the right-hand side of the museum entrance. There is no official account of their significance, so take your pick of two competing stories. According to one, they depict the many strange and wondrous animals to be found throughout the British Empire. The second, more popular, account holds that they represent the gentlemen members of the old Club.

Georgian opulence at **Newman House**.

Walk: Out of sight

St Stephen's Green is quite possibly the most famous patch of grass in Dublin: it is here that tourists and local office workers congregate to sun themselves in summer and to stretch their legs in the winter. And yet, right on its doorstep are some of the city's most beautiful gardens and charmingly secluded spots, where those seeking respite from the crowds of the Green come to get their daily fix of *rus in urbe*.

This exploration of the area's leafy secrets begins with the oft-overlooked **Iveagh Gardens** (*see p70*). At first glance, the gardens look private: they're ringed by high stone walls and their entrances are hidden. One door lurks behind the National Concert Hall (*see p185*) on Earlsfort Terrace, another on Clonmel Street; a few years ago, a third gate was created on Hatch Street, from which a flight of concrete steps (flanked by a wheelchair ramp) leads down to the southernmost end of the circuit of sequestered paths. From here, turn left (leaving the extraordinary mass of gnarled tree roots behind you) and head towards the gorgeous circular rose garden. Stop to smell the roses before continuing on to the miniature maze (a pleasingly symmetrical spectacle, and a welcome activity for those with kids in tow). From here, head north through the trees into the open section of the gardens, where two imposing statue fountains face each other across a sweep of perfectly manicured lawn. After the narrow paths and lichen-covered statuary of the south side of the gardens, the sense of space here is exhilarating. Wander in the direction of the northwest corner and exit the gardens on to Clonmel Street.

Turn right and head north up Harcourt Street before taking a left into Montague Street. This will soon lead you out on to Camden Street – the excellent Bóbó's burger bar (*see p108*) will be enticing you from the other side of the road. Be strong, walk on past and into Camden Row where, after a few paces, you will come across the tiny **St Kevin's Park** (*see p71*) squirrelled away to your right. Formerly the graveyard to the ivy-strangled relic of a church at its centre, this beguiling little park is almost always empty. Rumour has it that the area is haunted by the restless souls of the displaced band whose gravestones have been pushed to the side of the now neatly tended lawns – although, judging by the pious life stories told in the several plaques and memorials that are scattered around the place, it's hard to imagine any of this lot as the chain-rattling type. In fact, it's such a peaceful setting (a sensation heightened by the proximity of towering office blocks and busy roads) that St Kevin's can be one of the most relaxing places in Dublin to immerse yourself in a book or simply sit on a bench and enjoy the murmur of bees and twitter of birdsong.

But don't get too comfortable – there is one last hideaway to discover. Find your way back to where Camden Row joins Camden Street and turn right, heading south for a few hundred yards. As you walk you'll see that this is prime student territory, with bars advertising happy hours, cafés touting cheap deals and copy shops with special rates on theses crowding the pavement. Stop at No.61, home to the ecologically-minded, high-quality paper company, Daintree. Walk through the shop, past the shelves of speciality papers and bindings, and emerge at the back into the hidden courtyard of the **Cake Café** (*see p122*).

Leinster House

Kildare Street (618 3000/www.oireachtas.ie). All cross-city buses/Luas St Stephen's Green. **Open** *Tours* (when Parliament is not in session) 10.30am, 11.30am, 2.30pm, 3.30pm Mon-Fri. **Admission** free. **Map** p252 G4.

Leinster House is the seat of the Irish Parliament, made up of the Dáil (lower house) and the Seanad (senate or upper house). The first of Dublin's great 18th-century houses to be constructed south of the Liffey, Leinster was built by Richard Castle (between 1745 and 1748) for the Earl of Kildare, who became Duke of Leinster in 1766. The Seanad meets in the sumptuous North Wing Saloon; the Dáil in a rather prosaic room added as a lecture theatre in 1897. The house has two formal fronts – the Kildare Street frontage, designed to look like a townhouse, and a Merrion Square frontage – that are connected by a long central corridor. Leinster House has been claimed as the prototype for the White House in the United States (the White House architect, James Hoban, was born in 1762 in County Kilkenny). The entrance hall and principal rooms were redecorated towards the end of the 18th century with the help of James Wyatt. No cameras or recording equipment are allowed inside.

few paces, you will come across the tiny **St Kevin's Park** (*see p71*) squirrelled away to your right. Formerly the graveyard to the ivy-strangled relic of a church at its centre, this beguiling little park is almost always empty. Rumour has it that the area is haunted by the restless souls of the displaced band whose gravestones have been pushed to the side of the now neatly tended lawns – although, judging by the pious life stories told in the several plaques and memorials that are scattered around the place, it's hard to imagine any of this lot as the chain-rattling type. In fact, it's such a peaceful setting (a sensation heightened by the proximity of towering office blocks and busy roads) that St Kevin's can be one of the most relaxing places in Dublin to immerse yourself in a book or simply sit on a bench and enjoy the murmur of bees and twitter of birdsong.

But don't get too comfortable – there is one last hideaway to discover. Find your way back to where Camden Row joins Camden Street and turn right, heading south for a few hundred yards. As you walk you'll see that this is prime student territory, with bars advertising happy hours, cafés touting cheap deals and copy shops with special rates on theses crowding the pavement. Stop at No.61, home to the ecologically-minded, high-quality paper company, Daintree. Walk through the shop, past the shelves of speciality papers and bindings, and emerge at the back into the hidden courtyard of the **Cake Café** (*see p122*). Here, you have reached journey's end, so settle in for a cup of something hot and a slice of something nice and fattening (there'll be plenty of chances to walk it off on the way back to town).

National Library of Ireland

Kildare Street (603 0200/www.nli.ie). All cross-city buses/Luas St Stephen's Green. **Open** 9.30am-9pm Mon-Wed; 9.30am-5pm Thur, Fri; 9.30am-1pm Sat. **Admission** free. **Map** p252 G4.

Though the National Library is predominantly a research institution, some parts of it are open to the public. These include the grand domed Reading Room – the place in which Stephen Dedalus expounds his views on Shakespeare in James Joyce's *Ulysses* – and the Exhibition Room, which plays host to changing displays from the Library's extensive collections. There's also a walk-in genealogical service for people keen on tracing their family trees. At the time of writing, a multimillion euro extenion plan (to increase exhibition, reading and repository space) had been approved for the Library.

National Museum of Archaeology & History

Kildare Street (677 7444/www.museum.ie). All cross-city buses/Luas St Stephen's Green. **Open** 10am-5pm Tue-Sat; 2-5pm Sun. **Admission** free. *Tours* €2. **Map** p252 G4.

Established in 1877 by the Science and Art Museums Act, the National Museum is deservedly one of Dublin's most popular attractions. The 19th-century building designed by Thomas Newenham Deane is squeezed into a site to the side of the impassive façade of Leinster House. Its domed entrance hall, or Rotunda, looks like a Victorian reworking of the Pantheon, with windows on the upper gallery that jut inwards so that the space appears to cave in towards the spectator. The most striking exhibition among its many excellent pieces is *Or*, a collection of Bronze Age Irish gold displayed in vast glass cases on the ground floor. Further along there are a number of examples of extraordinarily intricate sacred and secular metalwork dating from the Iron Age to the Middle Ages, as well as displays of well-preserved artefacts from prehistoric and Viking Ireland, plus Ancient Egyptian artefacts on the first floor.

Merrion Square & around

Map p251

Between St Stephen's Green and Ballsbridge is the well-preserved heart of Georgian Dublin, the wealthiest quarter of the inner city. Loaded with shops, cafés and restaurants, Baggot Street is the district's main artery. The area around elegant **Merrion Square** (where a list of the former residents reads like a *Who's Who* of 19th-century Ireland) is arguably the prettiest. This is the most architecturally and culturally significant square in the district, and it seems as if every inch of space has been used for something beautiful. On its western edge is the back entrance to **Leinster House** (*see p72*), home of the Irish Parliament, flanked by the **National Gallery of Ireland** (*see p76*) and the fascinating **Natural History Museum** (closed for refurbishment until at least 2011). Up until a few years ago, it all used to look very different, as the Leinster Lawn ran from the road up to Leinster House, but the grass was ripped up to make way for a 'temporary' car park that is now beginning to look unpleasantly permanent. Nonetheless, the space is still adorned with an obelisk dedicated to the founders of the Irish Free State – Michael Collins, Arthur Griffith and Kevin O'Higgins.

Next door to the Natural History Museum is another entrance to the Parliament complex. It's quite the grandest entrance, too, despite being saddled with the spectacularly dull label 'Government Buildings'. This part of the complex is the last word in Edwardian bombastic opulence; once part of University College Dublin, it was neglected for years before being restored and occupied by the government in the 1990s. Its interior is just as lavish as its gleaming façade, although you'll have to take our word for that, as tours have been suspended.

The rest of Merrion Square is occupied by offices and organisations, with small oval plaques recounting the names of each house's famous former occupants: on Merrion Square South: WB Yeats at No.82, the poet and mystic George (Æ) Russell at No.84; the horror writer Joseph Sheridan Le Fanu at No.70; and Erwin Schrödinger, co-winner of the 1933 Nobel Prize for Physics, at No.65. The hero of Catholic Emancipation Daniel O'Connell lived at No.58 – look for the plaque reading 'The Liberator'. Elsewhere around the square is the Duke of Wellington's birthplace at No.24 and the site of the former British Embassy at 39 Merrion Square East – the embassy was burned down by protestors in 1972 in protest at the actions of the British army in Derry on Bloody Sunday.

The square itself has beautifully tended formal gardens, which seem labyrinthine until you get to the open space at the centre. For many years the Catholic Church planned to build a cathedral here; in fact, these plans were only properly abandoned in the 1970s. The square is sprinkled with art: at the southern end is a bust of Michael Collins, while at the north-western corner the figure of Oscar Wilde sprawls in multicoloured loucheness atop a rough rock and is surrounded by his favourite *bons mots*, scrawled as graffiti on two translucent columns. Perhaps, inevitably, this memorial has been dubbed the 'fag on the crag'. Wilde's statue looks over at his old home at 1 Merrion Square North (now the **Oscar Wilde House**, *see p77*).

The stretch from Merrion Square East south to Fitzwilliam Square was the longest unbroken line of Georgian houses in the world until 1961, when the Electricity Supply Board knocked down a row of them – 26 in all – to construct a hideous new building that continues to blight the area's architectural symmetry to this day. This architectural travesty was typical of local planning decisions in the 20th century: most of Dublin's finest houses were built by the British, and the developing Irish state showed a marked lack of respect for the city's colonial architecture. Only in recent years have efforts been made to protect the architectural heritage (although, even then, many would argue that the powers that be continue to give away the store in short term deals; *see p41* **With or without you**). In partial recompense for the destruction it caused, the ESB tarted up **Number Twenty-Nine** (*see p77*), restoring it as a nice Georgian townhouse museum, kitted out with all the latest in circa-1800 household fashion.

Just down Fitzwilliam Street from Merrion Square, **Fitzwilliam Square** is the smallest, most discreet and most residential of the city's Georgian squares. Completed in 1825, it's an

National Gallery. *See p76.*

immensely charming space – even though, unfortunately, only residents have access to its lovely central garden. That square leads on to Leeson Street (via Pembroke Street Upper), a wide, long thoroughfare that slopes down to the Grand Canal.

National Gallery of Ireland

Merrion Square West (661 5133/www.national gallery.ie). All cross-city buses/Luas St Stephen's Green. **Open** 9.30am-5.30pm Mon-Wed, Fri, Sat; 9.30am-8.30pm Thur; noon-5.30pm Sun. **Admission** free; donations welcome. **Map** p251 G4. This gallery houses a small but fine collection of European works from the 14th to the 20th centuries, including paintings by Caravaggio (in Room 42), Tintoretto, Titian, Monet, Degas, Goya, Vermeer and Picasso. A room is also devoted to painter Jack Yeats, who developed an impressionistic style particularly suited to the Irish landscape. Look out, too, for works by Paul Henry, Roderic O'Conor, William Orpen, Nathaniel Hone and Walter Osborne. The smaller British collection is also impressive, with works by Hogarth, Landseer and Gainsborough, and every January an exhibition of Turner's watercolours draws art lovers from all over the world. Giovanni Lanfranco's magnificent *Last Supper* (in the equally impressive Baroque Room – more prosaically, Room 44) is a sight worth goggling at, as many do on a daily basis. The gallery's fabulous Millennium Wing has also been a big draw since its opening; it provides a new entrance on Clare Street, light-drenched galleries, and the obligatory – albeit lovely – restaurant, café and gift shop. Regular

Ceremonial artefacts and documents at the **Jewish Museum**.

changing exhibitions range in subject from Samuel Beckett's interest in fine art to the history of print-making. There is also a strong educational pro-gramme at the Gallery, which encompasses talks and lectures (on subjects as diverse as the Great Masters and 'architectural intelligence'), as well as short courses led by local and visiting artists. It is worth consulting the website to see what events might be on during your visit – tickets may run to, say, €35 for an 'art and supper lecture', but can you put a price on cultural enrichment? Discuss. *Photo p75.*

Number Twenty-Nine

29 Fitzwilliam Street Lower (702 6165/www.esb.ie/ numbertwentynine). Bus 6, 7, 10, 45/DART Grand Canal Dock. **Open** 10am-5pm Tue-Sat; noon-5pm Sun. **Admission** *Guided tours* €6; €3 reductions; free under-16s. **Credit** MC, V. **Map** p251 H4.
This restored 18th-century merchant house is pre-sented as a middle-class dwelling circa 1790-1820. It stands proudly on the corner of one of the most ele-gant vistas in Dublin, a long neo-classical perspective stretching from Merrion Square West down Mount Street. From furniture – comfortable rather than opu-lent – and paintings through to toys and personal effects, the interior of this property is a treasure trove of Georgian style. Dublin history buffs will also be intrigued by the collection of prints, oil paintings and watercolours, many of which offer interesting per-spectives on the city itself and one or two of its key residents (James Petrie's haunting portrait of revolu-tionary Robert Emmet being a notable example).

Oscar Wilde House

American College Dublin, 1 Merrion Square (662 0281/www.amcd.ie). All cross-city buses. **Open** *Guided tours* by appointment only (min 25 persons). **Admission** €8. **No credit cards. Map** p251 G4.
Really somewhere that most people will observe from the outside, as the house is only open for view-ings for large groups. A major refurb has left it look-ing good, though, so if you do manage to arrange a viewing, you won't be disappointed. Wilde lived in the house until 1878, and more than a century later the building was taken over by the American College Dublin, which has restored floors, including the surgery and Lady Speranza's drawing room.

Around the Grand Canal

Map p250 & p251

Both Baggot Street and Leeson Street lead from St Stephen's Green down to the Grand Canal, a short distance away. The canal meanders gently around the city to the south, eventually flowing into the Canal Basin in the old industrial zone of Ringsend before joining the Liffey at the south docks. Built between 1756 and 1796, it was the longest canal in Britain and Ireland, stretching from Shannon Harbour in Offaly to Dublin Bay. It has not been used commercially since 1960, and nowadays its grassy banks are a focal point

for walkers, cyclists and, in summer, swimmers, who rather unwisely take to the water when the locks are full. In the winter months, great phalanxes of swans take shelter on the water.

In recent years, the Grand Canal towpaths have been repaired along the most pleasant stretch of the canal, which runs from Grand Canal Street up to Harold's Cross Bridge, and a new bridge has been constructed close to Ranelagh Bridge for the Luas tram service.

The area is best explored in a walk that takes in the poignant **Jewish Museum** (*see below*), which recounts the often-neglected history of the Jews in Ireland, as well as the **Shaw Birthplace** (*see below*), a fine tribute to GBS.

Jewish Museum

3 Walworth Road, Portobello (490 1857). Buses 16, 16A, 19, 19A, 22, 22A/Luas Harcourt. **Open** *May-Sept* 11am-3.30pm Tue, Thur, Sun. *Oct-Apr* 10.30am-2.30pm Sun. **Admission** free. **Map** p250 D6.
This collection of documents and artefacts relating to the Jewish community of Ireland includes a recon-struction of a late 19th-century kitchen typical of a Jewish home in the neighbourhood and, upstairs, a synagogue preserved with ritual fittings. The exhibi-tion tells about events such as the pogroms against the Jews of Limerick in the 1920s. The museum is well arranged and has moving displays: among its exhibits is a letter, dated 1938, from the Irish Chief Rabbi to De Valera asking for six highly educated Jewish refugees (mostly doctors) to be admitted, and its almost casual rejection.

National Print Museum

Garrison Chapel, Beggars Bush, Haddington Road (660 3770/www.iol.ie/~npmuseum). Bus 5, 7, 7A, 45, 63/DART Grand Canal Dock. **Open** 9am-5pm Mon-Fri; 2-5pm Sat, Sun. **Admission** €3.50; €2 reductions; €7 family. **No credit cards.**
Surprisingly enough, this display of printing equip-ment is not, in fact, mind-numbingly boring – which is a feat in itself. Truth be told, it's positively inter-esting. The Beggars Bush building was originally a barracks, and the central garrison houses the Irish Labour History Museum, filled with documents relating to labour and industrial history. The guid-ed tours are entertaining and informative. Note the excellent Bookbinders' Union banner bearing the legend: 'Bind right with might'. Enough said.

The Shaw Birthplace

33 Synge Street, Portobello (475 0854). Bus 16, 16A, 19, 19A, 122/Luas Harcourt. **Open** *May-Sept* 10am-1pm, 2-5pm Mon, Tue, Thur, Fri; 2-5pm Sat, Sun. **Admission** €7.25; €4.55-€6.10 reductions; €21 family. **No credit cards. Map** p251 E5.
On the plaque outside this neat Victorian house, Shaw is commemorated simply – some might say tersely – as 'author of many plays'. The house is a good example of a Victorian middle-class home, but those who aren't Shaw (or Victoriana) enthusiasts might find it all a little tedious.

O'Connell Street & Around

Broad and busy, Dublin's most famous street is still making history.

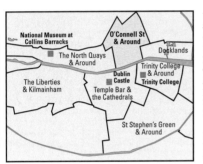

Any Dubliner worth his (or her) salt will proudly tell you that O'Connell Street is a very wide street. Some will go further. Some will say it is the widest street in Europe; others might even confidently claim it to be the widest in the world. But whatever its official status, the truth remains that O'Connell Street is indeed very wide – 46 metres (150 feet) – and its buildings are indeed tall (for Dublin). It is, without question, the most imposing thoroughfare in the city and, though it doesn't hold the parliament, it also tends to be the focal point of every political rally. But until recently it was going to seed, it had become a lucrative beat for petty criminals and junkies, its pavements mired in litter, half its fine buildings leased to burger joints, the other half knocked down.

These days, all that has changed. *Garda* patrol tirelessly, and the whole street has been placed under special planning and conservation control. Recent developments include the widening of footpaths, the removal of the old London plane trees and the planting of 200 new trees of various species, the restoration of monuments, the creation of a plaza in front of the **General Post Office** (or GPO, *see p81*) and, of course, the **Spire**. All this was done to the usual barrage of criticism (people hated the Spire, loved the old plane trees), but as the

Small world

The areas immediately surrounding O'Connell Street have become some of the city's most multicultural enclaves in recent years, but nowhere showcases Dublin's immigrant explosion quite like Parnell Street. Formerly a straggling, grey strip of down-at-heel bars and pound shops, it's been transformed into Dublin's Chinatown and Koreatown. Every second building on Parnell Street – and, for that matter, much of Moore Street – houses a Chinese or Korean restaurant, and nowhere in the city can you eat this well at this price. Chinese restaurants in Dublin used to be heavy, sombre, carpeted institutions, where punters paid a lot for food delivered with the decorous solemnity and creeping pace of dinner at Versailles; now, though, hordes of eager diners cram into these cheerful canteens, and freshly cooked dishes emerge swiftly from the kitchen. Most European capitals know this scene already, but it's still all new to Dublin: just when it was beginning to seem as if all good deals began and ended with Ryanair, finally there's the chance of getting delicious meals for under €10.

Then, just a short hop to the southwest is the vibrant Italian Quarter that has sprung up on both sides of Bloom Lane, snaking around on to the riverside at Lower Ormond Quay. Tasty little delis squeeze in among wonderfully authentic trattorias like **Enoteca delle Langhe** (*see p114*) or **Bar Italia** (*see p112*). Walking along this stretch on a summer's evening, among the pavement tables crammed with crowds tucking into authentic Italian *cucina* and glasses of fruity red, it is impossible to recognise the Dublin of ten years ago. But nor does it feel like just another fleeting foodie fad. This is a new facet of city life, and it's here to stay.

Shoppers in their droves on busy **Henry Street**. *See p80.*

street's now looking leafy, prosperous, more pedestrianised, much tidier (litter vans trawl assiduously) – in short, much more like the main street of one of Europe's richest countries – the naysayers have quietened down.

O'Connell Street

Map p251

O'Connell Street has its origins in the 17th-century Drogheda Street: laid out by the Earl of Drogheda, it was originally a third of the width of the current street and three-quarters as long. It was widened and lengthened in the 18th century, first by Ireland's foremost builder and millionaire, Luke Gardiner (who gave his name to Gardiner Street), and after his death by the Wide Streets Commission. On its completion in the 1790s, Sackville Street (as it was renamed) was one of the finest in Europe; Carlisle Bridge (now O'Connell Bridge) linked it to College Green and Westmoreland Street, and the whole area prospered as the city's commercial centre.

The street was such a focal point that in 1916 it was made HQ of the Easter Rising (*see p16*), during which many buildings were reduced to rubble. In the summer of 1922 it was the scene of fighting again, when the civil war broke out (*see p19*). In 1924, with the civil war now over, it was renamed O'Connell Street.

The street is bookended by sculptures of Ireland's two great constitutional nationalists – Daniel O'Connell and Charles Stewart Parnell. O'Connell's statue is the gateway to the street. Designed and built, through public subscription in the 1870s by John Henry Foley (who died before its completion), it's an imposing bronze monument of the Liberator flanked by four winged Victories (one of whom has a rather unfortunate bullet hole, right on her nipple, courtesy of the Easter Rising).

The whole centre median of the street, lined with trees, is like an outdoor art gallery. Among the permanent statues are those to Father Mathew (the temperance apostle who, incredible to relate, had between three and four million people abstaining from drink in 1840) and Oisin Kelly's fine, vigorous statue of the great trade unionist Jim Larkin throwing his arms out wide in an explosion of energy. Other statues form temporary exhibitions – in 2008, for example, the **Hugh Lane Gallery** (*see p82*) celebrated its centenary with Julian Opie's superb *Walking on O'Connell Street* LED installations.

The centrepiece is the **Spire**, built in 2003, an enormous stainless steel shard that jabs 120 metres (396 feet) into the sky. Its various nicknames ('stiletto in the ghetto', 'erection at the intersection', 'stiffy at the Liffey') are only ever used by cab drivers and tour guides – before the Spire came the 'floozy in the Jacuzzi' moniker for the particularly foul 1980s Joycean statue (now removed). But behind all the jokes, the Spire has an undoubted significance for many Dubliners, especially those old enough to remember the twin of Trafalgar Square's Nelson's column that originally stood in this spot, until it was blown up by the IRA in 1966 (on the 50th anniversary of the Easter Rising). At first the Spire's design was bitterly opposed, but now it finally seems to have won the city's affection (easy to see why when approaching from Henry Street on a sunny day).

The grey, columned building behind the Spire is the GPO, probably the most famous building in 20th-century Ireland. On these steps, on

Easter Monday 1916, Patrick Pearse read his proclamation for a free Irish Republic: 'In every generation, the Irish people have asserted their right to national freedom and sovereignty; six times during the past 300 years, they have asserted it in arms.' He was killed by a firing squad nine days later, but five years on, Ireland was independent. Pass by today, and you'll likely find some lone socialist workers voicing protests on the newly created plaza in front of it.

The grand department store across the street from the GPO is Dublin's beloved **Clery's** (*see p139*), formerly the Imperial Hotel. Clery's balcony was the position from which Jim Larkin made a stirring speech to his supporters during the general strike in 1913. On the corner here is O'Connell Street's lone literary statue – Joyce, of course, leaning on a stick. While directly opposite, the busy thoroughfare of **Henry Street** beckons with its many shops and cafés.

Turn right into Cathedral Street, one road up, and you get to **St Mary's Pro-Cathedral**, Dublin's main Catholic church, built in classical style in 1815. For a city with (give or take) 90 per cent devout church-going Catholics, it's a modest cathedral indeed, especially compared to the imposing Christ Church and St Patrick's,

both of which cater to Dublin's tiny Anglican community. But after independence, both churches were careful to keep relations cordial, and Catholic bishops seem perfectly happy with the Pro-Cathedral, which has seen numerous large funerals, including that of O'Connell himself in 1847.

Back to O'Connell Street, and the big, grand building at the top is the **Gresham Hotel** (*see p48*), which played a part in the Easter Rising – many fled here to seek refuge from the battle. Apparently, the rebel leader Michael Collins evaded capture during the war of independence by hiding out here on Christmas Eve 1920. Today you can have delicious (if highly priced) afternoon tea in the lovely, old-world lobby.

Besides statues, hotels and fast-food joints (still much in evidence, though reduced), the O'Connell Street area is strong on theatres and cinemas. It's marked top and bottom by the city's two leading theatres: the Abbey and the Gate.

The **Abbey Theatre** (*see p195*), on Abbey Street, was founded in 1904 by WB Yeats and Lady Gregory. It's Ireland's national theatre, but its location (in a building that is not considered one of renowned architect Michael Scott's best) has always been a sticking point. Finally, though, in December 2005, the government okayed a plan to move the theatre to George's Dock. Progress has been slow but, at the time of writing, a tender was being drafted to find an architect to design the new Docklands site – a sure sign that the wheels are turning at last. But for the forseeable future, the Abbey will remain in its O'Connell Street premises, alongside the smaller, more avant-garde and less commercial **Peacock Theatre** (*see p196*).

The **Gate Theatre** (*see p197*) stands at the other end of O'Connell Street, on the southeastern corner of Parnell Square. It has the most elegant, best-proportioned stage in Dublin, and its antecedents are as honourable and radical as the Abbey Theatre's – it was founded in 1929 by the remarkable, flamboyant British homosexual duo, Hilton Edwards and Michael McLiammoir.

At the top of O'Connell Street, beside the Gresham, the **Savoy** cinema (*see p164*) faces the old Carlton cinema. Built in 1928 as a Venetian-style theatre, then made over as 1970s kitsch, the Savoy is now, post-renovation, blandly comfortable and vacuously timeless. The Carlton has been shut for years. Though you'd hardly guess from its parlous condition, it's one of the city's most important post-Independence buildings and a rare Dublin instance of art deco design. It's boarded up, and renovation is delayed until 2012, but the O'Connell Street facelift won't be complete without it.

General Post Office.

Impressionists and Francis Bacon draw art lovers to the **Hugh Lane Gallery**. *See p82.*

General Post Office

O'Connell Street (705 7000/www.anpost.ie).
All cross-city buses/Luas Abbey Street. **Open**
8am-8pm Mon-Sat. **Admission** free. **Map** p251 F2.
Best known as the site of the Easter Rising in 1916,
the GPO remains a potent symbol of Irish independence. Designed by Francis Johnston in 1818, it was
almost completely destroyed by fire during the
uprising, and had barely been restored six years
later when the civil war did further damage to the
building. There are still bullet holes in the walls and
columns out front, and a series of paintings inside
depicts moments from the Easter Rising. In a
window, and visible from the outside, is the beautiful *Death of Cúchulainn*, a statue by Oliver Sheppard
commemorating the building's reopening in 1929.
Cúchulainn, the legendary knight of the Red Branch,
is used as a symbol by both Loyalist and Republican
paramilitary groups. Such terror did Cúchulainn
inspire in his enemies that, even after they had
succeeded in killing him, no one dared approach his
body until ravens landed on his shoulders. At the
time of writing, there was a talk of a dedicated museum on the 1916 Uprising being installed in the GPO.

Parnell Square

Map p251

O'Connell Street is bookended by the bustling,
multicultural Parnell Street (*see p78* **Small
World**) and the grey and sombre **Parnell
Square**, a large Georgian square made up
of museums and public buildings. The
imposing **Rotunda Hospital** takes up the
south side of the square. Founded in 1745 by Dr
Bartholomew Mosse as Europe's first maternity
hospital, it has occupied its current site since
1757 in a building designed by Richard Castle,
architect of Leinster House.

On the north side of the square, the **Garden
of Remembrance** was opened on the 50th
anniversary of the Easter Rising to honour
those who died for Irish freedom. The garden
is dominated by Oisin Kelly's huge, beautiful
sculpture *Children of Lir* – a representation of
an ancient Irish legend, in which four children
are turned into swans by their evil stepmother.

Opposite the garden is the Municipal Gallery
of Modern Art, more commonly known as the
Hugh Lane Gallery (*see p82*), housed in the
neo-classical Charlemont House. Re-opened in
May 2006 after much renovation, it hosts on
three floors its permanent collection of French
and Irish Impressionist art, alongside changing
exhibitions and Francis Bacon's London studio,
which is reproduced in the gallery.

Next door to the gallery, the **Dublin
Writers' Museum** (*see p82*) has an excellent
collection of letters, memorabilia, photos and
equipment from the city's many famous writers,
and adjoins the Irish Writers' Centre, which
hosts lectures, readings and literary receptions,
and serves as a resource for those researching

Irish literature. Recuperation from literary and artistic endeavours is provided by the excellent restaurant **Chapter One** (*see p112*) in the museum's vaulted basement.

If the Writers' Museum doesn't slake your literary thirst, make your way to nearby North Great George's Street, where the **James Joyce Centre** (*see below*) dedicates itself to the eponymous giant of Irish letters. North Great George's Street is a fine street of Georgian houses, on a steep slope. The stylish **Cobalt Café & Gallery** (*see p122*), at No.16, is an arty hangout that hosts occasional live preformances.

Dublin Writers' Museum

18-19 Parnell Square (872 2077/www.writers museum.com). Bus 3, 10, 11, 13, 16, 19, 22/Luas Abbey Street. **Open** *Sept-May* 10am-5pm Mon-Sat; 11am-5pm Sun. *June-Aug* 10am-6pm Mon-Fri; 10am-5pm Sat; 11am-5pm Sun. **Admission** €7.25; €4.55-€6.10 reductions; €21 family. **Credit** AmEx, MC, V. **Map** p251 E1.

It can be hard to showcase the real achievements of writers, but this small, jam-packed museum does pretty well, featuring unique and well-chosen memorabilia from Swift, Wilde, Yeats, Joyce, Beckett and others. Packed into its rather fusty wooden and glass display cabinets are some unusual and intriguing artefacts, such as the phone from Beckett's Paris apartment, and playbills from the Abbey Theatre's early days. There's a great display on Brendan Behan, including a long letter he wrote from California to a friend back home in Dublin, after he made it big. He wrote of a party he'd attended with Groucho and Harpo Marx, adding, 'It was in the papers all over, but I don't suppose the Dublin papers had it. They only seem to know when I'm in jail or dying.' There are also occasional temporary exhibitions and live performances to spice things up a bit.

Hugh Lane Gallery (Municipal Gallery of Modern Art)

Parnell Square North (222 5550/www.hughlane.ie). Bus 3, 10, 11, 13, 16, 19, 22/Luas Abbey Street. **Open** 10am-6pm Tue-Thur; 10am-5pm Fri, Sat; 11am-5pm Sun. **Admission** *Gallery* free. *Francis Bacon Studio* €7; €3.50 reductions; free under-18s. Half-price to all 9.30am-12.30pm Tue. **Credit** MC, V. **Map** p251 E1.

Celerating its centenary in 2008, the Municipal Gallery is named after Hugh Lane, nephew of Yeats's friend Lady Gregory and noted art patron who determined to leave his fine collection of French and Irish Impressionist art to the city (provided a suitable gallery was built to house it). Despite a number of vituperative poems from Yeats, Dublin Corporation did not come up with a gallery, forcing Lane to bequeath his pictures to London. At the eleventh hour he stipulated that Dublin could have them if they provided a gallery, but this codicil to his will was unwitnessed when he went down with the other passengers on the *Lusitania*, torpedoed by a German U-boat in 1915. London stuck to the letter of the law

for decades, but the matter was recently settled in Irish favour (though a number of the paintings still rotate between Dublin and London).

After extensive renovations, the gallery reopened in May 2006 and now uses the full three floors. Lane's collection of Manets, Coubets and Renoirs is on the ground floor (but don't miss Irish artists Walter Osbourne and Roderic O'Conor), as are Harry Clarke's marvellous stained-glass windows, and Francis Bacon's London studio, which, in a Herculean feat of excavation, was moved piece by piece from 7 Reese Mews and reconstructed here behind glass. Visitors gape at its half-completed canvases, dirty paintbrushes, bottles of booze, books, dust, magazines and sublime filth. Bacon was born in Dublin and brought up in Wicklow. He left at the age of 16 and, ever after, even the thought of Ireland induced a panic attack, but perhaps he retained some affection for it since his heir, John Edwards, bequeathed the studio to the Hugh Lane, where it has become a major attraction. The gallery has also upped its collection of paintings by Bacon. New since the renovation is a Sean Scully Room – the only space in Ireland dedicated to this major Irish-American contemporary artist. Also a big draw for the gallery is its highly succssful 'Sundays at Noon' programme of free musical concerts (there are around 30 a year, ranging from jazz and world groups to classical recitals – check the website for upcoming dates). *Photo p81.*

James Joyce Centre

35 North Great George's Street (878 8547/ www.jamesjoyce.ie). Bus 3, 10, 11, 11A, 13, 16, 16A, 19, 19A, 22/Luas Abbey Street. **Open** 10am-5pm Tue-Sat. **Admission** €5; €4 reductions; free under-14s. *Walking tours* €10; €8 reductions. **Credit** AmEx, MC, V. **Map** p251 F1.

Joyce never lived here, nor did Leopold Bloom, though a minor character in *Ulysses* – Denis Maginni – held dance classes here (but then in what building in central Dublin did a minor character in *Ulysses* not do *something* in?). How it came to be the Joyce Centre is that Senator David Norris noticed in the mid 1980s that this beautiful house was decaying, so, deciding to combine his passion for Joyce with his passion for Georgian architecture, he created a trust. The house took 14 years to renovate but, through careful adherence to old photos, it now looks just as it did in 1904, when Maginni would have been holding his dance classes – the ceiling on the first floor is one of the finest in Dublin. After being run haphazardly by Joyce's nephew, the centre is now under new management and has gained greater focus. The top floor has a recreation of Joyce's room in Zurich and a touch-screen history of the publication of *Ulysses*, while the terrace holds the door of 7 Eccles Street (Bloom's house), saved from the Mater Hospital's extension in Eccles Street. Highlights from the National Library's recent exhibition on Joyce are also on permanent loan to the Centre, and there are Joycean walking tours every Saturday (at 11am and 2pm).

The North Quays & Around

Riverside walks, urban regeneration and acres of parkland.

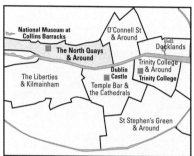

The North Quays is the collective name for the series of streets that run to the west of Docklands' **Custom House** (*p88*) along the northern embankment of the Liffey. Although it appears as one long street, the names change every block or so – Eden Quay, Bachelors Walk, Ormond Quay, Inns Quay – as do the individual characters of the discrete residential hubs that are scattered along this mile-long stretch. There are also several markets, including the remnants of the fabled Smithfield horse-trading fair, and the city's biggest green space (Phoenix Park) to be explored. It's busy, bustling and fascinating, and well worth your time.

North Quays

Map p250 & p251

After crossing the river on the O'Connell Bridge from the south side, take a sharp right along the river on to **Eden Quay**. You may be put off by the noise and fumes from the perpetual traffic jams, but persevere and soon the view of historic Marlborough Street will open up on your left. Here you will see both the historic **Abbey Theatre** (*see p197*) – one of the city's most beloved and controversial theatres, whose productions once caused rioting in the streets, but now tend toward the mainstream – and the **Flowing Tide** bar (*see p136*), a mainstay of thespian Dublin, which some northsiders claim has the finest pint in the city. That said, of course, Dubliners tend to discuss the question

of where to find the nicest stout with a dreamy intensity, while actually living by the motto that the best pint is the one within easy reach.

Turning left at the river after you cross O'Connell Bridge from the south, you find yourself on **Bachelors Walk**. Its rather charming name dates back to the 18th century, when it was a favourite promenade of young men of the neighbourhood. This strip was once the centre of the city's antique and furniture trade, and such shops that remain are worth a browse. On the wooden Liffey boardwalk here are three little huts manned by wonderfully grumpy staff selling coffee and sandwiches, which, weather permitting, you can enjoy alfresco on the little riverside benches.

After a few blocks, Bachelors Walk becomes Ormond Quay Lower, and the oft-photographed **Ha'penny Bridge** stands there charmingly, waiting to be snapped. It dates to 1816 and was once a toll bridge (no prize for guessing how much it cost to cross). Once you've taken that photo, you could do worse than turn into the literary haven that is the **Winding Stair**, a superb little bookshop with an equally impressive restaurant upstairs (*see p114 and p143*). Back on Ormond Quay, that paragon of modern sleekness you see before you is the **Morrison Hotel** (*see p48*, where the combination of New York chic and Irish friendliness makes a perfect place for a posh cocktail, although be warned: the fatal combination of delicious drinks and luxuriant sofas might lure you away from sightseeing. The elegant bridge in front of the Morrison is the **Millennium Footbridge**. Try to wander this way at night at some point, as it is strikingly lit.

Further down Lower Ormond Quay you'll pass the coffee shop **Panem** (*see p122*). It's a local treasure worth dropping into for coffee and for chef Ann Murphy's range of delicious soups and pastries. The road now becomes Upper Ormond Quay. Just before the Four Courts on Inns Quay is the **Chancery** bar (*see p137*), a popular 'early house', where the rough-and-ready pub life begins at 7.30am.

Like the Custom House, the original **Four Courts** building was designed in the 1790s

by James Gandon – although it was substantially rebuilt after it was burned in the 1922 Civil War. The court building houses the Supreme and High Courts, and only the entrance hall beneath the great cupola is open to visitors.

The courts have been at the centre of Dublin legal life for two centuries. From here, turn down Church Street to visit **St Michan's Church** (*see below*), one of the oldest churches in the city. Bram Stoker always said that viewing the macabre mummified corpses in its crypt inspired *Dracula*. This is one of several churches rumoured to contain the unmarked grave of executed rebel Robert Emmet.

St Michan's Church

Church Street Lower (872 4154). Bus 25, 26, 37, 39, 67, 67A, 68, 69, 79/Luas Four Courts/Smithfield. **Open** *Mid Mar-Oct* 10am-12.45pm, 2-4.45pm Mon-Fri; 10am-12.45pm Sat. *Nov-mid Mar* 12.30-3.30pm Mon-Fri; 10am-12.45pm Sat. **Admission** €4; €3-€3.50 reductions. **No credit cards**. **Map** p252 F4.
There has been a place of worship on this site since 1096, and the current building dates from 1686, though it was drastically restored in 1828 and again following the Civil War. Those with an interest in the macabre will love the 17th-century vaults composed of magnesium limestone, where mummified bodies – including a crusader, a nun and a suspected thief – have rested for centuries showing no signs of decomposition. You used to be able to touch one of the mummy's hands, and indeed sometimes still can if the guide is in a good mood.

Up to Smithfield

Map p250

The road on the north side of the Liffey now becomes Arran Quay, and you can turn right at any point into the atmospheric **Smithfield** district. A cobbled marketplace in the 17th century, it is now a warren of tiny Victorian streets that converge on the newly renovated Smithfield Square – Dublin's largest urban space at 1,300 square metres (14,000 square feet). A massive effort was made to arrive at the finished result: more than 300,000 cobblestones were lifted, cleaned by hand and replaced. Flickering light from gas braziers brings a somewhat incongruous but not unwelcome note of Dickensian romance to the square at night. At Christmas time it is filled with water and turned into an ice-skating rink, and there are markets here throughout the year. The monthly horse fair in Smithfield has largely been shifted to the suburbs over recent years, but it still breaks out on sporadic Sunday mornings. And while the towering **Smithfield Chimney** still stands guard over the area, it is no longer open to tourists – who used to be able

A whiskey whirl at **Old Jameson Distillery**.

to make the journey to its summit to take in the view of the city from 53m (175ft). At the time of writing, there were no plans to reopen the chimney as a tourist attraction, although the structure itself will remain.

While you're in the area, you can stop by the old **Cobblestone** pub (*see p136*) on North King Street (at the northern edge of the piazza) for a pint or sink a shot at the **Old Jameson Distillery** (*see below*) before taking in a movie at the Light House, Smithfield's superb new art-house cinema (*see p166* **To the Light House**). Or for something a little more upbeat, try the **Voodoo Lounge** (*see p137*) and the **Dice Bar** (*see p187*).

Old Jameson Distillery

Bow Street, Smithfield Village (807 2355/ www.oldjamesondistillery.com). Bus 25, 26, 37, 39, 67, 67A, 68, 69, 79/Luas Smithfield. **Open** 9.30am-6pm (last tour 5.30pm) daily. **Admission** (by guided tour only) €12.50; €6-€9 reductions; €25 family. **Credit** AmEx, MC, V. **Map** p252 E4.

Providing a hard-stuff counterpoint to the Guinness Storehouse, Dublin's other big alcohol-tied tourist attraction, the Old Jameson Distillery does its best to sell visitors on the cultural mythology behind John Jameson's fabled whiskey (always, in this case, spelt with an 'e'). A variety of displays and audio-visual demonstrations provide background; highlights include beautifully crafted models of distillery vessels. The tours could delve a little deeper, but at least you'll get to taste some of the stuff at the end.

Towards Phoenix Park

Map p250

Back along the river, the futuristic new suspension bridge at **Blackhall Place** (the James Joyce Bridge) was designed by Santiago Calatrava and opened in 2003. The balustrade curves down to a walkway of granite and toughened glass, and in these downbeat surroundings, it seems eerily postmodern – some would even say spectacular (although the description 'incongruously large' would also sum it up). If you head north along Blackhall Place, you arrive in **Stoneybatter**. This area is what much of Dublin used to be like – that is to say, fairly edgy, fairly grim and fairly depressed – so if you find yourself here at night, avoid dark areas (there are quite a few) and be careful.

Back along the quays and a little further west from Blackhall Bridge is Collins Barracks, which houses a branch of the splendid **National Museum** (*see p86*). This fine renovated 17th-century building is the oldest military barracks in Europe, but these days it's put to rather more genteel use, as a base for the museum's decorative arts collection. A short walk from the museum (follow Wolfe Tone Quay after it merges into Parkgate), the vast expanse of **Phoenix Park** sprawls for almost eight square kilometres (three square miles). The largest city park in

The **National Museum of Ireland**.
See p86.

Europe, it contains an invigorating blend of formal gardens, casual meadows, sports fields and wild undergrowth, as well as herds of deer. Inside the park is the official residence of the Irish president, Aras an Uachtarain, a Palladian lodge that originally served as the seat of the Lord Lieutenant of Ireland. (*See right*).

The formal **People's Garden** opens the south-eastern entrance of the park, while across the road the huge **Wellington Monument** by Sir Robert Smirke stands guard. A short walk north-west of here, the much-improved **Dublin Zoo** (*see below*) lures you to its menagerie. Opposite the zoo's main entrance is a lovely little wooden structure that serves excellent snacks. At the **Phoenix Monument** in the centre of the park, side roads and pathways will lead you to the **Visitors' Centre** (*see right*), the gracious 18th-century home of the American ambassador (not open to the public) and the towering **Papal Cross**, marking the spot where Pope John Paul II performed mass to the assembled multitudes during his 1979 visit.

If you don't feel up to walking back, leave by the North Circular Road entrance (at the top of Infirmary Road), and the No.10 bus will bring you back to O'Connell Street.

Dublin Zoo
Phoenix Park (474 8900/www.dublinzoo.ie). Bus 10, 25, 25A, 26, 51, 66, 67, 68, 69. **Open** *Jan* 9.30am-4.30pm Mon-Sat; 10.30am-4.30pm Sun. *Feb* 9.30am-5pm Mon-Sat; 10.30am-5pm Sun. *Mar* 9.30am-6pm Mon-Sat; 10.30am-6pm Sun. *Apr-Sept* 9.30am-6.30pm Mon-Sat; 10.30am-6.30pm Sun. *Oct* 9.30am-5.30pm

Mon-Sat; 9.30am-5.30pm Sun. *Nov-Dec* 9.30am-4pm Mon-Sat; 10.30am-4pm Sun. **Admission** €14.50; €5.20-€12 reductions; €42-€50 family; free under-3s. **Credit** AmEx, DC, MC, V.

One of the oldest zoos in the world (it was founded in 1830), Dublin's animal house is now home to 700 species, including endangered snow leopards and golden lion tamarinds. In terms of layout it is the epitome of a modern, eco-conscious facility, with tigers, elephants, chimps and hundreds more given all the time and space they need to feel (climate notwithstanding) right at home. The place is also run with children very much in mind, as evidenced by the Pets' Corner, the Zoo Train, and the ample picnic facilities and play areas. That said, though, it's far from miniature in scale: the impressive Asian Plains, for example, is a 32-acre (13-hectare) expanse of pasture and woodland, home to (among many others) some splendid white rhinos and the ever-expanding family of elephants (mother Yasmin gave birth to another son in early 2008). All in all, then, this is an excellent day out – just one word of warning: try to turn up as near to opening time as possible, as queues can be long and (especially for the junior contingent) joyless affairs.

National Museum of Ireland: Decorative Arts & History
Collins Barracks, Benburb Street (677 7441/ www.museum.ie). Bus 25, 25A, 37, 39, 66, 67, 90, 172/Luas Museum. **Open** 10am-5pm Tue-Sat; 2-5pm Sun. **Admission** free. **Map** p250 B2.

Housed in the breathtaking confines of the barracks formerly used by the British Army, this branch of the National Museum of Ireland contains the nation's most significant collection of decorative arts, as well as myriad displays devoted to Ireland's social, political and military histories. All of the exhibitions are complemented by informative, interactive multimedia displays, and are frequently supplemented by workshops and talks. The Earth Science Museum contains geological collections, fossils and even the odd chunk of dinosaur – kept well away from the china. There's also a permanent exhibition about the influential Irish designer Eileen Gray, which is excellent and well worth a look. But the latest, and arguably most involving, addition to the museum is the 'Soldiers and Chiefs' exhibition, which artfully documents the impact of four and a half centuries of warfare on the ordinary Irishman. *Photo p85.*

Phoenix Park Visitors' Centre
Phoenix Park (677 0095/www.heritageireland.ie). Bus 37, 39. **Open** *Mid Mar-Sept* 10am-6pm daily. *Oct* 10am-5.30pm daily. *Nov-mid Mar* 10am-6pm Mon-Wed, Sat, Sun. **Admission** free.

Housed in the old coach house of the former Papal Nunciature, this centre explains the history of Phoenix Park. Regular free tours of nearby Ashtown Castle, a 17th-century tower house, are offered, and tours to Aras an Uachtarain (*see left*) also depart from the centre on Saturdays throughout the year. For tour times and availability, call 677 7129.

Wellington Monument, Phoenix Park.

Docklands

Go with the flow.

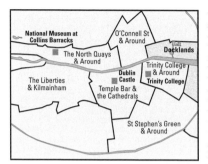

Spanning 1,300 acres (520 hectares) of land on the northern and southern banks of the Liffey, Dublin's Docklands were, until recently, languishing in a semi-derelict state and suffering from a long legacy of neglect and low employment. But all that changed when the Dublin Docklands Development Authority was created in 1997 and, after more than a decade of work, the area has been transformed. Smart office blocks, restaurants, wine bars and pubs have all flung open their doors in recent years. But what differentiates Dublin's dockside regeneration from similar projects across Europe is the emphasis that has been placed on quality of design: some of the most famous architects in the world have already begun or are due to start work on a variety of ambitious projects (*see p28*). All of which means that, in a city of historic charms, this riverside neighbourhood provides a refreshing glimpse into the future of an ever-evolving skyline.

Around Custom House

Map p251

At the easternmost end of Eden Quay, the **Liberty Hall** landmark (*see p88*) heralds the beginning of Dublin's Docklands. Next door to it is the **Liberty Hall Centre** (*see p181*), which combines a truly eclectic programme of cultural events and performances with a strong social conscience. On the corner, meanwhile, is Liberty Hall itself, the heart of Dublin trade unionism since 1912, when it was acquired by charismatic Liverpudlian Jim Larkin and his newly formed Irish Transport and General Workers Union. arkin became a folk hero

with his stand against unfair working practices at a time when 'working on the docks' was, quite literally, back-breaking stuff. And at the time, he was preaching to a very large audience indeed: in the early 20th century, cargo ships were crucial to Dublin's economic wellbeing, with thousands of dockers, coal carters and casual labourers employed from the teeming tenements nearby. And these were by no means the well-to-do quarters associated with Dublin's typical 'grand old dame' image of the period – in fact, one contemporary account goes so far as to describe the relationship between the Docklands' slums and the aforementioned dame as the 'suppurating ulcers covered by stinking rags under the hem of her dress'. The collapse of one tenement building led to the infamous 1913 lockout, which would become Larkin's greatest confrontation with the bosses. If you're interested in learning more, Joseph Plunkett's *Strumpet City* is an extremely readable account of the city in those times.

The neo-classical **Custom House**. *See p88.*

Beresford Place, to the east of Liberty Hall, leads to Gardiner Street, a prime example of the once-grand Georgian houses colonised by slum dwellers who lived in appalling conditions – sometimes up to 15 to a room. The street now provides considerably more salubrious accommodation to backpackers in its numerous guesthouses and hostels. And yet it was by no means an isolated example – the immediate vicinity was riven with abject poverty, especially in nearby Marlborough Street and Foley Street, which were among some of the most wretched and stagnant backwaters of destitution. Raw sewage, which was being pumped into the Liffey, followed by waste from the gasworks and the fertiliser plants of North Wall, had the combined effect of creating a miasma of pollution in the area that acted as a incubator for disease. Urban dereliction and decay set in and very little of any consequence was done to regenerate the area until the Custom House Docks Area Renewal Act of 1986 (which proved, as was the case with many similar Docklands projects in other European cities, to be the first step on a journey of gentrification culminating in what is now an enclave of wealth and prosperity).

The riverside walk continues past the ugly Butt railway bridge but more than makes up for it just a few steps further on with the grand neo-classical marvel that is **Custom House**. A Dublin landmark designed by James Gandon in 1791, its façade stretches for 114 metres (374 feet), with busts representing the gods of

Ireland's 14 major rivers decorating the portico. The green roof is of oxidised copper, and the extant foundations were wooden supports built on treacherous bog.

One could be forgiven for seeing metaphors here for Dublin's new-found wealth, and an ideal place for such rumination is to be found on the riverbank just in front of Custom House's riverside façade. Benches here provide an unhindered view of the Liffey and of the new, vast and gleaming glass-fronted Ulster Bank complex across the river.

Custom House Visitor Centre

Custom House Quay (888 2538). Bus 53A, 90A/ Luas Busárus/DART Tara Street. **Open** *Mid Mar- Nov* 10am-12.30pm, 2-5pm Mon-Fri; 2-5pm Sat, Sun. *Dec-mid Mar* 10am-12.30pm, 2-5pm Wed-Fri. **Admission** €1.50; €4 family. **Map** p251 G2.
This small, unsophisticated centre offers access only to a small area of the building (in and around the domed Clock Tower) but it is definitely worth a visit, if only for the extra perspective it gives on the building's elaborate and (for its time) extraordinary architectural features. Displays and a video relate the history of the building and its intrepid, dedicated architect James Gandon. *Photo p87.*

Liberty Hall

33 Eden Quay (874 9731/www.libertyhall.ie). Bus 53A, 90A/Luas Busárus/DART Tara Street. **Open** times vary. **Admission** prices vary. **Map** p251 G2.
Dublin's tallest building and the current headquarters of the Services, Industrial, Professional and Technical Union (SIPTU), Liberty Hall has a colourful past. The first building to be constructed on

George's Dock.

this site (not the one you see now, which was built in the 1960s following the demolition of the original) dated back to the beginning of the last century and played a dramatic part in many of the landmark events of Dublin's modern history. At various times, Liberty Hall was used as the headquarters of Jim Larkin's Irish Transport and General Workers Union, the base of operations for James Connolly, a printing house for the *Irish Worker* and an arms and munitions production line for the 1916 Easter Rising. And at the time of writing, yet more changes were in store for this historic site: a third incarnation of Liberty Hall has been mooted (and will be designed by local architects Gilroy McMahon) but dates are fluid (planning permission, demolition of the current site and sundry other red tape could take years to complete). So, for the time being at least, the current building will remain untouched. The building itself is not open to visitors but the Liberty Hall Centre (*see p181*) next door, which programmes a wide variety of musical and cultural events, is always worth a snoop around.

Beyond Custom House

Map p251

The next bridge east is Matt Talbot Bridge, named after a Dublin alcoholic who gave up the booze and wore a penitential hair shirt and chains for the rest of his days. Saint or lunatic? You decide. Here you could be in the financial district of any major international city. The glittering **International Financial Services Centre** dominates the waterfront in this area: the complex caters for 6,500 workers on any given day. At the water's edge, Rowan

Gillespie's beautiful **famine sculpture** is hauntingly evocative of Ireland's tragic past, when starving emigrants poured from these docks into ships that became known as 'coffin ships' since so many passengers never made it to their destinations. A replica of one such ship, the *Jeanie Johnston* (*see p90*), is often moored alongside the quay here. A painstakingly reconstructed replica of those ill-fated vessels, it sails the world as a kind of floating museum, and the crew are a cheery bunch who are filled with information.

Set slightly back from the riverside, just before you reach the impressive **chq** building (formerly the John Rennie-designed tobacco warehouse Stack A, now a thriving shopping mall; *see p28* and *p140*), are the landlocked basins of **George's Dock** and **Inner Dock**. As well as providing an attractive water feature for the many corporate HQs and office blocks that have sprung up in recent years around this mini financial hub, these two docks are also busy centres for local watersports clubs – at weekends, in particular, you'll see highly competitive matches of canoe polo being played here, much to the delight of passing strollers and (highly vocal) supporters pitching in with spirited advice from the dockside.

The many new apartment developments hereabouts are largely populated by young professionals. New shops, bars and restaurants appear constantly as the area's transformation continues. Many are part of international or national chains offering consistency rather

than excellence, but Ely (*see p111*) on Custom House Quay is a reliable independent. Check out Mayor Street too (behind the Clarion Hotel) and Excise Walk off North Wall Quay for more low-key eating and drinking options. And if you happen to be visiting on a Wednesday (between 11am and 3pm), you can also wander around the **farmers' market** on Excise Walk and Wall Quay; stock up on local cheeses and gourmet treats, and make yourself a picnic to eat beside the river.

And things, it seems, are just going to get better and better around these parts, with several huge new development projects planned for the coming years (*see p28*). Everything from new theatres and public spaces to hotels, offices and restaurants will be making an appearance on the Docklands skyline, many of them designed by big-name architects like Daniel Libeskind, Manuel Aires Mateus, Kevin Roche and Fosters + Partners. Even the good old Abbey Theatre (*see p197*) will be getting a new home down by George's Dock. Plans are also afoot to create the Royal Canal Linear Park along the Royal Canal. Paris architects Agence Ter's brief will see them conjure up floating gardens, playgrounds and a kayak centre.

Continuing along the river, an invigorating walk past cawing gulls, tall ships and navy boats brings you to the newly rebranded **O2** performance venue (*see p183*), formerly known as Point Depot. This area is best known locally for its residents' landmark victory over the seemingly unstoppable forces of capitalism: a few years back, there were plans to build yet more tower blocks where a row of eight artisan dwellings stands, but a determined group of locals fought them, and ultimately stopped the whole project. It is thanks to them, then, that there is still a photogenic view from the East Link Bridge, encompassing the sea in one direction and the Liffey bridges in the other.

Jeanie Johnston

Custom House Quay (066 712 9999/ www.jeaniejohnston.ie). Bus 53A, 90A/Luas Busárus/DART Tara Street. **Open** 10.30am-5pm Sat, Sun. **Admission** *Museum* €5. **Map** p251 G2.
Only in town at certain times of the year (the winter season is usually a pretty safe bet), the *Jeanie Johnston* is a working replica of Dublin's most famous famine ship (the boats that were used in the mid 19th century to transport victims of the famine to a brighter, better life abroad). The famine ships earned the grim nickname of 'floating coffins' due to the mortality rate of their frail and disease-ravaged passengers, but the *JJ* was a notable exception: despite carrying around 2,500 people on 16 separate voyages to America, she never lost a single soul. This remarkable feat, along with the blighted

period of Ireland's history that made it necessary, are the subjects of a small museum located inside the ship. Using data from the Lloyd's Survey, this replica vessel was painstakingly produced, timber for timber, to match the original, and upon completion in 2003 was broken in with a voyage to America, stopping at 20 ports in five countries along the way. Fascinating stuff.

South of the river

Map p249

From George's Quay on the southern bank of the Liffey, you get the best views of **Custom House** (*see p88*), which is impossible to appreciate in all its glory from the close-range vantage points of the northern bank. Further along the quay is a wonderful bronze statue of a docker hauling in a rope at the river's edge. A permanent reminder of the hard graft on which the Docklands were founded, and an apposite neighbour to the footbridge devoted to Sean O'Casey, 'playwright, humanist and chronicler of Dublin's poor'.

Heading further east along the crane-littered expanse of City Quay and Sir John Rogerson's Quay gives an idea of the sheer scale of the development still to come in the area. At the far eastern end of Sir John Rogerson's Quay is the U2 Tower, currently under construction. *See p28*. Similarly, heading south from here to the **Grand Canal Dock**, there is an overwhelming sense of another quarter about to break out of its chrysalis of construction to become a vibrant metropolitan hub. For centuries this area, where the Grand Canal and the Liffey join up at the bay, was the commercial powerhouse that made Dublin's economy what it was.
But when the focus of industry shifted to mechanised, container-driven ports, these docks inevitably fell by the wayside. Now, though, Martha Schwartz's vast **Grand Canal Square** (next to Grand Canal Dock) is one of the largest and most talked-about urban spaces in the city (its forest of giant red poles has provoked passionate reactions from both enthusiasts and detractors). And all around, office buildings are beginning to line the water's edge, and developers are cracking their knuckles as they prepare to take on the possibilities of the remaining prime riverside real estate.

Sadly, for those who are really entranced by the canals themselves, the erstwhile Waterways Visitor Centre (which used to tell you all that you ever wanted to know about them) is now closed for good, so the only option is to head down Grand Canal Quay in the direction of the towpaths that skirt the southern fringes of the neighbourhood surrounding St Stephen's Green and Fitzwilliam Square.

The Liberties & Kilmainham

A working-class neighbourhood rich in history.

Sightseeing

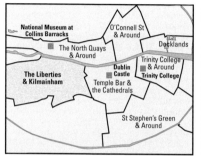

The tour buses sweep through, stopping only at the key attractions as they loop back round into town, but it's worth spending a little time getting to know this frequently overlooked part of the city. This is, after all, where the black stuff was made and where many a rebel came undone.

The Liberties

Map p248 & p250

Just beyond Christ Church, the Liberties (so-called because it was a self-governing area beyond the (then) city limits) is one of the oldest and liveliest districts of Dublin. Its markets, the vibrancy of the street life on its main artery of Thomas Street and its association with the Guinness family (see p92 **Through a glass darkly**) all lend it character – yet it remains among the most disadvantaged areas of the city, giving the lie, incidentally, to the local cliché that the south side of the city is complacently wealthy, the north side grindingly poor.

Originally a fiercely independent self-governing district, the Liberties grew up on the high ground above the river and just west of Dublin's medieval city walls. In the 17th century it was settled by Huguenots who developed the area as a centre for silk-weaving, but the introduction of British trading restrictions in the 18th century, along with increased competition from imported cloth, signalled the area's demise. By the 19th century it was a slum bedevilled by mass unemployment and outbreaks of violence,

often between the Liberty Boys (tailors' and weavers' apprentices) and the Ormond Boys (butchers' apprentices from across the river).

In recent decades the tight-knit community has been badly scarred by the heroin trade, and gentrification, so prevalent in other parts of the city, has only recently begun in earnest here. However, the rebuilding of the **Guinness Storehouse** (see p92) as a tourist attraction and (perhaps more importantly) the establishment in 2000 of MediaLab Europe in the old brewery complex suggest that the pace of change may accelerate. That said, the number of refugees that have settled in the Liberties in recent years only enhances the impression that this area is a microcosm of Dublin in flux.

If the Guinness Storehouse has ensured that Thomas Street has a steady stream of daytime tourists – usually easily identifiable by their Storehouse bags – then the **Vicar Street** music venue (see p181) is leading the charge in making the area a popular nightspot (and one favoured especially by students from the nearby National College of Art and Design). But at the same time, Thomas Street is the centre of the city's hard-drugs trade, and it has a persistently edgy undercurrent – despite a significant *Garda* presence.

Off Thomas Street, Francis Street is the heart of the Dublin antiques trade, and also the site of the 18th-century **Church of St Nicholas of Myra**, which features a stained-glass window in the nuptial chapel by Harry Clarke. Meath Street, further west, hosts an old-style street market of the type that has largely disappeared from the city. If you like getting off the beaten track and want to experience a vanishing side of Dublin, this is a good place to start. At the bottom of Meath Street is the Coombe, one of the area's main thoroughfares. The maze of streets between the Coombe and South Circular Road was once the heart of the Liberties, and it boasts wonderful names like Brabazon Street, Fumbally Lane and Blackpitts. Many of the tiny brick houses here are finally being renovated, and residents must be hoping that the rising economic tide will soon lift their boats too.

At the end of Thomas Street, James's Street is synonymous in Dublin's collective imagination with the black brew. The **St James's Gate Brewery** fills all available land north and south of James's Street, right down to the river, and has been producing Ireland's world-famous Guinness for over 250 years. There had been a brewery at St James's Gate since 1670, but it was largely derelict when Arthur Guinness bought a 9,000-year lease for the site in 1759 (a bargain at £45 per annum). Guinness started by brewing ale, but soon switched to a black beer made with roasted barley and known as 'porter', due to its popularity among porters at Covent Garden and Billingsgate markets in London. The new beer proved extremely successful – by 1838 Guinness at St James's Gate was the largest brewery in Ireland, and in 1914 it became the largest in the world. It now produces 4.5 million hectolitres of Guinness Stout each year; ten million glasses are consumed around the world every day. And, although the brand and brewery have now been subsumed into the multinational Diageo drinks conglomerate, the association between Guinness and Ireland remains as potent as ever.

Although most of the complex is closed to visitors, the brewery area is impressively atmospheric: vast Victorian and 20th-century factory buildings are surrounded by high brick walls and narrow cobblestone streets, and the air is suffused with the distinctive, warming odour of hops and malt. At the heart of the complex is the fabulous Guinness Storehouse.

Guinness Storehouse

St James's Gate (408 4800/www.guinness-store house.com). Bus 51B, 78A, 123/Luas James's Street. **Open** *Sept-June* 9.30am-5pm daily. *July-Aug* 9.30am-7pm daily. **Admission** €15; €8-€10 reductions; €30 family; free under-6s. **Credit** AmEx, MC, V. **Map** p250 B4.

It may no longer be part of the active brewery but this 'visitor experience', housed in a six-storey listed building dating from 1904, has become the popular public face of what is undoubtedly Ireland's most recognisable brand. The building is designed around a pint glass-shaped atrium and incorporates a retail store, exhibition space, function rooms, a restaurant and two bars. Much of the vast floor space is taken up with presentations on the history and making of the humble pint, which, although self-congratulatory in tone, are magnificently realised. Most entertaining, perhaps, is the advertising section – a testament to the company's famously imaginative marketing. The Storehouse tour includes a complimentary pint of the best Guinness you are likely to get, and there's nowhere better to drink it than in the Gravity Bar, at the very top of the building. This circular bar has a 360-degree window and offers the kind of spectacular view over Dublin that makes the rather steep entrance fee worthwhile. Despite the crowds, this really is a great place in which to linger.

Through a glass darkly

There can be few images as iconic in the world of brewing as that of the swirling black-and-white cloudscape of a pint of Guinness settling in its glass. Even the name itself has become synonymous with a certain kind of twinkly-eyed nostalgia for the vanishing glory days of 'Old Dublin'. But lurking behind the legend is a far more ordinary story of hard work, enterprise and a commitment to building an empire that has prospered for more than two and a half centuries.

In 1759, the founder of this Irish institution, Arthur Guinness, took out a 9,000-year lease on the St James's Gate brewery (the original document is still on display today). But the man who would go on to establish the huge Guinness fortune was, in fact, Arthur's great-grandson, Edward Cecil Guinness. Having bought out his brothers' shares in the brewery before he turned 30, Edward Cecil made Guinness a public company in 1886

(after he'd been made the first Earl of Iveagh), earning himself a vast personal fortune while still retaining more than 50 per cent of the shares. When he died in 1927 at the age of 80, his son Rupert took over as chairman, and was in turn succeeded by Benjamin Guinness, the third Earl of Iveagh, who died in 1992. As well as being head of the board at Guinness, Benjamin held the unique distinction of having been a senator, a member of the Oireachtas (Irish Parliament) and a member of the House of Lords in Britain.

Although the family holding in the company – now mostly owned by drinks behemoth Diageo – has been diluted to a mere three per cent, it is still enough to establish the family as the 26th richest in Britain. With over ten million pints being sold daily, some people's thirst for Guinness seems unquenchable. The story of this family is living testament to the adage 'Guinness is good for you'.

Black stuff tours and pints under the one roof of the **Guinness Storehouse.**

Kilmainham

Heading west from the brewery, you come to the Kilmainham district. If the Liberties epitomises Dublin at its most urban, Kilmainham offers a very different experience. The area is distinctly 'villagey'; the semi-rural ambience is helped by the amount of green space as well as the views across the river to the vast expanse of **Phoenix Park** (*see p86*). The main attraction here is **Kilmainham Gaol** (*see p94*), the notorious jail that housed every famous Irish felon from 1798 until 1924, when the new Free State government ordered its closure. Indeed, the list of those who spent time here reads like a roll-call of nationalist idols: Robert Emmet, John O'Leary, Joseph Plunkett, Patrick Pearse and Eamon De Valera, later the Taoiseach, who had the dubious honour of being the last ever prisoner released from here. The prison was shuttered then and has not been altered since. The boat in dry dock outside the prison is the *Asgard*, Erskin Childers's vessel, which successfully negotiated the British blockade and landed guns for the Irish Volunteers at Howth in 1912.

The other reason to head this far west is the Royal Hospital, brilliantly restored to house the **Irish Museum of Modern Art** (*see below*). The building dates from 1684 and was constructed as a hospital for military veterans.

A few minutes' walk west of the Gaol, and directly across the river from Phoenix Park, is Islandbridge, site of the **War Memorial Gardens** (*see p94*). The gardens slope down to the Liffey weir, where the rowing clubs of Trinity College and University College have their headquarters; and on fine days, the water is the scene of much smoothly executed coming and going.

Irish Museum of Modern Art

Royal Hospital, Military Road (612 9900/ www.imma.ie). Bus 51, 51B, 78A, 79, 90, 123/ Luas James's or Heuston. **Open** 10am-5.30pm Tue, Thur-Sat; 10.30am-5.30pm Wed; noon-5.30pm Sun. **Admission** free.

One of the most important 17th-century buildings in Ireland, the Royal Hospital was designed by Sir

Sightseeing

William Robinson in 1684 to serve as a nursing home for retired soldiers, and, famously, he modelled it on Les Invalides in Paris. It was founded by James Butler, Duke of Ormonde and Viceroy to King Charles II. In 1991 the place was reopened in the form of this modern art museum, with superb exhibition spaces distributed around its peaceful square. The displays are usually temporary shows, combined with a selection from a small permanent collection – a recent highlight was Carlos Amorales' mesmerising mix of haunting imagery and evocative piano music, *Dark Mirror*. On the ground floor, the Heritage section provides some fascinating and (in the case of the Gallipoli accounts) occasionally horrifying background on the Royal Hospital and the pensioners who lived there. The grounds include a beautifully restored baroque formal garden, as well as Bully's Acre (one of the city's largest cemeteries, containing ancient burial sites and a military graveyard) and 19th-century stable buildings.

Kilmainham Gaol

Inchicore Road (453 5984/www.heritageireland.ie). Bus 51B, 51C, 78A, 79, 79A. **Open** (guided tour only) *Apr-Sept* 9.30am-5pm daily. *Oct-Mar* 9.30am-4pm Mon-Sat; 10am-5pm Sun. **Admission** €5.30; €2.10-€3.70 reductions; €11.50 family. **Credit** MC, V.

Although it ceased to be used as a prison in 1924, this remains the best-known Irish lock-up and one of the most fascinating buildings in the country. It was here that the leaders of the 1916 Easter Rising, along with many others, were executed. If you harbour an interest in the 1916 Rising or, indeed, any previous rebellions in Ireland from the 18th century onwards, you'll find Kilmainham Gaol an awful lot

more informative and evocative than the National Museum. Various multimedia displays documenting the atrocious prison conditions of the past are grimly informative, but it is the lively guided tours that steal the show. Groups are led through the dank corridors, past bleak cells and into the highly evocative main hall (where some of the opening scenes of the original *Italian Job* were filmed). The sites of various executions, vigils, injustices and condemnations are conjured to vivid life, leaving you with a curious conflict of guilt and relief as you walk back out through the gates and into the free world.

War Memorial Gardens

Entrances: Con Colbert Road and South Circular Road, Islandbridge (888 3233/www.heritage ireland.ie/en/Dublin/WarMemorialGardens). **Open** 8am-dusk Mon-Fri; 10am-dusk Sat, Sun. **Admission** free.

Designed by British architect Sir Edwin Lutyens as a tribute to the 49,400 Irish soldiers who died in World War I (each end of the grounds is guarded by a granite bookroom containing manuscripts of the dead soldiers' names), these gardens retain an austere beauty. Covering eight hectares (20 acres) of the southern slopes of the River Liffey with granite columns, sunken circular rose gardens, pergolas, fountains and lily ponds, it is a masterfully landscaped space. But due to its slightly out-of-the-way location, few tend to bother with the journey up here, or indeed even seem to know of its existence, meaning that the gardens are rarely crowded. All of which is great news for the architecture buffs, clued-up tourists and local strollers who get the place all to themselves.

War Memorial Gardens.

Dublin Bay & the Coast

The call of the running tide.

A fair city it may be but Dublin also has a distinctly more outdoorsy side to it, thanks to its natural advantages of sea and mountains. They lend the city beauty whatever the weather and, on a good day, provide some really stunning views. Water gives the city a great air of bustle and activity, and even though much of the maritime manoeuvring is done for leisure, not commerce, there's still plenty of vitality among the quays and harbours.

The cheapest way to see the coast is still the best: take a DART from one end of the line to the other. Much of the trip is along the constantly changing seashore. The stretch from Sandycove to Bray is particularly attractive.

Northside

Clontarf

On the Northside, **Bull Island** is a fantastic nature and wildlife reserve reached by a spindly bridge off the Clontarf Road. Declared a UNESCO Biosphere in 1981, the island is barely 200 years old, formed by the gathering of sand when the Great South Wall was built in the 1700s. Sandbanks gradually became locked together by sea grass and other hardy plants, and the island's dunes and mudflats are now home to many types of bird and plant life. There's a beach that runs the length of the island, and in the summer orchids grow here in abundance.

Howth

There never seems to be anyone in Howth but women, children and old people, yet there's a robust feel to the place – and not just because of the bracing wind. Instead of the tinkle of yachts, there's the clunk of trawlers. This is a working village, not a picture postcard.

If you're in it for the long haul, jump on the No.31 bus, or walk along the shore road to the start of the eight-kilometre (five-mile) trail around the headland. The footpath cunningly avoids all the built-up areas. To the south are the Wicklow Mountains, to the north the Mountains of Mourne, sky above, sea below.

Beside the DART station is the West Pier, the best place to buy just-caught fish. A new marina beside the harbour means the boats

Handsome **National Transport Museum** tram.

stay in the water all year round, rather than exposing their unsightly hulls in winter.

The more rough and ready East Pier has a slender lighthouse at its end; a walk along the unprotected top tier is quite exciting, and from the pier end you can make out a Martello tower and a ruined church on the rocky, uninhabited island that is Ireland's Eye.

In the village itself is the ruined St Mary's Abbey, containing the 15th-century tomb of Christopher St Lawrence. His descendants still own Howth Castle; it's not open to the public.

National Transport Museum

Howth Castle Demesne (848 0831/832 0427/ www.nationaltransportmuseum.org). Bus 31, 31B/DART Howth. **Open** *June-Aug* 10am-5pm Mon-Fri; 2-5pm Sat, Sun. *Sept-May* 2-5pm Sat, Sun. **Admission** €3.50; €2 reductions; €9 family. **No credit cards.**

The National Transport Museum is filled with vehicles dating from the 1880s to the 1970s: trams, buses, commercial and military vehicles. Given the state of the city transport service today, it comes as a shock to discover that, a century ago, Dublin transport was among the most advanced in the world. *Photo p95.*

Malahide

The Northside's prettiest coastal village has the vast green spaces around its castle on one side and rolling ocean on the other. The Marina, where boats clink merrily at anchor, is a perfect spot for walking. The village itself has plenty of restaurants, coffee shops and boutiques, but bad parking; come by DART, rather than car.

Ardgillen Castle

Balbriggan (849 2212/www.iol.ie/~cybmanmc/). Bus 33/Balbriggan rail. **Open** *Apr-Sept* 11am-6pm Tue-Sun. *Oct-mid Dec, Feb, Mar* 11am-6pm Wed-Sun. *Mid Dec, Jan* 2-4pm Sun. **Admission** €6.50; €5 reductions; €13 family. **No credit cards**.

Robert Taylor, Dean of Clonfert, built this castle (it's really more of a country house with fancy embellishments) in 1738. It stands in 194 acres (79 hectares) of rolling pasture, woodland and gardens. There are regular tours of the castle; of particular interest is the library, with its marvellous Agatha Christie-style secret door hidden behind fake bookshelves (the clue to opening it is written on the spine of one of the fake books). Two coffee shops serve good cakes. But outdoors is the thing here: picnics, hide-and-seek, nature trails or romantic walks. Ardgillen is rarely too crowded; and when you've seen all you want to, a footbridge links the grounds to Barnageera beach.

Malahide Castle.

Malahide Castle

Malahide Castle Demesne, Malahide (846 2184/ www.malahidecastle.com). Bus 42/DART Malahide. **Open** *Apr-Oct* 10am-5pm Mon-Sat; 10am-6pm Sun. *Nov-Mar* 10am-5pm Mon-Sat; 11am-5pm Sun. **Admission** €7.50; €4.70-€6.30 reductions; €22 family. *Dublin Tourism combined ticket* €13; €8-€10.70 reductions; €36.30 family. **Credit** AmEx, MC, V.

The castle sits on 250 acres (101 hectares) – though much of it is given over to dull-looking playing fields – and the perimeter is just over three kilometres (two miles) long; a good distance for a walk, and largely sheltered by mature trees. Historic home of the de Talbots, the castle itself is an interesting hotchpotch of architectural styles: Norman and Gothic features co-exist with beautiful period furniture. There's an extensive collection of Irish portrait paintings, and faces from history stare down at every turn (some are on loan from the National Portrait collection, others are the family's own). One in particular – Van Wyck's commemoration of the Battle of the Boyne in 1690 – is poignant, showing the 14 family members who sat down to breakfast the morning of the battle before joining King James to fight William of Orange. Not one returned. In the basement is a dimly lit self-service café that serves really good, fresh, own-made food. There's also a model railway (open in the summer months only, except on Wednesdays), and outside is an excellent adventure playground.

Newbridge House & Traditional Farm

Newbridge Demesne, Donabate (843 6534). Bus 33B/Donabate rail. **Open** *Apr-Sept* 10am-5pm Tue-Sat; 2-6pm Sun. *Oct-Mar* 2-5pm Sat, Sun. **Admission** *House* €7; €3.50-€6 reductions; €18 family. *Farm* €3.80; €2.50-€2.80 reductions; €10 family. **Credit** MC, V.

This small, early Georgian house may appear modest from the outside but its style of furnishing is really rather grand: lots of Portland stone, stucco by Robert West, ceiling after the Francini brothers and endless family portraits. The beautiful Red Drawing Room and Museum of Curiosities are especially interesting. The latter is full of strange and sometimes ghoulish specimens: stuffed birds, bits of dusty coral, huge shells, scraps of Eastern fabrics, a tiny shoe worn by a Chinese woman with bound feet and a 'scold's bridle' – a belt to stop the mouths of witches and doomsayers. It is also possible to visit the traditional farmyard, forge, pigturesque pig sties and stables (which house a huge, fantastically ornate golden coach that looks as if it must have once been a pumpkin). A café selling basic refreshments is to the right of the first courtyard.

Skerries Mill Complex

Skerries (849 5208). Bus 33/Skerries rail. **Open** *Apr-Sept* 10.30am 5.30pm daily. *Oct-Mar* 10.30am-4.30pm daily. **Admission** €6.50; €3.50-€5 reductions; €13 family. **Credit** MC, V.

Newbridge House & Traditional Farm

Originally built in the 1500s, the complex has been restored, and now includes two large, working five-sail mills and one smaller four-sail watermill with bare stone walls and a thatched roof. The watermill is part of a range of stone buildings, and its many functions are outlined in different rooms such as the bakery, the weigh room and the engine room. There's a coffee shop in one of the lovely old stone buildings and a working bakery.

Talbot Botanic Gardens

Malahide Castle Demesne, Malahide (846 2456). Bus 42/DART Malahide. **Open** *May-Sept 2-5pm daily. Guided tour 2pm Wed.* **Admission** €4.50; free reductions. *Guided tour* €4.50. **No credit cards.**
Located within the vast grounds of Malahide Castle (*see left*), these gardens enjoy relative tranquillity even when the castle is rammed with summertime visitors. The Walled Garden (guided tours only, Wednesdays at 2pm) has a fine collection of rare plants from Australia and New Zealand. The conservatory, designed for an old convent in the 1800s and rescued from destruction, is an excellent import. Another must-see is the old Rose Garden; though surprisingly short of these flowers, it compensates with lovely magnolias and other bright blooms. There's also a lily pond and an enclosed nursery known as the Chicken Yard. Summer is the

best time to visit, but even in winter, thanks to careful and imaginative planting, there's always something to see.

Southside

Bray

There is a considerable amount of silly preconception in the way Bray gets sneered at by Dubliners who live in other parts of the city. Bray's reputation is somehow naff and dangerous at the same time: you might think of it as the Vinnie Jones of seaside towns. Maybe that's true if you're of cider-drinking age, but for the under-12s and sensible adults, the area makes for a perfectly jolly day out. The DART trip out will take you on a journey so beautiful that you will be in a Zen frame of mind by the time you arrive. Stroll along the promenade or stony beach, which have all the offbeat charm of an out-of-season seaside town, avoid the funfair and make for Bray Head. Follow the headland for a spectacular walk that takes you as far as Greystones, where you can turn and catch a DART or bus back again.

Dalkey

There's something faintly absurd in the way inhabitants still refer to this million-euro-a-millimetre area as a 'village' and cling to the conceit that it is a simple, rustic little place. And yet it's impossible to be cynical when confronted with this pretty seaside town's charm. Not for nothing have Bono, the Edge, Enya, Lisa Stansfield, Neil Jordan and plenty of hotshot businessmen chosen to buy property here. The influence of Dalkey's wealthy inhabitants can be seen in its many good restaurants, bars and delis.

The real fun here is outdoors. A walk along the main drag – start on Coliemore Road, then on up Sorrento Road and finally Vico Road – gives views of a section of coastline endlessly likened to the Bay of Naples. First is Coliemore Harbour, the launchpad for boats out to Dalkey Island during the summer. (On hot summer days the tiny, uninhabited island is the only place to be guaranteed freedom from the crowds. Although it can be tricky negotiating the slippery rocks at the water's edge, it's a perfect spot for a picnic.) Past Coliemore Harbour on the left is Dillon's Park, a grassy space with views out to sea and two larger-than-life-size goat statues. Next up is Sorrento Terrace, the city's most exclusive address, on a clifftop above the sea and with views as vertiginous as a crow's nest.

From Sorrento Terrace, turn on to Vico Road. The rocky Vico bathing spot is where many of the gentlemen swimmers from the Forty-Foot (*see right*) seem to have migrated, and it's unashamedly nudist. It's friendly and social for regulars and blow-ins alike, though the sharp rocks don't offer much scope for lounging.

From here, turn towards the upper route for Killiney Hill, on top of which stands a wishing stone and Queen Victoria's obelisk (although the proud boast of Republicans is that she never actually set foot on land to see it). From here you can explore the small forest above Burmah road, or walk (or abseil) down Dalkey Quarry.

Sandymount

There are plenty of beaches to visit, though not all are for swimming. No one would dip in the flat grey waters of Sandymount Strand, but if you fancy a walk in the blustery sea air, this is a good and popular spot. The hardy do the full Poolbeg Peninsula walk, taking in the Irishtown Nature Reserve, Sandymount Strand and finally the South Wall breakwater, at the end of which is a chunky red lighthouse.

Seapoint, Dún Laoghaire & Sandycove

Of the three popular year-round bathing spots on the Southside, Seapoint (the other two are the Forty-Foot and Vico) is perfect for swimming when the tide is high and laps over the two wide staircases, but the water's frustratingly shallow at low tide. Water quality is consistently good, though. On sunny days, the place is packed, mainly with families and children.

Dún Laoghaire, formerly called Kingstown in honour of the royal visit of George IV, is still in the throes of a makeover; the results so far are an excellent blend of old and new. The semi-pedestrianised main street still has its charity shops, greasy spoons and butchers, while the new Pavilion on the seafront covers the upmarket bar, stylish restaurant and fusion café end of things. What was for a long time just a satellite town around the car ferry port, filled with grotty B&Bs and hotels fallen on hard times, has reverted to its original role as a seaside destination; weekends here are busy and crowded. The ferry depot has been rebuilt and is decent-looking and unobtrusive.

The two piers are the focus for much of the activity. The more fashionable East Pier was always popular with South Dublin matrons for the bracing three-kilometre (two-mile) there-and-back walk, but is now a weekend destination for half the city. It takes in views of Dún Laoghaire's three members-only yacht clubs and new marina. The less popular West Pier is quite overgrown, but has its loyal fans.

From the East Pier, stroll along the seafront to Sandycove Green. A new path takes you past Sandycove beach – popular with the bucket-and-spade brigade – all the way to the **Forty-Foot**, a year-round bathing spot once famous for being nudist men-only. It was named after the Fortieth Foot regiment, who were quartered during the 19th century in the adjacent Martello tower, now the **James Joyce Museum** (*see below*). Battered 'Men Only' signs can still be seen, but nude bathing is increasingly rare.

James Joyce Museum

Joyce Tower, Sandycove (280 9265). Bus 59/DART Sandycove. **Open** *Apr-Sept* 10am-1pm, 2-5pm Mon-Sat; 2-6pm Sun. **Admission** €7.50; €4.70-€6.30 reductions; €22 family. **Credit** AmEx, MC, V.
Famously the setting for the opening chapter of *Ulysses*, in which Joyce mocks Oliver St John Gogarty as 'stately, plump Buck Mulligan', this Martello tower has been restored to match Joyce's description of it. Exhibits are a collection of memorabilia – walking stick, cigar case, guitar, death mask, letters. Best of all is an edition of *Ulysses* beautifully illustrated with line drawings by Matisse.

Eat, Drink, Shop

Restaurants	**100**
Cafés & Coffee Shops	**117**
Pubs & Bars	**123**
Shops & Services	**138**

Features

The best Restaurants	100
The burgers of Dublin	106
Believe the hype	115
The Best Cafés	118
The Best Bars	124
Oirish Original	128
The Best Shops	139
In one era, out the other	147
Get out of town	150

Cake Café. *See p122.*

Restaurants

Gain pounds with your euros.

As a barometer for the highs and lows of post-Tiger Dublin, the city's restaurant scene has always given pretty reliable readings. Not so long ago, for instance, an enormous surge in restaurant openings flooded the market with scores of new dining options, from the modest and gimmicky to the seriously high-flying. Some, but by no means all, have made it through to the more stable plateau of today's time-tested and solid bistros, brasseries, restaurants and (here and there) gastro temples.

Finally, it seems, the city's restaurateurs have realised that style over substance is an equation for short-term success only, and that good food needs integrity, not just an advertising budget. As ever, the fine-dining sector is working hard (Dublin is a paradise of stellar eateries for those who have the time and funds; *see p115* **Believe the hype**), but the good news is that casual neighbourhood restaurants are also starting to raise standards, attracting praise from both critics and consumers. Dublin is a small city (or large town), with big aspirations and a great sense of humour, and word spreads quickly if a restaurant is not up to scratch. Snooty service, especially prevalent during the recent boom years, has been replaced with better training and management presence. Customers have been shouting for better value, more fun and dishes they want to enjoy. Well, now they're getting it all.

Around Temple Bar

French

Les Frères Jacques

74 Dame Street (679 4555/www.lesfreresjacques. com). All cross-city buses/Luas Jervis. **Open** 12.30-2.30pm, 7-10.30pm Mon-Thur; 12.30-2.30pm, 7-11pm Fri; 7-11pm Sat. **Main courses** €30-€38. **Set lunch** €18 2 courses; €23 3 courses. **Set dinner** €39. **Credit** AmEx, MC, V. **Map** p252 E3 ❶
Die-hard fans (of whom there are many) don't mind Les Frères Jacques' location on this busy, slightly grotty street, nor are they deterred by its cramped interior. In fact, these things only seem to encourage their fondness for this classic French old-timer – and quite right they are, too. The seafood is spanking fresh, there's game in season, and the excellent cheese plates and own-made tarts are never less than delicious. At the weekend, a pianist eases the pain of the prices (though, it must be said, lunch remains great value). One of Dublin's best French restaurants.

L'Gueuleton

Fade Street (675 3708). All cross-city buses/Luas St Stephen's Green. **Open** 12.30-3pm, 6-10pm Mon-Sat; 1-3.30pm, 6-9pm Sun. **Main courses** €16.50-€28.50. **Credit** MC, V. **Map** p252 E4 ❷
Superb, unpretentious brasserie cooking has earned this charming little restaurant a good reputation over the years, and they've had the sense to not go tinkering with a winning formula. The classic french onion soup is still on the menu (alongside a revolving cast of grilled ribeye, slow-roast pork belly and tons of other tried and tasty favourites). Le Gueuleton has a very New York kind of vibe, and they don't take reservations, such is the demand for their simple, no-nonsense dishes. Occasionally, regulars complain about inconsistencies, but it doesn't

Hearty nosh for pennies at **Gruel**. *See p103.*

seem to deter them one bit. The food and wine are keenly priced. Good fun and the perfect place for a loud and opinionated group of friends.

Haute cuisine

Thornton's

Fitzwilliam Hotel, St Stephen's Green West (478 7008/www.fitzwilliamhotel.com). All cross-city buses/Luas St Stephen's Green. **Open** 7-10pm Tue, Wed; noon-2.30pm, 7-10pm Thur-Sat. **Main courses** €45-€55. **Set lunch** €45 2 courses, €55 3 courses. **Surprise menu** €125 8 courses. **Credit** AmEx, MC, V. **Map** p251 F4 ❸

One of the most talked-about fine-dining restaurants in Dublin, Thornton's is the culinary seat of celebrity chef Kevin Thornton, whose fiery appearances on RTÉ1's cook-off show *Heat* have put him firmly in the public spotlight. The restaurant itself (which is affiliated to, but has a separate entrance from, the Fitzwilliam Hotel; *see p39*) is a stylishly sombre medley of burgundy upholstered chairs, dark chocolate-coloured carpets and thick white tablecloths, with striking modern photography brightening the walls. It's all very comfortable and the staff are an attentive, knowledgeable lot, but the real reason to come here is to experience Thornton's exquisitely refined seasonal cooking. Despite the loss of Michelin star *numéro deux* (*see p115* **Believe the hype**), the eponymous Thornton continues to turn out some exciting dishes: warm Aran Island sea urchin or mallard duck crusted with pistachio and honey, with a nettle and thyme sorbet to cleanse the palate. Or, if you'd prefer not to know what you'll be eating, plump for the 'surprise menu', a spread of eight unannounced courses served at the dramatic 'chef's table',

which is positioned next to a massive circular window looking into the kitchen. Wines are, of course, sublime – but, like the food, they ain't cheap.

Indian & Nepalese

Jaipur

41 South Great George's Street (677 0979/ www.jaipur.ie). All cross-city buses/Luas St Stephen's Green. **Open** 5-11pm daily. **Main courses** €17-€23. **Credit** AmEx, MC, V. **Map** p252 E4 ❹

With branches on all three sides of the city, Jaipur is in danger of becoming a chain rather than a top-class Indian, for which it has always been liked. Service is extremely courteous, and food is light and tasty. Alongside a typical, albeit classily executed range of common or garden rubies are some excellent fish and seafood options (a rich Goan seafood curry, tamarind crab curry, sea bass steamed with curry leaves). Money has been spent on the interiors in all three branches.
Other locations 21 Castle Street, Dalkey (285 0552); 5 St James Terrace, Malahide (845 5455); 35 Main Street, Ongar Village, Dublin 15 (640 2611).

Montys of Kathmandu

28 Eustace Street (670 4911/www.montys.ie). All cross-city buses/Luas Jervis. **Open** noon-2.30pm, 6-11pm Mon-Sat; 6-11pm Sun. **Main courses** €16.50-€26.50. **Credit** MC, V. **Map** p252 E3 ❺

❶ Purple numbers given in this chapter correspond to the location of each place on the street maps. *See pp250-252.*

Nepalese cooking is a serious business and nowhere is it taken more to heart than at this excellent, city-centre restaurant. Among the *suruwat* (starters) are such delights as crab claws with onions, capsicum and fresh herbs, while *moukhay khana* (main courses) include all kinds of deeply flavoured and richly spiced curries, kebabs and stir-fries. To wash it down, the house Shiva lager was specially commissioned from a local micro-brewery to match the food. As for the decor, it's all very cosy, with pleasant, low-key staff to make you feel right at home. The perfect place, then, to get the ball rolling on a night out in town.
Other location 88 Rathgar Road, Dublin 6 (492 0633).

International

Fallon & Byrne
11-17 Exchequer Street (472 1000/ www.fallonandbyrne.com). All cross-city buses/ Luas Jervis/St Stephen's Green. **Open** 12.30-4pm, 6-10.30pm Mon-Thur; 12.30-4pm, 6-11pm Fri; 11am-4pm, 6-11pm Sat; 11am-4pm, 6-10.30pm Sun. **Main courses** €18-€34. **Credit** MC, V. **Map** p252 E3 **⑥**
Likely as not, your mouth will already be watering when you reach the restaurant of this foodie institution (you enter the building via the superb deli on the ground floor; *see p151*). It's a pleasant, business-like kind of space with an excellent menu of refined brasserie fare and some lovely wines to complete

the picture. Roast saddle of pancetta-wrapped rabbit stuffed with wild mushroom mousse would be a typical offering from the main courses. There's another, more casual operation in the basement where excellent cheese platters and charcuterie can be wolfed down with large glasses of affordable vino, or else a really quick café operation (but still with an emphasis on top-notch ingredients) on the ground floor, among the shelves of the food hall. All in all, F & B is a consistently excellent operation catering for pretty much every culinary need under one roof.

Farm
3 Dawson Street (671 8654). All cross-city buses/ Luas St Stephen's Green. **Open** 11am-11pm daily. **Main courses** €12.95-€23.95. **Credit** MC, V. **Map** p252 F4. **⑦**
Sensitive souls and rampant carnivores will be equally satisfied with the menu at this fresh, funky and attractively packaged new restaurant at the College end of Dawson Street. Good-quality ingredients are put to imaginative use in a variety of vegetarian dishes, from Asian green salad to tasty tarts. Meat-eaters, meanwhile, get to sink their teeth into less squeamish options with names like 'chicken on the run', or tackle thick, juicy steaks, all manner of burgers, grills and hearty mains. Pizzas are made with organic dough, and the kids' menu features plenty of health-conscious versions of classic junior crowd-pleasers (organic chicken nuggets and whatnot). Lime-green banquettes and table decorations in flowerpots complete the picture.

Larder.

Fitzers

50 Dawson Street (677 1155/www.fitzers.ie).
All cross-city buses/Luas St Stephen's Green. **Open**
11.30am-11pm Mon-Thur, Sun; 11.30am-11.30pm Fri,
Sat. **Main courses** €13.50-€26.95. **Credit** AmEx,
DC, MC, V. **Map** p252 F4 ❽

Understandably popular with those on their way to
or returning from shopping sprees on nearby Grafton
Street, this branch of the small family-run Fitzers
chain is also a good bet for a 'between museums'
break or even for a low-key dinner out with friends.
The menu (which rather responsibly points out what
may or may not contain nuts, be suitable for veggies
and vegans, or otherwise upset anyone) includes dishes like grilled sea bass with shaved fennel or spaghet-
ti tossed with feta, rocket, olives and tomatoes. It's a
professional and consistently busy operation, with
charming service, a pleasant interior and a small terrace with heaters.
Other locations Temple Bar Square, Temple Bar
(679 0440); Millennium Wing, National Gallery,
Merrion Square, Around Trinity College (663 3500).

Gruel

68A Dame Street (670 7119). All cross-city buses/
Luas Jervis. **Open** 9am-10pm Mon-Fri; 11am-10.30pm
Sat, Sun. **Main courses** €5.50-€8 lunch; €12.50-€15
dinner. **No credit cards. Map** p252 E3 ❾

Gruel continues to rule the eating-out agendas of
Dublin's bright but modestly-off young things. And
with its belly-filling bonanzas of hot roast-in-a-roll
(weekdays only), hearty weekend brunches, soup
served in huge bowls, pizza slices, own-made cakes
and brownies, all at affordable prices, it's easy to see
why. Its grown-up sister restaurant is next door
(Mermaid; *see right*), where you can expect something a little more formal, but you'll be missing out
on the charms of laid-back staff, higgledy-piggledy
interior design and, most importantly, roast turkey
with stuffing and cranberry crammed into hot own-
baked rolls. *Photo p101.*

Larder

8 Parliament Street (633 3581). All cross-city buses/
Luas Jervis. **Open** 7.30am-6pm Mon, Tue; 7.30am-
11pm Wed-Fri; 9am-11pm Sat, Sun. **Main courses**
€14.95-€19.95. **Credit** MC, V. **Map** p252 E3 ❿

It may be open all day and catering to a steady flow
of customers from breakfast to dinner, but it would
be unfair to write off the Larder as a mere café. It is
much more sophisticated than that. For a start, the
food is a cut above the normal café fare – whether
it's a warming dish of yellow bean chicken or
Moroccan meatballs with mint couscous, or a simple reinvention of a salad niçoise with chargrilled
tuna fillet on a caper-infused crunchy green salad.
Also, there are plenty of great wines to choose from
(as well as excellent smoothies, great teas and Illy
coffee) and there's no shortage of room to spread out
in the long dining room, with its rugged brick walls,
metal lampshades and towering shelves. Our pre-
ferred spot is right in the window, ensconced in the
scarlet wing-backed armchairs – the perfect place

from which to calmly observe the crowds of Temple
Bar hurry by as you sip a camomile and nana mint
tea and pick at a mixed berry crumble tart.

Mermaid Café

69-70 Dame Street (670 8236/www.mermaid.ie).
All cross-city buses/Luas Jervis. **Open** 12.30-3pm,
6-9.30pm Mon-Sat; noon-3pm, 6-9.30pm Sun.
Main courses €19.95-€32.95. **Credit** MC, V.
Map p252 E3 ⓫

With its rather lovely blue-painted storefront facade
and sweet little Sycamore Street running down one
side of it, the Mermaid is a pretty prospect from the
outside. And the good news is, it lives up to its initial promise. Don't come expecting culinary fireworks, perhaps, but you can certainly look forward
to a rich crop of well-executed dishes on the daily
menu. When we were last there, a feisty starter of
citrus-cured salmon with fennel and mustard seeds
was followed by excellent hake with a pine nut crust
and celeriac gratin. There are meaty dishes too
(steak, pork belly and whatnot) and some decadent
desserts (the pecan pie with maple ice cream is legendary). Basically, if you're a fan of tasty food and
fine wines, the Mermaid is always a safe bet.

Sixty6

66 South Great George's Street (400 5878/
www.brasseriesixty6.com). All cross-city buses/
Luas St Stephen's Green. **Open** 8am-3pm, 5-11pm
Mon-Thur; 10am-11.30pm Fri, Sat; 10am-11pm Sun.
Main courses €23.50-€28.50. **Credit** MC, V.
Map p252 E3 ⓬

A great-looking restaurant, Sixty6 is precisely the
kind of place most people would love to have right
on their doorstep. It's perfect for an impromptu meal
à deux, it can easily meet the demands of a special
occasion, and it's also the type of stylish, easygoing
brasserie that is just made for long, animated
evenings with a group of friends. Loads of original
touches (like the rows of antique china plates on the
walls, or the vaguely industrial tiles, lighting and
exposed air ducts around the bar) are undoubtedly
the fruits of an interior design that was a long time
in the planning, and the menu shows a similarly
considered and, ultimately, very successful knack
for hitting just the right note. Devilled chicken liv-
ers on rye toast or crispy lemon and cracked black
pepper calamari are typically tempting starters, to
be followed with mains such as duck breast stuffed
with apricot and prunes or chargrilled pork chop
with roast apple, pineapple and pomegranate salsa.
Puddings are lovely too (who could resist warm
banana bread with custard and caramel ice-cream?)
and the wine list crosses continents with confidence
and aplomb. And, what's more, you can even get
breakfast here. *Photo p105.*

Tante Zoé's

1 Crow Street (679 4407/www.tantezoes.com).
All cross-city buses/Luas Jervis. **Open** noon-midnight
Mon-Sat; 4-10pm Sun. **Main courses** €17.95-€32.50.
Credit MC, V. **Map** p252 E3 ⓭

With a happy-go-lucky steamboat aesthetic and more Creole and Cajun dishes than you could wave a washboard at, Tante Zoé's on Crow Street has been the default destination of birthday boys and girls, first-daters and festive families just about forever. Other restaurants have been and gone but this fun and noisy joint has kept on swinging, never altering its winning format of jambalayas, creoles, blackened salmon, Louisiana duck and the rest, with a healthy dollop of *bons temps* schtick chucked in for good measure. So go on, order yourself a jug of Cajun punch and get stuck into a big bowl of gumbo.

Town Bar and Grill

21 Kildare Street (662 4724/ www.townbarandgrill.com) All cross-city buses/ Luas St Stephen's Green. **Open** 12.30-11pm Mon-Sat; 12.30-10pm Sun. **Main courses** €25.95-€31.95. **Set lunch** €24.95 2 courses, €29.95 3 courses. **Credit** AmEx, DC, MC, V. **Map** p251 F4 ⓮
A few doors down from the impressive facade of the National Museum of Archaeology & History (*see pxxx*) on Kildare Street, this fashionable and (deservedly) popular restaurant is where a lot of Dublin's hard-earned cash gets spent. The basement dining room has an exclusive, moneyed feel, with thick linen cloths on the tables, expensive modern art on the walls and beautiful lights with giant pleated shades hovering like harvest moons in the half-light. The kitchen evidently has a soft spot for Italian ingredients, which crop up from the word go (in the form of the deliciously pungent olive oil that arrives with the pre-prandial breads). But the menu is largely international in flavour: white asparagus and artichoke with a soft-boiled egg and shaved pecorino being a typical starter; rump of lamb, yellow fin tuna and corn-fed chicken among the mains. The wine list is a labour of love, with an especially strong showing of Tuscan reds. *Photo p109.*

Italian

Il Baccaro

Meetinghouse Square (671 4597/www.ilbaccaro.com). All cross-city buses/Luas Jervis. **Open** 5.30-10.30pm Mon-Fri; noon-10.30pm Sat, Sun. **Main courses** €13.80-€23. **Credit** MC, V. **Map** p252 E3 ⓯
You'll not find the same quality of regional Italian *cucina* in this cute little den of a restaurant as you would at some of the city's more serious joints, but that's not to say that Il Baccaro on Meetinghouse Square is a dud. Far from it, in fact. This is a genuinely cheap, cheerful and fun spot before a night on the town, and as long as you're not expecting miracles, the food is perfectly nice. Bruschetta, crostini, bresaola and all the other usual suspects are to be found among the starters, pastas, polentas and cutlets among the mains. Wicker-clad chianti bottles, exposed brickwork, the odd mural and sunny tiles set the scene.

Sixty6. *See p103.*

The burgers of Dublin

It's a well-documented fact that Dublin has acquired a rich crop of exciting new restaurants in recent years, all of them playing their part in the inexorable rise in the quality of eating out. But what has been a less common feature of the city's restaurant explosion has been the appearance of good-quality budget eateries. Sure, there are a few notables around town (among them, the excellent **Lemon Crêpe & Coffee**; see p119) but it has usually fallen to such stalwarts as Pizza Express (branded in these parts as Milano) to cater for pre-cinema bites, birthdays, group get-togethers... What Dublin needed was a burger bar, or two.

Of course, some places have always been noted for their fine burgers (**Canal Bank Café**, for instance; see p109) and others have made a high street business out of it, notably the 1950s-style Eddie Rockets chain (with a look and menu that will be uncannily familiar to fans of the UK-based Ed's Easy Diners) but no one had set out to really grab hold of the idea and make it into something genuinely fresh and fun. Until, that is, **Jo'Burger** (pictured) and **Bóbó's** took the city's thrifty dining contingent by storm.

South of the canal, bang in the middle of student bedsit country, Jo'Burger has pulled off the impressive balancing act of looking cool but still managing to serve up a tasty, friendly and, above all, lively night out (and at a fraction of the price you'd pay in town). Long communal tables are surrounded by a hybrid decor of pop art murals, chintzy wallpaper and assorted retro lighting, while the menu (which arrives pasted into a 1970s annual – we got *Scorcher* and *Whizzer & Chips*) is devoted entirely to the burger in all its multifarious forms. It comes in a number of traditional styles, straight up or with any number of cheeses and relishes, or you can try Thai-flavoured or curried patties, with toppings as diverse as peanut chilli sauce and mango salsa.

Like everywhere, there are one or two drawbacks to Jo'Burger – such as the nightly DJs who keep the kids at party pitch and the old fuddy-duddies moaning, or the fact that there is always a massive queue snaking up the street on a weekend evening. But these are not real complaints, and besides, if you fancy somewhere a bit quieter, you can always head up the way to Bóbó's.

In a much more central location and, in many ways, with a slightly more substantial feel to it, Bóbó's is the other main contender for the city's burger buck. Taking the diner look and giving it a nifty kind of After Noah spin, this excellent little joint serves up peerless patties, 'proper chubby chips' and delicious malts, shakes and juices. Our favourite is the beautifully flavoursome Chimicurri (a fiery blend of chimicurri sauce and chorizo let loose on a fat slab of juicy burger). It may not be refined but this is the kind of food you can quickly develop strong and regular cravings for.

Jo'Burger. See p108.

Middle Eastern

Cedar Tree

11A St Andrew's Street (677 2121/www.cedartree.ie).
All cross-city buses/Luas St Stephen's Green. **Open**
5.30-11pm Mon-Wed, Sun; 5.30pm-midnight Thur-
Sat. **Main courses** €13.90-€25. **Credit** AmEx, MC,
V. **Map** p252 F3 **⑯**
A long-established, family-run Lebanese restaurant,
the Cedar Tree is as unpretentious and endearing as
they come. Sure, you might find a belly-dancing
floor show gets going while you're having your dinner, or some bloke may try to sell you a rose if you're
dining *à deux*, but somehow it doesn't seem to matter much here. It's just part of the holiday vibe. The
shishtaouk (marinated chicken) kebabs are delicious,
as are the *kafta halabieh* (chargrilled meatballs of
minced lamb, parsley, pine nuts and onion). Byblos
'house of mezze' next door is under the same own-
ership and serves lighter meals throughout the day.

Modern European

Bleu Bistro

Joshua House, Dawson Street (676 7015). All cross-
city buses/Luas St Stephen's Green. **Open** noon-3pm,
5.30-11pm Mon-Sat. **Main courses** €18.50-€29.
Credit AmEx, MC, V. **Map** p252 F4 **⑰**
A sassy metropolitan bistro with a particularly good
line in seafood, Bleu serves high-quality casual fare
with a twist. Its fans rave about the fare but moan
about how crowded it is – tables are close together
– and the erratic service. The delicious house fish
and chips make for great comfort food, while more
ambitious fare such as scallops with apple and
brown butter vinaigrette or zingy fishcakes cater to
sophisticated palates.

Tea Room

The Clarence Hotel, 6-8 Wellington Quay (407 0813/
www.theclarence.ie). All cross-city buses/Luas Jervis.
Open 7-11am, 12.30-2.15pm, 7-10.15pm Mon-Fri;
7.30-11.30am, 12.30-2.15pm, 7-10.15pm Sat; 7.30-
11.30am, 12.30-2.15pm, 7-9.15pm Sun. **Main**
courses €29-€42. **Credit** AmEx, DC, MC, V.
Map p252 E3 **⑱**
At the time of writing, planning permission has
been passed for some major changes at Bono and
The Edge's designer Clarence Hotel (*see p41* **With**
or without you), which is home to this posh
restaurant, but any work is a long way off and, for
the foreseeable future at least, it will be business as
usual at the Tea Room. This usually entails some
excellent cooking (such as roasted cannon of lamb,
creamed broad beans and chorizo tuile), some fine
wines and maybe a pre-prandial cocktail or two
in the louche Octagon Bar (*see p130*). Service is formal but accommodating, and the atmosphere, is
though decidedly upmarket, is never intimidating
(the place is owned by rock stars, after all). And
there's always a fair chance you'll find yourself next
to someone famous.

Oriental

Aya

49-52 Clarendon Street (677 1544). All cross-city
buses/Luas St Stephen's Green. **Open** 12.30-10pm
Mon-Fri; 12.30-11pm Sat; 1-9pm Sun. **Main courses**
€14-€30. **Set meal** €25 sushi. **Credit** AmEx, MC, V.
Map p251 F3/4 **⑲**
Very popular with brunching shoppers (there are
always a few European dishes on the conveyor belt),
as well as with Dublin's sushi lovers, Aya is a slick,
minimalist Japanese restaurant manned by discreet
uniformed staff. Yakitori, norimaki, tataki and sushi
– it all comes revolving past, and although the quality rarely creeps above average, there are certain
dishes on the menu itself (the beef tataki, say, or the
noodle dishes) that are reliably good. Deals can be
had during 'twilight' hours, when there is plenty of
grub to be offloaded from the conveyor belt. The deli
sells everything from not-very-Japanese egg mayonnaise sarnies to hot teriyaki dishes and lots of
Japanese condiments to take home.

Mao

Chatham Row (670 4899/www.cafemao.com).
All cross-city buses/Luas St Stephen's Green. **Open**
noon-10pm Mon, Tue; noon-11pm Wed-Sat; 1-30.9pm
Sun. **Main courses** €13.95-€21.50. **Credit** MC, V.
Map p252 F4 **⑳**
Two floors decked out in bold primary colours, generous portions of pan-Asian grub and a good location,
just set back from Grafton Street, make this outlet of
the Mao mini chain a sure-fire success with the city's
shoppers, pubbers and clubbers. The menu reads like
a Greatest Hits of oriental cuisine, with everything
from satay and wontons to nasi goreng and chilli
plum duck. There are wines and beers to choose from,
alongside an interesting selection of juices and non-
alcoholic drinks for those who want to save their
strength for the pub. The natural yoghurt, honey and
banana lassi is particularly moreish.
Other locations Dundrum Town Square, The
New Dundrum Town Centre, Dundrum (296 2802);
The Pavilion, Dún Laoghaire, Dublin Bay & the
Coast (214 8090).

Wagamama

King Street South (478 2152/www.wagamama.ie). All
cross-city buses/Luas St Stephen's Green. **Open** noon-
11pm Mon-Sat; noon-10pm Sun. **Main courses** €11.
75-€17.25. **Credit** AmEx, DC, MC, V. **Map** p251 F4 **㉑**
It's fun, convenient, tasty and healthy – in truth, the
Wagamama formula is what it is, so there are never
going to be any surprises, but as a lunch break from
shopping or a fuel-up station for a night out, it's hard
to beat. Big bowls of soupy ramen and teppan noodles are the chain's stock-in-trade, with tempting
back-ups in the form of mouthwatering teriyaki and
rich curries. To drink: fresh juices (apple and lime is
always a good one) and the usual soft drinks. Kids
get their own menu too, which features most of the
same ingredients, just made over with a deep fry
here, a breadcrumbing there.

Eat, Drink, Shop

Vegetarian

Cornucopia

*19 Wicklow Street (677 7583). All cross city buses/
Luas St Stephen's Green.* **Open** 8.30am-8pm Mon-
Wed, Fri, Sat; 9am-9pm Thur; noon-7pm Sun. **Main
courses** €8-€12.50. **Credit** MC, V. **Map** p252 F3 ❷
A stalwart for vegetarians, vegans, dairy intolerants
or anyone looking for healthy, wholesome grub,
Cornucopia is cramped, wooden and not exactly
glam. At lunch, the place is thronged with masses
of earnest twentysomethings vying for a place at one
of the few tables. Still, you'll be so thrilled with yourself after eating all those lentils, hearty soups and
salads that you won't mind sharing your personal
space with like-minded diners. For best results,
though, come mid morning, when the atmosphere is
more relaxed and you can dawdle over your organic porridge and freshly squeezed juice.

Around St Stephen's Green

American

Bóbó's

*22 Wexford Street (400 5750/www.bobos.ie).
All cross-city buses/Luas St Stephen's Green.*
Open 11am-11pm daily. **Main courses**
€7.50-€9.95. **Credit** MC, V. **Map** p251 E5 ❷
See p106 **The burgers of Dublin.**

Jo'Burger

*137 Rathmines Road Lower (491 3731/
www.joburger.ie). Luas All cross-city buses/Luas
Charlemont/Harcourt.* **Open** noon-11pm Mon-
Thur; noon-midnight Fri, Sat; noon-10pm Sun. **Main
courses** €8.50-€12. **Credit** MC, V. **Map** p251 E6 ❷
See p106 **The burgers of Dublin.**

Shanahan's

*119 St Stephen's Green West (407 0939/
www.shanahans.ie). All cross-city buses/Luas St
Stephens Green.* **Open** 6-9.45pm Mon-Thur; 6-
10.30pm; 12.30-2pm Fri-Sun. **Main courses** €41-
€55. **Credit** AmEx, DC, MC, V. **Map** p251 F4 ❷
There are those who believe this classy steakhouse
to be the finest restaurant in the city (admittedly,
they are almost always pinstriped men *d'un certain
âge* with a no-nonsense approach to dining out).
They are, of course, quite wrong. It's just that, when
you actually sit down and sink your teeth into one
of Shanahan's 12oz filet mignons, all of the reasons
why those people are so sorely misguided seem to
kind of evaporate from your mind. And all that
remains is a dreamlike state of steak-induced
shangri-la. Could it be because the meat is perfectly
aged, perfectly cut and cooked at scientifically cal-
culated temperatures in state-of the art broilers? Or
is it because the surroundings are so slick (the chandeliers, the gilt mirrors, the presidential Oval Office
bar)? Or perhaps it's the side orders of exquisite
creamed spinach and heart-stopping dauphinoise?

Maybe it's the vast and high-rolling wine list. The
truth is, no one really knows. The easiest thing to do
is just repeat to yourself as often as is necessary:
Shanahan's is *not* the best restaurant in Dublin,
Shanahan's is *not* the best restaurant in Dublin...
Photo p110.

French

Pearl

*20 Merrion Street Upper (661 3627/www.pearl-
brasserie.com). All cross-city buses/Luas St Stephen's
Green.* **Open** noon-2.30pm, 6-10.30pm Mon-Fri; 6-
10.30pm Sat, Sun. **Main courses** €21-€28. **Credit**
AmEx, MC, V. **Map** p251 G4 ❷
Great attention to detail that has gone into the design
of this elegant little restaurant, with its prettily upholstered furniture, its discreet modern art, funky
recessed fish tanks and its delightfully chic nooks.
Staff are a sophisticated bunch (as are, by and large,
the clientele) and the kitchen does its best to do them
justice. The bar area serves oysters, champagne and
(during the day) delicious soup, croque monsieurs
and steak sandwiches. Night-time gets fancier:
monkfish with ginger confit, perhaps or seared scallops served with coriander seeds, tomato sauce
vièrge and chervil. The extensive wine list is well
thought-out, affordable and dangerously tempting.

Haute cuisine

L'Ecrivain

*109A Lower Baggot Street (661 1919/
www.lecrivain.com). All cross-city buses/Luas St
Stephen's Green.* **Open** 12.30-2pm, 7-10pm Mon-
Fri; 7-11pm Sat. **Main courses** €45-€53 dinner.
Set lunch €40 2 courses; €50 3 courses. **Credit**
AmEx, MC, V. **Map** p251 G7 ❷
Classic Irish dishes get a truly gourmet twist at this
stalwart of Dublin's fine-dining scene: the oysters in
Guinness sabayon are legendary. Located in the
heart of the business and media district, it attracts
many suits at lunch, but in the evening it's the perfect spot for a romantic dinner or family celebration.
Any note of formality is truly Irish (that is, non-exis-
tent), and a good time is encouraged, often via the
piano downstairs in the bar. And while the cooking
here may be highly accomplished, it is also refreshingly lacking in pretension: spring lamb, for example, might be served in the form of a moussaka with
green peas, mint, feta and confit aubergine. On a
sunny day (they do happen sometimes), it is definitely worth bribing someone for a terrace table. *See also
p115* **Believe the hype.**

Restaurant Patrick Guilbaud

*The Merrion Hotel, 22 Merrion Street Upper
(676 4192/www.restaurantpatrickguilbaud.ie).
All cross-city buses/Luas St Stephen's Green.*
Open 12.30-2.15pm, 7.30-10.15pm Tue-Fri;
1-2.15pm, 7.30-10.15pm Sat. **Main courses**
€30-€50. **Set lunch** €38 2 courses; €50 3
courses. **Credit** AmEx, MC, V. **Map** p251 G4 ❷

Town Bar & Grill where the smart money eats. *See p105.*

Looking every bit as stellar as its two Michelin *étoiles* would suggest, Guilbaud's is pretty much the top table in town (although you may find it hard to properly enjoy your meal unless someone else is paying). The suited lunch clientele overcome this problem courtesy of their expense accounts but Dublin's gourmets and gourmands also line up alongside them, happy to exchange their own hard-earned cash for the chance to eat dishes like Wicklow venison fillet in mulled wine, served with apple polenta, crisp muesli, balsamic and grue de cacao reduction. But be warned: if you go off-piste here and start ordering cheese, dessert, and maybe that second bottle of wine, you will be forced to sell your house/partner/children to settle the bill. Although, of course, you might well consider that a fair exchange. *See also p115* **Believe the hype.**

International

Canal Bank Café
146 Upper Leeson Street (664 2135/www.canal bankcafe.com). All cross-city buses/Luas Charlemont. **Open** 10am-11pm Mon-Fri; 11am-11pm Sat, Sun. **Main courses** €14.95-€23.95. **Credit** AmEx, MC, V. **Map** p251 G6 ㉙
This smart and easy-going café on Upper Leeson Street has young, sassy staff and an American-influenced menu featuring omelettes, soups, burgers, steak sandwiches and quesadillas, as well as more grown-up dishes like lamb steak with couscous salad, sole on the bone or moules frites. Brunch is pleasant and the menu offers all you could want to eat the morning after. Be sure to ask for a window table.

Shanahan's, a corner of carnivore heaven. *See p108.*

Dobbins

15 Stephen's Lane (661 3321/www.dobbins.ie).
All cross-city buses/Luas St Stephen's Green.
Open 12.30-2.30pm, 6-9.30pm Mon-Fri; 6-10pm
Sat; noon-3pm Sun. **Main courses** €21-€34.50. **Set**
lunch €23.50 4 courses. **Credit** AmEx, DC, MC, V.
Map p251 H5 ③⓪
Full of politicos and men in suits, this is one of the
best places for a boozy lunch (and somewhere you
could easily end up buying dinner at too – time
seems to fly here…) The place reeks of money,
power and property deals. The wine list is endless,
and the food is all very meat and potatoes (rack of
lamb, crispy duck, suckling pig). Waiters seem to
have been here forever, the location is discreet and
fun is guaranteed.

Italian

Da Vincenzo

133 Leeson Street Upper (660 9906). All cross-city
buses/Luas Charlemont. **Open** noon-11pm Mon-Fri;
1-11pm Sat; 1-10pm Sun. **Main courses** €18.95-€28.
Credit AmEx, MC, V. **Map** p251 G6 ③①
This cosy old-timer is always busy. Try to book the
snug table on the left as you walk in (No.21) – it's
one of the nicest spots in town. Staff are lovely
enough to make you forget that the pasta dishes here
are, in fact, very average. You'd do well to order
pizza instead: it's well made and baked in a wood-
burning oven. Keep toppings fairly plain – a simple
margherita with some mushrooms and garlic is one
of the best options. Food can be prepared to take
away. This is one of those places you go to for the
atmosphere more than anything else.

Il Posto

10 Stephen's Green (679 4769/www.ilposto
restaurant.com). All cross-city buses/Luas St
Stephen's Green. **Open** noon-2pm, 5.30-10pm
Mon-Wed; noon-2pm, 5.30-10.30pm Thur, Fri;
noon-2.30pm, 5.30-10.30pm Sat; 5.30-10pm Sun.
Main courses €16.50-€28.50. **Credit** AmEx,
MC, V. **Map** p251 F4 ③②
An intimate, cosy and warm basement restaurant, Il
Posto serves decent Italian grub. Lunch can be a bit
disappointing (atmosphere-wise), except on a busy
Friday, but dinner makes up for it. Grilled swordfish
with lemon and olive oil, and good old chicken
supreme wrapped in pancetta are mighty tasty.
Portions are huge, the side orders are good (not just
an after-thought) and the place is usually hopping.

Modern Irish

Bang Café

11 Merrion Row (676 0898/www.bangrestaurant.
com). All cross-city buses/Luas St Stephen's Green.
Open 12.30-3pm, 6-10.30pm Mon-Wed; 12.30-3pm,
6-11pm Thur-Sat. **Main courses** €13.95-€36.
Credit AmEx, MC, V. **Map** p251 G4 ③③
The owners of this fashionable café have a good
pedigree: restaurants and fashion have featured
strongly in their lives. They drive fast cars, have
pretty blondes by their sides and wisely hired an ex-
chef from London's Ivy restaurant. The result is cool
minimalist interiors with brash art, chandeliers and
a menu that is full of dishes you want to eat. The
scallops with mousseline potatoes and pancetta is
an Ivy classic well translated, while pan-fried fillet
of Irish beef with sauteed girolles, braised shallots

and dauphinoise potatoes is the stuff comforting dreams are made of. Cocktails are good, and all the customers seem rather fabulous. Quite possibly the most fashionable restaurant in the city.

Cellar
Merrion Hotel, 22 Merrion Street Upper (603 0630/ www.merrionhotel.com). All cross-city buses/Luas St Stephen's Green. **Open** 7-10.30am, 12.30-2pm, 6-10pm Mon-Fri; 7-11am, 6-10pm Sat; 7-11am, 12.30-2.30pm, 6-10pm Sun. **Main courses** €14-€32. **Credit** AmEx, DC, MC, V. **Map** p251 G4 ❸
With its dramatic vaulted ceiling, its discreet, secluded vibe and its excellent wines, the Cellar certainly lives up to its name. It's an immaculate operation serving casual and contemporary classics (steamed lightly smoked salmon with asparagus, poached egg and lemon oil, for instance). It is also a good place for more conservative folk or lovers looking for a quiet nook (you'll find no loud music or squished tables here). In other words, this is a grown-up restaurant with good facilities, but the food and prices mean it's OK to go to dinner in jeans. It also has a gorgeous terrace for al fresco dining in the warmer months.

Tapas

Havana
3 Camden Market, Grantham Place (476 0046/ www.havana.ie). Bus 16, 19, 122/Luas Harcourt. **Open** 11am-10.30pm Mon-Wed; 11am-11.30pm Thur, Fri; 1-11.30pm Sat. **Main courses** €5.95-€12.95. **Credit** AmEx, DC, MC, V. **Map** p251 E5 ❸
A small tapas bar that's always ready for fun, Havana has pretty interiors, staff and customers. Food can be disappointing, though, but it's cheap, and the place has plenty of atmosphere. The music is hopping, and some customers tell of tables being cleared and dancing the night away. The microwave in the kitchen tells its own story but, as long as you aren't building up culinary expectations, you could end up having a great night here.
Other locations George's Street, Northern Suburbs (400 5990).

Thai

Diep Le Shaker
55 Pembroke Lane (661 1829/www.diep.net). All cross-city buses/Luas St Stephen's Green. **Open** noon-2.30pm, 5-11pm Mon-Thur; noon-11pm Fri; 6-11pm Sat. **Main courses** €13.50-€28. **Credit** AmEx, MC, V. **Map** p251 G5 ❸
Big, bright and busy, this tasty Thai always seems to be full to capacity. The large, open-plan atrium dining room can take the crowds, though, so it never feels claustrophobic and there's plenty of great stuff on the menu to distract you from other people's conversations. Red prawn curry, yellow chicken curry, stir-fried chicken with cashew nuts and dried chilli – all that, and plenty more. The Diep brand (there's also a noodle bar and a couple of home delivery

outposts) has come to be associated with comforting, delicious Thai classics, and it rarely disappoints. There are various cooling beers on hand to put out any chilli fires, as well as a list of fun and potent cocktails to help get the party started (we like the vodka-based Raspbery Watkins).
Other locations Diep at Home, 5 Main Street, Blackrock (497 6270); Diep at Home, Ranelagh Village (497 6270); Diep Noodle Bar, Ranelagh Village (497 6550).

Wine bars

DAX
23 Upper Pembroke Street (676 1494/www.dax.ie). All cross-city buses/Luas St Stephens Green. **Open** 12.30-2pm, 6.30-11pm Tue-Fri; 6-11pm Sat. **Main courses** €22-€33. **Set lunch** €24 2 courses, €27 3 courses. **Credit** AmEx, MC, V. **Map** p251 G5 ❸
Basement restaurants have to work a lot harder than their ground-floor colleagues – they need to lure their punters with a guarantee of good food, rather than just the (all too often meretricious) promise of it through an inviting window. Here you'll find said food in the guise of French 'tapas' by the bar or more formal fare in the dining room. Considered by many to be the city's best wine bar, DAX has great food, charming staff and plush interiors.

Ely
22 Ely Place (676 8986/www.elywinebar.ie). All cross-city buses/Luas St Stephen's Green. **Open** noon-11.30pm Mon-Thur; noon-12.30am Fri; 1pm-12.30am Sat. **Main courses** €13.50-€34.95. **Credit** AmEx, DC, MC, V. **Map** p251 G4 ❸
Cosy and smart, with brick walls, oversized armchairs and little nooks and crannies to sink into, Ely boasts a vast wine list that is possibly the best in the country. Thankfully, many bottles are available by the glass. The organic beef burger (sourced from the owner's organic farm), as well as some Irish classics like Kilkea oysters, bangers and mash and an Irish cheese plate, is the perfect accompaniment to over-sized glasses of wine. Good fun and never dreary, due to the fact that it is often filled with glowingly successful local moguls (as are its two branches down in the moneyed depths of Docklands).
Other locations chq, Custom House Quay (672 0010); Hanover Quay, Docklands (633 9986).

Hugo's
6 Merrion Row (676 5955). All cross-city buses/ Luas St Stephen's Green. **Open** noon-11pm Mon-Fri; 11am-11pm Sat, Sun. **Main courses** €17.50-€29. **Credit** AmEx, MC, V. **Map** p251 G4 ❸
With its smart aquamarine frontage and chic interior of gold patterned wallpaper, swag curtains, red-brick walls and (of course) rows of wine bottles, Hugo's is a welcome addition to an area that already has more than its fair share of wine bars. But then, this is the business end of town, with more than its fair share of suits to do the wine-drinking. Hugo's list is expansive but not expensive, with a good

showing of wines from around the world, and the food is no afterthought either. Plum-stuffed pork tenderloin, seared scallops with wilted greens and curry butter, and chicory, rocquefort and candied pecan salad were some of the stand-out dishes from our last meal here. The staff are friendly and efficient, and (on a warm summer's evening) the small table for two in the window is a great place to enjoy a glass or three of crisp rosé.

Peploe's

St Stephen's Green (676 3144/www.peploes.com). All cross-city buses/Luas St Stephen's Green. **Open** noon-10.30pm Mon-Sat. **Main courses** €10.50-€27.50 lunch; €13.50-€29.50 dinner. **Credit** MC, V. **Map** p251 F4 **⑩**

There is a reason – no, make that several reasons – why Peploe's is considered to be the best wine bar in town. First, it's a truly sophisticated joint, its rooms, decked out with wood, murals and crisp table linen, are patrolled by smartly kitted-out staff and resonate to the low hum of intelligent conversation and quietly swinging jazz playing somewhere in the background. It is fast the firm favourite for a fun Friday lunch – full of local heroes and business gurus – and has long been popular as a retreat for the city's cultured set to have their casual evening meals. Chef Sebastian Scheer turns out dishes like crêpe risotto with wilted rocket or loin of free-range pork with a pine nut and apricot gratin. The wine list is obviously very good and very long, and is well worth checking out, even if it's just for a glass of wine at the bar.

O'Connell Street & North Quays

Haute cuisine

Chapter One

18-19 Parnell Square (873 2266/www.chapterone restaurant.com). All cross-city buses. **Open** 12.30-2.30pm, 6-11pm Tue-Fri; 6-11pm Sat. **Main courses** €34-€38. **Set menu** €37.50 3 courses. **Credit** AmEx, DC, MC, V. **Map** p251 E1 **㊶**

The critics love it, the punters love it and so will you: a meal at Chapter One is easily the most accessible, affordable and enjoyable fine-dining experience in Dublin. The dining room is warm and tasteful, service is formal but easy-going, and the food is haute cuisine yet down to earth – plus the restaurant is located near to the Gate Theatre (*see pxxx*), which means that it also offers an excellent pre-theatre set menu. As for the cooking, it is nothing short of spectacular. A starter of sea bream might be served with caponata, pungent olive oil and a basquaise red pepper purée; among the mains, squab pigeon might get a white truffle and honey glaze, while hake and langoustine would be partnered by roast fennel, braised squid and a tomato and shellfish sauce. All followed, perhaps, by poached meringue with 'amaretto anglaise' and pistachio. Needless to say, the wine list is excellent, and the list of top-flight local meat, fish and vegetable suppliers speaks for itself. *See also p115* **Believe the hype**.

International

101 Talbot

101 Talbot Street (874 5011/www.101talbot.com). All cross-city buses/Luas Abbey Street. **Open** 5-11pm Tue-Sat. **Main courses** €14.50-€24. **Credit** AmEx, MC, V. **Map** p251 F2 **㊷**

Casual, but serious about its vegetarian customers, this long-running restaurant nourishes wise locals who pay little attention to food fads. Don't expect any razzmatazz, just straightforward, honest cooking geared to everyone from vegans to carnivores. Dishes include parsnip and sweet potato rösti, West African vegetable and peanut curry, and braised guinea fowl with roasted vegetables and Puy lentils. Chocoholics rave about the chocolate cake, while 101's proximity to theatreland also makes it an ideal spot pre- or post- performances.

Rhodes D7

The Capel Building, Mary Abbey (1-890 277 777/ 804 444/www.rhodesd7.com). All cross-city buses/ Luas Jervis. **Open** noon-10pm Tue-Sat. **Main courses** €19.50-€25.90. **Credit** AmEx, MC, V. **Map** p252 E2 **㊸**

The Spiky Haired One has put his name to this large and buzzy 250-seater, but you won't find him at the stove. This brasserie is an exercise in branding only, with Rhodes's head chef Paul Hargreaves running the operation. The menu is sensibly priced and gently appealing: salmon fishcakes with a smoked salmon, lemon and dill butter sauce; slow roast pork belly with apple, apricot, onion and sage tart tatin – that kind of thing. Expect a battalion of staff, plasma screens, a thumping piano and an outdoor terrace for smokers. Lunchtimes are busy with Ireland's finest lawyers; dinner, though, attracts large, noisy groups looking for pleasant food that won't break the bank. At the time of writing, a second outlet (Rhodes D4) was scheduled for the Boland's Mill development in Docklands.

Italian

Bar Italia

26 Blooms Lane (874 1000/www.baritalia.ie). All cross-city buses/Luas Jervis. **Open** noon-10.30pm Mon-Thur; noon-11pm Fri, Sat; 1-10pm Sun. **Main courses** €9.50-€27. **Credit** AmEx, DC MC, V. **Map** p252 E2 **㊹**

The foodies who own this Italian joint (that would be the team behind the brilliant Dunne & Crescenzi; *see p119*) seem to have the knack of giving people what they want. The little enclave surrounding the restaurant is known locally as the Italian Quarter and is fast becoming a great place to hang out for a glass of wine or a bite to eat before catching a flick

treacle bread €9.95
hrooms and fried
se €10.95
and boxty €9.95
d leaves €11.95
plate with our
rberries €13.95
d relish €12.50
t/Mount Callan

e salad €10.95
tomato chutney

toast €10.95

garlic butter and

oli €21.95
ne gravy €23.95
ard sauce €21.95
s and white

spuds and

Winding Stair. *See p114.*

Eat, Drink, Shop

or something fancier. Pasta, grilled meats and a good supply of vegetable dishes are what turn over Bar Italia's menu. It's cheap, comfortable and friendly.

Enoteca delle Langhe
24 Lower Ormond Quay (888 0834). All city buses/ Luas Jervis. **Open** noon-midnight Mon-Sat. **Main courses** €8-€19. **Credit** MC, V. **Map** p252 E2 **45**
The cuisine and wines of Piedmont (or more specifically the Langhe region of Piedmont) are at the heart of this excellent operation. If you love beautiful Italian wine, fresh, moreish cooking, and the convivial atmosphere of a group of Italian foodies doing what they love, then you should get down here. The tables and chairs are well spaced, comfortable and look reassuringly expensive. Cheese, tapenade, olives and salamis are served with plenty of bread (great to share, and cheap too). With an Italian deli, coffee shop and two more Italian restaurants in the same development, not for nothing is this area commonly known as the Italian Quarter.

Japanese

Yamamori Sushi
38 Lower Ormond Quay (872 0003/www.yama morisushi.ie). All cross-city buses/Luas Jervis. **Open** 12.15-11pm Mon-Wed, Sun; 12.15-11.30pm Thur-Sat. **Main courses** €15.95-€19.95. **Credit** AmEx, MC, V. **Map** p252 E2 **46**
A lot more spacious than it appears from its unassuming entrance, Yamamori Sushi stretches back into a light, bright atrium with a busy sushi counter and rows of packed tables waited on by efficient business-like staff. The sushi here (nigiri and norimaki) is excellent – the best in the city, in fact – but there's plenty more on offer for those who'd rather have something hot or, at the very least, cooked. Try the richly flavoured salmon teriyaki or the hearty *suki yaki* (thinly sliced marbled sirloin served in a cast-iron pan). Aside from the Kirin, saki and plum wine you might expect to see here, there's also a surprisingly full wine list.
Other locations Yamamori Noodles, 71 South Great Georges Street, Around Temple Bar (475 5001).

Modern Irish

Winding Stair
40 Lower Ormond Quay (872 7320/www.winding-stair.com). All cross-city buses/Luas Jervis. **Open** 12.30-3.30pm, 6-10.30pm daily. **Main courses** €19.50-€24.95. **Credit** MC, V. **Map** p252 E2 **47**
With its steel H-beams and darkwood floorboards, its white-painted brick walls and old service elevator, its bookshelves stacked with interesting reads and its river-facing windows, the Winding Stair looks a little bit like a Tribeca loft apartment or some arty atelier in Berlin. Hardly surprising, really, given that it's affiliated to the bookshop of the same name next door (*see p143*); but the reality is this is one of the capital's most popular restaurants, with a

reputation for putting well-sourced, high-quality ingredients to imaginatively good use. The menu is changed very regularly, if not daily, and might include starters such as own-made organic chicken and leek terrine with tomato chutney, and mains like smoked pollack poached in milk with white cheddar mash or roast neck fillet of pork with herbed white cabbage. The global wine list runs to several pages, including loads of great selections by the glass. Staff are enthusiastic about what they do, and their customers are too. *Photo p113.*

Polish

Gospoda Polska
15 Capel Street (086 6003383). All cross-city buses/ Luas Jervis. **Open** noon-10pm Mon-Thur; noon-11.30pm Fri, Sat; 12.30-10pm Sun. **Main courses** €12.90-€19.90. **Credit** MC, V. **Map** p252 E2 **49**
A welcome breath of fresh air on a stretch of Capel Street that is otherwise given over to sex shops and tatty boutiques, this smart new Polish restaurant is a cosy and quietly chic little outfit. Simple wooden furniture and discreetly patterned wallpaper are glammed up by the addition of a few chandeliers, while the menu pulls off a similar trick by offering traditional rustic grub alongside some snappier lunchtime options (paninis, salads and the like). But the predominant appeal of a place like this is the chance it offers to carb up on comfort food like 'hunting style' pork chops, potato cakes and big bowls of deliciously chunky soup, all washed down with gallons of crisp, strong lager.

Dublin Bay & the Coast

Haute cuisine

Bon Appetit
9 James Terrace, Malahide (845 0314/ www.bonappetit.ie). DART Malahide. **Open** *Restaurant* 6.30-9.30pm Tue-Thur, Sat; 12.30-2.30pm, 6.30-9.30pm Fri. *Café* 6-10.30pm Mon-Sat. **Main courses** *Restaurant* Set price €75. *Café* €21-€32. **Credit** AmEx MC, V.
The latest out-of-towner to be awarded a Michelin star, Bon Appetit is luring Dublin's gourmets away from the city centre with the promise of culinary fireworks from young Irish chef Oliver Dunne. And dishes such as boudin of duck and foie gras with celeriac purée and fresh peas or fillet of John Dory with new season asparagus, pine nuts and salted grapes have been ensuring that they do not leave disappointed. Café Bon, the high-quality bistro operation in the basement of the beautiful Georgian building (the restaurant is on the first floor) is a good bet for those who want to see what all the fuss is about without having to shell out haute cuisine prices. Here, you can expect more low-key offerings, such as grilled fillet of Irish beef with cherry tomatoes, 'Café Bon chips' and béarnaise sauce (fancy

steak and chips, in other words). But whether you're upstairs or down, the service is uniformly excellent and the wine list worthy of the bill of fare.

Modern Irish

Nosh

111 Coliemore Road, Dalkey (284 0666/ www.nosh.ie). DART Dalkey. **Open** noon-4pm, 6-10.30pm Tue-Sun. **Main courses** €10.95-€14.50. **Credit** MC, V.

A day trip to Dalkey is nice for anyone, be it locals, tourists or stargazers and celebrity stalkers. It's the Beverly Hills of Dublin. The pubs do a great trade, but for something a bit more sophisticated food-wise (but still very casual), Nosh fits nicely. It's light, bright, clean and friendly. Fish and chips, steak sandwiches and the like keep the blokes happy, while salads and pasta dishes satisfy the girls. It's consistently busy and has survived in a fickle village, where many restaurants have been and gone. When you go, you'll see why.

Believe the hype

Eat, Drink, Shop

A debate has been simmering, and occasionally boiling over, after the publication of the 2008 Michelin guide, in which Ranelagh's **Mint** restaurant (pictured; *see p116*) and Malahide's **Bon Appetit** (*see p114*) were both awarded their first stars. The cause of the controversy were claims that Mint had courted its star over the airwaves with a TV documentary (*The Pressure Cooker*) following the head chef as he battled to win a Michelin star. It was, Kevin Thornton (of **Thornton's**; *see p101*) has been quoted as saying, evidence that the revered Michelin guide has become increasingly commercial and that publicity stunts and good marketing can give new restaurateurs a leg-up to stardom. The fact that Thornton only recently lost his second Michelin star has poured a certain amount of hot fat on to what was already a lively kitchen fire. But whatever the truth of the matter, the key question

for gastro-curious visitors to the city is: should we believe the hype?

The simple answer to that question is a resounding yes. There is some truly amazing work being done on a daily basis in some of Dublin's top-end restaurants, and the fact that they have survived the fickle fortunes of gourmet dining and have gone on to become fixtures of the city's restaurant circuit is the categorical proof of the matter. Restaurants like **Patrick Guilbaud** (*see p108*) and **L'Ecrivain** (*see p108*) are the kind that people get on planes to eat at, while the city's most cherished fine-dining institution, **Chapter One** (*see p112*), continues to serve up superlative cooking at reasonable prices.

It may have taken a few internecine spats between Dublin's top toques to bring the matter to public attention but the fact remains that, hype or no hype, this is a city that is spoiled rotten with excellent eateries.

Seafood

Aqua

1 West Pier, Howth (832 0690/www.aqua.ie). DART Howth. **Open** 12.30-3pm, 5.30-9.30pm Tue-Fri; noon-3pm, 5.30-9.30pm Sat; noon-8.30pm Sun. **Main courses** €24.50-€29.50. **Credit** AmEx, MC, V.

This industrial first-floor building used to be the yacht club, although when you actually see it, you'll find it looks a lot more like a factory of sorts. But its distinctly urban appearance is softened by gorgeous sea views and a very warm, cosy bar area in front of a casual, uncluttered dining room (the venue for a great Sunday lunch complete with live jazz). On bright, sunny days, leave time for a nice stroll around the harbour; at night, it's all aglow and perfect for couples, although prices get heftier. Given the coastal location, fish is the order of the day: Dover sole on the bone, sea bass, slow-cooked organic salmon and the like. There's also meat for the carnivores and pasta for fussy kids.

Southern suburbs

French

French Paradox

53 Shelbourne Road, Ballsbridge (660 4068/ www.thefrenchparadox.com). Bus 7, 45A/DART Lansdowne. **Open** 10am-11.30pm Mon-Sat. **Main courses** €9-€36. **Set lunch** €14.50 2 courses. **Credit** AmEx, MC, V.

A wine shop, deli and almost accidental restaurant (that side of the business just evolved on its own), the adorable French Paradox is a joy to behold: lead-topped counters, orange leather banquettes and exposed brick walls make for a stylish backdrop. And to sharpen the appetite, the deli's platters of delicious Irish and French cheeses, cured meats and pâtés are everywhere you look. It's mouth-watering stuff. There's always one hot main course (a daube, stew or something similarly robust) but the way to get the most out of FP is to order several dishes, spread them out like a kind of indoor picnic and pick away. This is all about savouring, not so much with the troughing. But wine is this place's true raison d'être, and advice on that subject is plentiful (and not of the hectoring, snobby variety that one all too often encounters in sommeliers of posh restaurants). The wine-tasting evenings (every Tuesday) are great fun.

International

Itsa4 Sandymount

6A Sandymount Green, Sandymount (219 4676/www.itsabagel.com). Bus 2, 3, 18/DART Sandymount. **Open** noon-3pm, 5.30-10pm Mon-Fri; noon-3.30pm, 5.30-10pm Sat; noon-8pm Sun. **Main course** €12.50-€28. **Credit** MC, V.

Sandymount is a posh and pretty little village on the right side of town, where the locals can be a bit

demanding. And why not? They practically run the country. Itsa4 has been welcomed as a family-cum-neighbourhood restaurant serving up favourites like their chargrilled organic beef burger or the crispy skin salmon fillet in the comfortable surroundings of the dining room's booths or (in warmer weather) the garden. Organic dishes and Irish suppliers are a priority here. At night, get stuck into something a little fancier, like Indian spiced monkfish with yellow split pea dahl and coriander and cucumber yoghurt. All menus have a 'junior bites' section.

Other locations ItsaBagel, Epicurean Food Hall, Lower Liffey Street, Around O'Connell Street (874 0486).

Italian

Antica Venezia

97 Ashfield Road, Ranelagh (497 4112). Bus 11, 48/Luas Ranelagh. **Open** 5-11pm Mon-Thur, Sat, Sun; noon-2.30pm, 5-11pm Fri. **Main courses** €13-€29. **Credit** MC, V.

Good restaurants, good wine shops, good food shops: Ranelagh has become a little foodie nexus. Antica Venezia is staffed and (mainly) patronised by Italians – on some evenings, we have been completely surrounded by the sound of Italian being spoken (a welcome soundtrack to any meal). Food is predictable Italian fare (fresh antipasti, pastas aplenty – gamberoni, carbonara, amatriciana, arrabbiata, toscana, pesto, bolognese – and big pizzas) bolstered by a number of grilled meat dishes. Prices are quite reasonable, and the atmosphere makes for a romantic, if faintly kitsch, dining experience.

Modern Irish

Mint

47 Ranelagh Village, Ranelagh (497 8655/www.mint restaurant.ie). Bus 11, 11A, 18, 44, 44N, 48A, 48N/Luas Ranelagh. **Open** 6.30-10.30pm Tue, Wed, Sat; 12.30-2.30pm, 6.30-10.30pm Thur, Fri. **Main courses** €46-€48. **Set lunch** €45 2 courses, €50 3 courses. **Credit** AmEx, MC, V.

Chef Dylan McGrath's face is now a familiar sight to Dubliners, even those who haven't been lucky enough to visit this excellent fine-dining restaurant. The reason? McGrath is no stranger to RTÉ1 television channel (*see p115* **Believe the hype**) and his on-screen appearances have done a great deal to boost Mint into the media spotlight. Not, of course, that it needed the leg-up: this is the kind of cooking that speaks for itself. Sea bass, for instance, arrives with hot fennel mayonnaise and chilled fennel soup, while saddle of lamb comes with courgette flowers and pickled bell pepper. McGrath's signature dishes (foie gras with prune terrine, John Dory with Alfonso mango) are the ones everyone talks about, but everything here is good. The surroundings are very pleasant (as are the staff) and the wine list is a corker. Well worth those extra few minutes on the Luas (and that extra zero on the bill). *Photo p115.*

Cafés & Coffee Shops

Let them eat cake.

Bald Barista. *See p118.*

There was a time in the not too distant past when the average cup of coffee served up in a Dublin café would be the colour and approximate flavour of tepid dishwater. It did the job well enough – that is, it chased away the ghost of the previous night's Guinness and defibrillated the system each morning – but, as Dublin grew more prosperous and new cafés began to sprout up on every corner, doing the job was simply no longer enough. Soon everyone seemed to be powerwalking the pavements, take-out skinny latte in hand, or sitting on the terrace of some new coffee shop, sipping an espresso and munching on a muffin.

Dubliners have embraced caffeine culture like a long-lost friend. In this chapter, we have listed what we consider to be the most interesting cafés in urban Dublin. Whether it's their unique atmosphere, superior coffee or simply the fact that the staff are happy to let you linger for hours reading or chatting, Dublin's cafés provide a welcome alternative to the major chains. Order a cup of Guatemalan Maragogype, sit down and read on.

Around Temple Bar

Avoca

11-13 Suffolk Street (672 6019/www.avoca.ie). All cross city buses/Luas St Stephen's Green. **Open** 10am-5.30pm Mon-Sat; 11am-5pm Sun. **Main courses** €12-€17. **Credit** AmEx, MC, V. **Map** p252 F3 ❶

It can sometimes seem like a kind of manic pit stop for the grand prix circuit of shoppers who race through the popular Avoca store (*see p145*) in which this modern, casual café is located, but it's well worth the wait (and the jostling). Stick your elbows out and forge a path between lunching ladies and gaggles of young mums, and take your seat for a light meal of own-made soups and breads, or a more ambitious gap-filler from the ever-changing range of lovingly crafted pies and slow-cooked winter dishes. Or just have a chat, a coffee and a plate of scones with artisinal jams.

> ❶ Green numbers given in this chapter correspond to the location of each café on the street maps. *See pp250-252.*

Eat, Drink, Shop

Bald Barista

68 Aungier Street (475 8616). All cross-city buses/Luas St Stephen's Green. **Open** 6.30am-6pm daily. **Snacks** €2.50-€9.50. **Credit** MC, V. **Map** p251 E4 ❷

The barista in question is Buzz Fendall, a man on a mission to 'bring amazing coffee to Dublin'. And it is a mission that is accomplished on a daily basis at this busy, friendly café on Aungier Street. The making and serving of coffee here (which is done either by Buzz Fendall himself or by one of his personally trained protégés) is approached with a kind of gleefully pedantic zeal, and the results are sublime. Beans are sourced directly from individual farmers in carefully selected locations from around the globe (currently in Brazil, Sumatra and Ethiopia) and are freshly ground on site. Of course, there's more to the place than just coffee – snacks and more substantial dishes are on offer on the slickly appointed mezzanine dining area or on the diminutive terrace – but there's no denying the fact that the roaring takeaway trade and the permanently full house boils down to one thing and one thing only: the Bald Barista serves the best in Dublin. *Photo p117.*
Other location Avalon House, 55 Aungier Street (475 0001).

Bewley's Oriental Café

78 Grafton Street (672 7720/www.bewleys.ie). All cross-city buses/Luas St Stephen's Green. **Open** 8am-10pm Mon-Wed; 8am-11pm Thur-Sat; 9am-10pm Sun. **Main courses** €12-€16.50. **Credit** AmEx, DC, MC, V. **Map** p251 F4 ❸

It's not exactly a well-kept secret but this long-standing café on Grafton Street deserves its pole position on the tourist circuit, for its pedigree alone. Ernest Bewley first started brewing coffee and baking sticky buns for Dubliners over a century ago, when he opened the first of his Oriental Cafés. This flagship café opened its doors in 1927 and has since gone through many hands; it's now the only remaining café bearing the Bewley's name, and worth visiting – even if only to breakfast by the beauty of the original Harry Clarke windows on the ground floor.

Bite of Life

55 Patrick Street (454 2949). All cross-city buses/Luas St Stephen's Green. **Open** 8am-6pm Mon-Sat; 9am-5pm Sun. **Snacks** €3.80-€4.50. **No credit cards.** **Map** p250 D4 ❹

On the corner of Patrick Street and Bull Alley, this sunny yellow-painted café serves the strollers and lunchtime sun-seekers of St Patrick's Park (opposite) and the phalanxes of tourists headed for the cathedral itself (a couple of hundred metres away). There's not a great deal of room to sit down (just a small cluster of tables by the door), which means most people come to grab a doorstep ciabatta sandwich or an organic multi-grain toastie to eat in the park. Juices, smoothies, decent coffees and own-made cakes are added bonuses.

Brick Alley Café

25 East Essex Street, Temple Bar (679 3393). All cross-city buses/Luas Jervis. **Open** 9am-10.30pm Mon-Wed; 9am-11pm Thur, Fri; 9am-midnight Sat; 10am-10pm Sun. **Main courses** €5.95-€8. **No credit cards.** **Map** p252 E3 ❺

Only the name has changed at this delightful café (formerly the Joy of Coffee), which will come as a relief to its many loyal fans. Small and often crowded, the Brick Alley seats are still a little on the bum-numbing side but a tasty menu and the seriously excellent coffee more than make up for it. The food (which the owner describes as 'traditional', meaning lots of sarnies, and a few specials like Irish stew or lasagne) is good and filling.

Butler's Chocolate Café

24 Wicklow Street (671 0591/www.butlers chocolates.com). All cross-city buses/Luas St Stephen's Green. **Open** 8am-7.30pm Mon-Wed; 8am-9pm Thur, Fri; 9am-7.30pm Sat; 11am-7pm Sun. **Snacks** €1.80-€3.50. **Credit** AmEx, MC, V. **Map** p252 F3 ❻

Butler's credo (that 'chocolate could make the world a nicer place') is perhaps not as far-fetched as all that – at least, that tends to be our verdict each time we visit this sweet little branch on Wicklow Street of the city-wide chain. As the name suggests, this isn't simply a place to have coffee in. Alongside its excellent choice of coffee and superior cocoa, there's a luxurious range of handmade chocolates. Sadly, the sparse seating arrangement means Butler's is better suited to a quick pit stop than a long stay – however much you'd like to linger.
Other locations throughout the city.

The best Cafés

For Italophiles
Café Cagliostro (*see p122*); Carluccio's (*see p119*); Dunne & Crescenzi (*see p119*).

For something spicy
Govinda's (*see p119*); Silk Road (*see p121*).

For superior coffee
Bald Barista (*see above*); Dunne & Crescenzi (*see p119*); Léon (*see p121*).

For sweet treats
Butler's Chocolate Café (*see right*); Cake Café (*see p122*); Queen of Tarts (*see p121*).

For weary sightseers
Bite of Life (*see p118*); Gallery Café (*see p122*); Hugh Lane Café (*see p122*).

Carluccio's

*52 Dawson Street (633 3957/www.carluccios.com).
All cross-city buses/Luas St Stephen's Green.* **Open**
7am-10pm Mon-Fri; 8am-10.30pm Sat; 9am-10pm
Sun. **Main courses** €7.25-€16.50. **Credit** AmEx,
MC, V. **Map** p252 F4 ⑦

The Carluccio's formula is probably well-known to
most lovers of good-quality and affordably priced
regional Italian food, so it needs little introduction,
other than to say that this, the first branch to open
outside of England, is an absolute corker. A small but
perfectly stocked deli (*see p150*) acts as a foyer to the
smart two-tier café (OK, fine, *caffè*), where you'll find
everything from richly seductive coffee and all manner of cakes and breads to full-blown pasta dishes
(tortellini filled with braised venison, say), Italian
main courses (chargrilled lamb chops with peppers
or maybe *fegato e patate*) and various specials. Wines,
cans of San Pellegrino juice drinks and beers are on
standby to wash it all down.

Dunne & Crescenzi

*14-16 Frederick Street South (671 9135/
www.dunneandcrescenzi.com). All cross-city buses/
Luas St Stephen's Green.* **Open** 7.30am-11pm Mon-
Sat; 10am-10pm Sun. **Main courses** €9-€21.50.
Credit MC, V. **Map** p251 F4 ⑧

Despite the arrival of the much-discussed Carluccio's
(*see above*), D & C is the probably still the best Italian
café in town. Or, more accurately, Italian cafés – for

it actually occupies two adjoining spaces on this
street. Both are small, dark and crowded, and on a
busy day (which is every day), they can feel a touch
on the claustrophobic side. But the food is truly wonderful: the tasty, fresh and simple lunches include
cured and smoked meats, salads and panini; there's
also a full wine list and, of course, superlative coffee.
Other location 11 Seafort Avenue, Sandymount,
Dublin 4 (667 3252).

Govinda's

*4 Aungier Street (475 0309) All cross-city buses/
Luas St Stephen's Green.* **Open** noon-9pm Mon-Sat.
Main courses €6.95, €10.45. **Credit** AmEx, MC, V.
Map p252 E4 ⑨

Run by the Dublin Hare Krishna branch, this neat
little vegetarian café is actually a lot more fun than
it sounds, thanks to its upbeat, humorous staff and
the tasty spread at the buffet (choose from two sizes
of plate depending on how hungry you are). Even
if you're not a veggie, you'd be hard pressed not to
be tempted by the rich dahl, tasty samosas and
crunchy salads.
Other locations: 83 Middle Abbey Street,
Around O'Connell Street (no phone); 18 Merrion
Row, Around St Stephen's Green (661 5095).

Lemon Crêpe & Coffee Company

*60 Dawson Street (672 8898/www.lemonco.com).
All cross-city buses/Luas St Stephen's Green.*

Fashionable, fresh food for the health-conscious at **Nude**. *See p121.*

Open 8am-7.30pm Mon-Wed, Fri; 8am-9pm Thur; 9am-7.30pm Sat; 10am-6.30pm Sun. **Snacks** €5-€10. **No credit cards**. **Map** p252 F4 ⑩
With its zesty yellow walls and citrus-burst mural, Lemon certainly lives up to its name, and amid the tyranny of ciabatta and panini, a café specialising in crêpes comes as a welcome relief. Tasty sweet and savoury pancake-based snacks hit the spot (the Nutella, ice-cream and strawberry combination is heaven on a plate), and if you really want a sandwich or an omelette, they can do that too. The café is small and usually crowded, so you might prefer a table outside: a good spot for a very tasty morning coffee (made with 100 per cent Arabica beans).
Other location 66 William Street South (672 9044).

Léon
33 Exchequer Street (670 7238/www.cafeleon.ie).
All cross-city buses/Luas St Stephen's Green/
Jervis. **Open** 8am-10pm Mon-Wed, Thur; 8am-11pm Fri, Sat; 10am-10pm Sun. **Credit** MC, V. **Map** p252 F3 ⑪
Part of a trinity of excellent cafés in Temple Bar, this branch of Léon has a particularly charming old-world atmosphere (parquet flooring, mismatched dining room chairs, huge chandelier) and is a popular spot for an unhurried breakfast of first-class coffee and heavenly pastries (which are something of a Léon speciality). After noon a more elaborate menu of French bistro classic kicks in, but we prefer to come here first thing and scan the newspaper, coffee in hand, and enjoy the buzz of Dublin's own version of Left Bank café society.
Other locations 14 Trinity Street, Around Temple Bar (677 1060); 17 Wicklow Street, Around Temple Bar (671 7331).

La Maison des Gourmets
15 Castle Market (672 7258). All cross-city buses.
Open 8am-7pm Mon-Fri; 8am-6pm Sat; 11am-5pm Sun. **Main courses** €10-€14. **Credit** AmEx, MC, V. **Map** p252 F3 ⑫
This charming French pâtisserie (above an excellent bakery of the same name) is stylishly decorated in a palette of off-white and cool grey, and is the perfect environment in which to tuck into some sophisticated snacks (french toast with bacon for breakfast, savoury tarts for lunch, and cakes all day long). Service is authentically Parisian (in the sense that it can sometimes be slow and less than charming), but with pastries and coffee that taste this good, you'd be surprised how tolerant you can be.

Nude
21 Suffolk Street (677 4804/www.nude.ie). All cross-city buses/Luas St Stephen's Green. **Open** 7.30am-9pm Mon-Wed; 7.30am-10pm Thur; 8am-9pm Sat; 9am-8pm Sun. **Snacks** €5.50-€7.50. **Credit** AmEx, MC, V. **Map** p252 F3 ⑬
The glass roof and the wood-clad walls create an appropriately outdoorsy vibe for this busy and convenient outlet of the virtuous Dublin chain. Nude specialises in food that manages to pull off the not inconsiderable coup of tasting good while actually

doing you some good. Freshly squeezed juices of all varieties, paninis, superbly hearty 'bread bowl stews', wraps, and, of course, salads (the chick pea and chilli is a good one) are all in evidence – as is a small selection of snacks and sweets for unrepentant sinners. The long, canteen-style tables and hard benches may be stretching the ascetic thing a little too far for some, but if you want some quick vitamins, and you're prepared to pay a little extra for top-quality ingredients, then you'll love this joint.
Photo p119.
Other locations throughout the city.

Queen of Tarts
4 Cork Hill, Dame Street (670 7499). All cross-city buses. **Open** 7.30am-7pm Mon-Fri; 9am-7pm Sat, Sun. **Main courses** €5.75-€9.95. **No credit cards**. **Map** p252 E3 ⑭
The Queen of Tarts has recently extended its sovereignty with a large new branch just around the corner, no doubt to cope with the overflow of loyal Dubliners and tourists in the know who come in search of their daily fix of terrific grub. Breakfasts might be potato cakes or scones with raspberries or mixed fruit; the lunchtime savoury tarts are light, flaky and delicious. Everything is baked on the Cork Hill premises. For most people, though, the real glory is the wide range of cakes, crumbles, brownies and meringues.
Other locations 3 Cow Lane, Around Temple Bar (633 4681).

Silk Road
Chester Beatty Library, Dublin Castle (407 0750/ www.cbl.ie). All cross-city buses/Luas Jervis. **Open** *May-Sept* 10am-5pm Mon-Fri; 11am-5pm Sat; 1-5pm Sun. *Oct-Apr* 10am-5pm Tue-Fri; 11am-5pm Sat; 1-5pm Sun. **Main courses** €9.75-€12.50. **Credit** AmEx, MC, V. **Map** p252 E3 ⑮
Silk Road is set inside the fabulous Chester Beatty Library (*see p62*), and carries the museum's Eastern and Islamic theme into its menu. Come here for spice and heat, or the excellent range coriander-flecked salads, as well as for tall glasses of mint tea and honey-soaked baklava. The place tends to be pleasantly tranquil; nab a table beside the long, gleaming pool in the museum's atrium, and relax.

Simon's Place
George's Street Arcade, South Great George's Street (679 7821). All cross-city buses/Luas St Stephen's Green. **Open** 8.30am-5pm Mon-Sat. **Snacks** €3.90-€4.90. **No credit cards**. **Map** p252 E3 ⑯
There's a lot to be said for unpretentious local caffs (particularly in a city that has more than its fair share of foodie hype) and Simon's is just such a place. Great own-made soups, good coffee, vast sarnies, fresh and tasty salads and a casual vibe are the trademarks of this perennially popular joint. The layout is a little chaotic but the atmosphere is warm and busy. If you want to find out what's going on around town, this is the place to come to: there are fliers and posters everywhere. Get here late morning to sample the sublime cinnamon buns.

Around St Stephen's Green

Cake Café
Daintree Stationers, Pleasants Place (478 9394/ www.thecakecafe.ie). **Open** 8am-8pm Mon-Fri; 10am-6pm Sat. **Main courses** €6.50-€12.50. **Credit** MC, V. **Map** p251 E5 ⑰

In a concealed courtyard sandwiched between Pleasant's Place and the back of Daintree stationery shop on Lower Camden Street, this adorable new venture has already won itself a loyal following. Inside, it looks a little like a 1950s kitchen (in a good, Cath Kidston kind of way), while the terrace is an altogether funkier affair, with little eaves covered by murals and weird and wonderful designs, all overhung by a homemade scaffold of thick bamboo poles. But, whether you're inside or out, the food is the same consisting of the eponymous cakes (all own-made, all delicious), as well as biscuits, pies and cupcakes, a number of sandwiches, great salads (caramelised pear, blue cheese and walnut, say) and some more ambitious hot dishes. Everything is served on artfully mismatched crockery and the staff are delightful. A hidden treasure.

Gallery Café
National Gallery of Ireland, Merrion Square West (663 3500). All cross-city buses/Luas St Stephen's Green. **Open** 9.30am-5pm Mon-Wed, Fri, Sat; 9.30am-8pm Thur; noon-5pm Sun. **Snacks** €3-€7.50. **Credit** AmEx, DC, MC, V. **Map** p251 G4 ⑱

The National Gallery's Millennium Wing houses this bright, white, funkily furnished café, whose con-

Cake Café.

stant through-traffic of arty tourists gives it a pleasingly international vibe. There's nothing too filling on offer here, just coffee, tea, scones and snacks.

Around O'Connell Street

Café Cagliostro
Bloom's Lane, 24 Ormond Quay Lower (888 0860). All cross-city buses/Luas Jervis. **Open** 7am-5.30pm Mon-Fri; 8am-5.30pm Sat; 9am-5pm Sun. **Snacks** €4.50-€7. **Credit** MC, V. **Map** p252 E2 ⑲

Tiny and fabulous, Café Cagliostro is one of the main tenants in the Bloom's Lane courtyard, just off the quays. It features plain, stylish furniture and offers excellent coffee and hot chocolate, as well as a chaste but tasty selection of Italian sandwiches and desserts.

Cobalt Café
16 North Great George's Street (873 0313). All cross-city buses. **Open** 10.30am-4pm Mon-Fri. **Snacks** €4-€9.20. **Credit** MC, V. **Map** p251 F1 ⑳

Housed in a lovingly restored Georgian house, this handsome place is popular with local arty types and office workers. There is no kitchen on site so cakes, sandwiches and soups are bought in but are no less tasty for it. When it is not operating as a café, the Cobalt also hosts drama, music and small-scale performances (usually in a fairly minimal setting – there is no actual stage, chairs and tables are just cleared away to make room), which makes it a great place to catch people trying out new material. Performances tend to be on the weekends – ask staff for details.

Hugh Lane Café
Hugh Lane Gallery, Parnell Square North (222 5550/ www.hughlane.ie). All cross-city buses/Luas Abbey Street. **Open** 10am-6pm Tue-Thur; 10am-5pm Fri, Sat; 11am-5pm Sun. **Main courses** €7.75-€14. **Credit** MC, V. **Map** p251 E1 ㉑

It may be squirreled away in the basement of the excellent Hugh Lane Gallery (*see p82*) but this popular café is saved from pokiness by windows looking out on to an enclosed courtyard (complete with water feature) and by its breezy interior of light wood floors and smart white-painted walls. Local office workers and gallery-goers take time out here for coffee, cake, plates of good-quality antipasta, quiches and salads. A compact lunch menu is chalked up on the blackboard and there are also a few decent wines to choose from, if you're planning to make a meal of it.

Panem
21 Ormond Quay Lower (872 8510). All cross-city buses/Luas Jervis. **Open** 9am-5pm Mon-Sat. **Snacks** €2.40-€4.50. **No credit cards. Map** p252 E2 ㉒

It may be small but this superb café puts a lot of thought and effort into what it does. Hearty granola, moreish muffins and fresh croissants acompany excellent coffee at breakfast, while lunch dishes range from tasty foccacia sarnies and good soups to savoury pasties and a couple of daily pasta dishes. And it's all served up in a fun, stylish space overlooking the river.

Pubs & Bars

It's not all pint-sized, you know.

It's hard to think of another city in the world as synonymous with its pubs and watering holes as Dublin. The St James Gate brewery (despite its imminent downsizing) remains famous the world over, and visiting dignitaries and divas, even if they know nothing else about Ireland, can always be relied upon to pose for the press with a glass of Guinness in their hands.

Dublin writer Brendan Behan called himself 'a drinker with a writing problem'. Oscar Wilde, once a resident of Merrion Square, reckoned 'work is the curse of the drinking classes'. And, on one occasion, Tipperary-born actor Richard Harris claimed to have formed a group called Alcoholics Unanimous. 'If you don't feel like a drink' he explained, 'you ring another member and he comes over to persuade you'.

Yes, when it comes to the Irish and drinking, this is the city that launched a thousand quips. It should come as no surprise then to learn that Dublin has no shortage of bars, superpubs, dingy boozers and dives in which to pass the time of day, or just to wait for the next break in the rain. The decade-long party of the Celtic Tiger years may be over, but recession is grist for the mill for Irish barflies. If you happen to find yourself in a traditional music session, in fact, you'll find that economic hardship provides the subject matter for 90 per cent of Irish drinking songs!

WHERE TO DRINK

If what you're looking for is a pub with a bit of craic, you almost cannot go wrong. Any part of town will do. But here are a few pointers to get you started: the streets surrounding Grafton Street and Dawson Street are where Dublin's more fashion-conscious drinkers like to rest their Prada bags and sip Cosmopolitans. South from George's Street to Wexford Street and on to Camden Street there are dozens of bars popular with a younger, hipper crowd. Temple Bar at night is almost strictly the preserve of boorish British hen and stag parties (Americans: think 'frat party'), while the joints around Trinity College attracts middle-aged tourists by the busload. But there are countless exceptions to every one of these rules, so we suggest you pick a bar from our list that sounds like your kind of place and go there, regardless of where it happens to be located. And, once you've found it, take a moment to raise a glass to Brendan. That Irishman really could drink.

Around Trinity College

Ginger Man
40 Fenian Street (676 6388). All cross-city buses.
Open 11am-12.30am Mon-Thur; 11am-1.30am Fri, Sat; 5-11pm Sun. **Credit** MC, V. **Map** p251 H4 **❶**
This small, old-fashioned pub is just round the corner from Merrion Square, and great for a pint or two after a jaunt around the museums. The regular pub quizzes are good fun, the atmosphere is always relaxed – and you can dine until 9pm if you choose.

McDaid's
3 Harry Street, off Grafton Street (679 4395). All cross-city buses/Luas St Stephen's Green.
Open 10.30am-11.30pm Mon-Thur; 10.30am-12.30am Fri, Sat; 12.30-11pm Sun. **No credit cards. Map** p252 F4 **❷**
Popularly known as the Brendan Behan bar, McDaid's was once a haunt of the literary avant-garde, but is now more likely to be packed out with bus loads of people in search of a 'real' Dublin pub. It can get seriously busy on a Saturday night, when the Guinness fans jostle for space in the compact main bar.

Messrs Maguire
1-2 Burgh Quay (670 5777/www.messrsmaguire.ie). All cross-city buses/Luas Abbey Street. **Open** 10.30am-12.30am Mon, Tue; 10.30am-1.30am Wed; 10.30am-2am Thur; 10.30am-2.30am Fri, Sat; noon-midnight Sun. **Credit** AmEx, MC, V. **Map** p252 F2 **❸**
This quayside spot tries really hard, but never quite seems to get there. Downstairs has dark flooring, wood stools and affable barmen, while upstairs there's more ambience – despite the fact that it's obviously going for an old-school vibe. Still, it has its own microbrewery, so if you're tiring of the black stuff, you know where to make for.

Mulligan's
8 Poolbeg Street (677 5582/www.mulligans.ie). DART Tara Street. **Open** 10.30am-11.30pm Mon-Thur; 10.30am-12.30am Fri, Sat; 12.30-11pm Sun. **Credit** MC, V. **Map** p252 G2 **❹**
This legendary Dublin boozer really comes into its own on a Sunday afternoon, when you can sit back and watch the Guinness settle. Mulligan's on Poolbeg Street first opened its doors in 1782, and the tobacco-stained ceilings, glassy-eyed octogenarians

> **❶** Pink numbers given in this chapter correspond to the location of each pub and bar on the street maps. *See pp250-252.*

Eat, Drink, Shop

and a no-mobiles policy mean it retains authenticity and is gloriously unpretentious. Things get seriously packed on weekday evenings as workers from nearby offices flood in for their daily jar.

O'Neill's
37 Pearse Street (671 4074). DART Pearse.
Open noon-11.30pm Mon-Thur; noon-12.30am Fri, Sat. **Credit** AmEx, MC, V. **Map** p251 G3 **❺**
Pearse Street can feel a little quiet and desolate at night, but O'Neill's is one good reason to venture down this way. It's only a few minutes from College Green (but still well away from the crowds) and it's a fine bar in general, with lots of separate rooms and big glowing fires. The ventilation could be better. Gaggles of besuited folk drink here, but don't be put off: there are plenty of seats for all – and good pub grub too.

Around Temple Bar

AKA
6 Wicklow Street (670 4220). All cross-city buses/ Luas St Stephen's Green. **Open** 3pm-1am Mon-Thur; 3pm-2.30am Fri, Sat. **Credit** MC, V. **Map** p252 F3 **❻**
With a curious beehive motif informing its interior design, and space age taps to be negotiated in the bathroom, this subterranean bar remains weak on atmosphere and strong on loud music and expensive drinks – and seems to be past its prime. Still, it's a reasonably stylish place in which to down a pre-club cocktail or post-prandial bevvie.

Auld Dubliner
24 Anglesea Street (677 0527/www.thesmith group.ie). All cross-city buses/Luas Jervis. **Open** 10.30am-11.30pm Mon-Thur; 10.30am-12.30am Fri, Sat; 12.30-11pm Sun. **Credit** AmEx, MC, V. **Map** p252 F3 **❼**
If you're up for a laugh and a sing-song, and you're happy to drink with dewy-eyed tourists enthusing about the traditional music being played onstage, this place, smack-bang in the heart of Temple Bar,

is for you. There are bands playing traditional music upstairs, decent pints at the bar and coddle (a traditional Dublin sausage, bacon and potato stew) on the lunch menu. It can get very packed at the weekends.

Bailey
2 Duke Street (670 4939). All cross-city buses/Luas St Stephen's Green. **Open** noon-11.30pm Mon-Thur, Sun; noon-12.30pm Fri, Sat. **Credit** AmEx, MC, V. **Map** p252 F3 **❽**
Aching to be hip and thoroughly self-conscious, this is not the original Bailey of lore. Before it was torn down years back, the old Bailey featured in James Joyce's *Ulysses* (Leopold Bloom lived at 7 Eccles Street, which used to be one of the entrances to the bar) and was a vital organ in Dublin's literary life. Today, the new Bailey has decor and drinks prices in step with the chic clientele; the outdoor seating area is a great spot at which to while away an afternoon watching Dubliners on the move. Bring a well-stuffed wallet.

Ba Mizu
Powerscourt Townhouse Centre, 59 William Street South (674 6712/www.bamizu.com). All cross-city buses. **Open** noon-11.30pm Mon-Wed; noon-2.30am Thur-Sat; 12.30-11pm Sun. **Credit** MC, V. **Map** p252 F3 **❾**
Richly decorated in dark wood and some decidedly odd art, Ba Mizu is one of Dublin's better upscale watering holes. Subdued lighting and plush leather armchairs make the lobby bar perfect for a nocturnal rendezvous, while the back bar offers brighter and busier surroundings. Take a look underfoot and you'll notice there's a river running through the bar.

The best Bars

For boozing
Mulligans. *See p123.*

For celeb spotting
Kavanagh's. *See p137.*

For hipsters and hedonists
Octagon Bar. *See p130.*

For scoffing and quaffing
Southwilliam. *See p132.*

For trad music
Cobblestone. *See p136.*

Liquor up in **Davy Byrnes** for its literary connections. *See p127.*

Bank

20-22 College Green (677 0677/www.bankoncollege green.com). All cross-city buses. **Open** 10.30am-midnight Mon-Wed; 10.30am-1am Thur; 9.30am-1.30am Fri, Sat; 9.30pm-midnight Sun. **Credit** AmEx, DC, MC, V. **Map** p252 F3 ⑩

No prizes for guessing what type of business was once conducted on this premises. The central bar dominates the spacious lounge and professional types sprawl on the surrounding seating area. The design is tacky and the office party atmosphere means it won't be to everyone's taste.

Brazen Head

20 Bridge Street Lower (679 5186/www.brazenhead. com). Bus 21, 21A/Luas The Four Courts. **Open** 10.30am-12.30am Mon-Sat; 12.30pm-12.30am Sun. **Credit** DC, MC, V. **Map** p250 C3 ⑪

The Brazen Head claims to be Ireland's oldest pub (it's not) but it's been in operation since 1198 and the rebel Robert Emmett planned an uprising here in 1802. Today it offers trad music, real fires and the tastiest warm bar nuts in the country. Thinking positively, the high quota of tourists adds to its 'good time' atmosphere.

Bruxelles

7-8 Harry Street, off Grafton Street (677 5362). All cross-city buses/Luas St Stephen's Green. **Open** 10.30am-1.30am Mon-Wed; 10.30am-2.30am Thur-Sat; noon-1.30am Sun. **No credit cards. Map** p252 F4 ⑫

Bruxelles is one of those Dublin institutions that somehow manages to appeal to almost every punter – hairy, heavy metal fans, indie kids in skinny jeans, old codgers, students and tourists. The rockers and mods bars downstairs play a weird mix of tunes; upstairs is for those who just fancy a good pint and a chat. Although it needs a lick of paint, the place has pots of charm – and a useful outside seating area.

Café en Seine

40 Dawson Street (677 4567/www.capitalbars.com). All cross-city buses/Luas St Stephen's Green. **Open** 11am-2.30am daily. **Credit** AmEx, MC, V. **Map** p252 F4 ⑬

One of Dublin's first superpubs, Café en Seine has a decadent art deco theme reminiscent of 19th-century Paris. It's big enough to get lost in, so overcrowding is never a problem. The place is an after-work favourite among Dawson Street professionals, and is rumoured to have had the most expensive refurbishment in Dublin, which might explain the sky-high cost of a drink.

Cocoon

Royal Hibernian Way, off Grafton Street (679 6259/ www.cocoon.ie). All cross-city buses/Luas St Stephen's Green. **Open** 11.30am-2.30am Mon, Thur, Fri, Sat; 11.30am-11.30pm Tue, Wed; 4-11.30pm Sun. **Credit** MC, V. **Map** p252 F4 ⑭

Owned by Ireland's 'man-about-town' Eddie Irvine, Cocoon walks a fine line between stylish and tacky. TV screens tuned to music videos and fashion television hang on the walls while expensively-dressed clientele adorn the plush couches, availing of the free Wi-Fi and high-priced drinks. Worth stopping by for an early evening cocktail and a peek at post-Celtic Tiger Dublin in action.

Eat, Drink, Shop

Dakota

9 William Street South (672 7696/www.dakota bar.ie). All cross-city buses/Luas St Stephen's Green. **Open** noon-11.30pm Mon-Wed, Sun; noon-2am Thur; noon-2.30am Fri, Sat. **Credit** AmEx, MC, V. **Map** p252 F3 ⓯

Dimmed lighting and half-moon leather booths make Dakota one of Dublin's coolest and (predictably) busiest late-night bars. The long bar ensures you're never waiting too long for a drink, although it can get a bit hectic at the weekend. It's a great place for a sociable drink with friends (try to grab one of those booths) and reliably quiet during the day, with a cool warehouse feel. It also does excellent mixed platters of finger food – ideal for soakage if you're planning on making a night of it.

Davy Byrnes

21 Duke Street (677 5217/www.davybyrnes.com). All cross-city buses/Luas St Stephen's Green. **Open** 11am-11.30pm Mon-Wed; 11am-12.30am Thur, Fri; 10.30am-12.30am Sat; 12.30am-11pm Sun. **Credit** AmEx, MC, V. **Map** p252 F4 ⓰

In *Ulysses*, Leopold Bloom stops here for a gorgonzola sandwich and a glass of burgundy. 'He raised his eyes and met the stare of a bilious clock. Two. Pub clock five minutes fast. Time going on. Hands moving. Two. Not yet.' The clock is said to be kept at five minutes fast and the bar is now a regular for well-dressed Dubliners. Seating can be scarce, and the place is better suited to conversation than raucous revelry. The food – more fish and chips than gorgonzola and burgundy – is quite good, and not overly expensive. *Photo pp124-125.*

Dawson Lounge

25 Dawson Street (671 0311/www.dawsonlounge.ie). All cross-city buses/Luas St Stephen's Green. **Open** 12.30-11.30pm Mon-Thur; 12.30pm-12.30am Fri, Sat; 4-11pm Sun. **Credit** AmEx, MC, V. **Map** p251 F4 ⓱

A tiny downstairs bar at the bottom of a corkscrew staircase, the Dawson Lounge markets itself as the smallest bar in Dublin. Unsurprisingly, it's cosy in winter and summer. If you're at all claustrophobic, stay at street level; otherwise, climb down (and be careful negotiating the stairs on the way back up).

Dragon

64 South Great George's Street (478 1590/ www.capitalbars.com). All cross-city buses. **Open** 5-11.30pm Mon-Wed; 5pm-2.30am Thur-Sat; 5-11pm Sun. **Credit** AmEx, MC, V. **Map** p252 E3 ⓲

From the street, this mostly gay bar looks small, but get inside the former bank building and you'll find that it stretches back and back. Expect cool young things drinking bottled beer, Japanese prints, enormous fish tanks and pale wood aplenty. A great venue if there's a gang of you.

Duke

9 Duke Street (679 9553). All cross-city buses/Luas St Stephen's Green. **Open** 11am-11.30pm Mon-Thur; 11.30pm-12.30am Fri, Sat; noon-11pm Sun. **Credit** AmEx, MC, V. **Map** p252 F3 ⓳

If you feel daunted by the prospect of the hyper-trendy pubs nearby, the Duke offers something less pretentious. There's plenty of room on its two floors, the drinks are reasonable and the carvery lunch is one of the best in town.

Farrington's

27-29 Essex Street East (671 5135/www.thesmith group.ie). All cross-city buses/Luas Jervis. **Open** 10.30am-11.30pm Mon-Thur; 10.30am-12.30am Fri, Sat; noon-11pm Sun. **Credit** MC, V. **Map** p252 E3 ⓴

You get two bars for the price of one here. On the ground floor, thick wooden ledges, ornate mirrors and darkly lit spaces provide an idea of what an old Irish pub must have looked like; take the stairs and it's as if Habitat's chief designer had been let loose with an unlimited budget. Despite its location in Temple Bar, Farrington's tends to be quieter than its neighbours – though you'll still get the ubiquitous Temple Bar hen-night pub crawlers popping in, along with inquisitive tourists.

Foggy Dew

1 Fownes Street Upper (677 9328). All cross-city buses/Luas Jervis. **Open** noon-11.30pm Mon, Tue; 11am-12.30am Wed; 11am-1am Thur; 11am-2am Fri, Sat; 1pm-1am Sun. **No credit cards.** **Map** p252 E3 ㉑

Sitting adjacent to the looming Central Bank and named after an old Irish ballad, this is one of the rare pubs in Temple Bar that draws a healthy mix of tourists and Dubliners. Indeed, since its refurbishment, it has attracted in the same jokers who once dubbed it the 'Dodgy Few'. You'll hear the best of Irish and international alternative music playing throughout the night. Get here early and lay claim to one of the charming snugs.

4 Dame Lane

4 Dame Lane (679 0291/www.8sws.com). All cross-city buses/Luas St Stephen's Green. **Open** 5pm-2.30am Mon-Sat; 5pm-1am Sun. **Credit** AmEx, MC, V. **Map** p252 F3 ㉒

Though no longer as popular as when it first opened late in 2000, the two-floor 4 Dame Lane still brings plenty of people to its brazier-flanked doors. Though, with its cavernous interior, it can seem to lack atmosphere on quieter evenings. The eclectic mix of music and minimalist surroundings pulls a bohemian crowd as does the fact that there is no entry charge after midnight.

Front Lounge

33-34 Parliament Street (670 4112). All cross-city buses. **Open** noon-11.30pm Mon, Wed, Thur; noon-1am Fri; 3pm-2am Sat; 3-11.30pm Sun. **Credit** MC, V. **Map** p252 E3 ㉓

A comfortable distance from the madding crowd of Temple Bar, the Front Lounge offers a relaxed atmosphere for refined drinking: velvet couches, black marble tables and lots of beautiful people. The Back Lounge to the rear is a gay fave; check out the karaoke on Monday nights, Dublin's top camp event.

Eat, Drink, Shop

Oirish Original

Back in the mid-1990s, this writer hitched a lift in the west of Ireland from a young man in a shiny black Mercedes. His business, he said, was to rummage around the attics and outhouses of rural Ireland and retrieve whatever old junk he could find: old bicycles, obsolete household utensils and even discarded road signs. The assorted bric-a-brac thus collected was sold on for large sums to decorate the burgeoning ranks of Irish-themed pubs in Britain and across continental Europe. Rarely did the owners demand much money for the purchase of these items. In fact, many would offer him money for the trouble of removing them.

The business was such money-spinner, he predicted, that soon Ireland would be devoid of such junk and the industry would have to begin manufacturing these 'antiques' for itself. It sounded rather far-fetched at the time, but that is exactly what happened. Today the Irish pub brand is recognised n every corner of the world. But the authenticity of these places, and of the 'Irish' paraphernalia on their walls, is usually questionable at best. This writer once visited an Irish bar in a Quechuan village in Peru, where no one spoke English and the Irish-themed literature adorning the walls was written entirely in French!

What a lot of tourists probably don't realise, however, is that many of the 'traditional' Dublin boozers in which they'll be sampling the 'craic' will be as bogus as the word 'craic' itself. (The word 'crack' is actually a Hibernian derivation of the English word 'wisecrack'.

The Oirish spelling 'craic' was invented by the tourist industry sometime in the early 1990s.)

During the 1970s and '80s many pubs chose to redecorate and modernise their furnishings. When an influx of tourists subsequently arrived, expecting to sample some authentic Irish pub atmosphere, these premises elected to revert to the older style. To ensure the tourists got what they were expecting, the pub owners turned to the same companies who fitted out Irish pubs abroad.

One of the most egregious examples of this phenomenon is the Lotts pub on Liffey Street. It boasts all of the distinctive old touches you'd expect from a traditional Dublin pub, right down to the old legend 'Licensed to Sell Wine and Spirits' etched into the glass above the door. But, despite its appearance, The Lotts is not a faded relic of old Dublin. In fact, it only opened for business for the first time within the last decade.

Fear not though. There are still a great many authentic pubs for the discerning tourist to visit: among them **Toner's** (139 Baggot Street Lower), the **Cobblestone** (77 King Street North), the **Gravediggers** (1 Prospect Square), **Kehoes** (9 South Anne Street; *pictured*), and **Mulligans** (8 Poolbeg Street). But even if you've just ducked into a dusty old man's pub to avoid the latest shower, there is a failsafe test to determine whether this bar the real deal or not: the wallpaper. Genuine old time Dublin boozers have painted-over wallpaper on their walls. Pubs that are kitted out to look like genuine old time Dublin boozers, but aren't, don't. It's that simple.

Kehoe's.

Eat, Drink, Shop

Grogan's Castle Lounge

15 William Street South (677 9320). All cross-city buses/Luas St Stephen's Green. **Open** 10.30am-11.30pm Mon-Thur; 10.30am-12.30am Fri, Sat; 12.30-11pm Sun. **No credit cards. Map** p252 F3 ㉔ Grogan's has a relaxed, shabby charm, great Guinness and tasty toasted sandwiches: three good reasons for its customers – old regulars and a number of more youthful rogues – to drop in. It's the perfect bolt-hole in which to escape the hustle and bustle of Grafton Street. The sometimes bizarre artworks on the walls are for sale, often put there by punters. A Dublin drinking institution.

Hairy Lemon

42 Lower Stephen Street (671 8949). All cross-city buses/Luas St Stephen's Green. **Open** 10.30am-11.30pm Mon-Thur; 10.30am-12.30pm Fri, Sat; 12.30-11pm Sun. **Credit** MC, V. **Map** p252 E4 ㉕ While the decor in the older front bar may seem a little quirky, don't be put off spending an evening in this great little pub. The Lemon's popular any time of the week, and it can be hard to find a seat; but if you do, you're in for a fun night out. Incidentally, this is where Michael Flatley and the cast of Riverdance came to unwind during rehearsals for its first performance at Eurovision 1994.

Hogan's

35 South Great George's Street (677 5904). Bus 12, 16, 16A/Luas St Stephen's Green. **Open** 1pm-11.30am Mon-Wed; 1pm-1am Thur; 1pm-2.30am Fri, Sat; 4-11pm Sun. **No credit cards. Map** p252 E4 ㉖ Despite first impressions, this isn't a poseur's paradise. As befits the trendy Village Quarter, Hogan's is a lively bar filled with a hip and stylish late twenty-something crowd, listening to the hippest indie sounds. The upstairs bar can sometimes get uncomfortable, but thankfully there's the downstairs dancefloor to escape to.

International Bar

23 Wicklow Street (677 9250). All cross-city buses/Luas St Stephen's Green. **Open** 10.30am-11.30pm Mon-Thur; 10.30am-12.30am Fri, Sat; 12.30-11pm Sun. **No credit cards. Map** p252 F3 ㉗ Refreshingly laid-back, the International's long bar is always lined with Guinness-drinking regulars. An interesting crowd spills out on to the street in fine weather to sit on stools and swap stories. There are also regular comedy nights with some of Dublin's more notable comics occasionally dropping in.

JJ Smyths

12 Aungier Street (475 2565/www.jjsmyths.com). Bus 16, 16A, 19, 19A, 83/Luas St Stephen's Green. **Open** 10.30am-11.30pm Mon-Thur; 10.30am-12.30am Fri, Sat; 12.30-11pm Sun. **No credit cards. Map** p252 E4 ㉘ Downstairs, this is just a regular, unassuming old-fashioned Dublin boozer – and very nice with it. But it's also a famous jazz bar – head upstairs to hear some of the city's top jazz every night of the week (Thurdays and Sundays are best). The musical

associations don't end there: a plaque commemorating Thomas Moore, noted poet and recorder of Ireland's oral music tradition, is mounted beside the front door – this was his local. *See also p179.*

Kehoe's

9 South Anne Street (677 8312). All cross-city buses/Luas St Stephen's Green. **Open** 10.30am-11.30pm Mon-Thur; 10.30am-12.30am Fri, Sat; 12.30-11pm Sun. **Credit** MC, V. **Map** p252 F4 ㉙ If you suffer from a fear of small spaces, avoid the lavatories in Kehoe's. Designed with Lilliputians in mind, they are (literally) a low point in a pub that is otherwise rich with old-style character and delightful snugs. Friendly staff serve beautifully creamy Guinness, and the upstairs bar has changed little since John Kehoe died many years ago. At busy times a crowd gathers around the stairs, giving it the feeling of a convivial house party.

Long Hall

51 South Great George's Street (475 1590). All cross-city buses/Luas St Stephen's Green. **Open** 4-11.30pm Mon-Wed, Sun; 1-11.30pm Thur; 1pm-12.30am Fri, Sat; 1-11pm Sun. **No credit cards. Map** p252 E4 ㉚ This ornate Victorian gin palace has it all: jovial barman, old bloke at the bar with a pint of Guinness, smattering of characterful regulars. Indeed, the whole place looks as if it's been carved out of thick mahogany. From its antique chandeliers to its mirrored bar, the Long Hall has survived the recent neighbourhood renovations and is still regarded as one of Dublin's unmissable boozers.

Long Stone

10 Townsend Street (671 8102/www.thelongstone. com). All cross-city buses/DART Tara. **Open** noon-11.30pm Mon-Thur; noon-12.30am Fri; 2pm-2.30am Sat; 3-11pm Sun. **Credit** AmEx, MC, V. **Map** p252 G3 ㉛ The Long Stone is, depending on your tastes, a design catastrophe or an eccentric gem. It's got an odd ancient Celtic motif going on, with stained glass windows and giant druid's heads glowering down at you as you sip your pint of the black stuff. Its labyrinthine layout and outlandish aesthetic may not be to everyone's taste, but it's conveniently located a stone's throw from the Screen cinema on D'Olier Street and makes an ideal venue for a beer-fueled post-movie analysis.

Lord Edward

23 Christchurch Place (454 2158). All cross-city buses. **Open** 11am-11.30pm Mon-Thur; 11am-12.30am Fri; noon-12.30am Sat; 12.30-11pm Sun. **Credit** AmEx, MC, V. **Map** p252 D3 ㉜ After a visit to Christ Church Cathedral, cross the road and enter the calming Lord Edward. The round bar on the lower level is a typical old-fashioned boozer selling good Guinness, while the lounge upstairs is cosy and relaxed. The staff contribute to the pleasant atmosphere, as does the excellent porter; indeed, it's a fine spot in which to read the paper and enjoy

Eat, Drink, Shop

that craic you've been hearing so much about. Incidentally, the bar is named after Lord Edward Fitzgerald, a charismatic Irish rebel leader who was slain by the British on nearby Thomas Street on the eve of the 1798 Rebellion.

Market Bar

Fade Street, off South Great George's Street (613 9094/www.marketbar.ie). All cross-city buses/Luas St Stephen's Green. **Open** noon-11.30pm Mon-Thur; noon-12.30am Fri, Sat; 4-11pm Sun. **Credit** AmEx, MC, V. **Map** p252 E3 ⓷⓷

This little piggy went to market… The Market Bar on Fade Street was once a pig abattoir, and the grates in the floor used to flow with blood. The only thing flowing these days, though, is beer and plenty of it: this is one of Dublin's most popular bars. There's a no-music policy, so the noisy chatter of conversation wafts through the lofty space; be prepared to shout. Staff are cool but polite, and the tapas menu is good value and worth sampling; a creative smoking area has been rigged up under cover by the door.

Neary's

1 Chatham Street (677 8596). All cross-city buses/Luas St Stephen's Green. **Open** 10.30am-11.30pm Mon-Thur; 10.30am-11.30pm Fri, Sat; 12.30-11pm Sun. **Credit** MC, V. **Map** p252 F4 ⓷⓸

Rich mahogany tones, plush seating, heavy curtains and disaffected thespians from the nearby Gaiety Theatre give Neary's a unique atmosphere. The friendly barmen lovingly serve an excellent pint of plain (even skimming the head for the aesthetes among us). Upstairs is an elegant cocktail-bar style lounge, with some of the politest and friendliest bar staff in Dublin.

Octagon Bar

Clarence Hotel, 6-8 Wellington Quay (670 9000/ www.theclarence.ie). All cross-city buses/Luas Jervis. **Open** 11am-11.30pm Mon-Thur; 11am-12.30am Fri, Sat; noon-11pm Sun. **Credit** AmEx, MC, V. **Map** p252 E3 ⓷⓹

There are only a few bars in Dublin that can honestly be described as painfully hip, and Octagon is one of them. Situated in the sleek Clarence Hotel (*see p39*) owned by Bono and The Edge, this eight-sided bar has seen some very famous bums on its black leather stools and in its sleek, contemporary booths. For all its trend factor, though, the staff are friendly and good at what they do; even when it's crowded, you'll soon have a generous, well-made cocktail in hand. It's a bit expensive, but some things are worth paying for. Watch the media space for the proposed changes to the Clarence. *See p41* **With or without you**.

Oliver St John Gogarty

58-59 Fleet Street (671 1822/www.gogartys.ie). All cross-city buses. **Open** *Bar* 10.30am-2am Mon-Thur; 10.30am-2.30am Fri, Sat; 10.30am-1am Sun. *Lounge* 6pm-2.30am Mon-Thur; 3pm-2.30am Fri-Sun. **Credit** AmEx, MC, V. **Map** p252 F3 ⓷⓺

Named after the man parodied as Buck Mulligan in *Ulysses*, this place got its bar counter from the green room in the once-famous Theatre Royal. As well as that, there's an authentic flagstone floor and a large oatmeal grinder; the style here is nothing if not eclectic. Bands play traditional music nightly, and the seafood in the upstairs restaurant is very good. This is a great place to wind up in at the end of a Dublin pub crawl.

O'Neill's

2 Suffolk Street (679 3671/www.oneillsbar.com). All cross-city buses. **Open** 10.30am-11.30pm Mon-Thur; 10.30am-12.30am Fri, Sat; noon-11pm Sun. **Credit** AmEx, MC, V. **Map** p252 F3 ⓷⓻

O'Neills is the kind of place you wander into at 6pm and take seven hours to find your way out of. Yup, it's labyrinthine and chaotic, and there are enough pleasant nooks and crannies to make it an intimate spot, despite its substantial size; but it can be blighted by hordes of beer-swilling weekenders. The meat-and-two-veg lunch from the carvery is highly regarded by the hungover looking for soakage.

O'Shea's Merchant

12 Bridge Street Lower (679 3797). Bus 21, 21A/ Luas The Four Courts. **Open** 10.30am-11.30pm Mon-Wed; 10.30am-2am Thur-Sat; 12.30pm-2am Sun. **Credit** AmEx, MC, V. **Map** p250 D3 ⓷⓼

For those whose itineraries don't stretch to a couple of days outside of the capital, here's a taste of life beyond The Pale: Irish dancing, traditional Irish music, Gaelic football and hurling on the telly, decent Irish food and intriguing Irish 'country nights' on Wednesdays.

Palace

*21 Fleet Street (bar 677 9290/lounge 679 3037/
www.palacebar.com). All cross-city buses/Luas Abbey
Street.* **Open** *Bar* 10.30am-11.30pm Mon-Thur;
10.30am-12.30am Fri, Sat; 12.30-11pm Sun. *Lounge*
7-11.30pm Tue; 5-11.30pm Wed, Thur; 5pm-12.30am
Fri; 6.30pm-12.30am Sat; 6-11pm Sun. **Credit** MC, V.
Map p252 F3

The oldest bar in Dublin to have kept its original
form, the grand old Palace deserves a place on everybody's pub crawl. If it's authenticity you're after, this
place delivers, with its aged marble counter, mirrored alcoves and a reputation as a writers' hangout. Indeed, the walls are adorned with many
famous literary faces. This is a pub that rarely gets
uncomfortably busy.

Peter's Pub

*1 Johnston's Place (677 8588). All cross-city buses/
Luas St Stephen's Green.* **Open** 10.30am-11.30pm
Mon-Thur; 10.30am-12.30am Fri, Sat; 1-11pm Sun.
Credit MC, V. **Map** p252 E4

This is, quite simply, an oasis in a metropolitan
desert. Located just off increasingly fashionable
William Street South, the small modern pub offers
a decent sandwich, a legendary pint of plain and a
glimpse into the lives of Dublin's citizens. The small
interior – recently extended – is reminiscent of someone's living room and, accordingly, the emphasis is
on polite conversation. *Photo p132.*

Porterhouse

*16-18 Parliament Street (679 8847/www.porterhouse
brewco.com). All cross-city buses/Luas Jervis.* **Open**
11.30am-11.30pm Mon-Wed; 11.30am-2am Thur;

11.30am-2.30am Fri; noon-2.30am Sat;
12.30-11pm Sun. **Credit** MC, V. **Map** p252 E3
Dublin's oldest microbrewery pub sprawls casually
over three storeys. Its wooden decor may be exces-
sively rustic, but the Porterhouse makes up for that
with the quality of the beer. It sells only its own label,
but its stouts, lagers and ales are better than any
mass-produced beer; the Oyster Stout, made on the
premises with real oysters, is very good. It also
serves excellent pub food at reasonable prices, and
the Irish stew and bangers and mash will fill you up
without breaking the bank.

Ron Blacks

*37 Dawson Street (672 8231/www.ronblacks.ie).
All cross-city buses/Luas St Stephen's Green.*
Open 10.30am-11.30pm Mon-Wed; 10.30am-2.30am
Thur, Fri; noon-2.30am Sat; noon-11pm Sun. **Credit**
AmEx, MC, V. **Map** p252 F4
This looks like a gentleman's drinking club, with
dark mahogany panelling and voluptuous leather
seats – and, indeed, seems to be frequented by the
type of chap who doesn't mind being waited on. If
you can get over the guffawing professionals, it's
actually an attractive place in which to have a quiet
drink (albeit an expensive one). Not to be confused
with its more fun-loving neighbour: Ron Black's
Dawson Lounge, the smallest bar in Dublin.

Samsara

*La Stampa Hotel, 35 Dawson Street (671 7723/
www.lastampa.ie). All cross-city buses/Luas St
Stephen's Green.* **Open** noon-12.30am Mon-Thur;
noon-2.30am Fri, Sat; noon-1.30am Sun. **Credit**
AmEx, MC, V. **Map** p251 F4

Market Bar.

Prop up the bar with the punters at true local **Peter's Pub.** *See p131.*

North African-influenced superpub Samsara, like nearby Café en Seine (*see p125*), is astonishingly long, as you discover when you try to find the loos. It's smart and determined to be thoroughly sophisticated, but it should be avoided by anyone whose idea of hell is standing behind 17 people at the bar.

Sheehan's

17 Chatham Street (677 1914). All cross-city buses/Luas St Stephen's Green. **Open** 11am-11.30pm Mon-Thur; 11am-2.30am Fri, Sat; 12.30-11pm Sun. **Credit** MC, V. **Map** p252 F4 ㊹

This is a pleasant, glass-fronted bar that tends to attract your basic central-city crowd of lawyers, writers and a few other business/media types. Hosts a comedy club every Tuesday night from 8pm.

Southwilliam

52 South William Street (672 5946/www.south william.ie). All cross-city buses/Luas St Stephen's Green. **Open** noon-11.30pm Mon-Wed; noon-2.30am Thur-Sat; 3pm-1am Sun. **Credit** MC, V. **Map** p252 F4 ㊺

Very quickly after it opened its doors in 2007, Southwilliam – or Swilly as its pressed for time clientele have been known to call it – became a favourite with Dublin's trendier young tipplers. Its impressive array of imported beers and excellent selection of gourmet pies baked on-site make it an ideal spot to begin a night on the town. It can get a little crowded after 9pm, when the hipsters descend on the bar and the DJ starts up.

Stag's Head

1 Dame Court, off Dame Street (679 3687). All cross-city buses/Luas St Stephen's Green. **Open** 10.30am-11.30pm Mon-Thur; 10.30am-12.30am Fri, Sat; noon-11.30pm Sun. **Credit** MC, V. **Map** p252 E3 ㊻

The Stag's Head is hidden away on Dame Court, but easily found thanks to the pavement mosaic on Dame Street that points punters to its hallowed door. Inside it's all mahogany, stained glass and mirrors; enjoy the intimate Victorian smoking room while the gigantic stag's head hanging above keeps a vigilant watch over proceedings. The Stag's is a favourite among students of Trinity College, and film buffs may like to know that *Educating Rita* was shot here.

Temple Bar

48 Temple Bar (672 5286/www.thetemplebarpub. com). All cross-city buses/Luas Jervis. **Open** 11am-12.30am Mon-Sat; noon-12.30am Sun. **Credit** MC, V. **Map** p252 E3 ㊼

Two words sum up this bar: always packed. This wasn't always the case but the current situation is excellent news for the owners. One unusual feature is the outdoor area in the middle of the large bar – a good place for a cigarette break. Traditional music and singalongs make this a haven for foreign accents: don't expect to hear much Irish lilt.

Thomas Read

1 Parliament Street (671 7283/www.thomasread.ie). All cross-city buses/Luas Jervis. **Open** 10.30am-11.30pm Mon-Thur; 10.30am-2.30am Fri, Sat; 11am-12.30am Sun. **Credit** AmEx, MC, V. **Map** p252 E3 ⑱
Opposite the grandeur of City Hall sits Thomas Read, a bustling modern bar offering a varying choice of scenes. The main bar is trendy and modern, while downstairs is a mecca for young indie rockers, with regular free gigs. Pass through a back corridor and you're in the neighbouring pub, The Oak, which has an intriguing history; check out the frames around the walls.

Turk's Head

27-30 Parliament Street (679 9701/www.paramount hotel.ie). All cross-city buses/Luas Jervis. **Open** noon-1am Mon, Tue, Sun; noon-2.30am Wed-Sat. **Credit** AmEx, MC, V. **Map** p252 E3 ⑭
If you're in town for shallow, meaningless… discourse with someone of the opposite sex, the Turk's Head has your name on the door. Popular with twentysomethings, this pub/club (you decide) is huge, with two levels of bars and a large dancefloor. The Gaudi-inspired walls add to the impression of drinking in a cavern of Turkish delight, and nubile belly-dancers gyrate on Tuesdays. A little bit past its prime now, unfortunately.

Around St Stephen's Green

Bernard Shaw Bar

11-12 South Richmond Street, (085 712 8342). Bus 19, 122, 16, 16A/Luas Harcourt. **Open** 4pm-11.30pm Sun-Thur; 4pm-12.30am Fri, Sat. **Credit** Laser, MC, V. **Map** p251 E6 ⑩
A proper 113-year-old Irish boozer, the Bernard Shaw was taken over in 2006 by Dublin-based club promoters and label owners Bodytonic. The place has kept its frayed-around-the-edges charm, but the new owners have injected a newfound sense of fun into the place. DJs appear nightly, covering everything from rock to to hip hop, reggae to dubstep and disco. The bar is also a gallery space and regularly hosts quirky events such as car boot sales, music lectures, record fairs, film clubs, t-shirt & badge making classes and more.

Bleeding Horse

24 Camden Street Upper (475 2705). Bus 16, 16A, 19, 19a, 49n 83/Luas Harcourt. **Open** noon-12.30am Mon-Wed; noon-1am Thur; noon-2am Fri, Sat; noon-11.30pm Sun. **Credit** MC, V. **Map** p251 E5 ⑪
The Bleeding Horse has occupied this prominent Camden Street site for two centuries. These days it

attracts a pleasant crowd of local regulars and an energetic student group in almost equal proportions. The bar sprawls over several levels: the connecting rooms downstairs are covered with heavy beams and a dark, medieval atmosphere, and there's a fairly good restaurant upstairs. The place can get busy at weekends, when a younger crowd jams in before heading on to the nearby Harcourt Street clubs.

Corner Stone

40 Wexford Street (478 9816). Bus 55, 61, 62, 83/ Luas St Stephen's Green. **Open** 11am-11.30pm Mon-Thur; 11am-2.30am Fri; 4pm-2am Sat. **Credit** AmEx, MC, V. **Map** p251 E5 ㊾
The façade on this corner building has been restored in recent years and now forms a pleasing introduction to the (also remodelled) bar inside. The decor is contemporary but not ultra-fashionable, with subdued lighting and leather seats in cool shades. Lunches here are tasty, and the upstairs lounge hosts live music and late drinking at weekends.

Doheny & Nesbitt

5 Baggot Street Lower (676 2945). Bus 10, 11, 11A/ Luas St Stephen's Green. **Open** 10.30am-12.30am Mon-Thur; 10.30am-12.30am Fri, Sat; 12.30-11pm Sun. **Credit** AmEx, DC, MC, V. **Map** p251 G4 ㊿
At weekends, this glorious old pub is packed to the gills with lawyers getting squiffy and quoting Blackstone and law gossip at each other. If this doesn't appeal – and why would it? – you'll be pleased to know it's at its best during the week, when all is quiet, you can gaze at your reflection in the polished wood and enjoy a pleasant, contemplative drink. In summer and on rugby days it's mayhem again, with hordes of drinkers spilling out on to the street.

Flannery's

6 Camden Street Lower (478 2238). All cross-city buses/Luas Harcourt. **Open** noon-2.30am Mon-Fri; 1pm-2.30am Sat, Sun. **Credit** AmEx, MC, V. **Map** p251 E5 ㊴
Unashamed of its less-than-appealing exterior, Flannery's is at its busiest on the weekend, when a crowd of nurses, teachers and Gardai pack out the bar. Ideal for a night out with single friends before heading on to Copper Face Jacks down the road.

Ocean Bar

The Millennium Tower, Charlotte's Quay Dock, off Ringsend Road (668 8862/ww.oceanbar.ie). Bus 1, 2, 3/DART Grand Canal Dock. **Open** noon-11.30am Mon-Thur; noon-12.30am Fri, Sat; noon-11pm Sun. **Credit** MC, V.
This upmarket dockside establishment in the Millennium Tower claims to have Dublin's only waterfront public licence. Take advantage – the patios overlooking the canal basin are ideal for drinking if there's even a hint of sunshine though the wind off the water can be positively brisk – and the bistro serves decent food until 10pm. Ocean was once very much on its own here, but the cranes bristling on the other side of the water are evidence of the area's development.

Odeon

*57 Harcourt Street (478 2088/www.odeon.ie). Bus
14, 15, 16/Luas Harcourt.* **Open** noon-11.30pm Mon-
Wed; noon-12.30am Thur; noon-2.30am Fri, Sat; noon-
11pm Sun. **Credit** AmEx, MC, V. **Map** p251 F5 ⑤⑤

Take a Luas to the old Harcourt Street station. The
impressive façade of the Odeon is a sign of what to
expect once inside. There aren't too many seats, but
nobody really cares: people come here to see and be
seen on a sea of polished floorboards under vaulted
ceilings. It's not cheap by any means: you pay for
the atmosphere and the style. Odeon is especially
pleasant on a Sunday, when you can deliciously frit-
ter the afternoon away with free newspapers or
watch a classic film showing on the big screen. The
smoking area out front, where you can watch space-
age trams shuttle back and forth while you dream
of the future, is excellent.

O'Donoghue's

*15 Merrion Row (660 7194/lounge 676 2807/
www.odonoghuesbar.com). All cross-city buses/
Luas St Stephen's Green.* **Open** 10.30am-11.30pm
Mon-Thur; 10.30am-12.30am Fri, Sat; 12.30-11pm
Sun. **Credit** AmEx, MC, V. **Map** p251 G4 ⑤⑥

Impromptu jam sessions are a staple here, and outfits like the Dubliners play regularly. While the
music really pulls in the tourists, O'Donoghue's really pulls in all sorts of customers: genuine locals and
visitors, young and old. While the pub itself can be
a little claustrophobic (especially mid session)
there's an excellent back alley smoking area, where
you can (after a fashion) catch your breath.

Searson's

*42-44 Baggot Street Upper (660 0330/
www.searsons.ie). Bus 10.* **Open** 10am-11.30pm
Mon-Thur; 12.30pm-1.30am Fri, Sat; 4-11pm Sun.
Credit AmEx, MC, V. **Map** p251 H5 ⑤⑦

While all around it, pubs bow to the pressure to
refurbish and change direction, Searson's sticks to
its guns and its rather lovely classic Victorian decor.
Punters are professionals, regulars and twentysomethings, and there's an ample smoking area out the
back. A visit to Searson's before and/or after a rugby
game at Lansdowne Road is a must: the atmosphere
is usually hilarious.

Solas

*31 Wexford Street (478 0583). Bus 16, 16A,
19, 19A, 23/Luas St Stephen's Green.* **Open**
11am-12.30am Mon, Tue; 11am-1.30am Wed-
Sat; noon-12.30am Sun. **Credit** AmEx, MC, V.
Map p251 E5 ⑤⑧

An attractive spot to come to before hitting the
clubs along the Camden Street strip, Solas, itself just
north on Wexford Street, is trendy yet easy going.
It's an attractive place: the orange globe lamps are
warm, the crimson banquettes plush, and the cherry wood tables glossy. It also serves reasonably
priced pub food, and the menu leans vaguely
towards pub spice, with dishes like Szechuan beef and
chicken enchiladas. In general, it's cosy, inviting
and well worth a visit.

Smyth's

10 Haddington Road (660 6305). Bus 10.
Open 10am-11.30pm Mon-Thur; 10.30am-
12.30am Fri, Sat; 12.30-11pm Sun. **Credit**
MC, V. **Map** p251 H5 ⑤⑨

Close to the banks of the Grand Canal, Smyth's is a
real neighbourhood pub with a disarmingly laid-
back atmosphere. Though an ill-considered renovation a few years back did its best to garble the
atmosphere, it only partly succeeded, and Smyth's
remains a quiet, snug and comfortable boozer.
If you're strolling on the canal towpath, drop in.

Toner's

*139 Baggot Street Lower (676 3090). Bus 10,
11, 11A/Luas St Stephen's Green.* **Open** 10.30am-
11.30pm Mon-Wed; 10.30am-12.30am Thur-Sat;
12.30-11pm Sun. **Credit** AmEx, MC, V.
Map p251 G4 ⑥⓪

Toner's is an authentic Dublin pub that has survived
being tarted up over the years: the character that
made it popular to begin with still remains, the bar
itself is still pleasing, and the tarting up was done
with a mercifully light hand. At weekends Toner's
is packed to the rafters, but if you find yourself on
Baggot Street on a wet afternoon, there are few better places in which to take refuge. It also holds the
honour of being the only pub visited by WB Yeats.
How could you doubt his judgement?

Village

*26 Wexford Street (475 8555/www.thevillagevenue.
com). Bus 16, 16A, 19, 19A/Luas Harcourt.* **Open**
11am-2.30am Mon-Fri; 5pm-2.30am Sun. **Credit**
AmEx, MC, V. **Map** p251 E5 ⑥①

The Village is one of Dublin's newest and best
music venues, catering to a wider and more diverse
crowd than Whelan's next door (*see below*). The success of its nightly gigs, however, tends to distract
attention from the bar itself, which is attractive and
agreeable in its own right. The striking modern
frontage of the building allows lots of natural light
to flood the front room, and this then gives way to
the subdued red and orange lights and cool atmosphere of the main bar. You can eat here at any time
of the day, and eat well; Sunday brunch is accompanied by jazz bands.

Whelan's

*25 Wexford Street (478 0766/www.whelanslive.com).
Bus 16, 16A, 19, 19A, 122/Luas Harcourt.* **Open**
10.30am-1.30am Mon-Wed; 10.30am-2.30am Thur-
Sat; 2pm-1.30am Sun. **Credit** AmEx, MC, V. **Map**
p251 E5 ⑥②

Dublin's miniature music institution has recently
been refurbished to include a 200-capacity venue
upstairs. By doubling its number of gigs, Whelan's
has managed to cement its place as HQ for all things
indie. Its success is due in no small part to the guid-
ance of legendary broadcaster, author and promot-
er Leagues O'Toole, who has watched the venue
blossom from a small club hosting then-unknowns
such as Jeff Buckley to becoming Dublin's trendiest
after-show nightspot.

Solas.

Around O'Connell Street

Floridita

Irish Life Mall, Abbey Street Lower (878 1032/
www.floriditadublin.com). All cross-city buses/
Luas Abbey Street. **Open** noon-11.30pm Mon-
Thur; noon-2.30am Fri; 5pm-2.30am Sat.
Credit AmEx, MC, V. **Map** p251 G2 ⑥

From one boozy capital to another, one of
Hemingway's favourite Havana bars has opened
(under capitalist guise) in Dublin. The former Life Bar
has been transformed into the 'seat of the daiquiri'
where mixologists serve up mojitos and other Cuban
cocktail classics from a lengthy expensive menu that
would have made even Hemingway's eyes water.

Flowing Tide

9 Abbey Street Lower (874 4106). All cross-city
buses/Luas Abbey Street. **Open** 10.30am-11.30pm
Mon-Thur; 10.30am-12.30am Fri, Sat; noon-11pm
Sun. **Credit** MC, V. **Map** p251 F2 ⑥

A recent renovation has converted the much-loved
Tide from a reliable Dublin boozer with a raffish
edge into a trendy place with polished wood floors
and sleek chrome details. Perhaps the new look is
not to all tastes, but the essentials remain the same:
the staff and Guinness are as decent as ever, and the
bar's location means it still attracts a crowd of actors
and audience from the nearby Abbey Theatre.

Isaac Butt Café Bar

Opposite Busáras Station, Store Street (819 7636).
All cross-city buses/Luas Busaras. **Open** 5-11.30pm
Mon-Wed, Sun; 5pm-2.30am Thur-Sat. **Credit** MC,
V. **Map** p251 G2 ⑥

A range of techno club nights first made this bar
popular among students and backpackers, but the
emphasis has recently shifted to live indie music.
The warren-like bars provide comfortable refuge
from the cares of the world, and there's a big screen
for football matches. Beware, though: many unsus-
pecting voyagers have dropped in from the adjacent
bus station 'for a quick one', only to find themselves
tarrying long after the 5.11 to Cork has gone.

Kiely's

37 Upper Abbey Street (872 2100). All cross-city
buses/Luas Abbey Street. **Open** 10.30am-11.30pm
Mon-Wed, Sun; 10.30am-12.30am Thur; 10.30am-
2am Fri, Sat. **Credit** AmEx, MC, V. **Map** p251 E2 ⑥

The Abbey Street entrance leads to a snug, old-style
dark wooden bar that's good for quiet pints or watching football in peace. The back of the pub – with the
Liffey Street entrance – is 'K3' and couldn't be more
different. It's a large, trendy space with a cheery
twentysomething crowd. The juxtaposition should-
n't work as well as it does – but one thing both areas
have in common is excellent and well-priced food.

Patrick Conway

70 Parnell Street (873 2687). All cross-city buses/
Luas Abbey Street. **Open** 10am-11.30pm Mon-Thur;
10am-12.30am Fri, Sat; noon-11pm Sun. **No credit
cards. Map** p251 F1 ⑥

A thoughtful pick of interior mood-setters, including candlelight and drapes, gives this Victorian pub
a cosy, relaxed atmosphere. Plentiful seating in lovely booths, an unpretentious bunch of punters and
friendly bar staff are its biggest attractions. If you
fancy a quiet pint, this civilised place will fit the bill
very nicely indeed.

Pravda

35 Liffey Street Lower (874 0076/www.pravda.ie).
All cross-city buses/Luas Jervis. **Open** noon-11.30pm
Mon, Tue; noon-2.30am Wed-Sat; 12.30-11pm Sun.
Credit AmEx, MC, V. **Map** p252 E2 ⑥

An abundance of cyrillic script stencilled on the
walls does not an authentic Russian bar make; but
Pravda pulls off the ersatz Eastern European thing
pretty well. The building is large and rambling, and
the atmosphere is chilled during the day and vibrant
at night. It's a particularly nice place for an afternoon hot toddy, with its view of the Ha'penny Bridge
and the shoppers streaming past; but after 10pm the
volume of the music will drown out your inner
monologue. The place could do with a lick of paint.

Traffic

54 Middle Abbey Street (873 4800). All cross-city
buses/Luas Abbey Street. **Open** 3-11.30pm Mon-Wed;
3pm-2.30am Thur-Sat; 4-11.30pm Sun. **Credit** MC, V.
Map p251 F2 ⑥

While its decor is stylish and trendy, Traffic's glory
days as a style bar seem to have passed. However,
it's now becoming a favourite venue for aspiring DJs
and a good place at which to spot emerging talent or
down a quick one before moving on to the Academy.

Woolshed

Parnell Centre, Parnell Street at Capel Street (872
4325/www.woolshedbaa.com) All cross-city buses/
Luas Jervis. **Open** noon-11.30pm Mon-Wed; noon-
1am Thur, Fri, Sun; 10.30am-1am Sat. **Credit**
AmEx, MC, V. **Map** p251 E2 ⑦

This place proudly proclaims itself home from home
for 'Aussies, Kiwis and Saffas'. Drinking pints, playing pool and watching sport on TV fill up the day,
while at night bands of decidedly mixed quality line
up to crank up the volume (on the basis, apparently, that if it can't be good, it might as well be loud).
Nearly always fun, though.

Around the North Quays

Cobblestone

77 King Street North (872 1799/www.imro.ie). Bus
25, 26, 37, 39, 67, 67A, 68, 69, 79/Luas Smithfield.
Open 4-11.30pm Mon-Thur; 4pm-12.30am Fri, Sat;
1-11pm Sun. **No credit cards. Map** p250 C2 ⑦

The musicians' corner downstairs attracts traditional players whom you would pay to see elsewhere,
and the paying venue upstairs rarely books a duff
band (lo-fi, trad and folk tend to dominate). Overall
it's cosy, while eschewing unnecessary frills; if you
want to avoid excessive paddywhackery in favour
of genuine traditional Dublin pubbery, come here.

Hughes' Bar

19 Chancery Street, off Church Street (872 6540).
All cross-city buses/Luas The Four Courts. **Open**
7am-11.30pm Mon-Thur; 7am-12.30am Fri, Sat; 7-
11pm Sun. **Credit** AmEx, MC, V. **Map** p252 C2 🕖
Hughes sits next to the law courts. Some argue
there's a rough edge to it, but its excellent trad music
sessions make it worth a visit. Actor Brendan
Gleeson pops in from time to time and Bob Dylan's
backing band joined the house musicians recently
for the type of unplanned and informal gig for which
the pub is becoming known.

Jack Nealons

165 Capel Street (872 3247). All cross-city buses/
Luas Jervis. **Open** noon-11.30pm Mon-Thur, Sun;
noon-12.30am Fri, Sat. **Credit** AmEx, MC, V.
Map p252 E3 🕖
Popular with pre-clubbers, Nealons is stylish but
relaxed. The downstairs bar is usually less hectic
than upstairs, but at weekends you take a seat where
you can find it. If the drinks seem slightly on the
pricey side, the happily braying customers don't
object. Look out for the juggling barmen, whose
cocktail expertise may tempt you towards something more adventurous than a pint of plain.

Morrison Hotel Bar

Morrison Hotel, Ormond Quay Lower (887 2400/
www.morrisonhotel.ie). All cross-city buses/Luas
Jervis. **Open** 10.30am-11.30pm Mon-Thur; 10.30am-
12.30am Fri, Sat; noon-11.30pm Sun. **Credit** AmEx,
MC, V. **Map** p252 E2 🕖
This place is pure class. With an interior designed
by fashion guru John Rocha, the Morrison's extremely stylish bar has plenty of comfy black couches on
which you can sip cocktails and dreamily peer out
at the silvery Liffey mist. What's particularly good
about the place is its combination of the aforementioned quality with some of the friendliest bar staff
in the city. If you've got the cash, there's truly no
more salubrious spot at which to spend an evening.
Dress to impress and arrive early.

O'Reilly Bros aka The Chancery

1 Inns Quay (677 0420). All cross-city buses/Luas
The Four Courts. **Open** 7.30am-11.30pm Mon-Sat;
noon-11pm Sun. **No credit cards. Map** p252 D3 🕖
At first glance, the Chancery is a spit-and-sawdust
local with little to recommend it. It is, however, worthy of note as one of Dublin's early houses – bars
that are legally allowed to open at 7.30am to service
market traders and those who work nights. For that
reason, it's a popular final port of call for clubbers.
It can be an odd (some would say dispiriting) experience to enter a bar so early and find people behav-
ing as if it were the top of Saturday night, but it's
certainly worth knowing about.

Voodoo Lounge

39 Arran Quay (873 6013). All cross-city buses/Luas
Smithfield. **Open** noon-Mon-Wed; noon-2.30am
Thur, Fri; 4pm-3am Sat; 4pm-1am Sun. **No credit
cards. Map** p250 C2 🕖

Voodoo is a happening bar-club with garage bands
seven nights a week and DJs at weekends. (A board
in the window communicates the musical line-up.)
Inside, the masks, beads and other scary paraherna-
lia are dimly lit by candles and complemented by eerie
murals on supernatural themes. Happily, the likeable
staff ensure that the vibe remains positive. Plenty of
bottled beers, yummy pizza slices and an old Space
Invader machine make it worth trekking up the quays
for a bit of black magic.

Zanzibar

36 Ormond Quay Lower (878 7212/
www.capitalbars.com). All cross-city buses/Luas
Jervis. **Open** 5pm-2.30am Mon-Thur, Sun; 3pm-
1.30am Sun. **Credit** AmEx, MC, V. **Map** p252 E2 🕖
Few bars provoke such divisive reactions as this vast
booze jungle. Inside are palm trees and 'African' decorations; outside are queues of teens and early twentysomethings shivering in their finery. It's clear why
some dismiss Zanzibar as a meat market. And that's
why, even though the bouncers are heavyhanded and
staff are narky, the place continues to pack 'em in.
Its customers just don't know any better.

Around the Liberties & Kilmainham

Gravity Bar

James Street (471 4527/www.guinness-storehouse.
com). Bus 51B, 78A, 123/Luas James's Street. **Open**
(admission with tour only) *Jan-Mar, Oct-Dec* 9.30am-
5pm daily. *Apr-Sept* 9.30am-7pm daily. **Credit** MC,
V. **Map** p250 B3 🕖
The Guinness Storehouse is one of the most popular tourist attractions in Dublin. Not surprising, considering the highlight of the tour is the experience
offered by the Gravity Bar. Set at the top of a converted grain house, this very special bar commands
a 360° view of Dublin from floor-to-ceiling windows.
With the Guinness making the shortest journey in
the world from vat to glass, the beer is great, too.

The Northern Suburbs

Kavanagh's ('The Gravediggers')

1 Prospect Square, Glasnevin (830 7978). Bus
13, 19, 19A. **Open** 10.30am-11.30pm Mon-Thur;
10.30am-midnight Fri, Sat; 12.30-11pm Sun. **No
credit cards.**
Way off the beaten track, Kavanagh's is a Dublin
institution and thus, for many, worth the trek.
Owing to its location next door to Glasnevin cemetery, this famous boozer is better known as 'The
Gravediggers'. It has hardly changed in its 150-year
history, and one of its chief attractions is that you
can bring your pints out to the square on sunny
days. Loved by many (ask Brad Pitt) for its spit-and-
sawdust simplicity, it can be a little hard to find (a
taxi from O'Connell Street is probably your best bet)
but most definitely worth the effort.

(sidebar) **Eat, Drink, Shop**

Shops & Services

Counter culture.

Eat, Drink, Shop

Brown Thomas. An emporium of designer delight.

The Celtic Tiger may have lost most, if not all, of its teeth, but there's still more than a little bite left in Dublin's shopping scene. The retail industry is positively thriving here, economic downturn or not, and the choice of shops runs from smart, cosmopolitan delis to neat indie record stores. While the city holds its own against other European capitals, with plenty of big chain stores and heavyweight designers, Dublin still retains an independent edge: check out its seductive little boutiques and Irish labels to see what we mean.

Part of Dublin's appeal is its handy size. It's compact and navigable, so walking from one shopping area to another is a pleasure; and if you weary of the urban scene, you can jump on a Luas and hang out with the suburbanites at the mammoth **Dundrum Town Centre** (*see p140*).

In the city, a good place to start south of the River Liffey is Grafton Street. A smart pedestrianised thoroughfare, it draws eager consumers and hopeful buskers in equal measure, and is lined with a good selection of chain stores and shoe shops. Avoid it mid afternoon at the weekend, though, unless you particularly enjoy elbowing your way through huge crowds. For a taste of upmarket Dublin, try the exceptionally elegant **Brown Thomas** (*see p139*), a super-chic department store devoted to the world's most exclusive labels.

Nearby **William Street South**, **Castle Market** and **Drury Street** offer a hipper, trendier slice of retail life, with independent boutiques and a slower pace, while the pleasant jumble of **George's Street Arcade** is ideal for unearthing unusual second-hand gear, from books to bell-bottoms. Head down to the Old City at the northern edge of Temple Bar, and you'll find the fashionable **Cow Lane Market** (10am-5pm Sat), and hip little stores.

North of the river lies the long, busy and shop-filled **Henry Street**, the **Jervis Centre** (*see p140*) and the newly spruced-up **ILAC** (*see p140*), a formerly run-down shopping centre that's finally being given a much-needed renovation. Vastly less pretentious than the southside, the northside has a different atmosphere, and Moore Street, with its old-school market traders, offers a glimpse into the Dublin of old.

OPENING HOURS AND TAX REFUNDS

Shops are generally open from 9am to 6pm Monday to Saturday, and from around noon to 6pm on Sunday. Almost all stores stay open late on Thursday – usually until 8pm or 9pm.

MasterCard and Visa credit cards are widely accepted; AmEx and Diners Club cards are generally only accepted in the bigger stores.

Sales tax (VAT) is 21 per cent; visitors from outside the EU can get a refund at the airport.

One-stop shopping

Department stores

Arnotts

12 Henry Street, Around O'Connell Street (805 0400/ www.arnotts.ie). All cross-city buses/Luas Jervis. **Open** 9am-6.30pm Mon, Wed, Fri, Sat; 9.30am-6.30pm Tue; 9am-9pm Thur; noon-6pm Sun. **Credit** AmEx, DC, MC, V. **Map** p251 F2.

Once an uninspiring department store better known for school uniforms than stylish clothing, Arnotts has completely reinvented itself as a vast and gleamingly modern department store. An array of electrical goods, cookware and affordable fashion outlets fill the floors – it is here, for example, that you'll find Dublin's only branch of GAP.

Brown Thomas

88-95 Grafton Street, Around Temple Bar (605 6666/www.brownthomas.com). All cross-city buses/ Luas St Stephen's Green. **Open** 9am-8pm Mon, Wed, Fri; 9.30am-8pm Tue; 9am-9pm Thur; 9am-7pm Sat; 11am-7pm Sun. **Credit** AmEx, MC, V. **Map** p251 F4.

Plush, elegant and painfully fashionable, BTs is popular with travelling celebs, rich kids and the local glitterati. There are more designer labels than you could shake a stick of celery at (Herve Leger, Halston, and Balenciaga, to name a few), not to mention a personal shopping service, a dedicated Vera Wang bridal salon and more. The BTKids department fits out junior fashionistas, while the ultra hip BT2 sees that the young and young at heart get a good supply of trendy denim, club wear and logo Tees.

Clery & Co

18-27 Lower O'Connell Street, Around O'Connell Street (878 6000/www.clerys.com). All cross-city buses/Luas Abbey Street. **Open** 9am-7pm Mon-Wed; 9am-9pm Thur; 9am-8pm Fri; 9am-6.30pm Sat; noon-6pm Sun. **Credit** AmEx, DC, MC, V. **Map** p251 F2.

Despite an auspicious beginning (it was one of the first purpose-built department stores in the world when it was founded in 1853), Clery & Co has long since been overtaken by its swisher, more modern competitors. But, that said, its elegant premises (the wonderful old staircases, in particular) still exude a traditional charm and its decent selection of menswear (Kangol, Wrangler, YSL) and womenswear (Karen Millen, Miss Selfridge, Sisley, Topshop) keeps it in the race.

Dunnes Stores

Henry Street, Around O'Connell Street (872 3911/ www.dunnesstores.ie). All cross-city buses/Luas Jervis. **Open** 9am-7pm Mon-Wed, Fri, Sat; 9am-9pm Thur; 11am-7pm Sun. **Credit** AmEx, MC, V. **Map** p251 F2.

The ubiquitous Dunnes Stores (there are dozens of branches across the country) holds a special place in the hearts of Dubliners, thanks to its good-value, no-nonsense gear. It's exceptionally inexpensive, carries a good range of babies' and children's clothes, and is great for well-priced home entertainment gear and homewares that can be surprisingly stylish. Some of the larger stores (such as this one) also sell groceries.

Other locations throughout the city.

Marks & Spencer

15-20 Grafton Street, Around Temple Bar (679 7855/www.marksandspencer.com). All cross-city buses/Luas St Stephen's Green. **Open** 9am-8pm Mon-Wed, Fri, Sat; 9am-9pm Thur; 8.30am-8pm Sat; 11am-7pm Sun. **Credit** MC, V. **Map** p251 F4.

Occupying an enviable spot on busy Grafton Street with a smart black-painted storefront wrapping around the corner into quaint little Duke Street, this is a particularly classy branch of good old M&S. As always, it draws a broad mix of shoppers, from slipper-seeking pensioners to fashion-conscious types on a budget. The food hall is up to the usual high standard and there's also a ground-floor coffee bar offering classic espresso-based combos to drink in or take away.

Other locations 24-29 Mary Street, Around North Quays (872 8833).

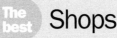
The best Shops

For everything under one roof

Avoca (*see p145*); Arnotts (*see p139*); Jervis Centre (*see p140*); Stephen's Green Centre (*see p140*).

For bright young things

Loft Market (*see p148*); Sabotage (*see p149*); Schuh (*see p150*); Urban Outfitters (*see p149*).

For good looks

Berry Bros & Rudd (*see p151*); Cathach Books (*see p143*); chq (*see p140*); Clery & Co (*see p139*); Fallon & Byrne (*see p151*); SitStil (*see p152*); Smock (*see p149*).

For something Irish

Avoca (*see p145*); Blarney Woollen Mills (*see p146*); Books Upstairs (*see p141*); Celtic Note (*see p144*); Sheridan's Cheesemongers (*see p151*).

Eat, Drink, Shop

Shopping and sculpture at **chq**.

Shopping centres

chq
*Custom House Quay, Docklands (673 6054/www.chq.
ie). All cross-city buses/Luas Busáras/DART
Connolly.* **Open** 7am-7pm Mon-Fri; 10am-6pm Sat;
noon-6pm Sun. **Credit** MC, V. **Map** p251 G2.
Not only is it impressive to look at (the building was
formerly a John Rennie-designed tobacco warehouse; *see p28*) but this sleek new shopping centre
is perfectly suited to Docklands' upwardly mobile
demographics. Smart, glass-fronted retail units
stock everything from designer homewares
(Meadows & Byrne) and upmarket gents' threads
(Henry Jermyn) to chic womenswear (Kohl, Pink
Room, Fran & Jane) and speciality teas (House of
Tea). There's also the usual clutch of coffeeshops
so you can rest your shop-weary feet.

Dundrum Town Centre
*Sandyford Road, Dundrum (299 1700/
www.dundrum.ie). Bus 17, 44C, 48A, 48N, 75/
Luas Balally.* **Open** 9am-9pm Mon-Fri; 9am-7pm
Sat; 10am-7pm Sun. **Credit** varies.
Fifteen minutes outside the city centre is the goliath
of Dublin shopping malls, the Dundrum Town
Centre. This pristine place is an unashamed temple
to consumerism and gets packed out with hungry
suburban shoppers at weekends. Midweek it's much
quieter and more pleasant, although you'd still need
a good few hours to scout it out. As well as the usual
range of well-known chain stores, there's a dinky but
disappointing boutique branch of Harvey Nichols
and a decent-sized House of Fraser. Hamley's, the
famous toy store, opened across three floors in 2008.
There are several cafés and restaurants, as well
as a cinema.

ILAC Shopping Centre
*Henry Street, Around O'Connell Street (704 1460).
All cross-city buses/Luas Jervis.* **Open** 9am-6pm Mon-
Wed, Fri, Sat; 9am-9pm Thur; noon-6pm Sun. **Credit**
varies. **Map** p251 F2.
There was a time when the ILAC Centre was a
byword for urban tawdriness, devoid of any charm,
bereft of shops you'd actually want to set foot in. But
those days are over. Extensive refurbishment and
revamping of the centre has left it looking every bit
the 21st-century mall. The Henry Street entrance is
now bright and airy, with a branch of H&M usher-
ing in the new era, alongside a supporting cast of
reliable big-name outlets like good old Debenhams.

Jervis Centre
*Jervis Street, Around O'Connell Street (878 1323/
www.jervis.ie). All cross-city buses/Luas Jervis.* **Open**
9am-6.30pm Mon-Wed; 9am-9pm Thur; 9am-7pm Fri,
Sat; 11am-6.30pm Sun. **Credit** varies. **Map** p251 E2.
With the kind of relentless mall lighting that makes
you feel as if you are suspended in a permanent light-
ning flash, this starkly modern shopping centre may
not be the most relaxing place in the world (crowds
are also a permanent fixture) but it is handily
located, and it's also full of equally handy, bite-sized
outlets. You'll find branches of big UK stores like
Argos, Debenhams and M&S, plus a fair selection of
clothes shops (Topshop and Next) and dozens of mall
staples, of the Sunglass Hut and Boots varieties.

Powerscourt Townhouse Centre
*59 William Street South, Around Temple Bar (671
7000/www.powerscourtcentre.com). All cross-city
buses/Luas St Stephen's Green.* **Open** 10am-6pm
Mon-Wed, Fri, Sat; 10am-8pm Thur; noon-6pm Sun.
Credit varies. **Map** p251 F3.
Despite its dead-centre location, the Powerscourt
Townhouse Centre is a remarkably calm, quiet and
elegant spot. With impressive plasterwork, exposed
brickwork and an imposing staircase, it's one of the
city's best 18th-century Georgian buildings. Enjoy
classical piano music in the background, sip a frothy
cappuccino in a café overlooking the light-filled
courtyard, or browse through a good selection of
antiques and curios, shoe shops, a photography
store and branches of French Connection and All
Saints. The achingly hip Loft Market (*see p148*) is
on the top floor.

Stephen's Green Centre
*St Stephen's Green West (478 0888/www.stephens
green.com). All cross-city buses/Luas St Stephen's
Green.* **Open** 9am-7pm Mon-Wed, Fri, Sat; 9am-9pm
Thur; 11am-6pm Sun. **Credit** varies. **Map** p251 F4.
Looming over Grafton Street on the edge of St
Stephen's Green, this overblown conservatory of a
shopping centre makes up in convenience for what
it lacks in charm. A wide selection of (more than 100)
shops extends over three floors and covers pretty
much all the bases, from a new ground-floor
Quiksilver outlet to the twee and comforting world
of the Art & Hobby shop.

Antiques

On the face of it, Dublin shopping attractions are bright, modern and mainstream; but scratch the surface, and you'll find a city with a thriving antiques trade. The area around Thomas Street and the Liberties has been marked out for redevelopment as Dublin's new Soho (south of Heuston Station, amusingly), but it's also where you'll find a seam of atmospheric, dusty and interesting antiques stores. **Francis Street**, near St Patrick's Cathedral, is where it all happens. Lined from top to bottom with a good selection of long-established stores, it's where Dublin's serious antiques hunters come to for a fix. Prices can range from reasonable to exorbitant, so it's a good idea to know your stuff; this place might look easygoing but it's all about experienced dealers and big business.

A little further south in the same area, **Clanbrassil Street** also has a scattering of smaller, cheap antiques and junk shops – the kind of places where you can spend a late sunny afternoon browsing around before going home with something that you never really wanted in the first place.

Books

Enjoy a bit of dust with your book browsing? Then try the excellent second-hand stalls in the **George's Street Arcade**, which tend to have a little bit of everything, from *Confessions of a Shopaholic* to *The Odyssey*. And at a fraction of the price of the larger, high-street stores.

General

Books Upstairs
36 College Green, Around Temple Bar (679 6687/ www.booksirish.com). All cross-city buses/Luas St Stephen's Green. **Open** 10am-7pm Mon-Fri; 10am-6pm Sat; 1-6pm Sun. **Credit** MC, V. **Map** p251 F3.
This worthy independent bookshop has been going for decades and it continues to attract discerning punters, visiting writers and resident academics with its notable stock of Irish literature, as well as interesting drama, philosophy, psychology, history and gay sections. The shop also stocks Irish interest books published in other countries as well as magazines and journals. There's also a regular selection of bargain titles.

Eason's
40 O'Connell Street, Around O'Connell Street (858 3800/www.easons.ie). All cross-city buses/ Luas Abbey Street. **Open** 9am-6.45pm Mon-Wed, Sat; 9am-8.45pm Thur; 9am-7.45pm Fri; noon-5.45pm Sun. **Credit** AmEx, MC, V. **Map** p251 F2.
Always busy, this long-established shop won't win any prizes for atmosphere, but it has a good selection of books over four floors.
Other locations throughout the city.

Hodges Figgis
56-58 Dawson Street, Around Temple Bar (677 4754). All cross-city buses/Luas St Stephen's Green. **Open** 9am-7pm Mon-Wed, Fri; 9am-8pm Thur; 9am-6pm Sat; noon-6pm Sun. **Credit** AmEx, MC, V. **Map** p251 F4.
With wall-to-wall books over three tightly packed floors, Hodges Figgis tends to have a good selection of special offers on throughout the year, as well as an extensive regular stock.

Cathach Books. *See p143.*

Spectacle Parade Opticians

designer eyeglass frames, sunglasses, repairs, eye tests, contact lens checks

24 Stephen St. Lower, Dublin 2
t: 01 400 5000 | f: 01 400 5020
e: info@spectacleparade.ie
w: www. spectacleparade.ie

Hughes & Hughes

Stephen's Green Centre, Around St Stephen's Green (478 3060/www.hughesbooks.com). All cross-city buses/Luas St Stephen's Green. **Open** 9.30am-6pm Mon-Wed, Fri, Sat; 9.30am-8pm Thur; noon-6pm Sun. **Credit** AmEx, MC, V. **Map** p251 F4.

A decent chain with an especially strong selection of Irish fiction, Hughes & Hughes also keeps its eye in with smaller sections on history, cookery and self-help. This branch has a particularly wide-ranging and well-presented stock of junior reading material. **Other locations** throughout the city.

Waterstone's

7 Dawson Street, Around Temple Bar (679 1260/ www.waterstones.co.uk). All cross-city buses/Luas St Stephen's Green. **Open** 9am-7pm Mon-Wed, Fri, Sat; 9am-8pm Thur; 11am-6pm Sun. **Credit** AmEx, MC, V. **Map** p251 F4.

A pleasingly labyrinthine layout gives this branch of the big UK chain a quirky appeal, and you could easily spend several hours in the small specialist rooms. Here, you can expect a good selection of titles, along with a varied programme of readings and signings throughout the year. **Other locations** Jervis Centre, Jervis Street, Around O'Connell Street (878 1311).

Winding Stair

40 Lower Ormond Quay, Around North Quays (872 6576/www.winding-stair.com). All cross-city buses/ Luas Jervis. **Open** noon-5pm Tue-Sun. **Credit** MC, V. **Map** p251 E2.

You'll find plenty of interesting titles at this beguilingly quirky bookshop, where chandeliers hang from the ceiling and wing-backed armchairs face each other across a coffee table piled high with perusable volumes. And sometimes there'll even be music from the ancient record player to keep you company as you browse the shelves of classic and contemporary fiction, design texts and imaginative children's books.

Second-hand & rare

Cathach Books

10 Duke Street, Around Temple Bar (671 8676/ www.rarebooks.ie). All cross-city buses/Luas St Stephen's Green. **Open** 9.30am-5.45pm Mon-Sat. **Credit** AmEx, MC, V. **Map** p251 F3/4.

Many a pleasant afternoon can be spent thumbing through the dusty, yellow-paged gems that fill the shelves of this charming shop. It's not cheap, but there's an admirable pick of first editions and signed copies from sons of the city like James Joyce and WB Yeats to far-flung scribblers like William S Burroughs. Cathach also sells rare maps and prints. *Photo p141.*

Greene's

16 Clare Street, Around St Stephen's Green (676 2554/www.greenesbookshop.com). All cross-city buses. **Open** 9am-5.30pm Mon-Fri; 9am-3pm Sat. **Credit** AmEx, DC, MC, V. **Map** p251 G4.

Set near the National Art Gallery, Greene's is now one of Dublin's bookish landmarks. An impressive number of literary giants have walked through its doors over the years, including Behan, Yeats and Beckett. Greene's is well known for its good selection of new, second-hand and antiquarian books. The storefront has changed little since 1917.

Secret Book & Record Shop

15A Wicklow Street, Around Temple Bar (679 7272). All cross-city buses. **Open** 11am-6.30pm Mon-Wed, Fri-Sun; 11am-7.30pm Thur. **No credit cards.** **Map** p251 F3.

This charming second-hand bookshop on Wicklow Street stocks a bit of everything: a few out-of-print paperbacks, recently remaindered titles and even the occasional stack of LPs. Despite its rather tongue-in-cheek name, it's not much of a secret, but is worth nosing out all the same.

Specialist

Connolly Books

43 Essex Street, Temple Bar (670 8707/ www.communistpartyofireland.ie). All cross-city buses/Luas Jervis. **Open** 9.30am-6pm Mon-Sat. **Credit** DC, MC, V. **Map** p251 E2.

Restored to its original location on Essex Street (after a temporary spell across the river in Bloom Lane), this political bookshop takes its name from James Connolly, Ireland's socialist pioneer. As you might expect, it stocks contemporary leftist writing (it is the official bookshop of the Communist Party of Ireland), plus books on Irish history, feminism and philosophy. It's popular with Gaelic speakers too.

Sub City

2 Exchequer Street, Temple Bar (677 1902). All cross-city buses/Luas Jervis/St Stephen's Green. **Open** noon-7pm Mon-Wed, Fri, Sat; noon-8pm Thur. **Credit** MC, V. **Map** p251 E3.

Proving that comics and graphic novels have a readership beyond that of arrested adolescents and lank-haired loners, this smart little comic store on Excequer Street really does have something for everyone. All the Marvel and DC titles are on display, from pricey collectors' editions to the €1 bargain crates, as well as more cerebral works such as Marjane Satrapi's *Persepolis* or Toufic El Rassi's *Arab in America*.

CDs & records

Beatfinder Records

4 Fownes Street Upper, Around Temple Bar (672 9355/www.beatfinderrecords.com). All cross-city buses/Luas Jervis. **Open** 11am-7pm Mon-Wed, Fri; 11am-8pm Thur; 11am-6pm Sat. **Credit** MC, V. **Map** p251 E3.

The name may have changed (the moniker Big Brother Records didn't sound quite so good in the age of reality TV) but the staff are still as friendly

Eat, Drink, Shop

Victory in vinyl at **Beat Finder Records**. *See p143.*

as ever. And they know their stuff, with a great independent selection of vinyl and CDs that covers all the bases from tech-house to punk-funk. It's a good place to catch up on club news, and the store has a nifty location in the heart of Temple Bar.

Celtic Note

12 Nassau Street, Around Trinity College (670 4157/www.celticnote.com). All cross-city buses/ Luas St Stephen's Green. **Open** 9am-7pm Mon-Wed, Fri, Sat; 9am-8pm Thur; 11am-6pm Sun. **Credit** AmEx, MC, V. **Map** p251 H5.

If you're after Irish stuff, then this is the place to come to (as you may have guesed from all those big posters of Glen Hansard and co in the window).

Helpful staff are on hand to answer any queries, and the stock also includes a decent pick of British and American folk artists.

Claddagh Records

2 Cecilia Street, Around Temple Bar (677 0262/ www.claddaghrecords.com). All cross-city buses/ Luas Abbey Street. **Open** 10.30am-5.30pm Mon-Fri; noon-5.30pm Sat. **Credit** MC, V. **Map** p251 E3.

Die-hard traditionalists will delight in Claddagh's excellent and extensive stock of Irish folk tunes. There's everything here from early trad recordings to the most recent releases. This is where to pick up a rare folk album, find out about traditional concerts or just catch up on what's happening in Irish music.

Golden Discs

Stephen's Green Centre, St Stephen's Green (872 4211/www.goldendiscs.ie). All cross-city buses/Luas St Stephen's Green. **Open** 9am-6pm Mon-Wed, Fri, Sat; 9am-9pm Thur; noon-6pm Sun. **Credit** AmEx, MC, V. **Map** p251 F4.

Handily located right opposite Grafton Street, this Stephen's Green Centre branch of Golden Discs (like the several others that are dotted around town) is fast becoming overshadowed by larger international chains, which may be in part because of its dedication to MOR stock. Still, it's not a bad record store, it's just not that inspiring.

Other locations throughout the city.

HMV

65 Grafton Street, Around Temple Bar (679 5334/www.hmv.co.uk). All cross-city buses/Luas St Stephen's Green. **Open** 8.30am-7pm Mon-Wed, Fri, Sat; 8.30am-9pm Thur; 10am-7pm Sun. **Credit** AmEx, MC, V. **Map** p251 F4.

As long as you expect the ear-drumming chart music and walls of teenagers that go with the HMV territory, you won't be diappointed by this comprehensive Grafton Street branch of the music, DVD and entertainment superstore. Gig tickets are often on sale here too.

Other locations throughout the city.

Road Records

16B Fade Street, Around St Stephen's Green (671 7340/www.roadrecs.com). All cross-city buses/Luas St Stephen's Green. **Open** 10am-6pm Mon-Wed, Fri, Sat; 10am-7pm Thur; 2-6pm Sun. **Credit** MC, V. **Map** p251 E4.

It might be a bit *High Fidelity* for some people's tastes but vinyl junkies will love this old-school music store for its great selection of leftfield tunes (with Irish independent artists getting plenty of shelf space), its small but perfectly formed interior and the good tunes on the stereo.

Tower Records

16 Wicklow Street, Around Temple Bar (671 3250/www.towerrecords.co.uk). All cross-city buses/Luas St Stephen's Green. **Open** 9am-9pm Mon-Sat; noon-7.30pm Sun. **Credit** AmEx, MC, V. **Map** p251F3.

Another chain, but thankfully this one has a good array of alternative and world music, plus jazz, traditional and country. It also sells music mags and foreign newspapers.

Children

General

If it's just clothes you're after, then try the children's departments in **Avoca** (*see right*), **Dunnes Stores** (*see p139*), **Marks & Spencer** (*see p139*) and **Arnotts** (*see p139*) – or even the pricier (but posher) **Brown Thomas** (*see p139*) for something special.

Mothercare

Jervis Centre, Jervis Street, Around O'Connell Street (878 1184/www.mothercare.co.uk). All cross-city buses/Luas Jervis. **Open** 9.30am-6pm Mon-Wed, Fri, Sat; 9.30am-9pm Thur; noon-6pm Sun. **Credit** MC, V. **Map** p251 E2.

The largest of several branches in Dublin, this Mothercare has a comprehensive supply of all the usual clothing, gizmos and gadgets. Pushchairs, nursery furnishings (including beds and cots), clothes (for mother and child) – it's all here. There's even a pre-packed 'hospital bag' stuffed full of everything a first-time mum will need on the big day.

Other locations throughout the city.

Toys

Banba Toymaster

48 Mary Street, Around North Quays (872 7100). All cross-city buses/Luas Jervis. **Open** 9.30am-6pm Mon-Wed, Fri, Sat; 9.30am-8pm Thur; noon-6pm Sun. **Credit** MC, V. **Map** p250 D2.

The young and young-at-heart are likely to lose their heads in this colossal pantheon of play. The tightly packed aisles roar with every big brand name you can think of, as kids cluster around the latest toys.

Early Learning Centre

3 Henry Street, Around O'Connell Street (873 1945/www.elc.co.uk). All cross-city buses/Luas Abbey Street. **Open** 9.30am-6pm Mon-Wed, Fri; 9.30am-8.30pm Thur; 9am-6pm Sat; 1-5pm Sun. **Credit** MC, V. **Map** p251 F2.

A well-known chain that's known for its bright, fun and educational toys (the Planet Protectors range is a stroke of genius), all designed to stimulate and engage babies, toddlers and youngsters.

Crafts & gifts

If you're after upmarket crafts, take a stroll around **Cow Lane** and **Temple Bar**; for traditional knitware, contemporary Celtic jewellery and Waterford Crystal, try **Nassau Street** near Trinity College.

Modern crafts

Avoca

11-13 Suffolk Street, Around Temple Bar (677 4215/www.avoca.ie). All cross-city buses/Luas St Stephen's Green. **Open** 10am-6pm Mon-Wed, Fri; 10am-8pm Thur; 10am-6.30pm Sat; 11am-6pm Sun. **Credit** AmEx, DC, MC, V. **Map** p251 F3.

Avoca is always ferociously busy at the weekends, but it's worth braving the crowds: this is one of the best-loved stores in town for a reason. As well as a good selection of clothing, the three-floor store bursts at the seams with pretty jewellery, unusual and wacky gifts (dog lead with built-in torch, anyone?), cute children's clothing and a good selection of non-fiction books (notably the range of cookbooks

Eat, Drink, Shop

from its famous County Wicklow café). Downstairs you'll find a small café and deli with delectable breads and tempting cakes (*see p117*). There are branches throughout Ireland (and even one in the States) but this is the sole outlet in Dublin.

Design Yard
48 Nassau Street, Around Trinity College (474 1011/www.designyard.ie). All cross-city buses/Luas St Stephen's Green. **Open** 10am-7pm Mon-Sat; 11am-6pm Sun. **Credit** AmEx, DC, MC, V. **Map** p251 F3.
It may no longer be in its quaint Cow Lane location but Design Yard's high-end contemporary art and jewellery is looking as good as ever. Everything from beautiful rings and necklaces to limited-edition sculptures and ornate lamps is on sale here, alongside an interesting revolving programme of art exhibitions taking in subjects ranging from Dublin streetscapes to conflict diamonds.

Pens & stationery

Pen Corner
12 College Green, Around Temple Bar (679 3641). All cross-city buses/Luas Abbey Street. **Open** 9am-5.30pm Mon-Fri; 10am-5pm Sun. **Credit** MC, V. **Map** p252 F3.
A classy stationer and supplier of top-notch fountain pens, this long-established Dublin shop is still going strong, furnishing those who are bored by email with the tools to do the job the old-fashioned way. Fountain pens (Mont Blanc, Cross, Waterman) are displayed in discreetly lit cabinets on the ground floor, while the elegant basement stocks fine art greeting cards and high-quality stationery (Moleskine and the like).

Traditional crafts

Blarney Woollen Mills
21-23 Nassau Street, Around Trinity College (671 0068/www.blarney.com). All cross-city buses/Luas St Stephen's Green. **Open** 9am-6pm Mon-Sat; 11am-6pm Sun. **Credit** AmEx, MC, V. **Map** p251 F3.
The main branch of this chain is actually located in the village of Blarney, so its name is not as shamelessly cheesy as all that. However, don't come here expecting the latest trends: what they stock is handwoven items like throws, sweaters and scarves, plus souvenirs of the Waterford Crystal and Royal Tara china varieties.

Louis Mulcahy
46 Dawson Street, Around Temple Bar (670 9311/www.louismulcahy.com). All cross-city buses/Luas St Stephen's Green. **Open** 10am-6pm Mon-Wed, Fri, Sat; 10am-8pm Thur.* **Credit** AmEx, MC, V. **Map** p251 F4.
It might be impossible to cram one of Mulcahy's oversized vases into your suitcase, but there's also plenty of smaller stuff here. His fine porcelain range has now been discontinued but there's still a good selection of attractive stoneware, not least the new Dearg line.

Woollen Mills
41 Lower Ormond Quay, North Quays (828 0301). All cross-city buses/Luas Jervis. **Open** 9am-6pm Mon-Wed, Fri; 9am-7pm Thur; 9.30am-6pm Sat. **Credit** AmEx, MC, V. **Map** p251 E2/3.
Spinning out the knitwear thang with considerable energy, the Mills has been going strong for well over a century now. Aran, cashmere, merino and mohair items are in plentiful supply, taking the form of sweaters, capes, scarves and cardies. Not exactly cutting edge but not dowdy, either.

Electronics

Cameras

Camera Centre
56 Grafton Street, Around Temple Bar (677 5594/ www.cameracentre.ie). All cross-city buses/Luas St Stephen's Green. **Open** 9am-6pm Mon-Wed, Fri, Sat; 9am-8pm Thur; 1-5.30pm Sun. **Credit** AmEx, DC, MC, V. **Map** p251 F4.
As well as the usual cameras, camcorders, binoculars and telescopes, Camera Centre also offers a one-hour film-processing service as well as facilities to develop digital photos.

Camera Company
9B Trinity Street, Around Temple Bar (679 3410/ www.cameraexchange.ie). All cross-city buses/Luas St Stephen's Green. **Open** 9am-6pm Mon-Wed, Fri, Sat; 9am-7pm Thur. **Credit** AmEx, MC, V. **Map** p251 F3.
Now known as the Camera Company (it used to be the Camera Exchange) this well-stocked shop has plenty of new and used camera equipment, with clued-up staff on hand to give advice.
Other locations 63 South Great Georges Street (478 4125).

Computer parts & repairs

Beyond 2000
2 Chatham Row, Around Temple Bar (677 7633/ www.beyond2000.ie). All cross-city buses/Luas St Stephen's Green. **Open** 9.30am-6pm Mon-Sat. **Credit** AmEx, MC, V. **Map** p251 F4.
A good, central resource for PC-related gizmos and software, this long-running computer store puts a friendly face on the business of getting technical. And if you're thinking of spending more than just a few quid, it could be worth checking the website for a downloadable discount coupon.

Fashion

While Dublin is packed with smart little boutiques, the city's shopping streets also throng with every possible chain store. Both ends of the market, in other words, are fairly comprehensively covered. Among the better mid-range chains in the city centre are the ever-dependable **GAP** (Arnotts; *see p139*), the serious label temple of **Urban Outfitters** (*see p149*) and modest **Muji** (5 Chatham Street, Around Temple Bar, 679 4591).

Chica

Units 3 & 4, Westbury Mall, Clarendon Street entrance, Around St Stephen's Green (633 4441). All cross-city buses/Luas St Stephen's Green. **Open** 10am-6pm Mon-Wed, Fri, Sat; 10am-7pm Thur. **Credit** MC, V. **Map** p251 F4.

One of two parts (there's another Chica store just around the corner at Unit 25), this upbeat, fun boutique sells evening and party wear to girls who want to stay just on the conservative side of boho. Expect sophisticated labels like APRIL,MAY and Sika. You'll find shoes, boots, bags and whatnot in the sister store.

Costume

10-11 Castle Market, Around Temple Bar (679 4188). All cross-city buses/Luas St Stephen's Green. **Open** 10am-6pm Mon-Wed, Fri, Sat; 10am-7pm Thur. **Credit** AmEx, MC, V. **Map** p251 F3.

Still one of the leading suppliers of hip and funky fashions to Dublin's discerning chicas, Costume pretty much has it all, from Roland Mouret and Temperley to Proenza Schouler.

In one era, out the other

Dublin may be known as something of a luxury shopping destination with more than its fair share of big-name stores and niche boutiques but it is also an increasingly popular destination for those on the scent of the past: antique hunters, retro fans and anyone looking to escape the cookie-cutter high-street norms will find much to admire in the city's vintage emporiums.

In terms of homeware, lighting and furniture, there is one name that rules the roost in Dublin: **Wild Child Originals** (*see p152*; pictured). Looking for an original Eames rocking chair or a vintage Bramin swivel chair? It's here that you'll find it, alongside a load of other pristine relics from the design archives of the 1950s through to the '80s, encompassing furniture of all shapes and sizes from studios in all corners of the world. And what's more, competitive shipping rates (not to mention the sheer gorgeousnes of the stock) mean that it's not, in fact, pure folly to be browsing here even if you are up to the last kilo on your baggage allowance home. Besides, there's smaller stuff too (from ornaments and kitsch stereos to space-age umbrella stands).

But if it's yourself rather than your home that you have come to furnish, then have a browse at **Rhinestones** (*see p149*), whose wonderful collection of sumptuous art deco and antique jewellery is nothing short of stunning. But check the tag before you fall in love with that precious 1930s necklace: some of the prices are as breathtaking as the stock.

For more jewellery and for high-quality vintage togs, visit **Jenny Vander** (*see p148*).

Wild Child Originals.

Eat, Drink, Shop

Urban Outfitters.

Henry Jermyn

16 Clare Street, Around St Stephen's Green (676 0501). All cross-city buses/Luas St Stephen's Green. **Open** 8.30am-6.30pm Mon-Wed, Fri; 8.30am-8pm Thur; 9am-6pm Sat; noon-6pm Sun. **Credit** MC, V. **Map** p251 G4.

Keeping the gents of nearby Merrion Square in hats and threads, this high-end tailor has an exclusive, gentleman's club aesthetic: oil paintings, ornate mantlepieces and other old-world trappings punctuate the racks of pinstripe suits and floor-to-ceiling shelves of double-cuffed shirts. The bespoke suits here are as good as you'll find anywhere in Dublin, and there's a suitably tasteful range of ties, cufflinks, umbrellas and felt hats (by Christys' & Company) with which to pamper one's inner Wooster.

Other locations chq, Custom House Quay, Docklands (636 0180); 45 Dawson Street, Around Temple Bar (671 1771).

Jen Kelly

50 North Great George's Street, Around O'Connell Street (874 5983). All cross-city buses. **Open** 8am-5.30pm Mon-Thur; 8am-4pm Fri. **Credit** AmEx, MC, V. **Map** p251 F1.

Not somewhere you can just wander into, couturier Jen Kelly's exclusive studio is geared more to those with the budget and ideas for a bespoke service. His opulent creations are famed for their rich use of velvet, fur, satin and Chantilly lace, and while they may be costly, they are worth every penny. All work is caried out on these elegant Georgian premises.

Jenny Vander

50 Drury Street, Around Temple Bar (677 0406). All cross-city buses/Luas St Stephen's Green. **Open** 10.30am-5.30pm Mon-Sat. **Credit** MC, V. **Map** p251 E3.

There's nothing fusty about this exquisite vintage clothing store, which carries an elegant range of

carefully selected threads, hats, shoes and accessories. The range of designer antique jewellery is particularly impressive. *See also p147* **In one era, out the other**.

Loft Market

Powerscourt Townhouse Centre, 59 William Street South, Around Temple Bar (671 7000). All cross-city buses/Luas St Stephen's Green. **Open** noon-6pm Fri, Sun; 11am-6pm Sat. **Credit** varies. **Map** p251 F3.

This NYC-style indoor fashion market has garnered a loyal following of local fashion junkies and hip students on the trail of the individual, one-off looks that are the stock in trade of the young designers and artists who share this space. There are plenty of vintage items (of clothing and jewellery) on sale too.

Louis Copeland

39-41 Capel Street, North Quays (872 1600/ www.louiscopeland.com). All cross-city buses/Luas Jervis. **Open** 9am-6pm Mon-Wed, Fri, Sat; 9am-8pm Thur. **Credit** AmEx, DC, MC, V. **Map** p251 E2.

Ireland's most famous tailor has been kitting out the chaps for over a century. As well as Copeland's own brand, the store also stocks suits from Hugo Boss, Armani and Canali.

Other locations 30 Lower Pembroke Street, Around St Stephen's Green (661 0110).

Louise Kennedy

56 Merrion Square, Around St Stephen's Green (662 0056/www.louisekennedy.com). All cross-city buses/ Luas St Stephen's Green. **Open** 9am-6pm Mon-Sat. **Credit** AmEx, MC, V. **Map** p251 G4.

Famed throughout the world for her exquisitely tailored suits and opulent eveningwear, Louise Kennedy is popular with a diverse range of women. Her stunning Georgian salon and home showcase her designs, as does an equally exclusive Belgravia outlet in London.

Tyrrell & Brennan

13 Lower Pembroke Street, Around St Stephen's Green (678 8332/www.tyrrellbrennan.com). All cross-city buses/Luas Harcourt. **Open** by appointment. **Credit** AmEx, MC, V. **Map** p251 G5.

Affable design duo Niall Tyrrell and Donald Brennan have broken the rigorous fashion mould with bold designs for real women. Don't expect any fuddy-duddy fashions here: this talented pair does a fine line in stylish ready-to-wear and made-to-order gear that's a big hit with Ireland's media types. And budding brides take note: some of the country's most glamorous wedding dresses are designed by T&B.

Urban Outfitters

4 Cecilia Street, Around Temple Bar (670 6202/ www.urbanoutfitters.co.uk). All cross-city buses/ Luas Jervis. **Open** 10am-7pm Mon-Wed, Sat; 10am-8pm Thur, Fri; noon-6pm Sun. **Credit** MC, V. **Map** p251 E3.

Taking it from the top: a floor of menswear asks serious cash for seriously trendy labels (Lyle & Scott, G Star, Fred Perry); in the middle, womenswear is equally cutting-edge, with Religion, Sessun, Paul & Joe and many others on the racks; on the ground floor, a thousand and one hip homewares and yet more clothes for the girls. There's also a small landing with an interesting selection of dance-music CDs and pop art canvases.

Fashion accessories

Jewellery

Powerscourt Townhouse Centre

(*see p140*) is home to all kinds of jewellers ranging from straightforward silversmiths to an assortment of eccentric antiques shops. **Johnson's Court** (off Grafton Street), on the other hand, is a good spot for small independent jewellers (as well as some larger, posher emporiums). Just don't forget your credit card.

Paul Sheeran

7 Johnson's Court, off Grafton Street, Around Temple Bar (635 1136/www.paulsheeran jewellers.ie). All cross-city buses/Luas St Stephen's Green. **Open** 9.45am-5.45pm Mon-Wed, Fri, Sat; 9.45am-7.45pm Thur. **Credit** AmEx, MC, V. **Map** p251 F4.

Don't be surprised if you bump into a celeb at this glamorous temple to all that glisters. Stocking some of the world's most exclusive brands in jewellery and watches, Sheeran's is a colossal emporium that oozes wealth and prestige.

Rhinestones

18 St Andrew's Street, Around Temple Bar (679 0759). All cross-city buses/Luas Jervis. **Open** 9.30am-6.30pm Mon-Wed, Fri, Sat; 9.30am-9pm Thur; noon-6pm Sun. **Credit** AmEx, MC, V. **Map** p251 F3.

See p147 **In one era, out the other.**

Richard Alan

58 Grafton Street, Around Temple Bar (616 8906). All cross-city buses/Luas St Stephen's Green. **Open** 10am-6pm Mon-Wed; 10am-8pm Thur; 9.30am-6pm Fri, Sat; noon-6pm Sun. **Credit** AmEx, DC, MC, V. **Map** p251 F4.

One for the ladies, this classy boutique on Grafton Street specialises in top-flight luxury clothing brands (Armani, Escada and the rest), as well as drop-dead gorgeous evening dresses by designers like Marc Bouwer. Plush stuff, then, with price tags to match.

Sabotage

20 Exchequer Street, Around Temple Bar (670 4789). All cross-city buses/Luas Jervis/St Stephen's Green. **Open** 10am-6.30pm Mon-Wed; 10am-8.30pm Thur; 10am-7.30pm Fri; 10am-6.30pm Sat; 1-6pm Sun. **Credit** MC, V. **Map** p251 E3.

Shockingly pink but reassuringly stylish, this hip womenswear boutique has two floors of party, club-by and everyday wear from labels like Numph and Uttam. There's also a good selection of funky giftware (cool crockery, tableware and whatnot). For something a little more grown-up, try Sabotage Too a few doors along (at No.14).

Smock

31 Drury Street, Temple Bar (613 9000/www.smock .ie). All cross-city buses/Luas St Stephen's Green. **Open** 10.30am-6pm Mon-Sat. **Credit** MC, V. **Map** p251 E4.

Having relocated in mid 2008 to this ultra chic Temple Bar site (a lovingly restored little townhouse on Drury Street that looks like it has been imported, brick by exposed brick from NYC's SoHo), Smock is still one of the hippest women's boutiques on this or any other block. Labels include Rittenhouse, Tsumori Chisato and Vivienne Westwood. Vintage jewellery and accessories are also sold.

Shoes

Birkenstock

36 Wicklow Street, Around Temple Bar (675 3766/ www.birkenstock.co.uk). All cross-city buses/Luas St Stephen's Green. **Open** 10am-6pm Mon-Wed, Sat; 10am-7.45pm Thur; 1-5pm Sun. **Credit** MC, V. **Map** p251 F3.

Give your feet a treat at this large Birkenstock emporium. Expect to find a good variety of styles from the German sandal and earthy footwear *meisters*.

Camper

10 Wicklow Street, Around Temple Bar (707 1501/www.camper.com). All cross-city buses/Luas St Stephen's Green. **Open** 10.30am-6.30pm Mon-Wed, Fri, Sat; 10.30am-8pm Thur. **Credit** MC, V. **Map** p251 F3.

Dublin's Camper store stocks a wide range of designs from the hip Mallorcan shoe company. It's a relatively small space, but the shoes are nicely displayed, with men's on one side, and women's on the other.

Schuh

47 O'Connell Street, Around O'Connell Street (872 3234/www.schuh.ie). All cross-city buses/Luas Abbey Street. **Open** 9.30am-6.30pm Mon-Wed, Fri, Sat; 10am-8pm Thur; noon-6pm Sun. **Credit** AmEx, MC, V. **Map** p251 F2.

Following a massive refit in summer 2008, this branch of Schuh is looking impressively spiffy. It's still a noisy and frenetically busy place but you'll find plenty of choice, with all the major skate brands, as well as Puma, Converse, Evisu and (exclusively stocked by Schuh) Red or Dead heels and pumps. **Other locations** throughout the city.

Food & drink

Delicatessens

Carluccio's

52 Dawson Street, Around Temple Bar (633 3957/ www.carluccios.com). All cross-city buses/Luas St

Get out of town

With untold miles of perfect trekking country and beautiful coastline right on its doorstep and enough annual rainfall to thoroughly test the best GORE-TEX on the market, Dublin is the natural home to a clutch of excellent outdoor clothing and equipment shops.

Leading the pack is the excellent **Great Outdoors** (*see p152*), whose main (Chatham Street) branch stocks a dazzling range of clothing, tents, backpacks, cooking and climbing gear, and every imaginable rugged accessory required for the taming of nature. Even if you're only in the market for a spot of light hiking, stop by here first: with everything

from lightweight fleeces and hiking socks through to heavy-duty waterproofs, you're bound to find something that will make life out there a little more comfortable. And if you're planning to take on the Irish Sea, then it's GO's sister branch (on Clarendon Street) that will be kitting you out in any of its bespoke departments devoted to diving, kayaking and surfing. Ask around too, as this branch sometimes organises kayaking trips or will be able to point you in the right direction.

Meanwhile, the **North Face** (*see p152*; pictured) specialises in its own brand of durable, lightweight and beautifully breathable outer clothing (much of which is ideal even for those not wishing to leave town but looking for good-quality, stowable shower protection). In a similar vein is **Patagonia** (*see p152*), where inspirationally 'right-on' stock extends to everything from organic cotton shirts and tote bags to backpacks and serious sleeping bags. The Patagonia global conscious is commendable, with a commitment to eco-friendly produce being the key tenet of the brand (there's even a carbon footprint tracker for its products on the website – you can't say fairer trade than that).

And if none of the above have what you need, then find your way to **Millets** (no, not *that* Millet's – a different one; *see p152*), where high-quality tents and camping equipment, and durable, waterproof footwear are the specialities.

Stephen's Green. **Open** 7am-10pm Mon-Fri; 8am-10.30pm Sat; 9am-10pm Sun. **Credit** AmEx, MC, V. **Map** p252 F4.

The first branch of the successful Italian deli and *caffè* chain to open outside of England, Dublin's Carluccio's does a good line in luxury Italian produce – from the fresh stuff (meats, cheeses, heavenly own-made *caponata* and so on) to the store-cupboard specials of high-quality oils, preserves and lots more. The small deli section is at the front of the busy café (*see p119*).

Fallon & Byrne

Exchequer Building, 11-17 Exchequer Street, Around Temple Bar (472 1010/www.fallonand byrne.com). All cross-city buses/Luas Jervis/St Stephen's Green. **Open** 8am-10pm Mon-Fri; 9am-9pm Sat; 11am-8pm Sun. **Credit** MC, V. **Map** p251 E3.

The Dean & DeLuca of Dublin, F & B is the foodhall of choice among the city's fashionable professionals and fastidious foodies. Its warehouse vibe and rows of high shelves jammed with international luxury deli items make shopping here a pleasure (particularly when combined with a delicious sarnie and top-notch coffee from the café counter). Whether you have a sudden craving for sun-blush tomatoes or you've run out of miso soup sachets, this is where you come to sort it out. There's also a restaurant and a wine cellar on the Exchequer Street premises (*see also p102*).

Magills

14 Clarendon Street, Around Temple Bar (671 3830). All cross-city buses/Luas St Stephen's Green. **Open** 9.30am-5.45pm Mon-Sat. **Credit** MC, V. **Map** p251 F4.

Always busy (and deservedly so), this appetising deli does a roaring trade in fine imported and own-made foods. Gorgeous fresh breads line the counter, salamis hang from the ceiling and expensive pastas fill the shelves. The staff are exceptionally knowledgeable and helpful.

Sheridan's Cheesemongers

11 Anne Street South, Around St Stephen's Green (679 3143/www.sheridanscheesemongers.com). All cross-city buses/Luas St Stephen's Green. **Open** 10am-6pm Mon-Wed; 10am-7.30pm Thur; 10am-7pm Fri; 10am-6pm Sat. **Credit** MC, V. **Map** p251 F4.

Coolea, Desmond, Lavistown: these are just some of the wonderful Irish artisinal cheeses that have people lapsing into Wallace-like trances of dairy-induced ecstasy at this Dublin branch of Ireland's premier cheesemonger. The Anne Street South premises are small, the fragrances are pungent and the staff are brimming over with expert advice. There's a good choice of English, French, Spanish and many other cheeses too, but that's hardly the point. Staff also man a Sheridan's stall between 10am and 5pm on Saturdays at the Temple Bar food market in Meeting House Square and at the People's Park, Dun Laoghaire on Sundays between 10am and 4pm.

Wine & alcohol

Berry Bros & Rudd

4 Harry Street, Around Temple Bar (677 3444/ www.bbr.com). All cross-city buses/Luas St Stephen's Green. **Open** 10.30am-6.30pm Mon-Wed, Fri, Sat; 10.30am-8.00 pm Thur. **Credit** MC, V. **Map** p251 F4.

Housed in the 19th-century splendour of the former Weights & Measures Building on Harry Street, this is surely Dublin's fanciest offy. The cellars are jammed with some 800 fine wines (many of which will be familiar to those who shop at BB&R's London branches). As ever, when it comes to wine, you get what you pay for, but bottles start at around the €6 mark.

Whelan's

23 Wexford Street, Around St Stephen's Green (475 2649). All cross-city buses/Luas Harcourt Street. **Open** 10.30am-10.30pm Mon, Tue; 10.30am-11pm Wed; 10.30am-11.30pm Thur-Sat; 12.30-11pm Sun. **Credit** AmEx, MC, V. **Map** p251 E5.

Not to be confused with the cracking pub of the same name next door (*see p134 and p183*), this Whelan's is nothing more exciting than a reliable, city centre off-licence.

Health & beauty

Cosmetics

Don't miss the vast, luxurious and sleek beauty counters at **Brown Thomas** (*see p139*) and **Arnotts** (*see p139*), as well as branches of the ever-dependable **Body Shop** (www.thebodyshop.co.uk), which are liberally scattered around town.

Face 2/Make-up ForEver

40 Clarendon Street, Around Temple Bar (679 9043/www.face2.ie). All cross-city buses/Luas St Stephen's Green. **Open** 9.30am-6pm Mon-Wed, Fri, Sat; 9.30am-7pm Thur. **Credit** AmEx, MC, V. **Map** p251 F4.

Home to the Face 2 and Make-up ForEver brands, this upmarket boutique sells myriad products from the two ranges, as well as offering courses to help punters acquire the professional touch, and various services (such as the 'wedding call out') designed to cover every make-up-related contingency.

Nue Blue Eriu

9 William Street South, Around Temple Bar (672 5776/www.nueblueeriu.com). All cross-city buses/ Luas St Stephen's Green. **Open** 10am-6pm Mon, Fri, Sat; 10am-8pm Tue-Thur. **Credit** MC, V. **Map** p251 F3.

If mainstream beauty brands leave you cold, you might find inspiration at this chic emporium filled with cult beauty products. Splurge on fragrances from E Coudray, make-up from Chantecaille and skincare products by La Prairie in a cool, stylish

Eat, Drink, Shop

environment. There are also treatment rooms to the rear of the shop – luxury facials and waxing treatments are specialities.
Other location chq, Custom House Quay, Docklands (636 0180).

Hairdressers

Natural Cut
34 Wicklow Street, Around Temple Bar (679 7130). All cross-city buses/Luas St Stephen's Green. **Open** 10am-7pm Mon-Sat. **No credit cards. Map** p251 F3.
If you're scared of sulky hairdressers wielding hair-straighteners and bottles of noxious gunk, try this soothing alternative. The salon also forgoes the shampoo and blow-dry route for a spray-and-snip technique. A cut starts at €70 (ladies) and €45 (men).

SitStil
17 Drury Street, Around St Stephen's Green (616 8887/www.sitstil.com). All cross-city buses/Luas St Stephen's Green. **Open** 9.30am-5.15pm Mon-Wed; 9.30am-7.15pm Thur; 9.30am-6.15pm Fri; 9am-4.15pm Sat.* **Credit** MC, V. **Map** p251 E3.
Relaxed and tastefully decorated with antique-style furnishings, this small, chic salon has a calm vibe: they even throw in an Indian head massage with every appointment. Cut and styling starts at €60 (ladies) and €35 (men).

Opticians

You can get eye examinations (and purchase good-quality budget eyewear and contact lenses) at branches of **Specsavers** (www.specsavers.com) all over the city.

Optika
1 Royal Hibernian Way, Dawson Street, Around Temple Bar (677 4705). All cross-city buses. **Open** 9.30am-6pm Mon-Sat. **Credit** MC, V. **Map** p251 F4.
You'll find swanky frames (Chanel, Prada and Tiffany) as well as a full contact lens service, eye tests and the rest at this hip optician.

Spectacle Parade
24 Lower Stephen Street, Around St Stephen's Green (400 5000/www.spectacleparade.ie). All cross-city buses/Luas Around St Stephen's Green. **Open** 9am-8pm Mon-Fri; 9am-6pm Sat; noon-6pm Sun. **Credit** MC, V. **Map** p252 E4.
Smart, modern and well stocked with designer frames (from Prada and Miu Miu to Alain Mikli and Tom Ford), Spectacle Parade has a variety of fashion-conscious eyewear, along with kids' specs, all manner of contact lenses and cool shades.

Interiors

INREDA
71 Lower Camden Sreet, Around St Stephen's Green (476 0362/www.inreda.ie). All cross-city

buses/Luas Around St Stephen's Green. **Open** 10.30am-6pm Mon-Fri; 11am-6pm Sat. **Credit** MC, V. **Map** p251 E5.
Design-literate lighting, furniture, homeware and kitchenware light up this small but stylish shop. Beautiful (and portable) home and kitchen accessories by String, iittala and Stelton will have spontaneous shoppers reaching for the plastic, while more serious, and less wieldy, purchases from the range of Ruben and Moooi furniture and lighting will probably require a little more forward planning.

Wild Child Originals
61 South Great George's Street, Around Temple Bar (475 5099/www.wildchildoriginals.com). All cross-city buses. **Open** 11am-7pm Mon-Wed, Fri; 11am-8pm Thur; 10am-6pm Sat; 1-6pm Sun. **Credit** MC, V. **Map** p251 E3.
See p147 **In one era, out the other.**

Sports & outdoor equipment

Foot Locker
28 Henry Street, Around O'Connell Street (872 1417/www.footlocker-europe.com). All cross-city buses/Luas Abbey Street. **Open** 10am-6.30pm Mon-Wed, Fri; 10am-8pm Thur; 9.30am-6.30pm Sat; noon-6pm Sun. **Credit** MC, V. **Map** p251 F2.
Booming music and wall-to-wall sports gear (from swimwear to specialist trainers) make this heavyweight chain a massive hit with teens.
Other locations throughout the city.

Great Outdoors
20 Chatham Street, Around Temple Bar (679 4293/ www.greatoutdoors.ie). All cross-city buses/Luas St Stephen's Green. **Open** 9.30am-6pm Mon-Wed, Fri, Sat; 9.30am-8pm Thur; 12.30-5.30pm Sun. **Credit** MC, V. **Map** p251 F4.
See p150 **Get out of town.**
Other locations 3 Clarendon Street, Around St Stephen's Green (672 7154/www.greatoutdoors.ie).

Millets Camping
61 Mary Street, Around North Quays (873 3571/ www.millets.co.uk). **Open** 9am-6pm Mon-Wed, Fri, Sat; 9am-7.30pm Thur; noon-6pm Sun. **Credit** MC, V. **Map** p251 E2.
See p150 **Get out of town.**

North Face
17 Temple Lane South, Around Temple Bar (672 7088/www.thenorthface.com). All cross-city buses/Luas Jervis. **Open** 10am-6pm Mon-Wed, Fri; 10am-8pm Thur; 10am-6pm Sat; noon-5pm Sun. **Credit** MC, V. **Map** p252 E3.
See p150 **Get out of town.**

Patagonia
24-26 Exchequer Street, Around Temple Bar (670 5748/www.patagonia.com). All cross-city buses/Luas Jervis/St Stephen's green. **Open** 10am-6pm Mon-Wed, Fri; 10am-8pm Thur; 9.30am-6pm Sat; 1-5pm Sun. **Credit** AmEx, MC, V. **Map** p251 E3.
See p150 **Get out of town.**

Eat, Drink, Shop

Arts & Entertainment

Festivals & Events	154
Children	159
Film	163
Galleries	167
Gay	171
Music	176
Nightlife	186
Sport & Fitness	191
Theatre & Dance	195

Features

Chapter and verse	158
To the Light House	166
A helping hand	175
A high price to pay	184
Indie Reign	188
Rules of the game	192

Light House. *See p164.*

Festivals & Events

A plan for all seasons.

Dublin has the art of pleasing everyone. In its cornucopian spread of festivals and events the city keeps readers, artists, boozers and sportsmen entertained. Recently, the ring of entertainment has grown and chocolate lovers, circus wannabes and film buffs have been invited into the fold.

There are quite a few annual events worth knowing about before you book your holiday. First, of course, there's **St Patrick's Day** (*see below*), still by far the biggest entry in the Dublin calendar. It's now celebrated with plentiful pints of the black stuff the world over, but Dublin is the fun's epicentre. As long as you can cope with the crowds, the weather and the queues, there's no better place to enjoy it.

Calmer heads prevail in the summer at the excellent **Dublin Writers Festival** and the **Bloomsday Festival** (for both, *see p155*): the latter celebrates the works of James Joyce, while the former pulls in some of the world's best writers. That sort of thing would bore the bejaysus out of most of the people packed into the stands for the **Six Nations** rugby tournament (*see right*) each spring, of course. But then, to each his own.

Winter

Christmas Eve Vigil

St Mary's Pro-Cathedral, Marlborough Street, Northside (874 5441). DART Connolly Station. **Admission** free. **Map** p251 F1. **Date** 24 Dec.
The majority of Christmas events here still focus on the religious festival itself. A Christmas vigil is held in St Mary's Pro-Cathedral by the Archbishop of Dublin, with the beautiful sounds of the Palestrina Choir at 9.30pm. Mass follows at 10pm.

Christmas Day & St Stephen's Day

Date 25, 26 Dec.
On Christmas Day, shops, pubs, restaurants and public transport all close down. On St Stephen's Day (known as Boxing Day in the UK, and in the US as 'the day after Christmas') most pubs reopen; there's little public transport; and the day ends with a big party. St Stephen's Day also sees the start of the Christmas Racing Festival at Leopardstown Racecourse.

Jameson Dublin International Film Festival

Information: 50 Upper Mount Street, Around St Stephen's Green (635 0290/www.dubliniff.com). **Tickets** phone for details. **Date** Feb.

Rising from the ashes of the much-maligned Dublin International Film Festival, this new event seems to be succeeding where the other failed. It celebrates the best of Irish and world cinema in screenings across the city, backed up by events that let fans meet Irish screenwriters, directors and actors.

Six Nations Rugby

Croke Park, Jones Road, Drumcondra, Northern suburbs (669 0950/www.rbs6nations.com/ www.crokepark.ie). Bus 3, 11, 11A, 11B, 16, 16A, 41, 51A. **Open** *Office* 9.30am-5.30pm Mon-Fri. **Tickets** available through the Irish | Rugby Football Union (www.irishrugby.ie) €24-€220. **Date** 7, 28 Feb.
This rugby competition between England, Ireland, Scotland, Wales, France and Italy is one of the biggest events in the Irish sporting calendar. Home games are played at Croke Park (*see p192*), and the atmosphere of a big match affects the whole of the city. Even when Ireland are not playing at home, match days are so partytastic that fans have been known to travel to Dublin solely to watch the game in a Dub pub. Accommodation is almost impossible to find at this time.

Spring

12 Points! Festival of Europe's New Jazz

Project Arts Centre, East Essex Street, Around Temple Bar (881 9613/www.project.ie/ www.improvisedmusic.ie/12points.php). **Tickets** €20 per three acts. **Date** March.
Organised by the Improvised Music Company, the new 12 Points! European Jazz festival offers a sassy mix of jazz from all points of the European compass. As well as the many gigs at venues across town, including Vicar Street (*see p181*) and the National Concert Hall (*see p185*), there are movies, workshops and exhibitions.

St Patrick's Day Parade & Festival

676 3205/www.stpatricksfestival.ie. **Date** 17 Mar.
It's the world's best excuse for a drink or seven: the feast day of a Welshman who ran the snakes out of Ireland. Over the past few years, the day has been comprehensively glammed up. The parade still forms the core of the celebrations, with some of Europe's brightest street performers and some of the world's loudest pyrotechnics. There's also a five day festival of top-class entertainment including concerts, exhibitions, street theatre, deafening fireworks and general frivolity. Pubs and bars are packed to the rafters from morning to night.

Arts & Entertainment

Convergence Festival

15-19 Essex Street West, Around Trinity College (674 6396/www.sustainable.ie/convergence). **Tickets** *prices vary, phone for details.* **Map** p251 E3. **Date** early-mid April.

This week-long event favours a simple, ethical approach to the business of urban living. Its programme features conferences, theatre, film screenings and exhibits, and themes that include slow food, sustainability, eco-design and plant medicine.

International Dance Festival Ireland

26 South Frederick Street, Southside (679 0524/ www.dancefestivalireland.ie). **Tickets** phone for details. **Date** April-May.

This innovative and often provocative annual event brings the best international dance companies to perform in the Abbey and the Project. Despite a rocky start (when an audience member sued the festival for programming a show that featured nudity and urination), the festival has been a success.

Summer

Women's Mini-Marathon

293 0984/www.womensminimarathon.ie. **Tickets** €15 walking or jogging; €22 running. **Date** early June.

This annual run is the largest event of its kind in the world, attracting upwards of 30,000 participants (not all of them female). It's less a competition than an opportunity to raise money for charity, and the vast majority of people walk rather than run the 10km (six-mile) course.

Dublin Writers Festival

881 9613/www.dublinwritersfestival.com. **Tickets** prices vary, phone for details. **Date** June.

Drawing together 50-odd writers and poets from all over the world, this increasingly high-profile literary event dishes up a banquet of readings, discussions and public debates. Programmes tend to be adventurous, with readings from heavyweights like Julian Barnes sitting comfortably beside an introduction to contemporary Arab writing. Try not to miss the Rattlebag poetry slam, where members of the public compete for a prize. *See p158* **Chapter and verse**.

Bloomsday Festival

James Joyce Centre, 35 North Great George's Street, Around O'Connell Street (878 8547/ www.jamesjoyce.ie). **Tickets** prices vary, phone for details. Date 16 June.

Held every year around 16 June, the date on which *Ulysses* is set, and taking its name from the novel's central character, the Bloomsday Festival commemorates Bloom's 'walking out' with a week-long celebration. Readings from Joyce, performances, excursions and meals help recreate the atmosphere of 1904 Dublin. Booking is strongly advised.

Docklands Maritime Festival

Liffey Quays, Docklands (818 3300/ www.dublindocklands.ie/maritimefestival). **Date** June bank holiday weekend.

A festival for sealovers and landlubbers. Maritime attractions include a flotilla of tall ships on the River Liffey while on land there's street theatre and a huge market for foodies.

A day in the life of the **Bloomsday Festival**.

Arts & Entertainment

Electric Picnic.

Music in the Park

222 2242/www.dublincity.ie.
Admission free. **Date** June-Aug.
The sun is shining, there's laid-back jazz or rousing opera in the background and all is right with the world. Dublin City Council's free open-air concerts and recitals in the city's parks have been a huge success. Bands can be heard Wednesdays and Friday lunchtimes at Wolfe Tone Park and Herbert Quay. Make your way to the Civic Offices Park on Wood Quay for Opera on Thursday lunchtimes in August.

Pride

Outhouse, 105 Capel Street (873 4932/ www.dublinpride.org). **Date** June.
Highlights of this week-long gay festival include a gay *céilidh*, drag contests, workshops, readings and theme nights in gay-friendly venues. The flamboyant centrepiece, however, is the Pride march itself, which troops from the Garden of Remembrance at the top of O'Connell Street to the grass-covered amphitheatre beside the Civic Offices at Wood Quay.

Dublin Circus Festival

Temple Bar Cultural Information Centre, 12 East Essex Street, Around Temple Bar (888 3610/www.templebar.ie). **Admission** free. **Date** Mid July. Some events require tickets and advance booking.
Roll up for a mix of performance art and traditional circus skills; the first 2008 season saw some unusual events. Not-to-be-missed shows included ants and butterflies performing acrobatically on a trapeze and leek dancing for the vegetable curious.

Temple Bar's Chocolate Festival

Temple Bar Cultural Information Centre, 12 East Essex Street, Around Temple Bar (888 3610/www.templebar.ie). **Admission** free. **Date** July. Some events require tickets and advance booking.
A festival in honour of the cocoa bean; somebody has seen sense. This new festival isn't all about licking slabs of the stuff though, it's a celebration of chocolate. Events include sensory exploration, chocie-related films, a chocolate carnival, a chocolate-themed literary event and a cocoa bean workshop. Start salivating now.

Jameson Movies on the Square

Meeting House Square, Around Temple Bar (888 3610/www.templebar.ie). All cross-city buses/Luas Jervis. **Admission** free. Tickets can be collected from the Temple Bar Cultural Information Centre, 12 East Street. **Map** p251 E3. **Date** July-Aug.
Life just got better. Saturday nights (plus an opening and a closing Friday session) will see big-screen movies shown in Meeting House Square. The 2008 billing included a comedy mix of the Commitments, Some Like it Hot, Life of Brian and Borat.

Oxegen

Punchestown Racecourse, Naas, Co Kildare (www.oxegen.ie/www.mcd.ie). **Tickets** check website for details. **Date** mid July.
Filling the gap left by the much-missed Witness festival, Oxegen is one of Ireland's only multi-stage festivals. Staged over three days at the Punchestown Racecourse in County Kildare (*see p193*), the 2008

line-up included the Kings of Leon, Editors, REM, Kaiser Chiefs, Stereophonics, Groove Armada, the Pogues and the Prodigy, among many others.

Dublin Horse Show
Royal Dublin Society, Anglesea Road, Ballsbridge, Southern suburbs (668 0866/www.rds.ie/horseshow). Bus 7, 7A, 45/DART Lansdowne Road. **Open** 9am-6.30pm Wed-Sun. **Admission** €33-€54; €27-€48 reductions. **Date** early Aug.

Offering some of the richest prizes in the world, this five-day showjumping event attracts high-profile visitors and competitors. The famous Nations' Cup, where international teams compete for the prestigious Aga Khan Trophy, is traditionally held on a Friday; Thursday is Ladies' Day.

Festival of World Cultures
Venues across the city (271 9555/www.festivalof worldcultures.com). **Date** 28-30 Aug 2009; 27-29 Aug 2010.

This annual arts and music festival is as international in scope as its name suggests (more than 50 countries take part). It may have a worthy aim (namely, promoting respect, understanding and awareness between different cultures) but it's also a really good laugh.

Electric Picnic
Stradbally Estate, County Laois (Tickets 0818 719 300/www.electricpicnic.ie). **Tickets** €240-€480. **Date** Last weekend in Aug/first weekend in Sept.

Billed as a boutique music and arts festival, the three-day Electric Picnic is in its sixth year. Old and new acts join the line-up in the music arena. Musical talent is joined by comedic talent for the International Comedy Club Stage and those looking for an holistic experience may embrace the Body & Soul Village. A performance art troupe, fire installation by David Best, poetry, political debate, a cooking stage and circus completed the rounded entertainment. For the first time, in 2008, a family ticket granted entrance to a specially designated family campsite. Music fans loved the 2008 music line-up – the Sex Pistols, Grace Jones, Franz Ferdinand, My Bloody Valentine, Goldfrapp and Underworld all took to the stage.

Liffey Swim
Rory O'More Bridge to Custom House Quay (www.dublincity.ie). **Date** Sat late Aug/early Sept.

Attempted generally by the very brave or the extremely foolhardy, this annual swimming race begins at the Rory O'More Bridge (near the Guinness Brewery) and ends 1.5 miles (2km) downstream at the Custom House (*see p88*). It was first undertaken by a handful of cold water enthusiasts back in 1920, and these days it attracts about 400 swimmers of all ages. It is organised by the Irish Amateur Swimming Association.

Autumn

All-Ireland Hurling & Football Finals
Croke Park, Jones Road, Drumcondra, Northern suburbs (836 3222/www.gaa.ie). Bus 3, 11, 11A, 11B, 16, 16A, 41, 51A. **Tickets** prices vary, phone for details. **Date** *Hurling* 2nd Sun in Sept. *Gaelic football* 4th Sun in Sept.

Arts & Entertainment

The north side of the city traditionally grinds to a halt on the second and fourth Sundays in September, as fans of Gaelic football and hurling travel from all over the country to Croke Park for their respective finals.

Dublin Fringe Festival

Selected venues across town (817 1677/ www.fringefest.com). **Tickets** prices vary, phone for details. **Date** Sept.

The Fringe is such an established event it hardly deserves the term 'fringe'. It's usually a mixed bag, but it has its moments. The festival is dedicated to providing a focus for new companies, though it also acts as a test bed where veteran companies can try out new material. The emphasis is on the unusual, and performances are innovative. The huge demand for venues during the event has sometimes forced companies to adapt quickly: previous performances have taken place in the city's public toilets and in parked cars.

Dublin Theatre Festival

677 8899/www.dublintheatrefestival.com. **Tickets** €6.50-€45. **Date** Sept-Oct.

This has been a showcase for the best of Irish and world theatre since its foundation in 1957. It not only provides a stage for emerging local talent, but also attracts international productions. Most of the city's theatrical venues host festival events, and the programme is usually varied; sometimes it follows a specific theme. Be sure to book in advance.

Adidas Dublin City Marathon

623 2250/www.dublincitymarathon.ie. **Date** Last Mon in October.

Ever since it first ran in 1980, the Dublin City Marathon has been hugely successful, attracting thousands of runners. The 26-mile (42km) course starts and finishes at the top of O'Connell Street and traces a route through Dublin's streets and suburbs. It starts at 9am, and you can cheer on the finishers a couple of hours later. Competitors should submit their entry form at least three weeks before the race.

Samhain Festival (Hallowe'en)

Dublin Tourism, Suffolk Street, Around Trinity College (www.visitdublin.com). **Date** 31 Oct.

Hallowe'en in Dublin is based on the traditional pagan festival of Samhain (pronounced: 'sow in'), a celebration of the dead that signalled the end of the Celtic summer. Dublin's Samhain Festival is one of Ireland's largest night-time events, attracting up to 20,000 people as the Hallowe'en Parade winds its way through the city from Parnell Square to Temple Bar and Wood Quay. The fireworks display afterwards is worth staying up for.

Chapter and verse

Normally, a city can lay claim to one of two kinds of literary glory: that of an illustrious past of poetry and penmanship, or else the mantle of 'creative capital', where today's stars of the printed page ply their trade and pool their wisdom. Dublin, it seems, can have a shot at both titles. While its pedigree has never been in doubt – the city's statues and heritage plaques read like a writerly *Who's Who* – its reputation as one of Europe's dynamic literary centres has been earned much more recently. And a large part of this

newfound kudos can be traced back to one, increasingly influential annual event: the **Dublin Writers Festival** (*see p155*).

These days, the Dublin Writers Festival is reeling in some serious heavyweights to give lectures,

participate in debates, and read from their latest works. And 2008 was no exception. Among the many events were an entertaining and wide-ranging talk by Tom Stoppard, a crowning of the year's IMPAC Dublin Literary Award winner (Rawi Hage) and readings from one of the greatest living exponents of the American short story, Tobias Wolff. And yet the flavour of the event is not exclusively literary, thanks to the programming of more eclectic events, such as 2008's debate on 'Irish Values'. A mixed bag of commentators (politician, historian and broadcaster) jousted and parried their way towards an insight into the current moral and social status of the nation.

Discussions, interviews and readings orbit the main events – which tend to take place in the **Project Arts Centre** (*see p198*) or the **Gate Theatre** (*see p197*) – at smaller venues around town, including some of the academic halls and classrooms on campus at Trinity. All of which bestows on the city a sense of scholarly and literary energy that spills over the boundaries of the festival itself, and to an increasing extent, percolates down through the other 51 weeks of the year.

Children

Major attractions for minors.

Dublin is a truly excellent city for a family holiday: it's the right kind of size, with the right kind of vibe, and it's full to bursting with child-friendly fun. Not only is it home to Europe's first purpose-built children's cultural centre – the **Ark Children's Cultural Centre** (*see below*) – but it now has the added bonus of a second, brand-new, fully interactive children's museum, **Imaginosity** (*see right*). And for those children who would rather eat a plateful of sprouts than be dragged around a museum, Dublin also has **Phoenix Park** (*see p85*), the largest city park in Europe, with the superb **Dublin Zoo** (*see p86*). If that doesn't wear them out, nothing will.

And then there's the seaside, in many ways still the surest bet for guaranteed family fun. Dublin has plenty of nearby beaches where sand castles can be built, kites flown and balls kicked. For all the information on the Bay area and the coast, *see pp95-98* and (for hotels) *pp36-52*.

INFORMATION
The 'Ticket' supplement with Friday's *Irish Times*, its Saturday magazine, and the *Sunday Independent*'s 'Living & Leisure' section, are all good sources of information, particularly for festivals, family days and other one-offs. The Dublin Tourism Centre's *Family Fun in Dublin* brochure has more long-term options, and www.dublinks.com has a good 'Kids' link. For children's shops, *see p145*.

Children's centres

These days, it seems you can't swing a paintbrush without splattering a child-oriented cultural programme or interactive display – everything from art lessons to workshops and junior lectures take place on a regular basis in many of the city's major museums. As well as the venues listed below, one of the best museums for kids is the **National Museum: Decorative Arts** (*see p86*), which holds regular events specifically designed to teach children about art and history.

Ark Children's Cultural Centre
11A Eustace Street, Around Temple Bar (670 7788/www.ark.ie). All cross-city buses/ Luas Jervis. **Open** *Office* 10am-5pm Mon-Fri. **Admission** €10 adults; €8 under-3s reductions. **Credit** MC, V. **Map** p252 E3.

Despite its slightly earnest mission statement (that 'all children, as citizens, have the same cultural entitlements as adults'), the Ark is, more than anything else, really good fun. It stages theatrical productions and exhibitions that have been created by children for children, while also running a regular programme of children's workshops with a wide but resolutely arty remit (how to build musical instruments, stage plays, productions and much more). All events take place during the day and make the most of the centre's fantastic amenities: there's an indoor theatre, an outdoor amphitheatre, gallery spaces and a workshop. Check the website or drop into the centre to see what activities are scheduled during your visit. *Photo p160-161.*

Imaginosity
The Plaza, Beacon South Quarter, Sandyford, Dublin 18 (217 6130/www.imaginosity.ie). Bus 46B, 11A, 75, 114/Luas Stillorgan. **Open** 1-5.30pm Mon; 9.30am-5.30pm Tue-Fri; 10am-6pm Sat, Sun. **Admission** €8 adults; €7 under-3s reductions; €6 toddlers (1-2yrs); €2 babies (6-12 mths). **Credit** MC, V.

The capital's newest child-oriented attraction, Imaginosity is a children's museum that has pretty much everything you need to get curious young minds fizzing with original ideas. It's a bright, light, fun building, from the 'reflecting pool' that runs beneath it (the structure stands on columns) to the colourful mosaics on its roof. There's a theatre space for junior dramatists, a 'climber' that spans two floors of scrambling and clambering opportunities, and a 'construction company' that offers kids the chance to get tooled up with plastic gear and hard hats and set about building, well, something. Really young ones can join in at a dedicated area where all manner of activities focus on motor skills, sensory exploration and language stimulation. In other words, if you've come to Dublin with the kids, you absolutely have to bring them here. And needless to say, everything from the food in the first-floor café to the layout of the loos has been devised with them in mind.

Eating & drinking

Dublin is not just a city for adults to come and gorge themselves on fine food and wine; junior gourmets (and not-so-gourmets) get more than their fair share here too. Starting at the obvious place: burgers are very much in vogue these days in Dublin, with **Jo'Burger** and **Bóbó's** (for both, *see p106* **The burgers of Dublin**) in the top spots (and with the added advantages of menus that will appeal to parents too), and **Canal Bank Café** (*see p108*) coming in a close second. The next best thing to burgers, of course, is pizza: try the **Farm** (*see p102*) for healthy versions, **Gruel** (*see p103*) for big, fat slices or the familiar comforts of Pizza Express (branded in these parts as **Milano**; check www.pizza express.com for branches). For something a little more exotic, there's always the excellent children's menu at **Wagamama** (*see p107*).

If they've been really, really good, you might consider taking the terrors to the superb **Lemon Crêpe & Coffee Company** (*see p119*), where waffles and pancakes come piled high with all kinds of Nutella-based gunge (also, sleep-deprived parents, take note: the coffee here kicks ass). Otherwise, take your pick from the city's many excellent cafés: the **Cake Café** (*see p122*) and **Butler's Chocolate Café** (*see p118*) would be obvious choices.

Sightseeing

A wander through Temple Bar at the weekend will usually unearth plenty of fun, even if it is only sampling the wares of the **market** in Meeting House Square, or wandering into one of the centre's many museums. One of the most popular museums for children is **Dublinia** (*see p67*), even if it is looking a little tattered around the edges these days. On a rainy day, make your way over to the **Natural History Museum** (*see p77*) – a genuine old-school Victorian museum, with not an interactive display in sight, just cramped glass cases full of skeletons, pickled creatures and stuffed animals. The ground floor of this fine old building houses the fauna of Ireland under the skeleton of a gigantic fin whale suspended from the ceiling. Upstairs (note, there's no lift, so prams and buggies must be left with the attendant downstairs) are creatures of the rest of the world. It's a dusty, old-fashioned and yet magical place – an archetype of museums as they once were. Children are fascinated by things like the sheer size of the giraffe or the strangeness of sea creatures and the ferocity of grizzly bears.

If it's a sunny day and you want to spend some time outside, **St Stephen's Green play area** is well equipped and orderly, with plenty of ducks to feed nearby, while **Trinity College** is spacious and pleasant for walks, although there are perhaps a few too many 'Keep Off the Grass' signs about. Still, the cricket greens, when not in use, provide plenty of space for charging around.

The plaza outside the General Post Office (*see p81*) on **O'Connell Street** usually has a few of the city's (free) rickshaws waiting to give

Ark. *See p159.*

people rides as far as St Stephen's Green or just over the bridge as far as Temple Bar. Naturally, kids love this, and the cyclists at the helm (typically students, jobbing Aussies and the like) tend to have a good line in child-friendly banter.

Further afield, the vast expanse of **Phoenix Park** (*see p85*) offers much to do in good weather, including the ever-distracting **Dublin Zoo** (*see p86*). The years have been kind to the zoo, which has regenerated into a jolly spot with increasing emphasis on conservation and safari-style attractions. New enclosures for many of the animals mean it is possible to observe them in something closer to their natural habitat.

And finally, heading beyond the city limits, the scenic coastal villages or towns – **Dalkey, Dún Laoghaire, Howth** or **Malahide** (*see pp95-98*) – all make for excellent day-trip destinations. Although, be aware that in most cases the beaches are pebbled – a notable exception being **Balbriggan Beach** on the northside, which is pretty, picturesque and has a sandy beach. Closer in, **Sandycove** (*see p98*) also fulfils this role on the southside, though it can be crowded on warm days.

Malahide Castle

Malahide Castle Demesne, Malahide (846 2184/www. malahidecastle.com). Bus 42/DART Malahide. **Open** *Apr-Oct* 10am-5pm Mon-Sat; 10am-6pm Sun. *Nov-Mar* 10am-5pm Mon-Sat; 11am-5pm Sun. **Admission** €7.50; €4.70-€6.30 reductions; €22 family. *Dublin Tourism combined ticket* €13; €8-€10.70 reductions; €36.30 family. **Credit** AmEx, MC, V.

The castle is exciting enough all on its own, and then there's the Fry Model Railway and Tara's Palace to make this a perfect junior his 'n' hers day out. The model railway features detailed replicas of Heuston and Cork railway stations, and a range of tiny, working trains that runs from vintage 1920s models to streamlined modern variants. Tara's Palace is a dolls' house built in the style of an 18th-century mansion. The basement café is excellent, and there's also a wooden adventure playground.

National Sealife Centre

Strand Road, Bray, Co Wicklow (286 6939/www. sealife.ie). DART Bray. **Open** *Mar-Sept* 10am-6pm daily. *Oct-Feb* 11am-5pm Mon-Fri; 10am-5pm Sat, Sun. **Admission** €10.95; €7.90-€9.95 reductions; €35 family; free under-3s. **Credit** MC, V.
This aquarium is constructed on a fairly humble scale, so there isn't much in the way of child-friendly wow factor. However, the wide variety of marine species, most of them native to these shores, means there's plenty to see, while the emphasis on conservation is commendable. There are baby sharks, seahorses and more. All in all, the National Sealife Centre is a great place to explore, and its commitment to children's education is exemplary (the recent Junior Sea Life Conference being a case in point).

Newbridge House & Traditional Farm

Newbridge Demesne, Donabate (843 6534). Bus 33B/Donabate rail. **Open** *Apr-Sept* 10am-5pm Tue-Sat; 2-6pm Sun. *Oct-Mar* 2-5pm Sat, Sun. **Admission** *House* €7; €3.50-€6 reductions; €18 family. *Farm* €3.80; €2.50-€2.80 reductions; €10 family. **Credit** MC, V.

An old-style cobbled farmyard with stables, a forge, hen coops, pig sties, bits of old farm machinery and a varied collection of animals – Newbridge has it all. There are even stables containing a huge, fantastically ornate golden coach that looks as if it must have once been a pumpkin. And little boys will find much to wrinkle their noses at in delighted disgust inside the Museum of Curiosities, which is crammed full of strange and sometimes ghoulish specimens, among them a 'scold's bridle' – a belt to stop the mouths of witches and doomsayers.

Sport & activities

For children who like the noise and excitement of karting, Dublin has a good racing venue. **Kart City** in Santry (*see p162*) has petrol-driven go-karts that really *go*, and are virtually impossible to flip over. Kids from six years and up can whizz around, but must be accompanied by an adult.

The Stillorgan **Leisureplex** (*see p162*) is the site of endless pre-teen birthday parties. Bowling, Quasar, bouncy castles, adventure playgrounds… you won't see them for hours.

Horse riding and water activities, each in their own way, make use of the city's best attributes: its littoral location and Dubliners' equine enthusiasms. The **Viking Splash Tour** is a riot of medieval fun and **Oldtown Riding Stables** (Wyestown, Oldtown, Co Dublin, 835 4755) has the advantage of being located near a lovely stretch of rural Ireland, which makes for some very pleasant riding.

Arts & Entertainment

Kart City

Old Airport Road, Clogharan, Northern suburbs (842 6322/www.kartcity.net). Bus 33, 41, 41B, 41C, 230, 746. **Open** 2-9.30pm Mon-Fri; 10am-9.30pm Sat, Sun. **Rates** *Adult track* €20/15mins, €26/20 mins, €32/25mins. *Junior track* €1/minute up to 30 mins. **Credit** MC, V.

Three tracks are available for four-wheel jeeps, kiddie karts and adult karting. Karting is not recommended for children under 12.

Leisureplex

Old Bray Road, Stillorgan, Southern suburbs (288 1656/www.leisureplex.ie). Bus 46A/Luas Stillorgan. **Open** 10am-1am Mon-Thur, Sun; 10am-3am Fri, Sat. **Admission** €1. **Credit** MC, V.

This noisy amusement chain offers all the usual activities like bowling, Quasar laser games and adventure play areas. At the Stillorgan centre kids can design and paint ceramics at Pompeii Paints, while Blanchardstown has dodgems for that old-fashioned fairground experience. **Other locations** Blanchardstown Centre, Northern suburbs (822 3030); Malahide Road, Coolock, Northern suburbs (848 5722); Village Green Centre, Tallaght, Southern suburbs (459 9411).

Viking Splash Tour

(707 6000/www.vikingsplash.ie). Starts from St Stephen's Green North (opposite Kildare Street), Bull Alley Street (by St Patrick's Cathedral). **Tours** *St Stephen's Green North* 10am, 11.30am, 2pm, 3.30pm daily. *Bull Alley Street* 10.30am, noon, 2pm, 3.30pm, 5pm daily. **Tickets** €20; €18 reductions; €10 under-12s; €60 family. **Credit** MC, V. **Map** p251 F4 and p250 D4.

If you're walking along the street one day and an old WWII 'duck' (a yellow canopied vehicle that looks a bit like a bathtub on wheels) draws up alongside you and its contents of over-excited children clad in plastic Viking helmets roar at you as loudly as they possibly can, don't be surprised. In fact, do be surprised, because scaring random pedestrians with synchronised roaring is one of the things that make the open-topped Viking Splash Tours such brilliant fun for kids (of all ages). Another thing is the fact that the vehicle can and does drive into the Liffey and go steaming off up towards Grand Canal Docks on its rumbustious tour of the city. Guides, who are (of course) dressed head to toe in Viking gear, give unfailingly funny commentaries that are worth the fee alone (and have the extraordinary talent of making dry historical facts sound fun).

Babysitting

Belgrave Agency

56 Mulgrave Street Dun Laoghaire, Co Dublin (280 9341/fax 280 9374/www.nannyie). **Open** *Bookings* 9am-5pm Mon-Fri. **Fees** *Agency* €36.30 booking fee. *Babysitters* €12-€15/hr. **Credit** MC, V.

A highly professional, reliable agency with consistently good reports, the Belgrave provides in-hotel babysitting services throughout Dublin. Just don't leave the booking until the last minute, partly because it's a popular service, and partly because the agency email forms in advance (for consent and giving some details about your children) that need to be downloaded, signed and sent back (via post, fax or email scans).

Viking Splash Tour.

Film

The Irish are watching them and making them like never before.

The surprise Irish movie sensation of 2007, *Once*, proved beyond any doubt that the nation's home-grown cinema is a force to be reckoned with. With its backdrop of Dublin streets, its Dublin-born director and a leading man plucked from the much-loved Irish band The Frames, *Once* did wonders for the city's cinematic self esteem. But then, in the last few years, Ireland's movie output has been grabbing headlines all over the place. In 2006, Ken Loach's *The Wind that Shakes the Barley*, about the Irish war of independence and civil war in the 1920s, took the Palme d'Or at Cannes and ignited a media row, with British papers accusing Loach of making a 'repulsive' film that 'drags the reputation of our nation through the mud'. Though many suspected the French of indulging in their national pastime of Brit and Yank bashing (the film drew clear parallels to the current situation in Iraq), scooping the top prize proved that Irish history could be a crowd-puller.

However, even more interesting than Loach's prize were two other films of the same period that also scooped awards: *Pavee Lackeen* and *Adam & Paul*. What got Irish cinema buffs excited about these two was not only the fact that the scripts, locations, cast and directors were all home-grown (*Pavee*'s director, Perry Ogden, is British but he's lived in Dublin for over ten years), but that both were partly financed by the Irish Film Board and both dealt with marginalised sectors of society – *Pavee* with travellers, and *Adam & Paul* with drug addicts. They were a refreshing antidote to the recent slew of romantic comedies – *About Adam*, *Goldfish Memories*, *When Brendan Met Trudy* – that make Dublin look bright, metrosexual, upbeat, feel-good... and not remotely like Dublin. Both were also low-budget and they blazed the trail for other independent low-budget, Irish films. Film in Ireland is still a nascent art, and the industry is tiny, but low-cost techniques help directors experiment and keep control. And maybe the rest of the country will get a look-in now that Hollywood's love affair with the west of the country (*The Quiet Man*, *Ryan's Daughter*) seems to be over, all Irish films begin and end in Dublin (or Belfast).

Meantime, Ireland's popularity as a film location continues – the government fought off competition from Eastern Europe, where labour is much cheaper, by raising the percentage of expenditure eligible for tax relief to 80 per cent for all films, up from pre-2006 levels of 55 per cent or 66 per cent. So 2006 saw the welcome return of loads of big-budget international projects, including *Becoming Jane* (about Jane Austen) and the *History of the Tudors*.

The **Irish Film Institute** (*see p164*) on Eustace Street is an excellent starting point for an exploration of Ireland's film heritage – classic films to watch out for are Robert Flaherty's *Man of Aran* (1934), Brian Desmond Hurst's *Playboy of the Western World* (1961), John Davies' and Pat Murphy's *Maeve* (1982) and Alan Clarke's *Elephant* (1989). The **Light House** (*see p166*) in Smithfield is the other place to catch the maverick and offbeat. The other city-centre cinemas – **Savoy** (*see p164*), **Cineworld** (*see below*) – are multiplexes offering the usual fare. Sadly, the tiny Stella in Rathmines, last bastion of the local cinemas that used to pepper the 'burbs, has finally closed down, leaving only multiplexes outside the centre.

The city plays host to a number of festivals throughout the year, including the Dublin Film Festival, the Dublin Lesbian and Gay Film Festival, and the Dark/Light Festival (www.darklight-filmfestival.com) in May or June, which emphasises digital films by up-and-coming filmmakers. A recent addition is the Jameson International Dublin Film Festival, which started in 2004 and offers a great mix of Irish, international, mainstream and offbeat pictures. For all festivals, *see pp154-158*.

GENERAL INFORMATION

New films open on Fridays, and movie listings appear daily in the *Irish Times* and the *Evening Herald*. The IFI also publishes its own guide, which you'll find in many cafés and bars, as well as at the cinema itself. Ticket prices vary, hovering around €8-€10 for new releases.

Cinemas

Cineworld
Parnell Centre, Parnell Street, Around O'Connell Street (872 8444/www.cineworld.ie). All cross-city buses. **Open** Box office 11.20am-9.30pm Mon-Thur, Sun; 11.20am-11.50pm Fri, Sat. **Tickets** €8-€10; €6-€8 reductions; €25-€28.40 family. **Credit** AmEx, MC, V. **Map** p251 F1.

Arts & Entertainment

Since it opened about a decade ago, this multiplex has been through more names than Prince (Virgin, UGC) but through each name change, it has remained exactly the same: the latest releases on the best screens, crystal-clear sound, chairs you can fall asleep in and super-sized tubs of popcorn. Definitely the best way to enjoy blockbusters' special effects, and there are so many screens that you can sometimes catch a rare indie too. Be sure to book or come well in advance.

Irish Film Institute

6 Eustace Street, Around Temple Bar (679 5744/ www.irishfilm.ie). All cross-city buses/Luas Jervis. **Open** *Box office* 2-8.30pm daily. **Tickets** €9; €6-€7.75 reductions. **Credit** MC, V. **Map** p251 E3.

The starting point for Irish cinema, the IFI is in a wonderfully converted 17th-century building in Temple Bar and has two screens, a bookshop and a public film archive; there's also a busy bar, which serves decent food and is a popular hangout in its own right. On offer is what you'd expect from a serious, non-commercial film buffs' centre: arthouse, indie, foreign-language, experimental, documentary, classic. The IFI operates a membership system, although in practice this means that only films that have not obtained a censor's certificate (usually those not on release elsewhere) are closed to the general public. Don't let this put you off: at just €20 per year, or €1 per day, the cost of joining is hardly prohibitive. All kinds of special programmes are operated under the IFI umbrella, such as its inspiring itinerary of educational screenings and the annual Reel Ireland run, which is where to catch the very latest work from the country's up-and-coming filmmakers.

Light House

Market Square, off Smithfield Square, Around North Quays (879 7601/www.lighthousecinema.ie). All cross-city buses/Luas Smithfield. **Open** *Box office* 1-9pm daily. **Tickets** €7.50-€9; €6-€7.50 reductions. **Credit** MC, V. **Map** p250 C2.

Foreign-language and art-house movies reign supreme at this welcome addition to the city's independent cinema scene. The theatres here are probably the most comfortable (and certainly the most stylish) in town. Special screenings and one-off events are also worth looking out for.

See also p166 **To the Light House**.

Savoy

16-17 O'Connell Street Upper, Around O'Connell Street (0818 776 776/www.savoy.ie). All cross-city buses/Luas Abbey Street. **Open** *Box office* 2-9pm daily. **Tickets** €9; €6-€8 reductions. **Credit** MC, V. **Map** p251 F1.

The Savoy, long a fixture of shabby 1970s chic that perfectly complemented the litter-strewn O'Connell Street has, like the street itself, finally had its facelift. These days, it's in a timewarp of wood panelling and fake chandeliers, and has gone from atmospheric to anodyne, but the seats are definitely more comfortable and the box office more responsive, so many

will accept the trade-off. The Savoy no longer has the largest screen in the city so isn't guaranteed the premières, but its location is prime, and it still trades on years of affection, so it remains integral to the festivals. Expect the usual mainstream blockbuster and rom-com programming.

Screen

D'Olier Street, Around Trinity College (0818 300 301/www.omniplex.ie). All cross-city buses/Luas Abbey Street. **Open** 2-9pm daily. **Tickets** €7; €6-€8 reductions. **Credit** MC, V. **Map** p252 F3.

Just round the corner from Trinity College, the Screen is scuffed, tatty, eternally studenty, and its programme is exactly what you'd expect: offbeat without being obscure; a mix of second-run, limited-release, foreign-language and arthouse pictures that can pack them in at busy times. Two of the three screens have seats for couples, so take someone you'd like to know better.

Out-of-town multiplexes

With the Stella gone, the 'burbs have nothing in the way of quaint, unusual or independent cinemas. So here, instead, is the best of the rest.

IMC Lower George's Street

Dún Laoghaire, Dublin Bay (information 280 7777/ bookings 230 1399/www.imccinemas.com). Bus 7, 7A, 45A, 46A, 46X, 59, 75, 111, 746. **Open** 1-8pm Mon-Fri; noon-8pm Sat, Sun. **Tickets** €9; €5.50-€6 reductions. **Credit** MC, V.

Ormonde Stillorgan

Stillorgan Plaza, Lower Kilmacud Road, Northern suburbs (1520 927 015/707 4100/www.ormonde cinemas.com). Bus 46, 46B, 63, 84, 84X, 86. **Open** 11am-7.30pm daily. **Tickets** €6.50-€8.70; €5.50-€7 reductions.; €20 family. **Credit** AmEx, MC, V.

Santry Omniplex

Old Airport Road, Santry, Northern suburbs (0818 719 719/www.omniplex.ie). Bus 16, 16A, 33, 41, 41B. **Open** noon-8.30pm Mon-Fri; 11am-8.30pm Sat, Sun. **Tickets** €9; €5.50-€6 reductions. **Credit** MC, V.

UCI Cinemas

Malahide Road, Coolock, Northern suburbs (1520 880 000/www.uci.ie). Bus 20B, 27, 42, 42B, 43, 103, 104, 127, 129. **Open** 12.30-8.30pm daily. **Tickets** €7.50-€11; €6.25-€7.75 reductions. **Credit** MC, V.

Other locations Blanchardstown Shopping Centre, Blanchardstown, Northern suburbs (1520 880 000); The Square, Tallaght, Southern suburbs (1520 880 000).

Vue

Liffey Valley Shopping Centre, Clondalkin, Southern suburbs (1520 501 000/www.myvue.com). Bus 78A, 210, 239. **Open** noon-10.30pm Mon-Thur, Sun; 11.30am-midnight Fri, Sat. **Tickets** €7.85-€9.95; €6.80 reductions; €27.20 family. **Credit** AmEx, MC, V.

The curtains are unveiled on the **Savoy**'s facelift.

To the Light House

When the **Light House** (*see p164*) cinema vacated its premises in Middle Abbey Street in 1996, Dublin lost one of its great cultural assets. Left with just the bastion of the **Irish Film Institute** (*see p164*) to shore up the art-house defences against Hollywood's perpetual ground-swell of blockbusters and rom-coms, the city endured more than a decade of pretty slim cinematic pickings. But in May 2008, all that changed, when a new, unrecognisably improved and completely relocated Light House opened up its doors again, this time in the hip hinterlands of Smithfield.

Designed by the award-winning DTA Architects, the new Light House is a stunning cinema. Its modest exterior (really no more than a nondescript entrance on an unobtrusive corner of the vast Smithfield Square) gives no hint of the signature building that lurks within. Walls and ceilings are bright and white or else clad in smooth black tiles; the staircase

is adjoined by a stepped lounge area; the corridors that connect the four movie theatres segue off into unexpected angular annexes, where unusual furniture and discreet lighting encourage filmgoers to linger and chat after the film. And the theatres themselves are all individually designed – some are decked out in a homage to traditionalism with blood-red walls and seats, or furnished with rows of brightly upholstered seats, all jumbled together in candy-coloured confusion.

Neil Connolly, joint owner of the Light House, is passionate about the future of independent cinema in Dublin. His reasoning behind the massive outlay of funds and resources that has been necessary to produce the current incarnation of the cinema is simple: 'If it is going to survive, cultural cinema needs the right habitat.' And judging by the influx of audiences (not to mention passers-by who drift in for a cappuccino and cake at the ground-floor café), there are a great many Dubliners who agree with him.

Light House cinema. *See p164.*

Galleries

Revival of taste in old and new.

Even if the Celtic Tiger is slinking off into the distance, tail between its legs, the market for Irish art is as bouyant as ever, with local galleries, both new and established, seemingly raking in the cash. A few years back, the market was confined to four or five serious buyers, who bought conservatively in the 1980s and early '90s – mostly 18th-century landscapes and works by the late 19th- and early 20th-century artists Jack Yeats, Sir John Lavery and Sir William Orpen. But now, not only are there hundreds of new buyers, but tastes have moved on, and there's a strong market at auction in 20th-century and contemporary work. Reflecting this change, Sotheby's hosted its first ever Contemporary Irish Sale in Dublin in autumn 2006, and now continues to do so every October.

Nevertheless, the tastes of Irish millionaires remain fairly conservative, making the cutting-edge work offered in contemporary commercial galleries like **Monster Truck** (*see p170*), **Gallery Number One** (*see right*) and **Green on Red** (*see p170*) extremely difficult to sell on the auction market. But such zeitgeist galleries are the exception rather than the norm – most galleries go for the solid and well established. The market is also insular – Ireland is, after all, an island, and the Irish like to buy Irish. Apart from Lavery, Orpen, William Scott, and one contemporary, Sean Scully (who now has a dedicated exhibition space in the **Hugh Lane**; *see p82*), most – if not all – of the Irish artists doing well in Dublin are virtually unheard of on the international markets.

Dublin's commercial galleries are mostly clustered round two areas in the centre: Temple Bar, which also houses two of the city's most innovative and challenging non-commercial galleries, the **Project Arts Centre** (*see p168*) and the **Temple Bar Gallery and Studios** (*see p168*); and Grafton Street and St Stephen's Green, where you'll find the **Kerlin** (*see p168*) and the **Rubicon** (*see p169*) for contemporary art, and the excellent **Gorry** (*see p168*) is the main standby for more traditional work (now that the splendid Solomon Gallery has moved out of town). But do stray off the beaten track for the adventurous Green on Red, tucked behind Trinity College, and Monster Truck and **Cross Gallery** (*see p170*) up in the Liberties. And if

you want a democratic street art fair, go to Merrion Square on Sunday afternoon – all and sundry are out, displaying their magnum opi. Most of the work runs from anodyne to garish to kitsch, but some of it is decent enough, and you can always haggle your way to a bargain.

Around Trinity College

Oisin Art Gallery

44 Westland Row (661 1315/www.oisingallery. com). DART Pearse/all cross-city buses. **Open** 9am-5.30pm Mon-Fri; 10am-5.30pm Sat. **Credit** MC, V. **Map** p251 G3.
This central, popular gallery recently moved to a beautiful new space right next door to its former home on Westland Row, and now it has a bit more room – there's even a spacious courtyard. Oisin deals in traditional and contemporary artists, including Christine Bowen, John Skelton, Katy Simpson, Ronan Goti, Cecil Maguire and Alan Kenny.

Around Temple Bar

Apollo Gallery

51C Dawson Street (671 2609/www.apollogallery.ie). All cross-city buses/Luas St Stephen's Green. **Open** 10.30am-6pm Mon-Sat; 1-6pm Sun. **Credit** MC, V. **Map** p252 F4.
From the sublime to the ridiculous – alongside a chance lovely portrait by Louis le Brocquy is the kind of kitsch you find in Sunday's open-air Merrion Square market. 'Eclectic' is the best description for the Apollo, but there really is something for everyone, and it's probably the only gallery in Dublin where you can still haggle, making it absolutely worth a visit.

Gallery Number One

1 Castle Street (478 9090/www.gallerynumberone. com). All cross-city buses/Luas Jervis. **Open** 11am-6pm Mon-Wed, Fri, Sat; 11am-8pm Thur; 1-6pm Sun. **Credit** MC, V. **Map** p252 E3.
Behind the smart modern frontage of this new gallery you'll always find an interesting selection of contemporary works by a wide range of artists. Connected to the hip Dublin-based design agency ebow, the Number One sets out to 'celebrate the link between art, music and popular culture'. The practical results of this mission statement might be anything from an exhibition of photographs taken by Pattie Boyd, self-proclaimed muse to Eric Clapton and George Harrison, through to a major show of paintings by Ronnie Wood. *Photo p169.*

Gallery of Photography

Meeting House Square (671 4654/www.irish-photography.com). All cross-city buses/Luas Jervis. **Open** 11am-6pm Tue-Sat; 1pm-5pm Sun. **Admission** free. **Map** p252 E3.

A gem of a space in the heart of Temple Bar. This gallery's permanent collection of 20th-century Irish artworks is run in conjunction with monthly exhibitions by Irish and international photographers. The bookshop is well stocked.

Gorry Gallery

20 Molesworth Street (679 5319/www.gorrygallery .ie). All cross-city buses/Luas St Stephen's Green. **Open** 11.30am-5.30pm Mon-Fri; 11am-2pm Sat (during exhibitions). **No credit cards. Map** p252 F4.

This gallery is a lovely space, where an old-world atmosphere is combined with some wonderfully eccentric touches. The Gorry sells Irish art from the 18th to the 21st centuries, and also specialises in painting restoration work.

Graphic Studio Gallery

Through the Arch, off Cope Street (679 8021/ www.graphicstudiodublin.com). All cross-city buses/Luas Jervis. **Open** 10am-5.30pm Mon-Fri; 11am-5pm Sat. **Credit** AmEx, MC, V. **Map** p252 F3.

Another Temple Bar gem, Graphic Studio Gallery's works on paper by Irish and international contemporary printmakers are displayed on two levels, in both group and solo shows. After taking in the good temporary displays, you can spend some time perusing a permanent selection of affordable works in folders, with prices starting at a very reasonable €90. This is an atmospheric space, running for more than ten years now, that offers affordable pieces by Jim Goulding, Mary Lohan, Louis le Brocquy, William Crozier and Tony O'Malley, alongside consistently strong work by local artists such as Cliona Doyle and John Graham.

Kerlin Gallery

Anne's Lane, Anne Street South (670 9093/www. kerlin.ie). All cross-city buses/Luas St Stephen's Green. **Open** 10am-5.45pm Mon-Fri; 11am-4.30pm Sat. **No credit cards. Map** p252 F4.

This gallery's focus is on conceptual, minimal and abstract work, and it has some of the country's most successful contemporary artists in its stable: these include Felim Egan, Mark Francis, Callum Innes, Brian Maguire, Fionnuala Ni Chiosain, Sean Scully and Sean Shanahan.

Kevin Kavanagh Gallery

3A Chancery Lane (874 0064/www.kevinkavanagh gallery.ie). All cross-city buses/St Stephen's Green. **Open** 10.30am-5.30pm Mon-Fri; 11am-5pm Sat. **Credit** MC, V. **Map** p252 E4.

Newly ensconced in these central premises, the Kevin Kavanagh Gallery exhibits works by well-respected contemporary Irish artists. Its emphasis is more on painting than on installation, and it regularly features works by noted local artists such as Gary Coyle, Mick O'Dea, Gemma Browne and Dermot Seymour.

Original Print Gallery

4 Temple Bar (677 3657/www.originalprint.ie). All cross-city buses/Luas Jervis. **Open** 10.30am-5.30pm Mon-Fri; 11am-5pm Sat; 2-6pm Sun. **Credit** MC, V. **Map** p252 E3.

Next door to the Temple Bar Gallery & Studios (*see below*), the OPG is a brightly lit space that is as much a showcase for printmakers as an opportunity to flick through folders of both international and Irish works. Look out for Mary Fitzgerald, Siobhan Cuffe, Anthony Lyttle, Cliona Doyle and John Graham.

Project Arts Centre

39 East Essex Street (679 6622/www.project.ie). All cross-city buses/Luas Jervis. **Open** Box office 11am-7pm Mon-Sat. **Credit** MC, V. **Map** p252 E3.

A conglomeration of custom-designed theatre and performance spaces as well as a gallery, Project (as it is known locally) was founded back in the 1960s but is probably still the most adventurous space in the city. Many exhibitions here are purely non-commercial but others also feature work for sale – the kind of work you would be hard pressed to find anywhere else in Dublin. Project has, on occasion, been criticised for being overly conceptual and isolationist – but surely every capital city needs a venue that can keep the flag of ultra-modernism flying. *Photo p170.*

Temple Bar Gallery & Studios

5-9 Temple Bar (671 0073/www.templebargallery. com). All cross-city buses. **Open** 11am-6pm Tue, Wed, Fri, Sat; 11am-7pm Thur. **Credit** MC, V. **Map** p252 E3.

Essentially a non-profit organisation, TBG & Studios (the most coveted artists' studios in Dublin) organises an end-of-year fundraising show (in November or December; call for precise dates) in which much of the work produced by its resident artists is sold. Even during the rest of the year, sales are not unheard of, and with a decent contemporary gallery space at ground-floor level in the heart of Temple Bar, this is just a great place to go and have a browse. If you like what you see in the gallery, you can schedule a studio visit and meet the artists, 30 of whom work upstairs. Displays here are invariably challenging and uninhibited.

Around St Stephen's Green

Hallward Gallery

65 Merrion Square (662 1482/www.hallward gallery.com). All cross-city buses/Luas St Stephen's Green. **Open** 11am-5.30pm Tue-Fri; 12.30-4.30pm Sat. **Credit** MC, V. **Map** p251 H4.

Despite being tucked into a Georgian basement, this space is surprisingly bright. Works here tend to be contemporary Irish art of the tried and tested variety. The quality is always very high, with many well-established artists on show – expect names such as Robert Ryan, Cormac O'Leary, Niall Wright, Maighread Tobin and John Brennan. A 2008 ceramics show featured some unusual, imaginative pieces.

Cutting-edge multimedia **Gallery Number One**. *See p167.*

Peppercanister Gallery

3 Herbert Street (661 1279). Bus 7A, 8, 10. **Open** 10am-5.30pm Mon-Fri; 10am-1pm Sat. **Credit** MC, V. **Map** p251 H5.

In a basement space just off Mount Street, this gallery is a family-run affair with an informal yet highly polished atmosphere. Its artists (mainly Irish) are usually contemporary or early 20th century – names such as Anne Donnelly, Neil Shawcross, Liam Belton and Breon O'Casey.

Royal Hibernian Academy

15 Ely Place (661 2558/www.royalhibernian academy.ie). All cross-city buses/Luas St Stephen's Green. **Open** 1-7pm Mon-Sat; 5-7pm Sun. **Admission** free. **Credit** MC, V. **Map** p251 G4/5.

Utterly transformed after a year of closure, the Royal Hibernian Academy reopened in late 2008 as a smart, sleek new gallery complete with a suite of artists' studios, a café and a bookshop. While it remains an essentially non-profit organisation, the RHA's commercial operation continues to function in the form of its annual exhibition (in May), which features more than 1,000 exhibits selected by jury, making it the best and most affordable opportunity in Dublin to acquire the work of highly rated emerging artists.

Rubicon Gallery

10 St Stephen's Green North (670 8055/www.rubicon gallery.ie). All cross-city buses/Luas St Stephen's Green. **Open** noon-6pm Tue-Sat. **Credit** MC, V. **Map** p251 F4.

Overlooking the treetops of St Stephen's Green, this elegant gallery focuses on international contemporary artists in all media. Blaise Drummond, Tom Molloy and Maud Cotter are typical examples.

Taylor Galleries

16 Kildare Street (676 6055/www.taylorgalleries.ie). All cross-city buses/Luas St Stephen's Green. **Open** 10am-5.30pm Mon-Fri; 11am-3pm Sat. **Credit** MC, V. **Map** p252 G4.

This beautiful gallery fills an entire townhouse. There's a feeling of real elegance to the space, which shows some of Irish modernism's heavyweights – figures such as Louis le Brocquy, William Crozier, Tony O'Malley and Brian Bourke – alongside work by artists like Mary Lohan and Timothy Hawkesworth.

Around O'Connell Street

Hillsboro Gallery

49 Parnell Square West (878 8242/www.hillsboro fineart.com). All cross-city buses/Luas Abbey Street. **Open** 10.30am-6pm Mon-Fri; 10.30am-4pm Sat. **No credit cards.** **Map** p251 E1.

Just around the corner from the Hugh Lane Gallery (*see p82*), the Hillsboro is beautifully situated in a restored Georgian townhouse. It specialises in contemporary Irish, American and European art, with various works by the 'St Ives artists' (William Scott, Nancy Wynne Jones and others) and paintings by Kenneth Noland and Larry Poons, among many, many others.

Around North Quays

Green on Red
26-28 Lombard Street East (671 3414/www.green onredgallery.com). All cross-city buses/Luas Busáras. **Open** 10am-6pm Mon-Fri; 11am-5pm Sat. **Credit** MC, V. **Map** p251 H3.
It may be a little off the beaten track, but this gallery is well worth seeking out, as many consider it to be one of the city's best. The high industrial ceiling complements the sparse contemporary works inside. Prices are a bit high as well, but the collection of works on paper will suit those on a budget. The gallery represents some of the best local and international contemporary artists, including Mark Joyce, Gerard Byrne, Paul Doran, Alice Maher and Corban Walker. Recent exhibitions have included the outstanding 'Dust Breeding' by Nigel Rolfe.

Liberties & Kilmainham

Cross Gallery
59 Francis Street (473 8978/www.crossgallery.ie). *Bus 51B, 78A, 123.* **Open** 10am-5.30pm Tue-Fri; 11am-3pm Sat. **Credit** MC, V. **Map** p250 D3/4.
If you happen to be in the Liberties, don't miss the Cross Gallery. The space, reminiscent of spaces on New York's Lower East Side, holds mostly abstract pieces. Its young director has a flair for choosing some of the best emerging Irish painters around. Names to watch out for are Simon English, Siobhan McDonald, Michael Coleman and John Boyd.

Monster Truck
73 Francis Street (no phone/www.monstertruck.ie). *Bus 51B, 78A, 123.* **Open** 1-7pm Mon, Tue, Fri-Sun; 6-8pm Thur. **No credit cards**. **Map** p250 D3/4.
The gallery arm of a co-operative of largely unknown local artists supported by the Royal Hibernian Academy (*see p169*), Monster Truck exhibits fresh, feisty new work in a variety of media. The turnover is high, with exhibitions set up every Wednesday (when the gallery is closed) and preview evenings every Thursday. Names to watch from recent shows are James Kirwan, Magnhild Opdoel, Nina Tanis and Kohei Nekata.

Project Arts Centre. *See p168.*

BLACKBOXING
Mariana Castillo Deball, L Budd et al., Rene Gabri & Ayreen Anastas, Peter Galison & Rob Moss, Bea McMahon, Garrett Phelan, Grace Weir, Mick Wilson

Exhibition: 2 November – 1 December 2007
'Unpacking Blackboxing': Friday 16 November
www.project.ie

Gay & Lesbian

Tail of the Pink Panther.

The economic boom that overtook Ireland in the mid-1990s was known as the Celtic Tiger and came just after homosexuality was decriminalised in the country, sparking a similar commercial boom on Dublin's gay scene that came to be known as the Pink Panther. Almost overnight, a scene that was once characterised by dingy backstreet bars and 'speakeasy'-type clubs became filled with superbars and club nights pumping it out seven nights a week, catering to a suddenly visible and confident clientele.

The Celtic Tiger has long since met its maker, but the Pink Panther is still stalking the city – or at least it seems to be. If you visit Dublin for a weekend, you'll be surprised at the size of the scene, but this has to do with the nature of Irish licensing laws rather than a massively diverse gay social experience. Bar licences in Ireland are like gold dust but once obtained they will cover an establishment of any size, tiny or humongous – so during the Celtic Tiger days there was an explosion in superbars that took over several buildings and packed as many punters in as possible.

Dublin is home to two gay superbars – **The George** and **The Dragon** – a hop, skip and a jump from each other on the same street. Owned by the same company, their sheer size, and the fact that on weekend nights you could hardly swing a cat for the numbers of happily homosexual revellers jammed into both venues, gives the idea that Dublin's gay scene is big, brash and still booming like crazy.

The other two gay bars in Dublin are by no means small. The **Front Lounge** on Parliament Street, all sofas and art on the walls, is home to a stylish post-work crowd who like to be noticed and a great cocktail menu. Meanwhile, **PantiBar** on Capel Street, owned by Ireland's most popular drag queen, attracts a wide range of punters, from dykes to bears, twinks to muscle Marys, and hosts Dublin's most popular weekly night, a cross between *America's Next Top Model* and *The Apprentice* that sees drag queens and kings battle it out to become Panti's PA (Performing Assistant). The show was won by Belfast drag newbie, Bunny in August of this year and kicks off again in May 2009.

The great thing about Dublin's gay bars is that they are incredibly friendly. It's difficult to sit down alone on a barstool without getting into conversation with someone, and while cruising is just as prevalent as in other gay bars in the world, the level of agenda-free chatter is up in the high decibels. There is no dedicated bar for girls who like girls, but The Front Lounge and PantiBar are your best bets for lesbian chatter.

Key times to visit gay Dublin are during the annual Pride festivities, which take place during the last two weeks of June; the Alternative Miss Ireland Contest livens up March, the International Dublin Gay Theatre Festival runs in May, the aLAF Lesbian Arts Festival is showcased in July and the GAZE: Dublin International Lesbian & Gay Film Festival (www.gaze.ie) is screened the first weekend in August every year.

Visitors should note that even more draconian licensing laws were introduced in Ireland in August 2008. All bars and clubs must now close their doors to punters at 2.30am, Monday to Saturday, and at 1.30am on Sundays. This will effectively put an end to Sunday night one-nighters on the gay scene, which have always been popular.

GAY NEWS & INFORMATION

Scene publications come and go, but at the moment *Gay Community News* (*GCN*) is the only free magazine on the shelves. Approaching its 21st birthday, it's a glossy monthly magazine, available in all the gay pubs and in lots of cafés and bookshops around the city (its main distribution point is the Irish Film Institute on Temple Bar's Eustace Street) and it's absolutely up to date about what's going on socially and culturally for gay people in the city.

There are no glossy gay or lesbian magazines published here, but *Gay Times*, *Attitude* and *Diva* are widely available. Two superb and constantly updated gay Irish websites are the Gay Community News website (www.gcn.ie) and www.queerid.com.

There is a Little Gay Map of Dublin, which not only points out the bars, centres, saunas and cafés, but has a wide-ranging quota of gay-friendly restaurants within its range. It can be found in most hotels in the city, the Dublin Tourist Office, the Temple Bar Tourist Information Centre and, of course, all gay venues.

George.

Bars

Front Lounge

33-4 Parliament Street, Around Temple Bar (670 4112). All cross-city buses. **Open** noon-11.30pm Mon-Thur; noon-12.30am Fri, Sat; 4-11.30pm Sun. **Credit** MC, V. **Map** p252 E3.

As sleek as a Porsche's bumper, The Front Lounge is a large, gay-friendly bar. Clientele-wise, expect hordes of handsome guys in suits and stubble and a gaggle of oh-so-interesting Sauvignon Blanc sippers. This is a mixed bar, and the queerest part is the raised section at the back, where local drag supersister, April Showers, hosts Casting Couch, a karaoke extravaganza on Tuesday nights.

Dragon

64 South Georges Street, Around Temple Bar (478 1590). All cross-city buses. **Open** 5pm-2.30am Mon; 5-11.30pm Tue, Wed; 5pm-2.30am Thur-Sat; 5-11pm Sun. **Credit** MC, V. **Map** p251 E3.

Formerly a cavernous dive, the Dragon has been completely revamped with over-the-top theatrical touches and an extravagant entrance flanked by red leather couches.

On weekend nights the long main bar heaves with young gay guys and their gal pals. There's a popular dancefloor and a welcoming outdoor courtyard that usually ends up as a talking house and a refuge for smokers. Regular in-house DJs play an assortment of funk, electro and house every night, but it can quieten down midweek even though the venue stages themed evenings. The Dragon is immensely popular (not to mention cruisey).

George

89 South Great George's Street, Around Temple Bar (478 2983/www.capitalbars.com). All cross-city buses. **Open** 12.30-11.30pm Mon, Tue; 12.30pm-2.30am Wed-Sat; 2.30pm-1am Sun. **Credit** AmEx, MC, V. **Map** p251 E3.

The hub of gay life in Dublin since the early '90s, The George has expanded in size twice over the intervening years to become two bars and a club that's a hotbed most nights, especially on Sundays, when the Shirley Temple-Bar hosts a notorious bingo session. The smaller bar to the side of the venue is nick-named Jurassic Park by locals because it attracts an older clientele, while the main bar has a raised stage, plenty of drag shows and PAs, and a dancefloor that's regularly packed to the gills. If you're gay and visiting Dublin, it's inevitable you'll end up here at some point.

Irish Film Institute Bar

6 Eustace Street, Around Temple Bar (679 5744/www.irishfilm.ie). All cross-city buses. **Open** 9.30am-11.30pm Mon-Thur, Sun; 10am-12.30am Fri, Sat. **Credit** MC, V. **Map** p251 E3.

The IFI Bar occupies the same building as an arthouse cinema. It's a sympathetic renovation of the old 17th-century Quaker meeting house, with an extended bar that encloses a large bright glass-roofed courtyard. There's also an outdoor beer garden popular with smokers. It has a significant gay and lesbian presence, and the institute is home to GAZE: Dublin International Lesbian & Gay Film Festival, a five-day cinematic event that takes place the first weekend of every August and is now in its 17th year.

Arts & Entertainment

Morrison Bar

Ormond Quay Lower (887 2400/www.morrison hotel.ie). All cross-city buses/Luas Jervis St. **Open** noon-11.30pm Mon-Thur; noon-11.45pm Fri, Sat; 4-11.30pm Sun. **Credit** AmEx, DC, MC, V. **Map** p251 E2.

With its high-end design, loungy brown leather sofas peppered with cushions, and its cool, laid-back atmosphere, the gay-friendly Morrison Hotel bar has become a very popular haunt for gays who like their drinks constructed by a mixologist and their bar snacks organic.

PantiBar

7-8 Capel Street, North Quays (874 0710). All cross-city buses/Luas Jervis St. **Open** 5-11.30pm Mon-Thur; 5pm-12.30am Fri, Sat; 4-11.30pm Sun. **Credit** MC, V. **Map** p251 E2.

Owned by the eponymous Panti, Ireland's doyenne of drag, PantiBar is an enormously popular addition to Dublin's gay scene. Housed in the former Gubu, the revamp has been minimal, but in inverse proportion to the injection of creative thinking. On any night of the week you'll find something fun and interesting happening from Make and Do-Do craft nights on Mondays, to Movies in Her Living Room on Wednesdays plus queer classics presented by Irish gay filmmakers to The Furry Glen bear night on the third Saturday night of the month. There's something for everyone here and almost everyone goes there at some stage in the night.

Panti is also a host of the Alternative Miss Ireland contest (http://alternativemissireland.queerid.net /homepage.aspx) that raises money for HIV groups.

Club nights

Glitz

Breakdown, below Break for the Border, Lower Stephen Street, Around Trinity College (478 0300/ www.capitalbars.com). Bus 16, 16A, 19, 19A. **Open** 11pm-2.30am Tue. **Admission** €7; €8 after midnight. **No credit cards. Map** p251 E4.

Pumping out the housed-up chart hits for the past five years now, courtesy of DJ Fluffy, Glitz also has a great line in campy B-list PAs – think X Factor runner-ups and Celebrity Big Brother losers by the dozen. The club itself has a central dancefloor surrounded by plentiful seats (ideal for a spot of people-watching); UK acts are regularly flown over to keep the beats going.

KISS

The Shelter at The Tivoli, Francis Street, (454 4472). Bus 78A, 123, 51C. **Open** 10.30pm-3am 3rd Fri of mth. **Admission** €10. **No credit cards. Map** p250 C3.

Going strong after an unprecedented three years (lesbian clubs usually come and go overnight), Kiss is for 'gay girls and their male friends'. The women tend to be more femme than butch, which might explain the club's most unusual feature – the slow sets. Chart remixes prevail for most of the time.

Purty Kitchen

Essex Street, Temple Bar (www.queerandalternative. com). All cross-city buses. **Open** 10pm-2am Sun. **Admission** €12. **No credit cards. Map** p251 E3.

Three floors of fun make this a destination for half of the beautiful gay guys and all the beautiful gay girls in Dublin. Good house music fills the top floor with DJ Paddy Scahill, there's chill out on the middle floor, and crazy handbag mixes from dragettes, Davine Devine and April Showers on the ground floor.

Q+A

Temple Bar Music Centre, Curved Street, Around Temple Bar (www.queerandalternative.com). All cross-city buses. **Open** 10pm-2am 2nd Sat, every 2nd mth. **Admission** €12. **No credit cards**. **Map** p251 E3.

The most popular one-nighter in Dublin only comes around every second month making sure the anticipation builds and builds. Recently, it abandoned its Temple Bar Music Centre home for a while, but it's back there now and packing in a young mix of gay boys and girls with big hair. It has an alternative karaoke section, indie, punk and electro on the main dancefloor, and PAs and promotions for Dublin's most alternative musicians.

Tea for a towelled two at the **Boilerhouse.**

Spice

Spy, South William Street, Around Grafton Street area (677 0945). All cross-city buses. **Open** 10pm-2am every Sat. **Admission** €12. **No credit cards.** **Map** p251 E3.

Pumping it out every Saturday night in the Spy complex in the Powerscourt Centre, Spice is one of the most popular weekly nights on the Dublin scene. With three dance areas featuring alternative music sets, from electro to retro chart, five bars and lounges, and beautiful people bumping to the beat all over the place, it's a weekend must.

Saunas

Boilerhouse

12 Crane Lane, Around Temple Bar (677 3130/www.the-boilerhouse.com). All cross-city buses. **Open** 1pm-5am Mon-Thur; 1pm Fri-5am Mon. **Admission** €20. **Credit** AmEx, MC, V. **Map** p251 E3.

Dublin's biggest sauna is equipped with a steam room, whirlpool, solarium, gym and café housed across five floors of a converted 19th-century grain store. There's even a specially designated heated decking area for smokers.

Dock

21 Ormond Quay Upper, Around North Quays (872 4172). All cross-city buses. **Open** 10am-4am Mon-Thur; 24hrs Fri-Sun. **Admission** €15 Mon-Thur; €20 Fri-Sun. **Map** p251 E2/3.

Sitting right beside the Inn on the Liffey on the river's North Quays, the Dock is a bit smaller than the Boilerhouse, but that only makes it more intimate. Best of all, if you've nothing planned for the weekend, it's open the entire 48 hours.

Information & advice

Gay Men's Health Project

19 Haddingdon Road, Ballsbridge, Southern suburbs (660 2189/www.gaymenshealthproject.ie). Bus 10. **Open** 6.30-8pm Tue; 6-7.30pm Wed.

A drop-in sexual health clinic for gay and bisexual men. The Gay Men's Health Project offers a service that is free, friendly and entirely confidential.

Gay Switchboard Dublin

872 1055. **Open** 8-10pm Mon-Fri, Sun; 3.30-6pm Sat.

Help and information for the gay community.

Lesbian Line

872 9911. **Open** 7-9pm Thur.

An advice and information line.

Outhouse

105 Capel Street, Around North Quays (873 4932/www.outhouse.ie). All cross-city buses. **Open** 12.30-10pm Mon-Fri; 12.30 6pm Sat; women's night 7-10pm Thur; men's night 7-10pm Fri. **Map** p251 E2.

A useful lesbian and gay meeting place, with social activities like book, youth and travelling clubs. See **A helping hand**, *below*.

A helping hand

At the back end of Capel Street, which is fast becoming the most cosmopolitan thoroughfare in Dublin, the city's lesbian, gay, bisexual and transgender (LGBT) Centre, Outhouse might seem at first to have a quiet existence, but a closer look shows a hotbed of community activity going down.

Over the four years it's been open, the centre has become the steady-beating heart of Dublin's queer community, underpinning the scene like a sensible pair of shoes that manage to look good too.

The converted tea merchant's house is now home to a basement theatre space used by theatre groups, music recitals and all sorts of arts-related and community-related events.

"We're very clear about making Outhouse a really good social space for the LGBT community," says Robotham. "We're particularly conscious of the youth sector of the gay community, who are not catered to on the social scene, and older people too. We want to make sure that everyone in Dublin's

diverse community and visitors to the city feel welcome to access the centre."

With that in mind the meeting rooms are stuffed to capacity seven days a week with a variety of groups, stretching from Alcoholics Anonymous to book groups; gay internationals to gay men into leather, uniform, bears and alternative sexual expression. There are also gay writers groups and the very successful youth group, BeLonG To, which currently attracts teenagers from all over the surrounding areas, into a welcoming and supportive atmosphere. The centre even provides a police outreach service, where people who have experienced homophobic crime or intimidation can report it without having to face into a police station.

And while all this activity is happening upstairs, the ground floor is home to a café and internet hub, which buzzes merrily away every day and evening of the week, and a library on the first floor where a more chilled-out vibe reigns supreme.

Music

Let the renaissance begin.

Dublin's reputation as a live music destination dates back to 1742, when the world premiere of Handel's Messiah was staged on Fishamble Street. In the modern era, the 1960s saw the emergence of a string of home-grown acts that mined the rich heritage of traditional Irish music: Thin Lizzy and Horslips. At the same time, a folk revival led by the Chieftains and the Dubliners reached its apotheosis in the early '70s with the trad supergroup Planxty, featuring Christy Moore. Then, in the wake of the punk upheaval in Britain, Dublin got its own collection of angry young men. Bob Geldof's Boomtown Rats voiced their frustration with political and cultural stagnation in Ireland, only to be kicked around by a bunch of blokes with big hair: U2. After them came Sinead O'Connor and Kevin Shields (the eclectic genius behind My Bloody Valentine), and with the grizzled addition of Shane MacGowan's Pogues, Dublin's place in the pantheon of international stars was set.

Then it all went quiet. On walls across town, the graffito 'Dublin is Dead' became the standard assessment of the Irish music scene. But recently, things have been looking up. The last few years have seen a burst of live music in the capital, and the hunger for new tunes has revitalised the city's music scene. Venues like the International Bar (see p179) have helped promote quality acts like Gemma Hayes, Adrian Crowley and Paddy Casey. The DIY punk scene brewing for so many years in small clubs around Dublin (such as JJ Smyth's and Ballroom of Romance) has delivered Redneck Manifesto, Large Mound and The Dudley Corporation; the electronica and dance scene has spawned Herv, Si Schroeder, Ti Woc and Somadrome; while the Future Kings of Spain, Turn and La Rocca take inspiration, and make plenty of lolly, from the US rock scene. Other 'breakthrough' bands of the recent past include Jape and Mumblin' Def Ro. All manner of electronica, from ambient to evil, has sprung up of late, thanks in part to the hard work of independent labels like Alphabet Set, Trust Me I'm A Thief.

The recent success in the US and Britain of Fionn Regan's debut album The End of History, meanwhile, has heralded the arrival of yet another Irish singer songwriter star – albeit one with much more to offer than the likes of Damien Rice or Mundy. Glen Hansard and Markéta Irglová have also emerged as leading lights, having won an Oscar in 2008 – and the international profile to go along with it – for their song Falling Slowly from the film Once (in which they both star).

Meanwhile, traditional Irish performers still knock out some of the best and most exciting music the country has to offer. The last decade has seen the emergence of a whole new generation of such acts (Lunasa, Solas, Martin Hayes and Dennis Cahill, Karen Casey and North Cregg, say), while bands like Kila combine Irish trad with the world music styles of Africa, the Far East and South America.

Ticket sales are fuelled by enterprises like Road Records and Claddagh Records (for both, see p144-145), which help acts convert local success to national and international acclaim; then there's the crop of new venues that host the bands, such as the Village, Liberty Hall, Crawdaddy and most recently Andrews Lane Theatre – all supplying a hungry local audience with new sounds.

Still, newest isn't always best, and most music fans agree that Whelan's (see p183), one of the most prestigious venues in the city, remains the best place at which to hear Dublin's brightest up-and-coming stars.

INFORMATION

To find out what's happening in town, pick up local free sheet the Event Guide for full listings of concerts in Dublin. You can find it in bars, cafés and record shops. Also check out Irish music promoters Comhaltas's website, http://comhaltas.ie.

TICKETS

While places like the O2 (see p183), Whelan's and Olympia (see p183) have their own box offices, other major venues and such smaller but established names as Vicar Street (see p181) rely on agencies for ticketed concerts. You can get tickets at Ticketmaster (0818 719 300/from outside Ireland 456 9569/www.ticketmaster.ie) in the St Stephen's Green shopping centre, which deals with just about every big event. The reservation service in the Tourism Centre on Suffolk Street can make credit card bookings (605 7729/www.visitdublin.com), and tickets can often be bought at record shops like Road Records and HMV (see p145).

Arts & Entertainment

Check Time Out's listings or call the venues directly to find out the best source of tickets.

WHERE TO GO
Most band venues are, conveniently enough, located in or around the city centre. A few of them, such as the Helix (*see p181*) and the National Stadium (*see p183*), are deep in the suburbs – but even those are only 30 minutes from the centre by bus. Larger-scale rock concerts are occasionally held in outdoor venues like Punchestown racecourse, Croke Park (now the default venue while Lansdowne Road is being renovated) and the RDS (*see p183*).

Bars, clubs & small venues

Ballroom of Romance
The Lower Deck, 1 Portobello Harbour, Around St Stephen's Green (475 1423). Bus 16, 16A, 19, 19A, 122/Luas Charlemont. **Open** times vary. **Admission** €10. **Credit** MC, V. **Map** p251 E6.

Bleu Note. *See p178.*

Arts & Entertainment

Jamming it at **JJ Smyths** where the bonhomie pulls in the crowd. *See p179.*

This monthly alternative live music club, taking place in an old man's pub, has showcased talented new indie acts. It's a pick 'n' mix – you could get the searing post-rock of Terrordactyl one night and the gentle glitch balladry of Si Schroeder the next. As a starting point for Irish alternative music, though, Ballroom of Romance is an essential venue.

Bleu Note

61-63 Capel Street, Around O'Connell Street (874 9753/www.thebleunote.com). All cross-city buses/ Luas Jervis. **Open** noon-11.30pm Mon-Thur; noon-2.30am Fri, Sat; noon-11pm Sun. **Admission** Sun-Thur €5-€7. Fri, Sat €10 after 10pm. **Credit** MC, V. **Map** p251 E2.

A new-ish live music venue, with the main floor completely dedicated to jazz, Bleu Note is a welcome addition to the city's live music scene. The second floor plays an eclectic mixture of blues, soul funk and Latin every Thursday to Sunday night. The club plays host every Monday night to The Essential Big Band, a seventeen piece swing ensemble. Bring your zoot suit and spats. *Photo p177.*

Bruxelles

7-8 Harry Street, off Grafton Street, Around Temple Bar (677 5362). All cross-city buses/Luas St Stephen's Green. **Open** 10.30am-1.30am Mon-Wed; 10.30am-2.30am Thur-Sat; noon-1.30am Sun. **No credit cards. Map** p251 F3.

The musical quality here can vary, but even so, this is a great pub: you'd do well to pop in for a drink anyway. Local blues acts play upstairs early in the week; there's dancing late at night down in the Zodiac Bar, and you'll be served a loud of helping of classic rock in the Heavy Metal Bar (which feels a good deal like Wayne's World, except without the irony). *See also p125.*

Cobblestone

77 King Street North, North Quays (872 1799/ www.musiclee.com). Bus 25, 26, 37, 39, 67, 67A, 68, 69, 79/Luas Smithfield. **Open** 4-11.30pm Mon-Thur; 4pm-12.30am Fri, Sat; 1-11pm Sun. *Bar music* from 9pm daily. *Back bar venue* from 9pm Thur-Sat. **Admission** *Bar* free. *Back bar* venue €10-€15. **No credit cards. Map** p250 C2.

Overlooking the vast square at Smithfield, this is an old-fashioned, friendly boozer that hosts trad music in its back bar. Upstairs is a surprisingly comfortable and intimate space that specialises in more serious gigs by good traditional and roots groups, as well as the odd rock act.

Eamonn Doran's

3A Crown Alley, Around Temple Bar (679 9114). All cross-city buses. **Open** noon-2.30am Mon-Sat; noon-1am Sunday. *Live music* phone for details. **Admission** prices vary; phone for details. **Credit** AmEx, MC, V. **Map** p251 E3.

Eamonn Doran's replaced the once-famous Rock Garden when its star dimmed in the late '90s. Owner Dermott Doran kept the metallic decor in the basement venue and refurbished the upstairs bar. Doran's is slowly gaining prominence as a starting point for such young Irish rock acts such as Halite, the Things and the Republic of Loose.

Hub

24-25 Eustace Street, Around Temple Bar (635 9991) All cross-city buses/Luas Jervis. **Open** *Live music* from 8pm. *Music club* 11pm-2.30am daily. **Admission** prices vary. **Credit** MC, V. **Map** p251 E3.

A new, small-scale rock venue in the city centre, this basement bar (below the Mezz Bar) has a small stage, which puts the musicians and audience pretty much face to face. Acts here tend to be local rock bands on the way up, plus a few low-key international acts.

Regular club nights like Skinny Wolves also play host to worthwhile Dublin acts such as Cap Pas Cap and Somadrome, as well as choice indie bands from further afield. Dublin needs small venues like this to give up and coming bands a chance, but the atmosphere is not high class, and the sound does tend to be woolly.

International Bar

23 Wicklow Street, Around Trinity College (677 9250). All cross-city buses/Luas St Stephen's Green. **Open** 10.30am-11.30pm Mon-Thur; 10.30am-12.30am Fri, Sat; 12.30-11pm Sun. *Live music* from 9pm Tue-Sun. **Admission** prices vary. **No credit cards**. **Map** p251 F3.

The International is a quaint old pub with a small but charming venue upstairs. In recent years, it has become more of a comedy space, with four nights of stand-up each week; but it still does jazz on Tuesday nights, experimental music with Lazy Bird on Sunday nights, and two trad sessions in the bar on Sunday afternoons and evenings.

JJ Smyth's

12 Aungier Street, Around St Stephen's Green (475 2565/www.jjsmyths.com). Bus 16, 16A, 19, 19A, 83/Luas St Stephen's Green. **Open** *Live music* from 9pm Mon, Tue, Thur-Sun. **Admission** prices vary. **No credit cards**. **Map** p251 E4.

One of the city's oldest jazz and blues venues, Smyth's does good music every night bar Wednesdays. There's an acoustic open-jam session on the first Tuesday of every month, and fine jazz is the order of the night on Monday, Thursday and Sunday. The keen, friendly crowd and cheap pints are added bonuses. *See also p129.*

O'Shea's Merchant

12 Bridge Street Lower, Liberties (679 3797). Bus 21, 21A/Luas The Four Courts. **Open** 10.30am-11.30pm Mon-Wed; 10.30am-2am Thur-Sat; 12.30pm-2am Sun. *Live music* from 9.30pm daily. **Admission** free. **Credit** AmEx, MC, V. **Map** p250 C/D3.

This sprawling pub and restaurant hosts live trad music and set dancing every night. It can be good fun with the right crowd but tends to attract large coach tours looking for that Oirish vibe.

Voodoo Lounge

39-40 Arran Quay, Smithfield, Dublin 7 (873 6013) Bus 25, 26, 37, 39, 67, 67A, 68, 69, 79/ Luas Smithfield. **Open** noon-2.30am Mon-Sat; noon-1am Sun. *Live music* phone for details. **Admission** prices vary. **No credit cards.** **Map** p250 C2.

Voodoo Lounge, owned by Huey Morgan of US one-hit-wonders The Fun Lovin' Criminals, is a NY-style booze emporium – cavernous and yet strangely pokey – complete with its own pizzeria. In recent years it has become a mainstay of Dublin's small, but reasonably vibrant, punk scene, regularly playing host to local face-melters like Easpa Measa as well as underground noise-bringers from the US and Europe, along with the occasional DJ set from the likes of Shane MacGowan. If you like your pizza slice

with a side order of punk rock, Voodoo Lounge is worth the ten-minute walk from the city centre. And Statik!, Voodoo's Thursday evening indie club, is definitely worth a punt.

Medium-sized venues

Ambassador

Top of O'Connell Street, Around O'Connell Street (0818 719 300/www.mcd.ie/venues). All cross-city buses/Luas Abbey Street. **Open** times vary. **Admission** prices vary. **Credit** *Ticketmaster* AmEx, DC, MC, V. **Map** p251 F1.

The Ambassador was a theatre, then a woefully underused cinema. As a rock venue, it keeps many of its old trappings: decor, balcony and a large stage. It's a big stage to fill, and it takes loud rock bands like the Queens of the Stone Age or charismatic indie acts like Beck to put the place to best use. The management has pretty much cornered the Dublin market in nu metal and hard indie rock; an acoustic act would be lost in this 1,200-seat venue.

Andrew's Lane

9-17 Andrew's Lane, Dublin 2 (679 5720). All cross-city buses/Luas Stephen's Green. **Open** times vary. **Admission** prices vary. **Map** p251 E/F3.

Formerly one of the few playhouses on Dublin's south side, Andrew's Lane reopened recently as a music venue. Theatre-lovers' loss has been music fans' gain, with Andrew's Lane already gaining a reputation as a welcome addition to the city's live music scene. So far, the fare has tended toward the leftfield end of the spectrum, with arty electronica acts like Matmos and Venetian Snares wooing the more adventurous punters. Andrew's Lane is shaping up to be an interesting venue.

Button Factory

Curved Street, Around Temple Bar (670 9202/ ww2.buttonfactory.ie). All cross-city buses. **Open** *Live music* 7.30pm (check for days). **Admission** prices vary. **Credit** MC, V. **Map** p251 E3.

The Button Factory is the rebranded and refurbished version of what was once the Temple Bar Music Centre, a home to hard rock bands where sound quality and atmosphere mattered less than beer and decibels. With a new layout, decor and sound system, the venue, which (re)opened in late 2007, is a useful addition to the Dublin music scene. Scratch DJ maestro Mr Scruff was delighting the punters in 2008. *Photo p181.*

Crawdaddy

Hatch Street Upper, off Harcourt Street, Around St Stephen's Green (478 0166/www.crawdaddy.ie). Bus 15A, 15B, 86/Luas Harcourt Street. **Open** times vary. **Admission** prices vary. **Credit** *Ticketmaster* AmEx, MC, V. **Map** p251 E5.

Medium-sized Crawdaddy is an exciting new venue that meets the demand for live music with an impressive roster of contemporary jazz, world music and rock. It can hold about 300 people, and ticket

The best guides to enjoying London life

(but don't just take our word for it)

'More than 700 places where you can eat out for less than £20 a head... a mass of useful information in a genuinely pocket–sized guide'

Mail on Sunday

'Armed with a tube map and this guide there is no excuse to find yourself in a duff bar again'

Evening Standard

'I'm always asked how I keep up to date with shopping and services in a city as big as London. This guide is the answer'

Red Magazine

'Get the inside track on the capital's neighbourhoods'

Independent on Sunday

'A treasure trove of treats that lists the best the capital has to offer'

The People

Rated
'Best Restaurant Guide'

Sunday Times

TIME OUT GUIDES WRITTEN BY LOCAL EXPERTS

timeout.com/shop

prices tend to be higher than average; but the place has the atmosphere of an intimate jazz club, and draws acts of the calibre (not to mention considerable, genre-busting diversity) of Courtney Pine, the Fall and Talvin Singh.

Helix

DCU, Collins Avenue, Glasnevin (700 7000/www.the helix.ie). Bus 11, 13A, 16, 16A, 19A. **Open** times vary. **Admission** prices vary. **Credit** AmEx, MC, V.
Part of Dublin City University's building complex, the Helix is a multi-venue arts centre in the leafy suburb of Glasnevin. Its three venues – Mahony Hall, the Theatre and the Space – cover the range from small gigs to bigger concerts. The smaller venues have fielded some of the bigger acts from Dublin's music scene, and recently hosted Van Morrison and Lou Reed. The only drawback is the distance – a good half-hour trip – from the city centre.

Liberty Hall Theatre

33 Eden Quay, Around O'Connell Street (872 1122/ www.libertyhall.ie). All cross-city buses/Luas Abbey Street. **Open** times vary. **Admission** prices vary. **Credit** AmEx, MC, V. **Map** p251 F2.
This theatre and music venue sits inside Ireland's main union hall, the famous Connolly Hall. It was very popular in the '70s (Paul Brady has released a live album he recorded here in 1978), but fell into disuse. The recent renovation turned its fortunes around, and the place now offers a refreshing programme of world music, jazz and rock. Long may its popularity continue.

Sugar Club

8 Leeson Street Lower, Around St Stephen's Green (678 7188/www.thesugarclub.com). Bus 46A/Luas St Stephen's Green. **Open** 8pm-midnight Mon-Thur; 8pm-2.30am Fri-Sun. **Admission** €10-€15. **Credit** AmEx, MC, V. **Map** p251 G6.

One of Dublin's most stylish venues, the Sugar Club has the feel of a hip US jazz bar. The audience gazes down on the musicians from tiered seats with tables. The programme ranges from cabaret and rock to jazz or singer-songwriter styles. Weekday crowds are mainly suits; keep an eye on listings for the likes of KT Tunstall and Crazy P.

Vicar Street

99 Vicar Street, off Thomas Street West, Around North Quays (information 454 5533/www.vicar street.com). Bus 123. **Open** *Live music* from 7.30pm daily. **Admission** varies. **Credit** *Ticketmaster* AmEx, DC, MC, V. **Map** p250 C3.
A modern venue with an old-style feel, Vicar Street has comfortable seating, sensitive lighting and a great sound system. It was recently expanded to hold 1,000 punters, but has lost none of its intimate atmosphere. The spacious pub in the front and the little bars hidden in the corridors are handy, too. Acts include Bob Dylan, Kanye West, Rufus Wainwright, Calexico and Al Green, as well as big-name jazz and comedy acts and top local musicians.

Village

26 Wexford Street, Around St Stephen's Green (475 8555/www.thevillagevenue.com). Bus 16, 16A, 19, 19A/Luas Harcourt. **Open** 11am-2.30am Mon-Fri; 5pm-2.30am Sun. **Admission** prices vary. **Credit** AmEx, MC, V. **Map** p251 E5.
This shiny venue opened in 2003 on the same site as the underperforming Mean Fiddler. The good people at Whelan's (*see below*) took it on and gave it a thorough makeover; the redesign and revamped sound system made it a cosy and enjoyable spot. It now has some of the most interesting musical offerings in town – the likes of Sufjan Stevens and Clap Your Hands Say Yeah. It does, however, suffer from some frankly baffling layout decisions: the toilets are located behind the stage, which means you may

Button Factory. *See p179.*

well have to circumnavigate a mosh pit to get to them. A minor quibble, though, in a club that has become central to Dublin's nightlife. Its Songs Of Praise rock karaoke event, held every Sunday evening, is a must-do.

Whelan's
25 Wexford Street, Around St Stephen's Green (478 0766/www.whelanslive.com). Bus 16, 16A, 19, 19A, 122/Luas Harcourt. **Open** noon-2.30am Mon-Sat; noon-1am Sun. **Tickets** €9.50-€25. **Credit** *TicketMaster* AmEx, MC, V. **Map** p251 E5.
One of the city's most prestigious venues, Whelan's has built an unassailable reputation among Dublin music fans. It's the stomping ground for most of the city's up-and-coming bands: Damien Rice, David Kitt, the Frames, Paddy Casey and Gemma Hayes all made their first appearances here. With a line-up that takes in Irish trad, English folk and American roots, this is a vital Dublin venue. *See also p134.*

Large venues

Gaiety
King Street South, Around St Stephen's Green (677 1717/www.gaietytheatre.com). All cross-city buses/Luas St Stephen's Green. **Open** *Live music* noon-2.30am Fri, Sat. **Admission** €12 Fri; €15 Sat. **Credit** MC, V. **Map** p251 F4.
The Gaiety is a spacious, old-time concert hall whose main trade is opera and theatre, but it has given space to rock performers like the Divine Comedy and Lambchop. A few years ago, it opened its lofty corridors to club nights, with live music and DJs in different rooms. Fridays feature Latin, salsa and world music, and Saturday nights revolve around funk, soul and groovy jazz.

National Stadium
145 South Circular Road, Southern suburbs (453 3371). Bus 19, 22. **Open** *Office* 9am-4pm Mon-Fri. **Tickets** prices vary. **Credit** *Ticketmaster* AmEx, MC, V.
The National Stadium was a popular venue in the 1970s and '80s, with everyone from Led Zeppelin to Van Morrison playing here. It holds a seated audience of 2,200 and has a large stage, but has never had a great sound system. Gigs here are now quite rare; it has largely returned to being a sports venue.

Olympia
72 Dame Street, Around Temple Bar (679 3323/tickets 0818 719 330/www.mcd.ie/venues). All cross-city buses/Luas Jervis. **Open** *Box office* 10.30am-6.30pm Mon-Sat. *Music* usually 8pm, midnight Tue-Sun; phone for details. **Tickets** prices vary. **Credit** AmEx, MC, V. **Map** p251 E3.
The Olympia is one of Dublin's old music halls. It's a fabulous place, with red velvet seats and theatre boxes on either side of the stage; the design is perfect for music and the acoustics are excellent. Famed for its late-night gigs, it's become more of an established music venue in recent years, hosting the likes

of Radiohead, Bowie and Blur. These days late-night gigs only happen on Saturdays and usually feature tribute bands like the Australian Doors.

Amphitheatres

02
East Link Bridge, North Wall Quay, Around North Quays (general enquiries 676 6144/www.theo2.ie). Tara Street or Connolly DART/rail. **Open** *Box office* 10am-6pm Mon-Sat. **Tickets** *prices vary.* **Credit** AmEx, DC, MC, V.
The Point Theatre, Dublin's largest indoor music venue, closed its doors in the summer of 2007 to undergo a complete overhaul and rebranding as The O2, having been bought by the entertainment behemoth Live Nation. When it reopens in December 2008, the venue will feature a 14,000 capacity arena, a more intimate 2,000-seater theatre, a hotel, a shopping centre and an underground car park. Whether or not any improvements will have been made to the venue's acoustics – a perennial bugbear for serious music fans – remains to be seen.

RDS Showgrounds
Ballsbridge, Southern suburbs (668 0866/www.rds.ie). Bus 5, 7, 7A, 8, 45/DART Lansdowne Road. **Open** times vary. **Tickets** prices vary. **Credit** *TicketMaster* AmEx, MC, V.
One of the city's main sites for festival-size concerts, these sprawling grounds have hosted the Red Hot Chili Peppers and the re-routed Lisdoonvarna festival. It has a capacity of 40,000, but while this is one of Dublin's longest-standing open-air venues, its main activity is showjumping, so food and drink facilities depend on each gig's promoters. Seats in the stands provide the best view, but standing on the grass in front of the stage means better sound.

Classical music

Though Dublin music buffs are fond of the fact that Handel's *Messiah* had its premiere here in 1742, the city's contribution to classical music is largely undistinguished. The city has no opera house, and despite the occasional success of productions such as *Salomé* and *Tosca* at the Gaiety, Dublin really doesn't compare with other European cities.

Still, the situation is far from hopeless. Though classical music doesn't have the high profile of other art forms here, there's still plenty being made. The **National Concert Hall** is home to the **RTÉ Concert Orchestra** and the **National Symphony Orchestra**. Performances by contemporary chamber ensembles such as Vox 21, the **Crash Ensemble** and popular choir **Anúna** can often be seen at the likes of the **Project Arts Centre** and the **Helix**.

Other regular events around town include the RTÉ Proms (208 3434/www.rte.ie), a feast of international music held each May, and the triennial Dublin International Organ & Choral Festival. And yes, there's an annual performance of the Messiah in commemoration of its debut here every Easter Tuesday at 1pm, on Fishamble Street.

Opera companies

Opera Ireland
The Schoolhouse, 1 Grantham Street, Around St Stephen's Green (478 6041/www.operaireland.com).
Founded in 1941, Opera Ireland is as close as Ireland gets to a national opera company. Guest performers have included Placido Domingo, José Carreras and even Luciano Pavarotti, who made his international debut with the company in a 1963 production of Rigoletto. After transforming itself in the 1980s into a more eclectic outfit, the company is as much at home with Verdi and Shostakovich as with Mark-Anthony Turnage's *Silver Tassie*. Its two short seasons at the Gaiety Theatre are in autumn and spring.

Opera Theatre Company
Temple Bar Music Centre, Around Temple Bar (679 4962/www.opera.ie).
Founded in 1986, this company is the national touring company of Ireland. In addition to producing four tours a year, it also runs the Opera Theatre Studio, a training facility for young singers. It has achieved national and international success with baroque and early classical operas, as well as 20th-century works. It occasionally commissions new operas by Irish composers.

Orchestras, choirs & ensembles

Anúna
283 5533/www.anuna.ie.
Best known for its association with the Riverdance group, this gifted Celtic choir has toured worldwide. Founder and artistic director Michael McGlynn has been at the helm since 1987; the choir's intricately arranged vocal harmonies sell CDs by the truckload. Anúna performs regularly in Dublin; check listings.

Crash Ensemble
O'Reilly Theatre, Belvedere College, Great Denmark Street (858 6644/www.crashensemble.com).
Largely responsible for putting cool back into classical, this outfit fuses the likes of Philip Glass and Steve Reich with dance, video and electronica. It regularly commissions and performs works by new Irish composers. The group, which celebrated its 10th anniversary in 2007, was founded by Donnacha Dennehy, Andrew Synott and Michael Seaver.

A high price to pay

Perhaps it's because we've yet to feel the pinch of the global economic slowdown, but Irish people remain peculiarly stoical when it comes to being ripped off. It's not that we're any more fond of it than we are of, say, the often outlandish vicissitudes of our weather. It's just that we've come to the conclusion that complaining about it would be equally fruitless.

The increasingly exorbitant price of concert tickets has become a pressing concern. It's long been obvious that concertgoers in Ireland are being charged considerably more to see live acts than their neighbours in the UK and in the rest of the EU. A performance by US rapper Snoop Dogg on his Autumn 2008 European tour, cost €45 to attend in Amsterdam and €53, four nights later, in Dublin. This is not an isolated example – an increasing number of acts cost more to see live in Ireland than elsewhere in Europe. But why should this be so, and who is at fault?

A portion of the blame, it seems, can be located at each of the links in the supply and demand chain – from the acts, to the promoters, to the venues to the fans

themselves. There are three major promoters on the Irish music scene – Aiken, MCD and Pod Concerts – who, between them, have the market more or less sewn up. Intense competition among these behemoths often leads to bidding wars for popular acts. The performers' fees have to be recouped, and necessary evils like advertising, crew fees and venue hire must be factored in. (That said, vertical integration is an increasing factor in the entertainment sector, with all three promoters now owning their own venues). Like almost every product or service, these things cost appreciably more in Ireland than they do in the rest of Europe, and so the price of concert tickets ends up ballooning.

As is inevitably the way with such things, it's the consumer who's left to pick up the tab. The national trait of fiscal stoicism is again a factor here: Irish fans might complain but they will still stump up the cash. Although the live music sector has not yet gotten quite as out of hand as the Dublin property sector, most concertgoers will tell you that they have occasionally feared having to take out a small mortgage to see their favourite acts.

RTE National Symphony Orchestra broadcasting to the Republic.

National Chamber Choir

700 5665/www.dcu.ie/chamber.
Based on the Northside campus of Dublin City University, this professional choir puts on many concerts throughout the year. Its repertoire runs from Seiber and Thompson to Handel, and in summer and winter it can be heard on several Thursdays at the National Gallery of Ireland.

RTÉ Concert Orchestra

208 3347/www.rte.ie/performinggroups/rteconcert orchestra/.
Considerably less ambitious than its big sister the NSOI, the RTÉ Concert Orchestra is defined by its broadcasting remit. It has the largest audience of any Irish classical music outfit, thanks to Ireland's winning streak in the Eurovision Song Contest in the 1990s, when the orchestra was called upon to play to TV audiences of 300 million.

RTÉ National Symphony Orchestra

208 3347/www.rte.ie/performinggroups/ nationalsymphonyorchestral.
The National Symphony Orchestra was founded in 1926 to provide music for radio broadcasts, and it's still run by radio and TV network RTÉ. The NSOI has developed greatly over the past few years.

Venues

In addition to the venues listed below, concerts are often held in the city's theatres (*see pp197-198*). The O'Reilly Hall (858 5665) at Belvedere College is sometimes used for concerts by the RTÉ orchestras, and the Irish Museum of Modern Art in Kilmainham (612 9900/ www.modernart.ie) occasionally rents out its impressive annexe hall to independent ensembles. There are also beautifully sung

daily services and choral concerts at St Patrick's Cathedral and Christ Church Cathedral. Finally, don't miss Latin mass at St Mary's Pro Cathedral, sung by the Palestrina Choir every Sunday (except July and August) at 11am.

Hugh Lane

Parnell Square North, Around O'Connell Street (222 5550/www.hughlane.ie). Bus 3, 10, 11, 13, 16, 19, 46A, 48A/Luas Abbey Street. **Open** 10am-6pm Tue-Thur; 10am-5pm Fri, Sat; 11am-5pm Sun. **Admission** free. **Credit** MC, V. **Map** p251 E1.
This ample hall in the Hugh Lane Gallery hosts the long-running and stylish Sunday at Noon concerts. The series features jazz, contemporary and classical music from Ireland and abroad, and runs from October to June.

National Concert Hall

Earlsfort Terrace, Around St Stephen's Green (417 0000/www.nch.ie). All cross-city buses. **Open** Box office 10am-7pm Mon-Sat. **Credit** AmEx, DC, MC, V. **Map** p251 F5.
Dublin's main venue for orchestral music was established in 1981, in the Great Hall of what was then University College Dublin. It retains the bland flavour of a lecture theatre, though its acoustics are generally considered excellent. Its annexe, the John Field Room, hosts performances of chamber, jazz, traditional and vocal music.

RDS Concert Hall

Royal Dublin Society Showgrounds, Ballsbridge, Southern suburbs (668 0866/www.rds.ie). Bus 7, 5, 45. **Credit** *TicketMaster* AmEx, MC, V.
This overly large but fairly serviceable hall is set in Ireland's main showjumping arena. In its favour, the venue is large enough to accommodate a modestly sized opera company, but it lacks a certain cosiness.

Nightlife

More grooves despite the new curfew.

The laid-back crowd at the **Dice Bar**.

It's now over a decade since Dublin established itself as one of Europe's premier party destinations. By the time Britney, J-Lo et al rolled into town for the MTV Music Awards in 1999, the city could legitimately claim to be the going out capital of Europe. Since then, Dublin has seen its crown snatched by quirkier, cheaper capitals like Prague and Tallinn. Worse still, in August 2008, despite numerous protests, Facebook petitions and a campaign by clubbers (called Give Us The Night), the government closed the loophole that had allowed some clubs with theatre licences to stay open well past 3am. Despite this, a typical weekend in Dublin will prove that, when it comes to letting their hair down, the Irish are still up there with the best.

It all started with that EU cash infusion in the early 1990s. A few clubs opened up, and it wasn't long before the word spread that there was cheap booze to be had in Dublin. Suddenly, people were coming from all over the planet to check out 'Europe's new party capital'. More clubs and bars opened to satisfy demand, causing word to spread further. Dublin was hot.

It was too good to last, of course, and by the end of the 20th century, Dublin's bars and clubs had reached critical mass. The city was awash with 'booze tourists', fun-loving types who took advantage of the cheap budget flights, the favourable exchange rates and that famous Irish hospitality (which, in truth, was beginning to wear a bit thin under the non-stop onslaught of drunken international stag parties). Temple Bar was becoming a no-go area for locals and sane tourists, particularly at weekends. There was vomit on the pavement and syringes in some of the lavatories. Still, huge new bars were opening all over town, most of them designed with partying tourists, rather than character, in mind. At the same time, prices were skyrocketing: the price of a pint almost doubled in just a few years. It seemed like the party might be over. For Dubliners, staying in became the new going out.

But these things happen in cycles, and as the crowds thinned, the people who had made Dublin's party reputation in the first place began to resurface, and the party started up again. These days Dublin's nightlife is

Arts & Entertainment

geared towards more discerning patrons, and the city offers a dynamic variety of venues, but you need to know where to look to find the best.

Most of them are within ten minutes' walk from the banks of the Liffey. On the south side, the best concentration of bars and clubs is around George's Street and Wicklow Street. Camden Street and South William Street are also able to hold their own when it comes to thriving bars. On the north side, the layout is a little more random, but Abbey Street, just off O'Connell Street, has some interesting new bars and clubs. One thing that didn't survive, though, is Temple Bar. Once the centre of the clubbing universe, it's largely dead now. These days, locals only recommend Temple Bar to the sort of tourists they don't want to see in their favourite clubs.

Clubs & dance bars

Academy
57 Abbey Street Middle, Around O'Connell Street (877 9999/www.theacademydublin.com). All cross-city buses/Luas Abbey Street. **Open** 11pm-2.30am Mon-Fri; 10.30pm-2.30am Sat; 11pm-1am Sun. **Admission** €10-€15. **Credit** MC, V. **Map** p250 F2.
Formerly Spirit nightclub, the new-look Academy on Abbey Street Middle has been reborn largely as a live venue. Still, there is much to love here for clubbers: ditching the complacent vibe that befell its naff predecessor, the Academy comes to life on Saturday nights. Spinning current club favourites and festival tracks, popular DJs including FM104 DJ Al Gibbs are on hand to provide the ultimate Saturday night soundtrack. Think CSS and Klaxons rubbing proverbial shoulders with Felix da Housecat and Roger Sanchez.

Button Factory
Curved Street, Around Temple Bar (670 9202/ www.buttonfactory.ie). All cross-city buses. **Open** times vary, check local listings. **Admission** prices vary. **Credit** AmEx, MC, V. **Map** p252 E3.
Until recently, the Button Factory was the famed Temple Bar Music Centre, one of the foremost music venues in the city. After a pricey revamp, the Button Factory is decidedly more plush and relaxed than its grungy predecessor. Now, this 1,000-capacity venue hosts a wide selection of club nights: indie to salsa to house to hip hop. Try Nightflight's house/funk/techno night on Fridays, Transmission (indie/pop) on Saturdays and Club NME (trendy indie/rock/electro) on Thursdays.

Carnival
11 Wexford Street, Around St Stephen's Green (405 3604). Bus 16, 16A, 19, 19A, 122. **Open** 5pm-midnight Mon-Fri; noon-midnight Sat, Sun. **Admission** free. **No credit cards. Map** p251 E5.
Owned and run by Eamon Doran's – the same crowd that looks after the Dice Bar *(see right)* – Carnival

is the top spot on the Camden Street 'strip' if you like your bar music to be a stew of indie, jazz and soul, your lighting cavernous, and your things young and pretty. One drawback is that the bar tends to go from yawningly empty on a weeknight to jam-packed by 8pm on a weekend. If you're coming on a Friday, get in early.

Dice Bar
Queen Street, off Arran Quay (633 3936). All cross-city buses/Luas Smithfield. **Open** 5-11.30pm Mon-Thur; 5pm-12.30am Fri, Sat; 3.30-11pm Sun. **Credit** MC, V. **Map** p250 C2.
A red neon sign reading 'Phat Joint' protrudes from the downbeat wall outside, and the bar itself has a vaguely illicit, Noo Yawk street vibe, courtesy of owner Huey from the Fun Lovin' Criminals. We could reel off a list of the rock stars who've dropped in here for a snifter, but the Dice is not about being star-struck. Best thing about it? Possibly the cool tunes, the laid-back crowd or the post-goth decor illuminated by dozens of church candles; but for us it's the bouncer's afro, a work of tonsorial art worthy of a preservation order. *Photo p186.*

Fitzsimons
Fitzsimon's Hotel, Around Temple Bar (677 9315/ www.fitzsimonshotel.com). All cross-city buses. **Open** 11pm-2.30am Mon-Thur; 10.30pm-2.30am Fri, Sat; 11pm-1.30am Sun. **Admission** €5-€8 Mon-Thur, Sun; €10-€13 Fri, Sat. **Credit** AmEx, MC, V. **Map** p252 E3.
Since it's in the centre of Temple Bar, Fitzsimons is popular with tourists and plays chart hits. The large basement club gets very crowded at weekends, and most of the crowd seems to have wound up here by accident, or because they aren't familiar enough with the city to pick a triendier place. Still, Fitzsimons boasts one of the best rooftop bars in the city – a bonus on the few days that the sun shines in the capital. Turn up drunk.

4 Dame Lane
4 Dame Lane, Around Temple Bar (679 0291). All cross-city buses. **Open** 5pm-2.30am Mon-Thur; 5pm-2.30am Fri, Sat; 5pm-1.30am Sun. **Admission** free. **Credit** AmEx, DC, MC, V. **Map** p251 E3.
Pitching itself somewhere between a DJ bar and a nightclub, Dame Lane is a two-level, New York loft-style space, popular with club kids during the week and a hip, more professional crowd at the weekend. The bar downstairs is ideal for a quiet-ish drink, while upstairs is good for an incredibly loud drink. Neither really has a dancefloor, but that never seems to stop people, and as the night progresses, every inch of floor fills up. It can get claustrophobically crowded, but then, let's face it, so can pretty much everywhere else.

Gaiety
King Street South, Around Trinity College (677 1717/www.gaietytheatre.com). All cross-city buses. **Open** midnight-2.30am Fri, Sat. **Admission** €12 Fri; €15 Sat. **Credit** MC, V. **Map** p251 F4.

One of the city's oldest and largest theatres by day and a mega club by night, this big, Victorian place has several spaces for bands, DJs and films. There are lots of bars, and the warren-like structure of this beautiful old building means you almost need a map (or at least a local guide) to find your way around. The Gaiety is a particularly good destination for fans of Latin and jazz, or indeed for an older crowd.

George

89 South Great George's Street, Around Temple Bar (478 2983/www.capitalbars.com). All cross-city buses. **Open** 5pm-2.30am daily. **Admission** €8 Wed, Thur after 10pm; €10 Sat, Sun. **Credit** AmEx, MC, V. **Map** p251 E4.

This is the gayest gay club in Dublin, but it's still straight-friendly: on a good night the George is as much fun as any straight club will be. If you're in town on a Sunday at about 6pm, check out the George's famed drag bingo and cabaret.

Globe

11 South Great George's Street (671 1220/ www.globe.ie). Bus 12, 16, 16A, 55/Luas St Stephen's Green. **Open** 3pm-2.30am Mon-Sat; 5pm-12.30am Sun. **Credit** AmEx, MC, V. **Map** p252 E3. Populated with students taking advantage of the free Wi-Fi, fashion victims in vintage Dior tank tops and the odd celebrity (Robbie Williams comes here, apparently, when he's in town), the Globe is nothing

Indie reign

A few years ago, Dublin's dance scene was in rude health; the streets of the capital were swarming with techno, dance, euro-pop, progressive house and high-octane disco offerings. At the same time, however, truly thrilling guitar music clubs were few and far between. During Ireland's ongoing love affair with singer-songwriters, indie fans were all dressed up with few places to go.

Yet a new coterie of tastemakers have decided to wrong this right; if you're a fan of the sort of stylish, sweat'n'leather indie/electro nights found in London's Camden or Soho, you'll find much to like in Dublin's new-look nightlife.

Just like the 46A bus, you wait and wait and then a whole troupe of indie clubs arrive at once... a dream scenario for any muso who doesn't want to get their feet wet during the summer's many festivals.

The club that arguably sparked this rebirth is **Antics**, a perennial favourite held each Wednesday in Crawdaddy (10pm-2.30am). Serving up a clatter of rock delights from The National and Queens Of The Stone Age to the Yeah Yeah Yeahs, Antics caters for a twenty-something, skinny-jeaned set.

Currently, the indie illuminati are also heading in their droves to the **Southwilliam** (on South William Street) – held the first Thursday of each month (9.30pm-2.30am) – prides itself on its 'no music policy' agenda. DJs from esteemed local acts like The Jimmy Cake and Halfset mix up a beguiling stew of old rarities and current darlings (think MIA and The Rapture rubbing shoulders with The Slits and Devo).

A few doors down on South William Street, **Spy** was once the sole preserve of house/dance DJs, and served as the location for

after-shows for the glitzy likes of Beyoncé and Justin Timberlake. Now, it is home to three most exciting pop/rock club nights. Friday Night's Summer Of Love is a mixed bag, where DJs spin everything from disco to vintage rockabilly. Despite its name, the fun continues year-round. Ex-JJ72 bassist Sarah Fox and pals preside over Soundcheck every Thursday (7-11pm). Here, 2-for-1 cocktails and dessert treats are served up alongside a white-hot playlist of electro-clash and up-to-the-second indie. Afterwards, the party continues courtesy of Gift DJs, who take over the reins until closing time with their own guitar-driven club night (11pm-2.30am).

As if things couldn't get any better, Dubliners are regularly treated to a steady stream of incoming indie rock dignitaries who serve up one-off club sets of their own. Kings Of Leon, the Go! Team and Sam Fogarino (Interpol) have stolen into the city and wowed crowds with eclectic DJ sets. New Order star Peter Hook, ex-Sex Pistol Glen Matlock and former Specials star Terry Hall are the latest in a long line of former indie icons keen to share their record collections with audiences. As with most things in life, catching these gigs is all about knowing where to look: keep an eye on listings for The Academy, The Village and Whelans on the off-chance that the decks may be manned by a familiar face.

Despite this rash of activity and Dublin's indie scene finally finding its feet, a new set of licensing laws have just been instated, meaning an early curfew for clubs across the board on Sunday nights. It's a less-than-ideal turn of events... no-one likes to be told when to go home, after all. Still, we're sure you'll find some creative ways to spend the wee hours of the morning.

Arts & Entertainment

if not varied. Sit yourself down at one of the long wooden tables, order a pint and a chunky sandwich and do what everyone else is doing: people-watch. A wide range of foreign beers and an eclectic mix of music spun by in-house DJs enhance the experience.

Hub
23 Eustace Street, Around Temple Bar (670 7655). All cross-city buses. **Open** 8.30pm-2.30am daily. **Admission** €3-€10. **Credit** MC, V. **Map** p251 E3.
This basement club and live music spot is the least tourist-oriented venue in Temple Bar. In fact, the average tourist would probably find the Hub a little unnerving. It hosts up-and-coming live acts until 11pm, then turns into a club. The vibe depends on what bands have played that night, but if you like it messy and rock 'n' roll, you won't be disappointed. Check out Trashed on Tuesday, a wicked stew of indie, electro and mash-up. Keep an eye on local listings and gig posters for details.

Kennedy's
31-32 Westland Row, Around Trinity College, (679 9077/www.theunderground.ie). All cross-city buses. **Open** 10am-11.30pm Mon-Thur, 10am-2.30am Fri, Sat. **Admission** prices vary. **Credit** MC, V. **Map** p250 G3.
Thanks in part to resident electro/house DJs like Calvin James, Simon Hayes and Dave Salacious, new life has been breathed into this bar-cum-club venue on Westland Row. Given its proximity to Trinity College, expect a few students, but for the most part the crowd here is terminally trendy. The club night menu changes regularly, so best to consult local listings to see who is playing. For the time being, this place is so hip it hurts.

Lillie's Bordello
Adam Court, Grafton Street, Around Trinity College (679 9204/www.lilliesbordello.ie). All cross-city buses. **Open** 11.30pm-2.30am Mon-Sat. **Admission** €15 non-members. **Credit** AmEx, MC, V. **Map** p251 F4.
You have to be 'somebody' to get in, and once inside, there are lots of reserved areas to negotiate. It looks to us like the crowd is just a bunch of hairdressers who think they're VIPs. If there are any celebs in here, they're safely tucked away in one of the reserved suites, being bored to death by Dublin's self-appointed elite. Staff are precious, and although the music can be good, everyone's far too worried about striking a pose to really let their hair down.

McGruder's
18 Thomas Street, Around St James' Gate (453 9022). Buses 123, 78A/Luas James's. **Open** noon-11.30pm Mon-Wed; noon-2am Thur; noon-2.30am Fri, Sat; noon-1am Sun. **Admission** €10-€15. **Credit** MC, V. **Map** p250 C3.
Uniquely located in the up-and-coming Dublin 8 area near the Guinness Storehouse, McGruder's is the capital's best-kept secret. The venue is home to arguably the best beer garden in the capital – expect impromptu parties and barbecues if the weather is good. Club nights are a mixed bag, from Blues/Soul (most

Sin é. *See p190.*

Fridays) to house, drum 'n' bass and indie rock. A favourite for trendy locals and students from the nearby National College of Art & Design, McGruder's has a relaxed policy. If you're lucky, you may end up stumbling in on one of its all-day techno sessions.

PantiBar
7-8 Capel Street, North Quays (874 0710). All cross-city buses/Luas Jervis. **Open** 5-11.30pm Mon, Wed, Sun; 5pm-2am Tue; 5pm-2.30am Thur; Fri, Sat. **Admission** free. **Credit** MC, V. **Map** p252 E2.
This is a new-school gay bar – which means, apparently, that you can't really tell that it's a gay bar: PantiBar is more about postmodern interior design than camp and cross-dressing. As with most gay-friendly bars, the music is the best pop party tunes. Owned and run by Dublin's best-loved drag queen Panti, who takes to the stage for what is arguably the most popular drag show each Thursday. From intimate acoustic sessions to the intriguingly-titled 'Furry Glen Bear Nights', there is something on Pantibar's slate for everyone.

Pravda
35 Lower Liffey Street, Around O'Connell Street (874 0090). All cross-city buses/Luas Jervis. **Open** 4-11.30pm Mon, Tue; Wed 4pm-2am; 4pm-2.30am Thur; 2pm-2.30am Fri; noon-2.30am Sat; 2-11pm Sun. **Admission** free. **Credit** MC, V. **Map** p251 E2.
One of the more consistent spots on the north side of Dublin's River Liffey, this Russian-themed bar has comfy seating and a fine selection of vodkas, all surrounded by Soviet iconography. The bar hosts numerous themed music nights during the week, from funk to live bands. Thursday's riotous King Kong Club is arguably the high point in Pravda's week, teeming as it is with gorgeous, fun-loving young things.

Ri-Ra

Dame Court, off South Great George's Street,
Around Temple Bar (671 1220/www.rira.ie).
All cross-city buses. **Open** 11.30pm-2.30am Mon-Sat.
Admission €5-€10; free from 11pm-11.30pm Sat-
Thur. **Credit** AmEx, DC, MC, V. **Map** p251 E4.

This place is a safe bet all week. Mondays are particularly busy with Strictly Handbag (soul and '80s
dancefloor fillers), while man-about-town Ollie Cole
rustles up an indie/electro storm with his weekly
Ruby Tuesdays offering (every Tuesday, oddly
enough). Ri-Ra has been in business for more than
a decade and has acquired a small army of regulars
who set a friendly tone. The music policy is wonderfully varied, but the general theme is 'tunes to party
to'. The door policy and dress code are relaxed.

Sin é

14-15 Ormond Quay (878 7078). All cross-city
buses/Luas Jervis. **Open** 11.30am-12.30am Mon-
Wed; 11.30am-2.30am Thur, Fri; 1pm-2.30am Sat;
1pm-12.30am Sun. **Credit** MC, V. **Map** p250 E2.

Located on the north side of the quays, two minutes'
walk from Capel Street Bridge, Sin é survived initial
fad-dom to secure an enduring place as one of
Dublin's most popular bars. An eclectic playlist,
crowds usually heavy in Spanish and Italian students and dim lighting make for wild, wild nights.
The only gripe would be the early closing of the
smoking area to the rear; for the rest of the evening,
smokers have to trudge through the sweaty crowd
to get to the entrance. *Photo p189.*

Solas

31 Wexford Street, Around St Stephen's Green (478
0583/www.solasbars.com). Bus 15, 16, 19, 19A, 55,
61, 62, 83/Luas Harcourt. **Open** 11am-2am Fri, Sat;
11am-11.30pm Mon-Thur, Sun. **Admission** free.
Credit AmEx, MC, V. **Map** p251 E5.

One of the city's best DJ bars, Solas is still a good
spot at which to kick off your night. Renowned for
its sunny rooftop bar, the vibe at this Camden
Quarter hotspot is brilliantly laid back. Music starts
earlier than in many other bars courtesy of a roll
call of resident DJs, and it often seems to lean
towards the jazzy-funky side of things. It's a fun
place, but its principal drawback is a tendency to get
absurdly crowded at weekends.

Southwilliam

52 South William Street, Around St. Stephen's Green
(672 5946/www.southwilliam.ie). All cross-city buses.
Open 11.30pm Mon-Wed; noon-2.30am Thur-
Sat; 5pm-1am Sun. **Admission** free. **Credit** AmEx,
MC, V. **Map** p252 G4.

Southwilliam is growing in popularity by the day,
thanks to a host of diverse club events. Run largely
by local music industry figures, bloggers, stylists,
musicians and DJs, the attention to detail is what
sets the Southwilliam apart as a club venue. Often,
free mini pies are served up during some of the better club events. Expect a varied, anything-goes
music policy in this stylish, shabby chic haunt.

Spy/Wax

Powerscourt Townhouse Centre, William Street
South, Around Temple Bar (677 0014/www.spy
dublin.com). All cross-city buses. **Open** 6pm-2.30am
Mon-Sat; 9pm-1am Sun. **Admission** *Spy* free Mon-
Fri; €8 non-members after midnight Sat. *Wax* €5-€8
Mon-Sat. **Credit** MC, V. **Map** p251 F3.

Two flash, upmarket clubs in one: Spy upstairs,
Wax downstairs. Spy is for those who like to watch
and be watched rather than sweat on the dancefloor;
Wax is all about the dancefloor, it's more of a weekend club, and the music is predominantly house and
hip hop. This is an ideal spot for showing off,
and the cocktails are fab. Spy has a dress code and
a fairly strict door policy, but Wax goes the other
way: if Spy is haute couture, Wax is jeans.

Tripod

Old Harcourt Street Station, Harcourt Street,
Around St Stephen's Green (478 0225/0166/
www.pod.ie). All cross-city buses. **Open** 7.30pm-2.30am
Admission €10-€25. **Credit** MC, V. **Map** p251 F6.

Formerly the famed Red Box, Tripod is one of the
city's newest kids on the block. The club doubles up
as a live venue, but is still renowned for its explo-
sive club nights. Each Friday, 515 DJs rustle up a
techno/house/dance set; on Saturdays, expect more
commercial/chart-based fare. Situated within the
Pod complex, which also houses Crawdaddy, the
labyrinthine Tripod is designed to create an explo-
sive atmosphere, especially on nights when big-
name guest DJs like Carl Cox, Erick Morillo and
James Lavelle visit.

Tripod.

Sport & Fitness

Playing hard in the capital.

Going to the dogs at **Shelbourne Park**. *See p193.*

Work still continues at the most famous of Dublin's sporting facilities, **Lansdowne Road Stadium** (*see p193*), but otherwise it is business as usual in this sports-obsessed city. So take a seat in the stands and get an insight into what Dublin life is really about: from a visitor's point of view, sport can provide a fast track into an area of the city's grass-roots culture that is refreshingly free of tourist gloss. Racing, rugby, soccer and the indigenous games of Gaelic football and hurling are all popular and accessible spectator sports.

To find out what's going on while you're in town, check the *Irish Times*, which prints a detailed daily sports diary. If you want in-depth knowledge of Irish sporting culture, two books by the country's top sports journalists, Tom Humphries' *Laptop Dancing and the Nanny Goat Mambo* and Con Houlihan's *More Than a Game*, are both superbly written.

Spectator sports

Gaelic football & hurling

Gaelic football is a cross between rugby and soccer, while hurling most closely resembles hockey. Both games are fast, furious and not for the faint of heart, and following a match can be confusing, so if you're headed for the stands, *see p192* **Rules of the game** for the low-down on a few of the basics.

Games are run by the **Gaelic Athletic Association** (*see p192*), an amateur organisation that holds a unique place in Irish life. There are Gaelic Athletic Association clubs in every parish, and the top players of each are selected for inter-county competition. Counties play for the league in winter and the more important **All-Ireland Championship** in summer. Big games are quintessentially Irish occasions that bring colour and passion to the streets and pubs, and if you see a preponderance of sky-blue football shirts with the three-castle city crest, you'll know that the local favourites are doing the business.

Dublin (aka 'the Dubs') play some matches at **Parnell Park**, but the big games are played at the home of the GAA, **Croke Park**. Also, until the regeneration work at Lansdowne has been completed, Croke Park will be hosting all **Six Nations** matches, as well as various other rugby and soccer matches.

Croke Park

Jones Road, Drumcondra, Northern suburbs (836 3222/www.crokepark.ie). Bus 3, 11, 11A, 16, 51A. **Open** *Office* 9.30am-1pm, 2.15-5.30pm Mon-Fri. **Tickets** €25-€60; €5-€25 reductions. **No credit cards**.

Gaelic Athletic Association

Croke Park, Jones Road, Drumcondra, Northern suburbs (836 3222/www.gaa.ie). Bus 3, 11, 11A, 16, 51A. **Open** *Office* 9.30am-5.30pm Mon-Fri.

Parnell Park

Clantarkey Road, Donnycarney, Northern suburbs (836 3222/www.hill16.ie). Bus 20, 27, 27B, 42, 42A, 42B. **Open** Times vary. **Tickets** €6-€15; €5 reductions; free under-14s. **No credit cards**.

Greyhound racing

The greyhound tracks at Harold's Cross and Shelbourne Park have bars and reasonable food

Rules of the game

Gaelic football's closest living relative is Australian-rules football and while it may appear to the unschooled eye that the only rules are to inflict the worst possible injuries on your opponents, this is not actually (entirely) true. The ball (slightly smaller than a soccer ball) may only be carried in the hand for a distance of four steps, after which it must be either 'hand-passed' (whacked with hand or fist) or 'solo-ed' (bounced on the foot and caught again; although this may only be done a maximum of two consecutive times).

To see Dubliners at their most passionate, their most convivial (which is not just a nice way of saying 'drunk', although it's partly that) and their most vocal, you need to get yourself down to **Parnell Park** (*see p192*) or, better still, **Croke Park** (*see p192*) to watch a hurling or a Gaelic football match. Frankly, either one will do – both are equally insane, in terms of sheer violence and propensity for grievous physical injury (the two aspects of these dearly cherished sports that whip the crowds into their greatest frenzies). Even the meekest and mildest end up shouting and screaming like spectators at the Colosseum. And you will too.

The rules are fairly simple: in both games, teams of 15 players compete on a playing field with both rugby goalposts and soccer nets. Getting the ball in the net is worth three points (a goal), while putting it over the crossbar earns one. How each sport achieves this, however, is decidedly different.

Tackling is (in theory) not a contact manoeuvre (grabbing an opponent is against the rules, 'bumping' is allowed). In **hurling** games, meanwhile, the ball, or *slíothar*, is hit or carried along by a hurley stick, but may also be kicked or slapped with the palm of the hand. The clash of the ash and the aggressive momentum of the game make it incredibly exciting to watch; and the fizzing velocity of the ball (small, hard and covered in horse hide) make it a dangerous game to play. Today it vies with Gaelic football as the country's biggest sport.

It seems incredible that these two arcane sports are still more popular than football or rugby, but then the Irish are a nation of proud traditionalists. A fragment of the ancient Brehon Laws show that hurling was played (and regulated) as early as the eighth century. It was banned by the English Crown in the 12th century, but when the British weren't looking the game continued to thrive.

offerings, as well as (between them) racing events six nights a week. Further information can be obtained from the **Greyhound Board** (Bord na gCon) at Shelbourne Park (*see below*).

Harold's Cross Racetrack

151 Harold's Cross Road, Harold's Cross, Southern suburbs (497 1081/www.igb.ie). Bus 16, 16A. **Open** *Racing* 6.30-10.30pm Mon, Tue, Fri. **Tickets** €8; €5 reductions. **No credit cards.**

Shelbourne Park

Lotts Road, Ringsend, Southern suburbs (497 1081/www.igb.ie). Bus 2, 3. **Open** *Racing* 6.30-10.30pm Wed, Thur, Sat. **Tickets** €8; €5 reductions. **Credit** MC, V.
Photo p191.

Horse racing

At Dublin's year-round horse races, the atmosphere in the stands, betting rings and bars is hard to beat. The **Curragh** racecourse (*see below*) is the home of flat racing, hosting classic races, including the prestigious Irish Derby each summer. Steeplechasing is the major focus of racing in Ireland, though, and the Grand National takes place in April at **Fairyhouse** (*see below*) in County Meath. Then there's the National Hunt Festival each spring at **Punchestown** (*see below*), while the four-day Leopardstown Festival, starting on Boxing Day at Leopardstown (*see below*), is one of the country's social highlights.

For race-day transport, call **Dublin Bus** (873 4222, www.dublinbus.ie) for Leopardstown, and **Bus Éireann** (836 6111, www.buseireann.ie) or **Iarnród Éireann** (836 6222, www.irish rail.ie) for the others.

Curragh Racecourse

Curragh, Co Kildare (045 441 205). Special bus services. **Open** *Race times* 2-2.15pm Sat, Sun. **Tickets** €15-€65. **Credit** AmEx, DC, MC, V.

Fairyhouse Racecourse

Ratoath, Co Meath (825 6167/www.fairyhouseracecourse.ie). Special bus services. **Open** Times vary with fixture. **Tickets** €14-€18; €7-€11 reductions. **Credit** MC, V.

Leopardstown Racecourse

Foxrock, Co Dublin (289 0500/www.leopards town.com). Bus 46A/DART Blackrock, then 114 bus. **Open** times vary with fixture. **Tickets** €15-€30; free under-14s. **Credit** MC, V (for pre-bookings).

Punchestown Racecourse

Naas, Co Kildare (045 897 704/www.punches town.com). Special bus services. **Open** Time vary with fixture. **Tickets** €15-€18; €8-€10 reductions; free under-14s. **Credit** MC, V.

Rugby union

Rugby in Dublin always used to be associated with the city's elite private schools, but the recent swing to professionalism has widened its appeal: provincial rugby in particular has really taken off. Leinster compete at Donnybroook in the **Inter-Provincial Championship** and the **Celtic League** (against teams from Scotland and Wales), but it's the hugely successful European cup contest that has been getting the most attention lately.

At the international level, the **Six Nations Championship** (*see p154*) is the highlight of the rugby calendar, and match weekends inspire cheerful debauchery. The national side will still play at Croke Park while Lansdowne Road is being regenerated (a project that will rumble on until at least 2010). Contact the **Irish Rugby Football Union** (668 4601, www.irishrugby.ie) for more details.

Lansdowne Road Stadium

62 Lansdowne Road, Ballsbridge, Southern suburbs (www.lrsdc.ie). DART Lansdowne Road. **Open** for Six Nations tickets, contact Croke Park (*see p192*).
Plans that were first announced as long ago as September 2004 should (fingers crossed) finally come to fruition at the beginning of 2010, according to the latest information at the time of writing. The project to develop Lansdowne Road into a world-class 50,000-capacity stadium has been keenly anticipated by displaced fans (who continue to watch national and international games at Croke Park; *see p192*). Hopefully, the wait will have been worth it.

Soccer

When the national soccer team is doing well, their matches can bring the city to a standstill. On a local level, check out the **Eircom League**, where crowd enthusiasm and gritty passion take precedence over the ostentatious glamour and self-indulgence that is so often associated with top English sides these days. Your best bet for atmosphere and facilities is **Dalymount Park** in Phibsborough, home to Bohemians FC (*see below*).

Contact the **Football Association of Ireland** (676 6864, www.fai.ie) for information about fixtures.

Bohemians FC

Dalymount Park, Phibsborough, (868 0923/www. bohemians.ie). Bus 10, 19, 19A, 38, 120. **Tickets** €20; €5-€10 reductions. **No credit cards.**

Shamrock Rovers

Unit 9C, Centre Point Business Park, Oak Road, Southern suburbs (460 948/www.shamrockrovers.ie). **Tickets** €15; €8-€10 reductions; free under-12s. **No credit cards.**

Arts & Entertainment

Following their relegation from the Eircom Premier Division, the Rovers continue to find themselves in the reduced circumstances of the First Division. But games are still great fun and worth turning up to.

Shelbourne FC
Tolka Park, Richmond Road, Drumcondra, Northern suburbs (837 5536/www.shelbournefc.ie). Bus 3, 11, 11A, 13, 16, 16A. **Tickets** €15; €10-€5 reductions. **No credit cards**.

Active sports & fitness

Gyms & fitness centres

Contrary to any popular misconceptions about their Guinness consumption, the Irish are as into physical fitness, gyms and workouts as anybody else, so there are plenty of modern, well-equipped workout facilities in Dublin.

Crunch Fitness
UCD Campus, Belfield, Southern suburbs (260 3155/www.crunchfitness.ie). Bus 10, 11, 46A. **Open** 7am-10pm Mon-Fri; 10am-5.30pm Sat, Sun. **Rates** €12 per visit; €6.50 student. **Credit** MC, V.
The University College Dublin health centre is fully equipped with CV machines and free weights, and it hosts regular aerobics classes.

Thérapie.

Markievicz Leisure Centre
Townsend Street, Around Trinity College (672 9121/www.dublincity.ie). All cross-city buses/Luas Abbey Street. **Open** 7am-10pm Mon-Thur; 7am-9pm Fri; 9am-6pm Sat; 10am-4pm Sun. **Rates** *Swim* €5.50. *Gym* €6. **Map** p252 G3.
This centre on Townsend Street, which is run by the Dublin Corporation, is relatively inexpensive; it has a fully equipped gym, swimming pool and sauna.

YMCA Gym
Aungier Street, Around Temple Bar (478 2607/www.ymca.ie). Bus 16, 16A, 19, 19A. **Open** 7.30am-10pm Mon-Fri; 9.30am-4.30pm Sat. **Rates** €8-€9. **Credit** MC, V. **Map** p252 E4.
Conveniently central, and the great advantage for visitors who want to work off the holiday weight is that anyone can use its small fitness classes on a pay-as-you-go basis.

Golf

More than 60 golf courses sprawl across County Dublin, including some of the finest links in the world. Most accept visitors, but green fees vary greatly. Corballis near Donabate has two decent cheap courses: **Corballis Links** (843 6583, www.golfdublin.com), which is always in good nick and has the potential to reduce any golfer to tears, and the **Island** (843 6205, www.the islandgolfclub.com), which is one of the city's most dramatic golfing venues. **Hollystown** (820 7444, www.hollystown.com) in Mulhuddart is pleasant but deceptively simple, and it boasts a lovely clubhouse. The upmarket **Portmarnock Hotel & Golf Links** (*see p52*) is also superb.

Contact **Dublin Corporation** (222 2222, www.dublincity.ie) for details of cheaper courses and prices (including pitch-and-putt). A complete list of private courses, along with pretty much anything else you need to know about golfing in Ireland, can be obtained from the website of the **Golfing Union of Ireland** (www.gui.ie).

Wellbeing

Thérapie
8 Molesworth Street, Around Temple Bar (472 1222/www.therapie.ie). **Open** 8am-8pm Mon-Fri; 9am-6pm Sat; 10am-6pm Sun. **Rates** varies with treatment. **Credit** MC, V. **Map** 252 F4.
Neither spa nor gym, Thérapie is a one-stop shop for the body, whether it's pampering you require (there is a long menu of beauty treatments involving top-flight products like Dermalogica and Elemis) or if you want to book an appointment for one of the various non-surgical skin treatments. Check the website for up to date information on special offers.

Arts & Entertainment

Theatre & Dance

The scenes may change but Dublin's theatres never lose the plot.

Last chance to see performances at the historic **Abbey** theatre building.

Dublin's theatrical landscape is shifting. In 2008, the much-loved, long-standing **Andrew's Lane Theatre** closed its doors to become, of all things, a nightclub (*see p179*), while the grand old **Abbey** (*see p197*) is pressing ahead with plans to forsake its historic premises in favour of plush new quarters in Docklands. And it will be getting an illustrious neighbour, in the form of Daniel Libeskind's proposed Grand Canal Theatre (*see p28*) – yet another new building project underway by the riverside. And in more modest ventures, both the **Gaiety** (*see p197*) and the **Gate** (*see p197*) have recently lavished millions of euros on spiffy new refurbs.

But then a progressive, dynamic attitude towards the theatre has always been at the heart of Irish life. If Ireland has a reputation for literature, it's mostly down to its dramatists. There's one Irish lion among novelists – Joyce – and one among the poets – Yeats – but it's only when you get to the stage that the names start tripping off the tongue: Sheridan, Wilde, Shaw, O'Casey, Beckett, Behan, Friel,

McDonagh. We could go on. From 1771 (Goldsmith's *She Stoops to Conquer*) to 1913 (Shaw's *Pygmalion*), most of the comedies written for the London stage were by Irishmen. Since Shaw, Irish plays have tended to be regional and idiomatic (with the great exception of Beckett), and they need Irish actors. Admittedly, Synge's *Playboy of the Western World* was performed to great acclaim in Chinese in Beijing in March 2006, but it's impossible to think of O'Casey, Behan or Friel being performed in anything but Irish accents.

INFORMATION AND TICKETS

The *Dublin Event Guide* and Thursday's *Irish Times* both contain listings and reviews; the *Dubliner* carries reviews of the bigger productions. Most Dublin theatres and companies produce their own leaflets, generally found in tourist centres, hotels and cafés. In addition, the *Golden Pages* phone directory has a particularly useful theatre information section.

Bewley's Café Theatre.

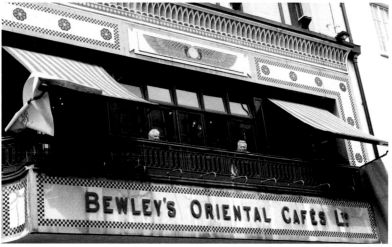

Theatre

Tickets for some theatrical and dance productions are available through **TicketMaster** at HMV on Grafton Street (*see p145*), though it charges a booking fee (0818 719 300, from outside Ireland 456 9569, www.ticket master.ie). Other tickets should be bought directly from the individual theatres.

Classics from the Irish canon – *The Importance of Being Earnest, Waiting for Godot* and the like – are performed with steady regularity and varying quality by the the **Abbey** and the **Gate**. Every decade or so, Dublin audiences are treated to an iconic performance of one of these, which then proves an impossible act to follow.

The best bets for new, avant-garde work are the **Peacock** in the Abbey (*see right*) and the **Project Arts Centre** (*see p198*), which host independent experimental companies such as **Irish Modern Dance Theatre** (*see p198*). The triptych of classy, state-of-the-art theatres in the Northside suburbs – the **Helix** (*see p198*), the **Draíocht** (*see right*), the **Civic Theatre** (*see right*) – generally act as receiving houses for touring productions.

Venues

Abbey

26 Abbey Street Lower, Around O'Connell Street (box office 878 7222/www.abbeytheatre.ie). All cross-city buses/Luas Abbey Street. **Open** *Box office* 10.30am-7pm Mon-Sat. **Tickets** €20-€30; €14-15 reductions (Mon-Fri). **Credit** AmEx, MC, V. **Map** p251 G2.

Internationally renowned theatre designer Jean-Guy Lecat has transformed the auditorium of this, the nation's premier theatre. Where there used to be a balcony there is now elegantly sloping seating, with no awkward corners left for bad sightlines and dodgy sound. And while plans for its move to Docklands have been finalised, the actual realities of transposing the Abbey to its new location were, at the time of writing, far from looming on the horizon. For the time being at least, the Abbey will remain in its original historic setting.

Established by WB Yeats and Lady Gregory in 1904 to further the nationalist cause, the theatre opened to glorious controversy – Synge's *Playboy of the Western World* (1907) and O'Casey's *Plough and the Stars* (1926) were considered so shocking in conservative Dublin (in particular Synge's use of the word 'shift' to mean knickers) that they were met with riots. Contemporary playwrights would kill for that kind of publicity, but unfortunately things haven't been so exciting since: the Abbey still gets loads of column inches but mostly from people railing against its creative mire – 'Abbey-bashing' is a favourite national pastime, and very tedious it is too. For talk of a more constructive nature, check out the regular programme of Abbey Talks (in which guest speakers reflect on everything from the role of a national theatre to interpreting *The Brothers Karamazov*). *Photo p195.*

Bewley's Café Theatre

78 Grafton Street, Around Temple Bar (086 878 4001/www.bewleyscafetheatre.com). All cross-city buses/Luas St Stephen's Green. **Open** *Lunchtime shows* 1pm Mon-Sat. *Evening shows* 8pm performance days. **Tickets** *Lunchtime* €14 (incl soup and bread). *Evening* €15. **No credit cards.** **Map** p252 F4.

Dublin's only year-round venue for lunchtime drama, this café theatre is an elegant and intimate space that has a reputation for staging exciting, innovative productions of both classics and new Irish works. In addition to the lunchtime shows, evening productions (cabaret, jazz and comedy) take place here from time to time, and it really comes into its own during the Dublin Fringe Festival (*see p158*).

Civic Theatre

Tallaght Town Centre, Tallaght, Southern suburbs (462 7477/www.civictheatre.ie). Bus 49, 49A, 50, 54A, 56A, 65, 65B, 77, 77A/Luas Tallaght. **Open** *Box office* 10am-6pm Mon-Sat. **Tickets** *Main auditorium* €20; €15-€16 reductions. **Credit** MC, V.

The windy suburbs of Tallaght may be a far cry from theatreland, but trekking out to this 350-seater – a bright state-of-the art space with a studio, restaurant, bar and gallery – can be rewarding. This is primarily a receiving house for established provincial and international touring productions.

Draíocht

Blanchardstown Centre, Blanchardstown, Northern suburbs (885 2622/www.draiocht.ie). Bus 38, 38A, 39, 39X, 236, 237, 239, 270. **Open** *Box office* 10am-6pm Mon-Sat. **Tickets** prices vary. **Credit** MC, V.

This well-appointed suburban theatre also has studio space, an art gallery, a handy bar and a brand-new café. Like the Civic (*see left*), Draíocht acts as a receiving house, playing host to a broad range of performing and visual arts, both national and international, from stand-up comedy, dance and children's shows to music recitals and dynamic contemporary theatre.

Gaiety

King Street South, Around Temple Bar (677 1717/www.gaietytheatre.ie). All cross-city buses/Luas St Stephen's Green. **Open** *Box office* 10am-8pm Mon-Sat. **Tickets** €12.50-€75. **Credit** AmEx, MC, V. **Map** p252 F4.

The Gaiety is a lovely Victorian chocolate box-style theatre that hosts the Christmas pantos and the spring opera season. It also caters for classic Irish plays and West End shows during the Dublin Theatre Festival (*see p158*). But the problem for many Dubliners is that, having been brought up going to the Gaiety's panto every Christmas, it becomes increasingly difficult to take any of their other productions seriously – 'Oh no, he didn't!' you want to shout as soon as you settle into those velvet seats, never mind that it's Hamlet's ghost on stage…

Gate

1 Cavendish Row, Parnell Square, Around O'Connell Street (874 4045/www.gate-theatre.ie). All cross-city buses/Luas Abbey Street. **Open** *Box office* 10am-7pm Mon-Sat. **Tickets** €27-€35. **Credit** AmEx, MC, V. **Map** p251 F2.

The Abbey's misfortune is the Gate's opportunity. While the national theatre has been foundering since the start of the millennium, its younger, sassier rival has gone from strength to strength. The year 2006 was triumphant, opening with Ralph Fiennes and Ian McDiarmuid in Friel's classic *The Faith Healer*, then moving seamlessly into a Beckett season – showcasing John Hurt, Michael Gambon and Barry McGovern – to celebrate the writer's centenary. And the staging in 2008 of Pinter's *No Man's Land* (also featuring Gambon, alongside David Walliams) was a similarly glittering success. The Gate's director, Michael Colgan, runs a shrewd operation, mixing international stars with local greats in quality productions that have theatregoers queuing for returns. He's helped by having the most elegant, spacious theatre in the city (which was being further improved with the construction of a new €5.2

Arts & Entertainment

million wing at the time of writing) and by a rambunctious, cosmopolitan legacy. The Gate was founded in 1928 by the flamboyant, legendary, homosexual duo Hilton Edwards and Micheál MacLiammóir (both English, MacLiammóir gaelicised his name), who for 40 years fed an eager public with an uncompromising diet of avant-garde experimental Irish and international plays. That cosmopolitan legacy allows Colgan to cast his net wide, unlike the poor Abbey, which, as the 'national theatre', seems to be condemned to unadulterated Irish fare.

Helix

Dublin City University, Collins Avenue, Glasnevin, Northern suburbs (700 7000/www.helix.ie). Bus 11, 13, 19A. **Open** *Box Office* 10am-6pm Mon-Sat. **Tickets** prices vary. **Credit** MC, V.
This performance space on the northern campus of Dublin City University is home to three separate venues, and hosts a wide variety of theatre, music and popular entertainment. Programming is eclectic: the Helix has hosted everything from big bands to ballet and Dame Kiri Te Kanawa, while gigs by heavyweights like Van Morrison and Lou Reed have bolstered the venue's reputation even further.

Olympia

72 Dame Street, Around Temple Bar (679 3323/ www.mcd.ie/olympia). All cross-city buses/Luas Jervis. **Open** *Box office* 10.30am-6.30pm daily. **Tickets** prices vary. **Credit** AmEx, MC, V. **Map** p252 E3.
This old-style variety theatre – it was Dublin's first music hall – retains its physical characteristics (many of them authentically worn) but has largely parted company with straight theatre. It's an occasional venue for well-known international stand-up comedians (Jimmy Carr made a recent stop here), but these days its cavernous auditorium usually reverberates with the sound of big-name rock and pop acts.

Project Arts Centre

39 Essex Street East, Around Temple Bar (box office 881 9613/www.project.ie). All cross-city buses/Luas Jervis. **Open** *Box office* 11am-7pm Mon-Sat. **Tickets** prices vary. **Credit** MC, V. **Map** p252 E3.
PAC began 40 years ago as a visual arts project in the foyer of the Gate (*see p197*), before settling into these refurbished premises in 2000. The building's three multi-functional performance and exhibition spaces host theatre, dance, video and film, contemporary and popular music, cultural debates and performance pieces, making this Dublin's main venue for the new, the innovative and the cutting-edge.

Tivoli

135-138 Francis Street, Kilmainham & Liberties (454 4472). Bus 50, 78A. **Open** *Box office (during show)* 10am-8pm Mon-Sat. **Tickets** prices vary. **Credit** MC, V. **Map** p250 D4.
This place hosts all manner of live entertainment, from serious drama to musicals. Irish and international shows feature in equal measure, but don't expect to see anything radical.

Dance

There's *Riverdance* and then there's dance in Ireland. And dance companies in Ireland have suffered, and continue to struggle. Why? Because, while the Irish are undoubtedly partial to watching their children hop around in traditional outfits, there's no actual tradition of sitting still on seats and watching dancers move through a narrative. A short-lived national ballet company dissolved in 1989 and there hasn't been one since. In its stead, a few small, dedicated and talented companies keep the art of dance alive.

Dance companies

Many of the city's most daring and critically acclaimed dance performances are staged at the **Project Arts Centre** (*see left*); check the website for current programming.

Dance Theatre of Ireland

Bloomfields Centre, Lower Georges Street, Dún Laoghaire, Dublin Bay (280 3455/www.dance theatreireland.com).
Known for the arresting visual quality of its work, this group performs material devised by its two artistic directors, Robert Connor and Loretta Yurick. Recently, the dancers have added a multimedia dimension to their performances, with interactive digital technology and fantastic backdrops.

Irish Modern Dance Theatre

Rear 44, East Essex Street, Around Temple Bar (671 5113/www.irishmoderndancetheatre.com).
Performing ambitious new works to original music by young composers, IMDT, run by progressive Dublin-born choreographer John Scott, collaborates frequently with artists such as the dance filmmaker Charles Atlas, and it has strong links with international dance companies.

Traditional Irish dance

Traditional Irish dancing is still a big thing, but not in Dublin. But, if you are confined to the capital, you can still stumble across the odd impromptu session. You're guaranteed a set at **Cultúrlann na hÉireann** (*see below*), but it's smoothly touristic, rather than spontaneous. Still, if it's your first experience of the genre, you may well find it highly entertaining.

Cultúrlann na hÉireann

32 Belgrave Square, Monkstown, Dublin Bay (280 0295/www.comhaltas.e). Bus 7, 8. **Open** *Dancing* 9pm Fri. **Admission** €9.50. **No credit cards.**
Cultúrlann na hÉireann (the Irish Cultural Institute) hosts popular large ceilidhs or communal dances, just like in the good old dance-hall days. Expect a mix of committed locals and curious tourists.

Trips Out of Town

Getting Started   200
Newgrange &
    the Boyne Valley   201
The Wicklow Mountains   207
Kilkenny & Around   213

Avoca. *See p211.*

Getting Started

Take a hike.

Glendalough, 'valley of two lakes'. *See p209.*

With such a wealth of outstanding scenery, prehistoric sites and delightful country sleepovers don't overlook the green hills of the fair Isle while staying in the city. In fact, just about the time you find yourself considering checking out the Museum of Banking, perhaps it might be a good idea to rent a car (or hop on a train or bus) and get out of town.

The countryside around Dublin is a lure in itself: to the north, in **Newgrange**, rolling green hills hold mysterious ancient burial sites (*see pp201-206*), while, to the south, the **Wicklow Mountains** surround gorgeous Glendalough (*see pp207-212*). Further south still is beautiful **Kilkenny**, with its arts shops, towering castles and rambling ruined abbeys (*see pp213-219*). All are within a couple of hours' journey from the city.

GETTING AROUND

The best way to see the countryside is by car. You can get to the major towns by train or bus, but then you miss out on the lovely scenery and the quaint villages in the surrounding countryside, as most are not accessible by public transport. Some sights are well out of any town and quite isolated, and there's no way to reach them without your own transport. For our list of car rental agencies in Dublin, *see p225*. Otherwise, the train service **Iarnród Éireann** and the bus service **Bus Éireann** (for both, *see pp220-222*) each have wide-ranging coverage to the bigger towns, although connections between rural stations are often lacking. Buses leave from the Central Bus Station (**Busárus**) on Store Street (*see p220*), while trains depart from **Heuston** and **Connolly** stations (*see p221*).

INFORMATION

The **Irish Tourist Board** (Bord Fáilte, *see p235*) has local outposts in most of the bigger cities, and some small towns have their own tourist offices. In Dublin, your first point of call should be the **Dublin Tourism Centre** (*see p235*), where you'll find reams of literature and maps, as well as advice on hotels, car hire and good routes to take. Those interested in countryside walks should check out **Waymarked Ways of Ireland** (www.walkireland.ie) with its helpful and bang up to date information.

Newgrange & the Boyne Valley

Travel back to the dawn of Ireland's legendary past.

With its quiet, hilly pastures dotted with fluffy white sheep, the area just north of Dublin may look like your typical Irish countryside, but it is much more than that. This is where Ireland began. This is the home of the **Hill of Tara** – Ireland's Olympus, where kings ruled the country 1,000 years ago, aided, it was said, by fairies.

By then, though, the land was already very old. County Meath's rich soil has attracted settlers for more than 8,000 years, and archaeologists have uncovered burial grounds and ruined settlements that indicate this was a thriving region millennia ago. The best known of the ancient sites is **Newgrange**, with its mysterious carvings and huge stone passage tomb. Nearby, the **Hill of Slane**, a lofty 150-metre (492-foot) mound, overlooks one of the loveliest parts of the Boyne Valley. On this hill, according to tradition, a Welsh priest lit a Christian fire in direct defiance of the pagan Irish King Laoghaire, thus beginning the first confrontation between religious orders in a country that was to see more than its fair share of them over the centuries.

The chief town of County Meath is **Navan**, but nearby **Kells** is better known because of its famous Book of Kells, the hand-illustrated gospel manuscript on display at Trinity College (*see p58*) in Dublin.

Still, even given the lush, rolling green hills, the charming villages and the bracing sea views, everybody really comes this way for one thing: namely, Newgrange.

Newgrange & Knowth

The ancient site at **Newgrange** is both mythological and real: it's one of the most important Stone Age sites in Europe and also, in Irish lore, the home of the Tuatha de Danainn, cave-dwelling worshippers of the goddess Danu. The deep cavern is covered in strange, geometric patterns (of the sort you'll find reproduced on jewellery sold at Glastonbury), and the meanings of the mysterious zigzags, ovals and crazy spirals have never been fully explained.

What is known for certain is that the ancient passage mounds were built 5,000 years ago, when most tools were made of bone, flint and metal, and then not discovered again until 1699. But how and why the members of a small farming community moved rocks weighing 50 tons over massive distances through inhospitable terrain remains a mystery.

For many, the most interesting part of Newgrange is probably this: the tomb's passageway descends 19 metres (62 feet), and the only time light reaches its depths is on the shortest day of the year. The cavern was, therefore, designed to align with the winter solstice so that when the sun rises on 21 December, a ray of light sweeps down the long passageway and strikes the back chamber, where it is believed that the ashes of the dead were once kept.

You can learn more about it all at the helpful **Brú na Bóinne Visitor Centre** (*see p203*), near the town of Donore. The centre also covers (and provides access to) the ancient site of **Knowth**. Like Newgrange, Knowth is a passage mound decorated with spirals, triangles, concentric circles and other stone carvings. Most unusually, though, Knowth, has two passage graves, and its central mound has two chambers – one pointing east and the other west; the eastern passage is an impressive 40 metres (130 feet) long. Like Newgrange, Knowth was designed with the sun in mind, but here light shines on the centre chamber during both spring and autumnal equinoxes. While both Newgrange and Knowth are generally referred to as 'passage tombs', and both undoubtedly functioned as burial places, archaeologists think there may have been much more to them than that; they're just not sure what. They may have been temples or even astronomical observatories.

Access to both Newgrange and Knowth is now handled by the visitor centre. You park at the centre and then are shuttled to the sites from there. In the summertime this system can lead to very long waits, so be prepared. Some swear that if you show up early, you can dodge the masses; we're not so sure, but if you show

Space-age access to Stone Age remains at **Knowth**. *See p201.*

up late, you might not get to see anything at all. Since you may have to wait for ages, it's a good thing the centre has a museum, informative videos, full-scale models, camp re-creations and decent grub.

If you can't deal with the crowds, you might want to try **Four Knocks** (Na Fuarchnoic), a much smaller, less well-known ancient tomb near the town of Naul. You can explore it at your leisure and picnic on the grassy roof: it's wonderful to have a 5,000-year-old site to yourself. The key is held by Fintan White and is available (for a refundable deposit) until 6pm daily. Fintan lives about a mile away from the site; for directions and further details, visit www.knowth.com/fourknocks.htm.

Once back at the site (follow the signs from Naul), follow the gorse-lined track. The tomb consists of a heavy iron door and a short passage leading into a wide, pear-shaped chamber. Just inside the main chamber to the left of the entrance is the oldest-known representation of a human face in Europe, as well as many other strange symbols carved in

the stone. You'd do well to bring a torch, but if you forget, check the ledge on the left to see if one's still kept there.

The passage graves are near the **Boyne Valley**, where the Battle of the Boyne took place in 1690. In 1688 the Catholic King James II was deposed in favour of his Protestant daughter Mary. In a bid to regain his throne, James fought William of Orange's army at Oldbridge, but his troops were routed, and he had to flee to France. This is where you will find **Slane Castle**, whose grounds were landscaped by famed British gardener 'Capability' Brown.

On the **Hill of Slane**, outside the town, Saint Patrick lit an Easter bonfire in 433 as a challenge to the authority of the Kings of Tara; the subsequent spread of Christianity eroded the power of the pagan rulers. A statue of Patrick marks the spot today.

You can see the other side of that story when you're heading back towards Dublin on the N3. On the way, you'll pass the **Hill of Tara**, once the seat of the High Kings of Ireland. Tara is the spiritual capital of ancient Ireland and the fount of much folklore. Entrance to the site is free, and there's a visitors' centre inside the church at the top of the hill where you can learn more about the ancient rulers.

The *Táin Bó Cúailnge* ('Cattle Raid of Cooley') is set around these parts. First written in the eighth century, it has been described as Ireland's *Iliad*. It tells the story of Queen Maeve of Connaught's efforts to obtain an exceptional Brown Bull from the people of Ulster (100 fighting men could rest in its shade and thrice 50 boys could sport on his broad back), and how she is foiled ultimately by one of Ireland's great folk heroes, Cú Chulainn.

Near the Hill of Tara, the town of **Trim** is well worth a visit. Best among its many sights is **Trim Castle**, an impressive Anglo-Norman castle. Hugh de Lacy began work on its construction in 1172; when completed, the castle's 20-sided tower had walls three metres (11 feet) thick. It was built to be impregnable – three storeys high, protected by a ditch, a curtain wall and a moat – but the English nevertheless managed to get in (twice) during the English civil war. It was abandoned after Cromwell and his cronies departed. If you think the castle looks familiar, that might be because you've seen *Braveheart*, in which it was used as a stand-in for York.

The building across the river from the castle is **Talbot Castle**, a grand manor house that dates back to 1415.

If you feel up to a walk from here, you can follow the Dublin road from Trim Castle, crossing the river to the ruins of **St Patrick's Church** (follow the signs). This lovely medieval ruin has well-preserved gravestones, including a 16th-century tomb known locally as the 'jealous couple'; this comes from the fact that the effigies on the tomb lie with a sword carved in between them.

Get maps and local information from the handy local **visitor centre** (*see p204*), which also has a small historical display.

About 20 kilometres (12 miles) north of Trim (or 12 miles west of Newgrange), in the north-west of the county on the N52, is the market town of **Kells**. This community was first established as a religious settlement in 550, and is most famed for its Book of Kells. The book is now kept in Trinity College (*see p58*), which reduces the town's power of tourist attraction somewhat, although there are some fine Celtic crosses here as well as a Round Tower. There's also the lovely old **Church of St Columba** in the town centre, which is most notable for standing where the monastic settlement that first received the Book of Kells once stood.

Brú na Bóinne Visitor Centre

Donore (041 988 0300/www.heritageireland.ie).
Open *Nov-Feb* 9.30am-5pm daily. *Mar, Apr, Oct* 9.30am-5.30pm daily. *May-mid June* 9am-6.30pm daily. *Mid June-mid Sept* 9am-7pm daily. **Admission** *Centre* €2.90; €1.60-€2.10 reductions; €7.40 family. *Centre & Newgrange* €5.80; €2.90-€4.50 reductions; €14.50 family. *Centre, Newgrange & Knowth* €10.30; €4.50 children. *Centre & Knowth* €4.50; €1.60-€2.90 reductions. **Credit** MC, V.

Slane Castle

Slane (041 988 4400/www.slanecastle.ie).
Open *May-Aug* noon-5pm Mon-Thur, Sun. **Admission** €7. **Credit** MC, V.

Trim Castle

Trim (046 943 8619). **Open** *Easter-Oct* 10am-6pm daily. *Nov-Easter* 10am-5pm Sat, Sun. **Admission** *Keep (with guided tour)* €3.70; €1.30 children; €8.70 family. *Grounds only* €1.60; €1.10 children; €4.50 family. **No credit cards**.

Where to eat & drink

County Meath is not famed for its cuisine. You can pick up makings of a picnic in Kells at the Tesco on the High Street. If you prefer somebody else to cook for you, **Pebbles** (Newmarket Street, Kells; closed Sun, no phone) is a decent greasy-spoon diner popular with the locals.

For more stylish fare, try the **Vanilla Pod**, which uses fresh, local ingredients in its modern Irish cuisine (Headfort Arms Hotel, Kells, www.headfortarms.ie, 046 924 0084, €14.95-€23.95). Lots of pubs have adequate food, particularly in Trim, Slane and Kells. In Kells, the **Ground Floor Restaurant** (Bective Square, 046 924 9688, main courses €9.95-€25.50) is an excellent bistro with good food and a great atmosphere.

Where to stay

Near Newgrange try the **Bondique House** in Cullen (Beauparc, 041 982 4823, rates €80-€100), which has affordable rooms, some with en suite. Alternatively, in Trim, the **Castle Arch Hotel** (Summhill Road, 046 943 1108, www.castlearchhotel.com, rates €140) has a grand entrance, 24 recently refurbished rooms and a popular restaurant.

Tourist information

Kells Heritage Centre & Tourist Office

The Courthouse, Headfoot Place, Kells (046 924 7840/www.meathtourism.ie).
Open *May-Sept* 10am-5.30pm Mon-Sat; 2-6pm Sun. *Oct-Apr* 10am-5pm Mon-Sat.

Trips Out of Town

Navan Tourist Office

*Solstice Arts Centre, Railway Street, Navan,
(046 907 3426/www.meathtourism.ie).* **Open**
Mar-Dec 10am-5pm Mon-Sat.

Trim Visitor Centre

*Castle Street, Trim (046 943 7227/www.meath
tourism.ie).* **Open** 9.30am-5.30pm Mon-sat;
noon-5.30pm Sun.

Getting there

By bus

There are buses to Navan and Slane several
times a day from Busáras (€10.80 return; 45mins). A
number of tour buses run from Navan to Newgrange
and Knowth. There are also bus tours from Dublin;
check at the tourism centre, located on Suffolk Street.

By car

For Bru na Boinne, Newgrange and Knowth, take
the N2 out of Dublin to Slane. The N3 leads from
Dublin to Navan and the Hill of Tara. For Four
Knocks, take the M1 towards Belfast, then turn on
the R122 towards Naul. Four Knocks is well
signposted from Naul.

Drogheda & Carlingford

Driving due east from Newgrange, you'll get
to the town of Drogheda in about 15 minutes.
Increasingly vibrant since the onset of Ireland's
EU-financed heyday, Drogheda is still a bit
tattered around the edges. But then it deserves
to be, since it's had the daylights kicked out of
it for the last 1,000 years.

The town was founded by the Normans, and
was the country's political and ecclesiastical
capital in the 14th and 15th centuries, but the
Black Death swung its scythe here in 1348,
killing hundreds, and the plague arrived again
in 1479. Then, most infamously of all, Oliver
Cromwell's New Model Army came for a visit
in 1649, and became the first ever to
successfully penetrate the town's encompassing
walls. Once they got in, Cromwell's men busily
set about butchering thousands of Drogheda's
Catholic inhabitants in many creative ways.

Start any tour of the town by picking up
information at the tourist office on Mayoralty
Street (*see p206*). From there, head to the
Drogheda Heritage Centre, on Mary Street.
As well as information on the town's long, dark
history, it also has a piece of the old city walls
on its grounds, and local lore holds that the
centre stands on the site where Cromwell's
hordes finally broke through the wall.

Heading up West Street in the city centre,
you really can't miss the Gothic **St Peter's
Catholic Church**, the permanent home to the
head of the Catholic martyr St Oliver Plunkett,
rather gruesomely preserved in a glass altar
and holding up surprisingly well, given that it's
more than 300 years old. The door to the cell
where he was imprisoned before being hanged,

Hill of Tara. See p202.

drawn and quartered – and, just to make sure, beheaded – in 1681 is neatly mounted nearby. Why did he meet such a grim fate, you ask? Plunkett was a Catholic archbishop believed to have conspired with the French. Something of a fatal combination in those days.

Around the corner and up the hill a bit, on William Street, is another, smaller St Peter's – this one a Church of Ireland version. This is where Catholic residents of Drogheda fled when Cromwell rampaged through the town. Many hid in here, but to no avail: his troops locked the doors and set the church alight. The church is not always open, but the graveyard is quite interesting and, so we are reliably informed, the vicar knows reams about Cromwell, if you happen to catch him in situ.

Not far from here, traffic flows through the **St Largeness Gate** at the top of Laurence Street – a remnant of the town's old walls, and the finest example of a 13th-century barbican you're likely to come across around here.

Heading north from Drogheda on the N1, signs will direct you to **Monasterboice**, a sixth-century monastery of which little is left except a round tower 27 metres (90 feet) high, and two of the most impressive Celtic crosses in existence. The better preserved of the two is **Muiredach's Cross**, the first one you encounter when you enter the churchyard. Its elegant tenth-century biblical carvings remain quite clear: on the western face are,

from the top down: Moses with Hur and Aaron, the Crucifixion, St Peter receiving keys from Christ, doubting Thomas, and finally the arrest of Christ. On the eastern side are, from the top: the wise men, Moses fetching water from the stone, David and Goliath, Cain killing Abel, and the fall of Adam and Eve.

The ruin adjoining Monasterboice is **Mellifont Abbey**, founded by Cistercian monk St Malachy in 1142, and closed by Henry VIII in 1539. There's not much left of the building now, but the ruins are evocative, and you can make out what was there once upon a time.

Back on the M1, take the exit for the Dundalk bypass and go to the Ballymascanlon Roundabout, where you can take the last exit for Carlingford. About half a mile from here, you'll see the **Ballymascanlon House Hotel** on your left. This hotel is worth visiting, not just because it's pleasant, but also because it has the 5,000-year-old proleek dolmen on its grounds. Dolmens are stone tables unique to Celtic countries, with three portal stones supporting a horizontal roof. In the past, visiting this one involved much clambering over fences and crawling through undergrowth, but the route is now well tended (though there's a mild hazard in the form of flying golf balls from the hotel's course). There's nothing there but the rocks, so this is one for those who care about such things. If you want to know your future, lob a stone (gently) towards the top;

St Patrick at Hill of Tara. *See p202.*

St Patrick's Church. *See p203.*

Trips Out of Town

local lore has it that if you throw a stone on the roof of the dolmen and it stays there, you'll be married within a year.

From here, it's only a short distance to the charming seaside town of **Carlingford**. Well, a short distance by car, anyway; dedicated hill walkers might want to look for signs for the **Táin Trail**, a scenic 17-kilometre (10.5-mile) walk from Ravensdale to Carlingford (or vice versa). If you choose to do the whole thing, it usually takes two days; on the other hand, if you drive, you can be there in a few minutes.

The name Carlingford derives from the Norse *Carlinn Fjord*, and, sitting as it does between the bay and a lough, this is indeed a fjord town. Its pretty boats, magnificent panoramic views, narrow winding streets, ancient buildings and cosy olde-worlde pubs make it an extremely pleasant place in which to while away a day or two, far from Dublin's bustle. There are a few sights to take in, although just soaking up the atmosphere is what you really come here for. Near the town centre, the **Mint** (on Tholsel Street) is a 15th-century tower house with mullioned windows decorated with pre-Norman Celtic motifs. Also of note is **King John's Castle**, by the lough; the eponymous king stayed here soon after it was built in 1210.

Mellifont Abbey & Monasterboice

Tullyallen (041 982 6459). **Open** *May-Oct* 10am-4.45pm daily. *Nov-Apr* visitors' centre closed. **Admission** €2.10; €1.10 children; €5.80 family. **No credit cards**.

Where to eat & drink

In Drogheda, try the **Westcourt Hotel**, on West Street. You'll find the backpackers hanging out at the **Salt House** restaurant at the Green Door Hostel (*see below*). If you fancy a drink, **Peter Matthews** pub (universally known as McPhails) is the liveliest place in town, while **Carbery's**, on North Strand, is good for trad music, especially on Sunday afternoons.

Along with some fabulous pubs, Carlingford also has a couple of excellent restaurants including the superb **Ghan House** (042 937 3682, www.ghanhouse.com, main courses €29.50), and the **Oystercatcher Bistro** (Market Square, 042 937 3989, main courses €18-€25, closed Mon-Wed Oct-May), where the fresh brown bread and oysters are a local speciality, and the magic ingredient in the Oystercatcher Porridge is a shot of whiskey.

Where to stay

The cheapest rooms are to be found in Drogheda, which has a number of hostels, including the endlessly popular **Green Door**

Hostel (13 Dublin Road, 041 983 4422, www.greendoorireland.com, rates dorm €18, €32). It's the backpackers' favourite, with all the hostel extras (lockers, linens, TV lounge) and the laid-back Salt House restaurant for cheap, hot meals. If you want to spend a bit more, try the **Westcourt Hotel** in the centre (West Street, 041 983 0965, www.westcourt.ie, rates €65-€135).

You can stay out in the countryside at the **Ballymascanlon House Hotel** (Dundalk, 042 935 8200, www.ballymascanlon.com, rates €185). The hotel is excellent, and the restaurant does good traditional Irish food. There is also an 18-hole golf course and a leisure centre. If you prefer your rural life quieter, try **Glebe House** (Dowth, 041 983 6101, rates €95), an ivy-covered country house about 15 minutes' drive from Drogheda, with big, beautiful rooms and fireplaces.

In Carlingford, the **Oystercatcher** not only does good food (*see above*), but also has bright, wood-floored rooms (rates €90-€120). **Beaufort House** (Ghan Road, 042 937 3879, www.beauforthouse.net, rates €70-€86) is a pleasant guesthouse near the water, while the **Carlingford Adventure Centre & Holiday Hostel** (Tholsel Street, 042 937 3100, www.carlingfordadventure.com, rates €26-€36 per person) is an IHH hostel with good food, lots to do, dorm beds and a few private rooms. Finally, there are good **campsites** at Giles' Quay and Ravensdale if you fancy roughing it.

Tourist information

Cooley Peninsula Tourist Office

Carlingford (042 937 3033/www.carlingford.ie). **Open** 10am-5pm Mon-Sun.

Drogheda Tourist Office

Mayoralty Street, Drogheda (041 984 5684). **Open** 9am-5pm Mon-Fri; 9am-4.30pm Sat.

Getting there

By car

From Dublin take the M1 to Drogheda (about 45mins). For Carlingford take the M1 to Dundalk and follow signs to Carlingford on the R173 (1hr 30mins). A €1.50 toll will be charged on the M1.

By bus

Bus Éireann runs a regular service from Dublin-Drogheda (041 983 5023, in Dublin 836 6111; 1hr 15mins). For Carlingford, change at Dundalk.

By train

There is a regular daily train service to Drogheda from Dublin on the Dublin-to-Belfast line. The train station is located just to the east of the town centre (041 983 8749).

The Wicklow Mountains

Moors, mountains and stately piles.

The green and hilly countryside of Wicklow starts just a dozen or so miles south of central Dublin, making it one of the easiest and quickest day trips from the city. There's plenty to do there, whether you prefer to picnic by the river in the **Vale of Avoca** (*see p211*) or hike through the isolation around **Glendalough** (*see p209*): this is country living. Take some good walking shoes (and some waterproofs).

A raised granite ridge runs through the county, peaking at two of the highest mountain passes in Ireland – the **Sally Gap** and the **Wicklow Gap** – and the scenery is dramatic. Ramblers, hikers and rock climbers will be in their element here, as you can strike out on foot on the well-marked **Wicklow Way** (*see p209*), which wanders past mountain tarns and secluded glens. (Pick up a map at any tourism office, and then choose a stretch of the path to explore). If you've got a car, head down to the picturesque villages of **Roundwood**, **Laragh**, and **Aughrim**, or splash about on the **Blessington Lakes** (*see below*).

Blessington & around

The roads south of Dublin rapidly leave the dreary south-western suburbs behind; and a green, mountainous landscape opens up swiftly. Between the road and the hills lie the lovely **Blessington Lakes**. These deep expanses of water cover thousands of acres and have attracted Dubliners for generations. Well, a few generations, anyway: they're not natural lakes, but man-made reservoirs created when the Poulaphouca Dam was built in the 1940s to supply Dublin's water. Several deep valleys were drowned in the process; the smooth lake waters hide whole villages long-since covered over in the name of progress. If you want to hit the water, the **Blessington Adventure Centre** (04 590 0670) provides equipment and instruction for canoeing, kayaking, windsurfing and sailing, as well as archery and abseiling. The village of **Blessington** is a pleasant spot, loved for its wide main street, quaint market square and grand Georgian buildings.

Russborough House and its demesne lie just a few miles south of Blessington on the N81. This vast Palladian mansion, built in 1741, its lush grounds still intact, commands a wide sweep of the countryside. Inside the building,

designed by Richard Castle, who also created nearby Powerscourt (*see p210*), is a fine, diverse, vast art collection including works by Vernet, Vermeer, Guardi, Goya, Gainsborough and Rubens. Amassing artworks was the hobby of mining magnate Sir Alfred Beit, a member of the de Beers diamond family, who bought the house in 1952 almost exlusively because he thought the paintings would like nice there.

Of course, planting hundreds of priceless paintings in a country that has long been torn by sectarian violence might look like a bad idea in hindsight… and so it was. Over the last few decades, Russborough has been the victim of several brazen and highly successful robberies. In 1974 the IRA made off with 16 of the paintings, and more were stolen in 1986. Then, astonishingly, there was a third robbery in 2001, carried out in broad daylight. The 16 paintings originally stolen were all subsequently retrieved, but after the third-time unlucky heist, the authorities at Russborough decided to call time before the house was stripped bare, and the more precious parts of the collection are now safely (we hope) on display at the National Gallery in Dublin (*see p76*). Still, much gorgeous art remains at Russborough, but you get the distinct impression that staff who lead the guided tours do not welcome jokes about burglaries. Something in their thin, tense smiles tends to give it away.

Once you've soaked up the art, a wander in the demesne is recommended: walks across the grounds offer any number of views down into the valley and across to the mountains.

South of Blessington and the lakes, the road continues towards Baltinglass, a pretty town on the banks of the River Slaney. There are a number of fine detours at this point, and the best of the bunch is the much-signposted **O'Dwyer Cottage**. Michael O'Dwyer (1771-1826) was a leader of the 1798 Rising (*see p15*) and took refuge in the Wicklow uplands after the rebellion failed. He was hunted by the British for years, finally run to ground in 1803 and transported to Australia. The cottage is the scene of one of O'Dwyer's most daring escapes: in 1799 he was hiding here when British troops got word of his location; as they approached, he fled, leaving his companions to defend the house to their death.

The main reason for taking this brief detour, though, is not the cottage itself, but the gorgeous landscape surrounding it: this is the **Glen of Imaal**, a narrow and atmospheric space that winds into the hills and offers splendid views across the fields to Lugnaquilla.

O'Dwyer Cottage
Derrymuck, Knockancarrigan, Co Wicklow (045 404 781/www.wicklow.ie). **Open** *Late June-late Sept* 2-6pm daily. **Admission** free.

Russborough House
Blessington, Co Wicklow (045 865 239/www.russborough.ie). **Open** Guided tours *May-Sept* 10am-5pm daily. *Apr, Oct* 10am-5pm Sun. **Admission** €10; €5-€8 reductions. **Credit** MC, V.

Where to eat & drink

Grangecon Café, on Blessington's main street (045 857 892, closed Sun, main courses €7-€14) is worth seeking out for its delicious and sophisticated cuisine at café prices. Otherwise, there are pubs in and around Blessington that have good food, including **O'Connor's**, on the main street. If you really want to splash out on a dinner, though, head to **Rathsallagh House** in Dulavin (*see below*) for traditional Irish fare.

Where to stay

If you fancy a treat, **Rathsallagh House** is a grand country hotel and golf club at Donard, just off the main road midway between Baltinglass and Blessington (045 403 112,

www.rathsallagh.com, rates €135-€160). If you're staying for a week, you can rent one of the rustic, self-catering stone cottages from the good people at **Fortgranite** (on the R747 near Baltinglass, 059 648 1396, rates €350-€650 per week), a working farm in the Wicklow foothills near Baltinglass.

Tourist information

Blessington Tourist Office
The Square, Blessington (045 865 850). **Open** *Sept-Apr* 9.30am-5pm Mon-Fri. *May-Aug* 9.30am-5pm Mon-Fri; 11am-3pm Sat.

Getting there

By bus
Dublin Bus (872 0000) runs from Eden Quay in Dublin to Blessington on its suburban 65 route. Bus Éireann (836 6111) offers service to Blessington on the routes to Waterford and Rosslare Harbour.

By car
The N81 from Dublin runs through west Wicklow, between the western edge of the mountains and the horse-racing flatlands of Kildare. The drive to Blessington takes about 45mins.

Glendalough & around

The lovely area known as Glendalough (which translates from the Irish as 'the valley of two lakes') was the refuge of the sixth-century saint

and hermit Kevin, who founded a monastery in the valley. By medieval times, Glendalough's fame as a seat of learning had spread across Europe, and countless monks toiled in the monastery's scriptoria, churning out precious books and works of scholarship. Unfortunately, its success, as with so many early Irish religious sites, was also its downfall, and Glendalough came to the attention of the Vikings, who pillaged it repeatedly between 775 and 1071. But it was always rebuilt, stronger than ever, until 1398, when the English finished what the Vikings could not do and virtually wiped the settlement off the map. Attempts were made to resuscitate it, and it limped on in some form until the 17th century as barely a shadow of its former greatness; then it was abandoned altogether.

Approaching Glendalough from Dublin, the road passes through the saddle known as the Sally Gap, to the high moors and into farmland and forests that give way to woodland and meadows as the land drops into the narrow glacial valley. The place is powerfully atmospheric under any sky and at any time of the year: its Round Tower rises from the trees – its door three metres (ten feet) above the ground – and the scant, evocative remains of other buildings are dotted here and there across the valley floor, encircled by hills and wreathed in isolation and silence. Late on a summer evening, or under frosty winter skies, the beauty of Glendalough is truly captivating.

Not that the valley today is truly isolated or silent: this is a very popular tourist attraction, so tour buses are legion in summer. It's worth arriving very early or rather late in order to have some quiet in which to think.

Most people come to Glendalough to walk. The Wicklow Way passes through the valley on its way south, and other trails meander through the woods around two lakes: the **Lower Lake** tends to be more crowded in high summer (most of the sights are clustered around it), so take the short walk up to the **Upper Lake** if you're looking for tranquillity. The nearest town of any size is **Laragh**.

On the Lower Lake you'll find the **Round Tower** and the **cathedral**, which date to the ninth century. There's a 12th-century **Priest's House** and the excellent **St Kevin's Church**, which dates to the sixth century. The **Visitors Centre** (*see p210*) is quite comprehensive and succeeds admirably in communicating the essence and unique history of the valley. On the other side of the centre from St Kevin's Church the lovely 12th-century **St Saviour's** is well worth a visit.

Up by the Upper Lake is the Romanesque **Reefert Church**, from which you can follow stone steps to the **Pollanass Waterfall** and a cave known as **St Kevin's Bed**. Even further along the road are a few ancient remains of **Teampull na Scellig**, 'the church of the rock', believed to be the oldest structure in the area.

Glendalough.

Trips Out of Town

The scenic roads (R755 and R760) heading back north towards Dublin from Glendalough skirt the pretty village of **Roundwood**, whose altitude of 230 metres (754 feet) lets it claim to be the highest village in Ireland. A few miles north of Roundwood, and only ten miles from Dublin itself, is **Enniskerry**, a tidy, thriving town built around a sloping market square and thronged with weekenders in the summer. Enniskerry was formerly the satellite settlement for the great estate of **Powerscourt** (*see below*), which borders the village to the south. The stately pile at Powerscourt is splendid, with beautifully managed grounds sprawling for miles of lush gardens, smooth lawns and shady woodland walks – all ideal for picnicking.

The house itself is a sad story. You can tell from looking at its exterior that it was once magnificent – it was designed in the 18th century by Richard Castle, the architect of Russborough House (*see p207*) and Dublin's Parliament building. The same family lived in the building for 350 years, until the 1950s. After they moved out, Powerscourt was finally to be opened to the public. Its renovations took more than 20 years (clearly, nobody was in a hurry). Then, in 1974, on the day before it was finally scheduled to open, it caught fire and the interior was completely destroyed. Parts of the house are now open to the public, but not much.

The café at Powerscourt is run by the brilliant Avoca chain, and serves up rich cakes, hot soups and healthy salads at reasonable prices with a breathtaking view.

Powerscourt House & Gardens

Enniskerry, Co Wicklow (01 204 6000/www.powers court.ie). **Open** *Mar-Oct* 9.30am-5.30pm daily. *Nov-Feb* 9.30am-dusk daily. **Admission** €8; €5-€7 reductions. **Credit** MC, V.

Where to eat & drink

Both **Lynham's** (main courses €8-€15) and the **Glendalough Hotel** (main courses €8 lunch, €25 set dinner; for details for both, *see below*) have good restaurants and bars, and both offer reasonable food that stretches beyond hamburgers; the former has a fire crackling on chilly days.

If you pop into the charming village of Roundwood, the **Roundwood Inn** (on the R755, 01 281 8107) is a well-restored 18th-century coaching inn, with good pub food.

Where to stay

Around Glendalough, you can try **Lynham's of Laragh** (040 445 345, www.lynhamsof laragh.ie, rates €130-€190), which has 18

pleasant bedrooms at relatively reasonable prices. Nearer to Glendalough itself is the lovely **Glendalough Hotel** (040 445 135, www.glendaloughhotel.ie, rates €150-€210).

There are no hotels at Powerscourt, but there are plenty in Enniskerry. Try the small, pretty **Powerscourt Arms Hotel** in the centre of the village (01 282 8903, rates €90-€110).

Near the tiny town of Dunlavin, the **Tynte House** is a well-preserved 19th-century family farm with a variety of rooms, apartments and self-catering cottages to rent at good prices (045 401 561, rates €70, €435-€520 per week self-catering high season, €260-€330 low season).

Tourist information

Glendalough Visitors Centre

Glendalough, Co Wicklow (040 445 325/ www.heritageireland.ie). **Open** *Mid Mar-mid Oct* 9.30am-5.15pm daily. *Mid Oct-mid Mar* 9.30am-4.15pm daily. **Admission** €2.90, €1.30-€2.10 reductions; €7.40 family. **No credit cards.** There is a tourism office inside this centre, but access to Glendalough itself is free, so you need not visit the centre (which is not free) if you don't want to. There is another visitors' centre at the Upper Lake (040 445 425) in the high season.

Getting there

By bus

St Kevin's Bus Service (281 8119) runs from Dublin's Royal College of Surgeons on St Stephen's Green to Glendalough, departing 11.30am and 6pm daily (€12.65 return). Dublin Bus 44 (872 0000) makes the hop from Hawkins Street to Enniskerry. Bus Éireann (836 1111) offers tours of Glendalough and Wicklow (Apr-Oct, €22.86); buses leave from Busáras. Alpine Coaches (286 2547) runs a summer service from Bray DART station to Powerscourt and Glencree.

By car

The Military Road (R115) – so called because it was built with the intention of hunting down the rebels who sought refuge in the mountains after the 1798 Rebellion – leaves the southern suburbs of Dublin at Rathfarnham and passes over the high moors before descending into the valley of Glendalough. The drive takes about an hour. This is wild country indeed: in winter, the Sally Gap is always the first in the region to be closed by snow. Returning by R755 or R760 will take you through Enniskerry.

Avoca & Wicklow Town

Eastern Wicklow is, for the most part, mild pastoral landscape, softened by the influence of the nearby sea. This is where you'll find **Avondale House & Forest Park**, the country seat of Charles Stewart Parnell, a 19th-century leader of the nationalist movement, near the small town of **Rathdrum**. The house was built in 1777 and decorated in a plain but elegant Georgian style, although the Wedgwood Room and rich plasterwork are startling exceptions to its understated rule. For many people, though, the beautifully landscaped country park surrounding the house is the highlight. It stretches for miles and is an ideal spot for a walk; several routes are laid out on nature trails in the forest park. As the place is relatively far from Dublin, its footpaths and trails are never crowded. Facilities include a restaurant, gift shop, children's play area and deer pen.

From here it's just a short drive to the small village of **Avoca**, which has managed to capitalise amazingly well on its limited charms to become a major tourist attraction in this part of Ireland. The village was the location of the BBC soap opera *Ballykissangel*, and always pulled in hordes of tourists at the height of the programme's success. The main draw for most visitors are the **Avoca Handweavers Woollen Mills**. These are, of course, tourist-oriented but still worth a visit for the excellent crafts, the colourful clothes and for the ubiquitous, but good, Avoca Café food, if nothing else.

From here, the coastal road back towards Dublin makes for a lovely drive. There's nothing especially rugged or spectacular on this stretch of the Irish coast; what you get instead are beautiful beaches and small coves that attract Dubliners through the summer – the glorious three-kilometre (two-mile) stretch of **Brittas Bay** is probably the best example. Heading on, **Wicklow Town** is agreeably bustling, with narrow, steep streets climbing up from a pebble beach and fine harbour. The district is home to interesting sights, including the **Wicklow Gaol** and the lovely **Mount Usher Gardens**.

The gaol was built in 1702 and all manner of inmates passed through its portals. As you would expect, it hosted many participants in the 1798 Rising; later, prisoners were held here before being transported to Australia. The gaol is an impressive and literate attraction, so you'll emerge knowing more than you would probably care to about the gruesome conditions of prison life in the 18th and 19th centuries; it also draws in the background of the 1798 Rising and the famine admirably.

Mount Usher comes as something of a relief after all that grimness: it's another world entirely. The gardens were laid out in 1860 in a lovely informal style, and now unroll over a large area along the banks of the River Vartry. Happily, there's the usual clutter of craft shops and tearooms.

Fame and fabrics at **Avoca**.

If you want to get in some exercise, take a walk up the splendid three-kilometre (two-mile) coastal trail that runs from Wicklow Town's seafront and beach past the gaol to Wicklow Head, where it takes in the granite lighthouse at the end. And, incidentally, you can also spend the night at the solid old lighthouse, which is one of the properties in the Irish Landmark Trust portfolio.

To continue further from here, turn towards **Aughrim** and follow the narrow roads north through the beautiful and isolated Glen of Imaal, before rejoining the main N81 road to Dublin. If you're looking for yet more spectacular scenery, this is the way to go, and Aughrim has hotels, food and drink.

Possible detours include the seaside town of **Greystones** (also on the DART line from Dublin) and the less attractive but more trendy seaside town of **Bray**; the two towns are linked by a six-kilometre (3.7-mile) cliff walk.

Avoca Handweavers
Avoca, Co Wicklow (040 235 105/www.avoca.ie). **Open** 9am-6pm daily. **Credit** AmEx, MC, V.

Avondale House & Forest Park
Rathdrum, Co Wicklow (040 446 111/www.coillte.ie). **Open** *May-Aug* 11am-5pm daily. *Mar, Apr, Sept, Oct* 11am-4pm Tue-Sun. **Admission** *Grounds* €5 per car. *House* €6; €4-€5.50 reductions; €17.50 family. **Credit** MC, V.

Mount Usher Gardens
Ashford, Co Wicklow (040 440 116). **Open** *Mar-Oct* 10.30am-6pm daily. **Admission** €7; €3-€6 concessions; free under-5s. **Credit** MC, Laser, V.

Wicklow Gaol
Wicklow Town, Co Wicklow (040 461 599/www.wicklowshistoricgaol.com). **Open** *Mar-Oct* 10am-6pm daily. **Admission** €7.30; €4.50-€6 reductions; €19 families. **Credit** MC, V.

Where to eat & drink

Yes, we keep banging on about it, but the **Avoca Café** is pretty darn good, and therefore worth visiting for lunch if you're sick of fish and chips (040 235 105, main courses €6-€13). In nearby Arklow, the bar in the **Woodenbridge Hotel** (040 235 146, main courses €13-€25) is an excellent option for traditional pub food in wonderfully historic surroundings and you can pull out the stops and try its highly regarded restaurant (set menu €39). Both Michael Collins and Eamon de Valera dined here in their day.

In Wicklow Town it's a short walk from the tourist office (*see right*) to the **Bakery Café & Restaurant** on Church Street (040 466 770, main courses €12-€28), which does very good bistro food. The **Old Court Inn** (040 467 680, mains €11-€19, closed Mon) in the Market Square is known for its superb seafood. Or you could try **Tinakilly House** (Rathnew, 040 469 274, main courses €30-€35), which specialises in truly fine, country-house cooking. **Philip Healy's** is the liveliest pub in Wicklow Town (Fitzwilliam Square, 040 467 380).

In Aughrim, the Brooklodge Hotel (*see below*) and its **Strawberry Tree** restaurant are the best, and most expensive, game in town (main courses €36-€40), but undoubtedly worth it.

Closer to Dublin, if you stop off in Greystones you'll want to eat at the **Hungry Monk** (Church Road, 01 287 5759), known for its outstanding seafood (main courses €20-€38).

Where to stay

In Aughrim, you can stay at the **Brooklodge Hotel** (040 236 444, www.brooklodge.com, rates €210-€240). It isn't cheap, but the food and standards are very high if you can afford it.

Near Wicklow Town, the **Woodenbridge Hotel** (040 235 146, www.woodenbridge hotel.com, rates €45-€75) has pleasant rooms with questionable decoration schemes in historic environs. In Rathnew there's the **Tinakilly House**, which is posh but lovely, with a fine foodie reputation (040 469 274, www.tinakilly.ie, rates €250).

The **Wicklow Head Lighthouse** is a fabulous place to stay: it offers comfortable self-catering accommodation for up to six people, and amazing views across the Irish Sea, though you should book ahead (Irish Landmark Trust, 25 Eustace Street, Temple Bar, Dublin, 01 670 4733, www.irishlandmark.com, rates €440 per week low season, €1,175 per week high season).

Tourist information

Wicklow Town Tourist Office
Rialto House, Fitzwilliam Square, Wicklow Town (040 469 117). **Open** *June-Sept* 9am-6pm Mon-Sat. *Oct-May* 9.30am-1pm, 2-5.15pm Mon-Fri.

Getting there

By bus
Bus Éireann's 133 service (836 6111) travels between Dublin and Avoca, including Wicklow Town and the Meetings. Buses are rarest on Sundays.

By car
Take the N11 south in the direction of Wexford and Rosslare, and then follow the signs.

By train
Trains from Dublin to Rosslare Harbour stop at Wicklow Town (040 467 329). Call for information.

Kilkenny & Around

Find art in the countryside.

Just beyond the Wicklow Mountains, a couple of hours' drive from Dublin, you're in the real Irish countryside. Roads ascend dark green foothills and tumble down into lush valleys where rushing rivers are bothered by nothing more troublesome than thirsty horses and old fishermen. This is a peaceful region, but not immune from tourists, all drawn to Kilkenny Town's many art and pottery stores, and Wexford's small villages and adorable shops.

Here you can relax in the rural tranquility and take your time exploring the grandeur of **Kilkenny Castle** and **Rothe House**, and the lost wonder of **Jerpoint Abbey** (*see p216-217*).

County Wexford

Enniscorthy

There's little to make you linger in the small stone-built river town of Enniscorthy at the northern edge of County Wexford, save for the **National 1798 Visitor Centre**. This interesting, interactive museum explains the events that took place in the spring of 1798, when a group of republican rebels seized the town and declared their independence. What

followed was a phenomenon in which 20,000 men and women flocked to the village from throughout the country and joined the group's unsuccessful raids on the nearby towns of New Ross and Arklow. With the British sending in thousands of well-armed reinforcements to put down the revolt, the poorly armed rebels took positions on Vinegar Hill, where they made an ill-fated last stand on 21 July. Five hundred rebels were killed or injured that morning; the rest fled into the countryside. Thousands of men and women were slaughtered by the English troops in the subsequent days. Within days it was all over, and the British had reassumed control. With interactive exhibits – some more impressive than others – the centre does a good job of explaining what led to the rebellion (in one section you can listen to a debate between Edmund Burke and Thomas Paine). But it's all generally targeted at school groups. If you wish to explore it all further, you can reach **Vinegar Hill** itself by crossing the bridge in town and taking the first right after Treacy's Hotel, then following the signs. Or you could join a guided walking tour from the Castle Hill Crafts Shop (053 913 6800) on Castle Hill. Tours, which are thorough and interesting, last an hour (€5; €3 reductions).

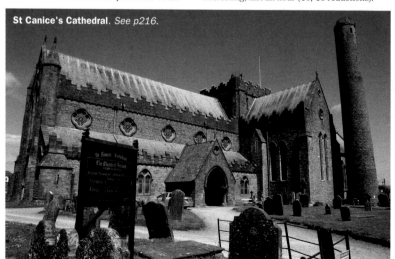

St Canice's Cathedral. *See p216.*

The noble, granite **Kilkenny Castle** and its manicured gardens. *See p216.*

Wexford Town

County Wexford is loved by sun worshippers and boaters for its stretches of often empty beach, while charming **Wexford Town** makes an excellent base for exploring the countryside. The town's array of statues are your first indication that this place has a heroic reputation for resisting authority; in the mid 17th century the locals stood up to Oliver Cromwell's soldiers when the English troops arrived to occupy the town. They lost, of course, and Cromwell handled the victory with his usual flair: he gathered 1,500 of the town's 2,000 residents and slaughtered them. This massacre – which took the lives of every one of the county's Franciscan friars – made Wexford a beacon of Irish resistance for centuries. It was here that the 1798 Uprising took hold, before spreading out into the countryside.

Start your exploration by getting maps at the **tourist office** (*see p216*) on Crescent Quay, where you can also enquire about free guided walks organised by the Wexford Historical Society. The statue near the office is the likeness of Admiral John Barry, who at 14 emigrated from Wexford to the US, where he is credited with founding the US Navy and firing the last shot in the American War of Independence.

In the centre of the town (at the intersection of Common and Main streets) the square known as the **Bull Ring** has a memorial stone that commemorates the rebels of the 1798 Uprising. Not far from the square, on North Main Street, the impressive Venetian Gothic building is the grand **St Iberius Church**.

A few parts of the medieval town walls remain intact, and you can visit the **West Gate** (on Westgate Street), one of the six original tollhouses. Not far from there, on Slaney Street, are the ruins of **Selskar Abbey**. Henry II is believed to have spent Lent 1172 at the abbey doing penance for the murder of Thomas à Becket, but its historical significance did not interest Cromwell, who had it destroyed in 1649.

Outside Wexford Town

Eight kilometres (five miles) north of Wexford Town at Ferrycarrig, the **Irish National Heritage Park** is a pseudo-historical theme park whose tours take you from Neolithic to Norman times in 90 minutes or fewer; there's even a replica Viking longboat at anchor on the River Slaney just outside. Grown-ups might prefer to head north to the more rustic pleasures of **Curracloe Beach**, a long, beautiful stretch of sand and dunes just made for lounging with a good book on a sunny day.

On the road to Rosslare, the 19th-century **Johnstown Castle** combines a research centre and the Irish Agricultural Museum with some delightfully lush, Italianate gardens. Deep in the woods around it is a ruined medieval tower house that makes for spectacular photographs.

If you continue south towards the Hook peninsula, the next points of interest are the evocative ruins of **Dunbrody Abbey**, a 12th-century Cistercian monastery founded, it is said, by the uncle of the Norman conquerer Strongbow. Its excellent visitors' centre connects with more ruins – those of the once-lovely **Dunbrody Castle** with its full-size hedge maze.

It's not far from here to the 15th-century **Ballyhack Castle**, less castle than tower house with a hazy history that may or may not have something to do with the Knights Templar, depending on who's talking. Just to the east of Ballyhack, the well-preserved ruins of the 12th-century **Tintern Abbey** (named after the bigger and more famous abbey in Wales) stand mournfully; it's often overlooked but well worth a vist.

Ballyhack Castle

Ballyhack (051 389 468). **Open** *5 June-17 Sept* 10am-6pm daily. **Admission** free.

Dunbrody Abbey, Castle & Visitors' Centre

Dunbrody Abbey, Horse Wood, Campile (051 388 603/www.dunbrodyabbey.com). **Open** *May-mid Sept* 10am-6pm daily. **Admission** *Abbey* €2; €1 reductions; €5 family. *Visitors' centre* €4; €2 reductions; €10 family. **No credit cards**.

Irish National Heritage Park

Ferrycarrig (053 912 0733/www.inhp.com). **Open** *Apr-Sept* 9.30am-6.30pm daily. *Oct-Mar* 9.30am-5.30pm daily (last admission 4.30pm). **Admission** €8; €6.50 reductions; €20 family. **Credit** AmEx, DC, MC, V.

Johnstown Castle & Gardens

4 miles (6.5km) south-west of Wexford Town (053 914 2888). **Open** *Garden* 9am-5pm daily. *Museum Apr-Nov* 9am-5pm Mon-Fri; 11-5pm Sat, Sun. *Dec-Mar* 9am-12.30pm, 1.30-5pm Mon-Fri. **Admission** *Garden* €5 per car; pedestrians €2. *Museum* €6; €4 reductions; €20 family. **No credit cards**.

National 1798 Visitor Centre

Mill Park Road, Enniscorthy (053 923 7596/ www.iol.ie~98com). **Open** *Mar-Sept* 9.30am-5pm Mon-Fri; 1-5pm Sat, Sun. *Oct-Feb* 9.30am-4pm Mon-Fri. **Admission** €6; €3.50 reductions; €16 family. **Credit** MC, V.

Tintern Abbey

Near the village of Saltmills, off the R734 road (051 562 650). **Open** *Mid May-late Oct* 9.30am-6pm daily. **Admission** €2.10; €1.10-€1.30 reductions; €5.80 family. **No credit cards**.

Where to stay

In Wexford Town, pick between **St George Guesthouse** (George Street, 053 914 3474, www.stgeorgeguesthouse.com, closed 23 Dec-Jan, rates €70-€90) or the 200-year-old surroundings of **Westgate House** (Westgate, 053 912 2167, rates €70), where you can sleep in a four-poster bed. A good budget option is **Kirwan House Hostel** (3 Mary Street, 053 912 1208, www.wexfordhostel.com, closed Dec-Feb, rates per person €21 dorm, €30). Elsewhere, you can try **Ballinkeele House** (off the N11 north of Wexford at Oylgate, 053 913 8105, www.ballinkeele.com, €150-€170, closed Dec-Jan), a grand, 19th-century manor converted into a luxurious guesthouse and surrounded by sprawling gardens.

Where to eat

Forde's Bistro (The Crescent, Wexford Town, 053 912 3832, main courses €19.95-€38) is arguably the town's most popular restaurant, with an emphasis on French cooking techniques and seafood. Try some of the finest food in the county in the town of Rosslare at **La Marine Bistro** in Kelly's Resort Hotel (053 913 2114, www.kellys.ie, closed Dec-Feb, main courses €25-€45), where Eugene Callaghan turns out brilliant dishes at decent prices. Kelly's Hotel is a four-star establishment with extensive leisure facilities, and yet its prices are not particularly high (rates €160-€210).

Tourist information

Tourist Office
Crescent Quay, Wexford Town (053 912 3111/ www.wexfordtourism.com). **Open** *July, Aug* 9am-7pm Mon-Fri; 10am-6pm Sat; 11am-5pm Sun. *May, June, Sept* 9am-6pm Mon-Sat. *Oct-Apr* 9.15am-5pm Mon-Sat. There are also offices in New Ross (051 421 857) and Enniscorthy (053 923 4699).

Getting there

By bus
There are up to 11 Bus Éireann trips daily between Dublin and Wexford Town (3hrs), and 12 between Wexford and Rosslare Harbour (30mins). Ardcavan Coach (053 912 4900) also runs a daily Dublin-Wexford Town service (2hrs 30mins). Wexford bus station (053 912 3939) is next to the railway station.

By train
The Dublin-Rosslare Harbour service stops at Wexford Town's O'Hanrahan Station (053 912 2522, 3hrs). A regular local train service connects Rosslare Harbour and Wexford Town. All trains for Rosslare Harbour depart from Dublin's Connolly Station.

By boat
Irish Ferries (0870 517 1717 from the UK) runs a ferry service from Pembroke in Wales to Rosslare; Stena Sealink (0870 570 7070 from the UK) handles the Fishguard-Rosslare route. There are also ferries to Le Havre and Cherbourg in France; contact Transport et Voyages (042 669 090).

Kilkenny & around

Compact and picturesque, with cobbled streets and a singular medieval atmosphere, Kilkenny is a busy, pleasant town, filled with good pubs and restaurants. It's also a major crafts centre and the locus for summer festivals, most notably the Kilkenny Country Roots festival in May, and the Arts Festival in August.

The main reason the town packs 'em in year after year is obvious as soon as you arrive, as the imposing granite edifice of **Kilkenny Castle** overlooks the River Nore with a kind of determined nobility. Historians believe a castle or fort stood on the site long before Strongbow's son-in-law built a castle here in 1192, but one has certainly been around ever since. The existing outer walls date from Strongbow's time, but the rest of the building has been rebuilt, restored and renovated often since then. The most recent work was completed in 2001 and made the building more impressive than ever. The castle grounds are a pretty, well-manicured park leading to a castle yard filled with artists', potters' and jewellers' studios. None of this has escaped the notice of the operators of tour buses, but don't be scared away by the crowds: it's worth a visit and, if you stay long enough to get hungry, the restaurant is excellent.

Like the castle, the large, medieval **St Canice's Cathedral** has also undergone many changes over the centuries, but the chancel, transept and nave date from the 13th century. Enough has been retained for it to rate as a fine example of early Gothic architecture. For those ambitious enough to climb it, the adjoining tower offers tremendous views.

Elsewhere in Kilkenny, the charming **Tholsel** ('toll stall') on Main Street is an 18th-century council chamber still used as an office. On Parliament Street, the sturdy Elizabethan **Rothe House** has been tastefully restored and is now a museum displaying period costumes and a few assorted artefacts; it's not terribly interesting, but the old building is gorgeous and merits a visit on its own: it has unusual octagonal chimneys and plenty of original detail. The restored mediaeval garden opened in April 2008.

So much of Kilkenny is as it has always been that parts of the town seem lifted from history books. Even the **tourist office** building on Rose Inn Street is of note: it's one of the few Tudor almshouses in Ireland.

Attractive though Kilkenny Town is, tear yourself away – the rest of the county is all pretty villages and meandering rivers and should not be missed. With an old watermill and stone bridge, the riverside town of **Kells** (not to be confused with its more famous namesake north of Dublin) is a lovely place. It's near the ruins of **Kells Priory**, a remarkably complete monastic settlement where most of the ruins date from the 14th and 15th centuries, and only a few minutes' drive from the extraordinary **Jerpoint Abbey** (follow the signs from the town centre). This Cistercian complex was founded in 1160 and thrived until it was suppressed by Henry VIII. It may be in ruins, but the carvings on the walls and tombs are exquisite: as you walk around its ancient columns, you can make out long-faced saints, sombre bishops, playful kittens and doe-eyed ladies. In some places the early pigment remains, giving a glimpse of how colourful and lavish the place must have been in its day. Staff in the small museum are friendly and well informed about the history of the abbey and the surrounding area, so it's a good place at which to seek recommendations for other sites nearby.

If ancient abbeys are your thing, there are further Cistercian settlements at **Holy Cross Abbey** in Kilcooley and **Duiske Abbey** at Graiguenamanagh, a delightful village near the Waterford border whose name means 'the granary of the monks'. Duiske was extensively restored in the 1970s and is now used as the parish church, but its door dates from the 13th century, as does the rather striking effigy of a knight kept behind glass.

If you have time you might want to make a side trip to the small valley town of Inistioge, even though it's slightly out of the way. It's an exquisite village by the River Nore with a wonderful aura of peace, especially down by the river and on its wide and ancient ten-arch stone bridge.

North of Kilkenny is the **Castlecomer Discovery Park** in the former grounds of the 17th-century Castlecomer House estate. Amid 80 acres of woodlands and lakes, walking, trout fishing, a children's adventure playground and a history of coal exhibition can be enjoyed.

Castlecomer Discovery Park

The Estate Yard, Castlecomer, Co. Kilkenny (056 444 0707/www.discoverypark.ie). **Open** *May-Aug* 9.30am-6pm, *Sept, Oct, Mar, Apr* 10am-5pm, *Nov-Feb* 10.30am-4.30pm. **Admission** €8; €5-6 reductions; €18 family; under 4s free. **Credit** MC.

Rothe House.

Trips Out of Town

Jerpoint Abbey

Thomastown, Kilkenny (056 772 4623/www. kilkennytourism.ie). **Open** *Mar* 10am-5pm daily. *June-mid Sept* 9.30am-6.30pm daily. *Mid Sept-Oct* 10am-5pm daily. *Nov* 10am-4pm daily. *Dec-Feb* by appointment only. **Admission** €2.90; €1.30-€2.10 concessions; €7.40 family. **No credit cards.**

Kilkenny Castle

The Parade, Kilkenny (056 770 4100/www. kilkennytourism.ie). **Open** *Guided tour only* *Apr-May* 10.30am-5pm daily. *June-Aug* 9.30am-7pm daily. *Sept* 10am-6.30pm daily. *Oct-Mar* 10.30am-12.45pm, 2-5 pm daily. **Admission** €5.30; €2.10-€3.70 reductions; €11.50 family. **Credit** AmEx, MC, V.

Rothe House

Parliament Street, Kilkenny (056 772 2893/www. rothehouse.com). **Open** *(last admission 4.15pm)* *Apr-Oct* 10.30am-5pm Mon-Sat; 3-5pm Sun. *Nov-Mar* 10.30am-4.30pm Mon-Sat. *Garden* 10.30am-4.30pm Mon-Thur, 10.30am-4pm Fri; 2-5pm Sun. **Admission** *House* €5; €3-€4 reductions; €10 family. *Garden* free. **Credit** MC, V.

St Canice's Cathedral

Irishtown, Kilkenny (056 776 4971/www.kilkenny tourism.ie). **Open** *Apr, May, Sept* 10am-1pm, 2-5pm Mon-Sat; 2-5pm Sun. *June-Aug* 9am-6pm Mon-Sat; 2-6pm Sun. *Oct-Mar* 10am-1pm, 2-4pm Mon-Sat; 2-4pm Sun. **Admission** €4; €3 reductions. **Credit** MC, V

Where to eat

In Kilkenny, **Café Sol** on William Street (056 776 4987, main courses €22-30) offers splendid lunches and beautiful afternoon teas in a delightfully decorated room. In a centuries-old building on narrow Butterslip Lane, **Pordylos** is a cosy, restaurant, serving imaginative modern food (off High Street, 056 777 0660, main courses €16-€40). **Lacken House** (Dublin Road, 056 776 1085, five-course dinner €59) is where you go for elegant dining in a stately Victorian building. For the hippest locale in town, though, you'll have to head for **Zuni** (26 Patrick Street, 056 772 3999, www.zuni.ie). Have a cocktail in the bar before enjoying some slick food in the main restaurant (main courses €19.95-€28).

Where to stay

In Kilkenny there are plenty of B&Bs on Parliament Street, Patrick Street and the roads leading out of town. Again, Zuni (*see above*) has sleek modern rooms done out in soothing colours (rates €100-€150). If you can't get in there, try the **Butler House** on Patrick Street, a fanciful 18th-century house with sweeping staircases and marble fireplaces (056 776 5707, www.butler.ie, rates €140-€220). A cheaper option is the **Metropole Hotel** (High Street,

056 776 3778, rates €70-€120), which offers B&B in 12 rooms; or you could try **Lawcus Farm Guesthouse** (off the N10 on the Kells Road just outside Kells, 056 772 8949, www. lawcusfarmguesthouse.com, rates €100), a rustic, 200-year-old stone cottage at the edge of the King's River, nicely renovated into a quiet country paradise.

Tourist information

Kilkenny Tourist Office

Shee Alms House, Rose Inn Street (056 775 1500). **Open** *May-Oct* 9am-6pm Mon-Sat; 9am-6pm Mon-Sat; 11am-5pm Sun (July, Aug only). *Oct-Apr* 9.15am-5pm Mon-Sat.

Getting there

By car

Take the N7 out of Dublin as far as Naas in County Kildare; follow the N9 through Carlow to the junction at Paulstown; then take the N10 into Kilkenny Town.

By bus

Regular Bus Éireann services (051 879 000) connect Dublin with Kilkenny (2hrs).

By train

Trains run several times daily from Dublin's Connolly Station to Kilkenny (2hrs).

Black stuff bliss.

SEAN SCULLY
GALLERY
←

Directory

Getting Around	220
Resources A-Z	226
Further Reference	237
Index	239
Advertisers' index	244

Features

Bus & rail tickets	221
Dublin by Bus	223
Travel advice	226
Average temperatures	236

Hugh Lane Gallery. *See p82.*

Directory

Getting Around

Arriving

By air

Dublin Airport is about 13 construction-plagued kilometres (eight slow miles) north of the city, and is managed by **Aer Rianta** (814 1111, www.dublinairport. com). It's small, but packed with shops. The airport also has currency exchange facilities and car rental desks, plus a tourist information office (open from 8am to 10pm daily) that can provide maps and information as well as accommodation booking. For getting to and from the airport, *see p221*. For left luggage (storage), *see p229*. For lost property facilities, *see also p229*.

The following run regular flights to Dublin:

Major airlines
Aer Lingus *0818 365 000/ UK tel 0870 876 5000/ www.aerlingus.ie*
Air Canada *679 3958/ UK tel 0871 220 1111/ www.aircanada.com*
Air France *605 0383/ UK tel 0871 66 33 777/ www.airfrance.com*
Alitalia *UK tel 0871 424 1424/ www.alitalia.it*
bmi (British Midland) *283 0700/UK tel 0870 264 2229/ www.flybmi.com*
British Airways *1-890 626 747/ UK tel 0844 493 0787/ www.ba.com*
City Jet *605 0383/ UK tel 0870 142 4343/ www.cityjet.com*
Continental Airlines *1-890 925 252/UK tel 0845 607 6760/ www.continental.com*
Delta Airlines *407-3165/ UK tel 0845 600 0950/ www.delta.com*
Lufthansa *844 5544/ UK tel 0871 945 9747/ www.lufthansa.com*
Ryanair *0818 303030/ UK tel 0871 246 0000/ www.ryanair.com*
US Airways *1-890 925 065/ UK tel 0845 600 3300/ www.usairways.com*

By coach

Travelling by coach in Ireland is a good deal cheaper than travelling by rail, though the Irish road network is still not as good as it might be. The largest nationwide coach service is **Bus Éireann** (836 6111, www.buseireann.ie), which operates out of Dublin's Central Bus Station (Busáras). Private bus companies include **Rapid Express** (679 1549, www.jjkavanagh.ie).

Central Bus Station (Busáras)
Store Street, Northside (recorded information 836 6111 6am-11pm daily/www.buseireann.ie). **Open** *in person* 9.30am-6pm daily. **Map** p251 G2.
The information desk here can provide details of local and national bus and coach services, as well as tours, including all services to Northern Ireland.

By ferry

Ferries are still likely to remind you of backpacking trips, but even in these days of cheap trans-channel flights, some people prefer them – if only for the views and the lure of spending time out on the water. While those on driving tours may find that it makes economic sense to take the car along (especially if travelling in a group), it's no longer cheap to cross by boat: two people with a car can expect to pay around £242 return to sail from Liverpool to Dublin in high season. Note that some lines give a 20 per cent discount to members of youth hostel organisations.

Ferries from Dublin sail to Holyhead (North Wales), the Isle of Man and Liverpool. There are two ferry ports in and around Dublin: **Dublin Port**, about three kilometres (two miles) from the centre (on Alexandra Road, 887 6000, www.dublinport.ie, bus 53, 53A to/from the centre), and **Dún Laoghaire** for the Stena Line (*see below*).

Irish Ferries
2-4 Merrion Row, around St Stephen's Green (reservations & enquiries 1818 300 400/ UK tel 0870 517 1717/www.irish ferries.com). **Open** 8.30am-9pm Mon-Fri; 9am-4pm Sat; 10am-2pm Sun. **Credit** AmEx, DC, MC, V. **Map** p251 G4.
This company operates the world's largest car ferry, the *Ulysses*, which can carry more than 1,300 cars and has 12 decks to explore on the run between Dublin Port and Holyhead in North Wales.

P&O Irish Sea
UK 0871 66 44 999/within Ireland 01 407 3434/www.poirishsea.com). **Open** 8am-8pm Mon-Fri; 8am-6.30pm Sat, Sun. **Credit** AmEx, DC, MC, V.
Operates between Dublin Port and Liverpool.

Stena Line
Ferry Terminal, Dún Laoghaire Harbour, Dublin Bay (reservations & enquiries 204 7777/UK tel 0870 570 7070/www.stenaline.com). **Open** 8.30am-7pm Mon-Sat. **Credit** AmEx, DC, MC, V.
Stena's massive ferry carries up to 1,500 passengers on its regular runs between Dún Laoghaire and Holyhead.

By train

The national railway network is run by **Iarnród Éireann** (836 6222, www.irishrail.ie).

Trains to and from Dublin use **Connolly Station** or **Heuston Station**, both on the city's north side. As a rule of thumb, Connolly serves Belfast, Rosslare and Sligo; Heuston serves Galway, Westport, Tralee, Killarney, Kildare, Cork, Limerick, Ennis and Waterford. The Enterprise service to Belfast is clean, fast and comfortable, but it's not representative; some other InterCity services can be slow, grotty and uncomfortable.

Bikes may be carried on most mainline routes; ask where to store them, as regulations vary with the type of train.

To & from the airport

By bus

As there's no rail service to Dublin Airport, the only public transport is Dublin Bus (see p222), which runs the very useful **Airlink** coach service (873 4222/www.dublinbus.ie). There are two routes: the **747** (5.45am-11.30pm Mon-Sat; 7.15am-11.30pm Sun) runs from the airport to O'Connell Street (in the centre of the city) and Central Bus Station, while the **748**

(6.50am-9.30pm Mon-Sat; 7am-10.05pm Sun) runs from the airport to Central Bus Station, Tara Street (DART Station), Aston Quay (in the centre), Wood Quay (by Christchurch) and Heuston Rail Station. On the 747 route, buses run every ten minutes Monday to Saturday, and every 20 minutes on Sunday. On the 748 route, buses run every 30 minutes daily. The **747** buses run 5.15am-10.50pm Monday to Saturday and 7.35am-11.15pm on Sunday; the **748** runs 7.15am-10.30pm Monday to Saturday and 7.50am-10.50pm on Sunday. Both journeys take around 25 minutes to the centre of town and 40 minutes to Heuston Rail Station; tickets, which can be bought from the driver, are €6/€10 return (€3 for children/€5 return).

Two non-express buses, the **16A** and **41**, also serve the airport (€2 single); timetables are displayed at the bus stops outside the airport's Arrivals terminal. Take note: no large items of baggage are allowed on these buses.

By car

To get into town from the airport, follow signs to the M1, then take it south toward Dublin. When you get to the

M50 ring road, either loop around to enter Dublin from whichever side is closest to the part of town you need, or stay on the M1, which becomes the N1 when it enters the city limits. The journey into town takes about 20 minutes, although the frequent construction on the M1 may slow you down, particularly during rush hour.

By shuttle

The big, blue private **Aircoach** service (844 7118/www.aircoach.ie, open 9am-5.30pm Mon-Sat) runs from the terminal to Ballsbridge in the southern suburbs via the city centre (O'Connell Street). A second route runs from the airport to Leopardstown taking in the city, Donnybrook and Stillorgan: its buses run hourly between midnight and 4am; every 20 minutes 4-6am and 8pm-midnight; and every ten minutes 6am-8pm. The trip usually takes 40 minutes, but can take up to an hour at rush hour.

It's marginally more expensive (€7 single, €12 return, €1 5-12s, free under-5s), but makes up for that by being impressively prompt, pleasant and reliable. You can buy tickets just outside the arrivals lounge. Aircoach also sells **The Dublin Pass** which provides a guide book and entry to over 30 attractions for €31 across the city.

By taxi

Taxis are plentiful and a journey into the city centre will usually cost around €25-€30.

Public transport

Iarnród Éireann runs the **DART** electric rail and suburban rail services, while **Dublin Bus** (Bus Atha Cliath) is responsible for the city

---

Bus & rail tickets

Combined pre-paid tickets can be the cheapest way to get around Dublin, especially if you're going to be doing a lot of travelling. These can be purchased from the offices of Dublin Bus and DART (see p222), from central newsagents and at the Dublin Tourism Centre (see p235).

● **One-day Short Hop**: unlimited bus, suburban rail and DART travel – €9.30; €14.20 family.

● **Three-day Short Hop**: Three days unlimited bus, Suburban Rail & DART travel across the city – €18.20.

● **Weekly Short Hop**: unlimited bus, suburban rail and DART travel – €31.50.

● **Weekly Rambler**: unlimited bus travel for one week across the city – €23.

Directory

buses. Several combined bus and rail tickets are available, so work out where and how much you want to travel and see which type suits best.

Bus

Bus stops look like tall green or blue lollipops. They usually (though not always) display a timetable but rarely have a shelter. 'Set down only' means the bus only lets passengers off there, so don't hang around waiting; look for a bus sign that doesn't bear those three words. Note a Dublin curiosity: you board buses at the front and get off at the front, too: the middle doors seldom open.

More than 150 bus routes crisscross the city centre, so you'll usually find a bus stop close by. Timetables at bus stops are often defaced, so your best bet is to get up-to-date versions from Dublin Bus's offices on O'Connell Street (*see right*). Buses are generally reliable and frequent, but most only keep loosely to their schedules, so allow plenty of time – especially in rush hour and during the whole of Friday afternoon.

Fares are set by city zone, or 'stage'. There are more than 23 stages in and around Dublin, and you can check timetables to see what stage your destination is in. Fares are €1.05 for a journey within stages one to three, €1.50 for stages four to seven, €1.70 for stages eight to 13, and up to €4.30 to take a bus from the centre to a far-flung suburban stage. For some useful bus tips, *see right* **Dublin by bus**.

You can buy tickets or bus passes from tourist offices and newsagents, or you can pay the driver the appropriate fare on boarding the bus in coins only. If you choose to do the latter, exact change is a good idea: drivers can't give change, though they will issue you a ticket for the amount of

the overpayment, and you can then have this money returned at Dublin Bus, 59 Upper O'Connell Street. If you need to buy a ticket, board on the left-hand side of the front entrance; the right-hand side is reserved for passengers who have pre-paid bus passes, which are easier and cheaper. If you plan to do a lot of travel by bus, it's a good idea to buy one of these passes. Options include a one-day pass (€6), three-day pass (€11.50), five-day pass €18.50, seven-day pass (€23) and one-day family pass (€10). All offer unlimited use of all Dublin Bus services for their specified period. There's also a range of student offers, for which you need ID and a Travelsave stamp from the Dublin Bus offices. For other passes, *see p221* **Bus & rail tickets**.

Nitelink

Normal bus services end at around 12.30am, but Nitelink buses run every night except Sunday along many different routes from the city centre to the suburbs. Services leave from D'Olier Street, Westmoreland Street and College Street, starting at around 12.30am, then departing every half hour or so until around 4.30am. The fare is €5. Check with tourist offices or Dublin Bus for timetables and routes.

Dublin Bus

Head Office, 59 Upper O'Connell Street, Northside (information & customer services 873 4222/www.dublinbus.ie). **Open** 8.30am-5.30pm Mon; 9am-5.30pm Tue-Fri; 9am-2pm Sat. **Map** p251 F1.

Rail services

The **DART** (Dublin Area Rapid Transit, www.irishrail.ie) and **Suburban Rail** lines provide a faster and arguably more pleasant alternative to buses for journeys beyond the city centre. Central DART stations include **Connolly**, **Tara Street**, **Pearse** and **Grand Canal Dock**. Most of the DART runs outside the city centre, serving the north and south suburbs from Greystones and Bray in the

south to Howth and Malahide in the north. The DART is supplemented by Suburban Rail routes that range as far as Dundalk in County Louth, Arklow in County Wicklow, Mullingar in County Westmeath and County Kildare. See the map on *p255* for more stations.

Rail tickets are available from all DART and Suburban Rail stations, as well as from the **Rail Travel Centre** (*see p223*). On buying a single or return rail ticket, specify the final destination so the ticket can be validated for a connecting bus service if that is required.

A new transport option is the **LUAS** tram system (1-800 300 604/www.luas.ie). This state-of-the-art light rail system connects you to the city centre, many of Dublin's top tourist attractions and the best shopping areas. Luas (the word is Irish for 'speed') has two routes. The red line runs from Connolly Rail Station to Tallaght in south-west Dublin. The green line runs from St Stephen's Green in the centre to Sandyford in the southern suburbs. An extension to the red line will be complete by the end of 2009.

Luas operates 5.30am-12.30am Mon-Fri, 6.15am-12.30am Sat and 7am-11.30pm Sun. Single fares start at €1.50; a one day adult pass costs €5. Combined Luas and Dublin Bus tickets cost €6.80. Buy tickets before boarding; there are ticket machines on the platform at every stop.

DART (Iarnród Éireann)

Connolly Station, Amiens Street (703 2358/703 2359/recorded information 836 6222/www.irishrail.ie). **Open** 7am-10.20pm Mon-Sat; 8am-9.30pm Sun. **Map** p251 H1.

LUAS

Red Cow Roundabout, Clondalkin, Dublin 22 (1-800 300 604/www.luas.ie). **Open** 7am-7pm Mon-Fri; 10am-2pm Sat. **Credit** (over €5) MC, V. **Map** p256.

Dublin by bus

Nearly all buses in Dublin display the mysterious legend 'Via An Lar'. This odd mingling of Latin and Irish is arguably deliberately misleading and off-putting to the uninitiated. But, in fact, it simply means 'via city centre' (*an lar* means 'city centre' in Irish) and it holds the key to understanding Dublin's ostensibly intricate bus system.

There are dozens of bus routes through the city and dozens of route numbers, with As, Bs and Xs added for good measure. But the system is not half as wilfully and hellishly confusing as it might appear. The main rules of thumb are these: nearly all buses cross the city from north to south; and nearly all are channelled through, or depart from, O'Connell Street and its immediate riverside environs – Eden Quay, Beresford Place, Aston Quay, D'Olier Street, Westmoreland Street and Dame Street. If you bear in mind Dublin's relatively small city centre, this means that you are never very far from the bus stop you need.

Most of the sights can be walked to but if you're planning to go to some of the outlying attractions such as the Phoenix Park and Kilmainham, then a bus might come in handy. And when the weather's bad, sometimes walking just isn't a lot of fun, so we've included some of the most useful bus routes below.

City Centre to National Botanic Gardens and on to Helix Concert Hall
Buses 13 and 13A (catch them at Merrion Square North and O'Connell Street).

City Centre to Guinness Brewery and on to Kilmainham
Bus 78A (departs from Aston Quay and Essex Quay).

City Centre to Heuston Station
Bus 25X (departs from Westmoreland Street).

City Centre to Dún Laoghaire, via University College
Bus 46A (departs from O'Connell Street and D'Olier Street).

City Centre to Howth Village and Howth Summit
Buses 31 and 31B (both depart from Eden Quay).

City Centre to Smithfield, Four Courts and Parkgate Street
Buses 25 and 26 (depart from Wood Quay).

City Centre to Phoenix Park Visitors' Centre at Ashdown Castle
Buses 37 and 39 (depart from Dame Street).

Rail Travel Centre
35 Lower Abbey Street, Around O'Connell Street (836 6222/ www.irishrail.ie). **Open** 9am-5pm Mon-Fri. **Credit** AmEx, DC, MC, V. **Map** p251 F2.

Taxis

A multitude of taxi companies operate and taxis tend to be plentiful (though finding one on Saturday nights can be tricky). Expect to pay high prices round the clock. There are 24-hour ranks at Abbey Street and Upper O'Connell Street on the northside, and at Aston Quay, College Green and St Stephen's Green (north). Taxis can often be found outside major hotels.

If you have any complaints about taxis, contact the **Irish Taxi Drivers' Federation** (836 4166).

Fares
Some private companies offer fixed rates for certain journeys and don't charge a pick-up fee; licensed cabs run on a meter. The minimum charge is €3.80 for the first kilometre or 170 seconds between 8am and 8pm. Between 8pm and 8am Monday to Saturdays and all day on Sundays and public holidays the initial rate is €4.80; each additional kilometre is charged at 95c (8am-8pm) or €34c per minute and €1.25 per kilometre or 44c per minute from 8pm-8am, and all day on Sundays and public holidays. Extra charges of €1 are levied for extra passengers. (One child under 12 travels free; 2 or 3 children will be charged an extra €1). You'll be charged an extra €2 if you hire a taxi by phone.

Phone cabs
Castle Cabs *802 2222*
City Cabs *872 2222*
Co-Op Taxis *676 6666*
Pony Cabs *661 0101/ www.ponyexpress.ie*

Chauffeur services
Charlemont Chauffeur Service *087 270 0506/ www.charlemontchauffeur.com*
Emerald Limos *087 223 1350/ www.emerald-limo.ie*
The Limousine Company *843 9055/ www.thelimousinecompany.ie*

Directory

Driving

Dublin's roads are truly hellish: traffic jams at rush hour (morning and night) make the daily commute a grind for locals, and driving an ordeal for visitors. Worse still, the street signs in Gaelic and English are too dark and the writing too small for the names of the streets to be easily read in either language – which means it's all too easy to get very lost, very quickly. The system of one-way streets in the centre – often not shown on maps – can get drivers unfamiliar with the city into a flat spin. Then there's construction disruption. Also, public transport is quite good in Dublin, so there's even less reason to drive; buses are reliable and frequent, and have a special lane for faster trips; the DART rail system will whisk you out to the coast in a few short minutes. Most people who spend all of their time in the city don't even bother renting a car. If you bring your own car, or rent one on the spot, do drive carefully. And be sure to get out of town. Country roads may not always be of the highest standard, but they're rarely choked with traffic and construction.

EU, US and international driving licences are valid in Ireland. Speed limits are 50kph (31mph) in urban areas, 80kph (50mph) in suburban areas, 100kph (62mph) on main roads (excluding urban areas and motorways) and 120kph (75mph) on dual carriageways and motorways.

Seatbelts must be worn by drivers and all passengers of cars and light vans. The alcohol limit, as in the UK and most US states, is 80 milligrams per 100 millilitres of blood.

Americans and Australians take note: as in Britain, cars drive on the left-hand side of the road.

Breakdown services

There are many garages in Dublin that will help if you have a breakdown. The following places all offer 24-hour support.
Automobile Association
56 Drury Street, Around Temple Bar (617 9999/www.aaireland.com)
Glenalbyn Motors *460 4050*
RAC *1 800 805 498/ www.rac.ie*
Kane Motors *833 8143*

Parking

Parking spaces in the centre of Dublin are expensive and can be difficult to find. Expect to pay at least €2 per hour in the centre. Computerised billboards throughout the city list availability in the major car parks. All on-street parking in the city centre is pay-to-park: there should be an automatic ticket machine on each street. Be warned: clamping is widely used, even in residental areas.

Vehicle hire

Unless you're a committed (and patient) car driver, there's no point hiring a car for your stay in Dublin. However, if you plan to travel outside the capital, a vehicle is essential, since public transport is far less reliable and infrequent away from the city. You must have a valid driving licence and a credit card in order to hire a car. All the car hire companies listed here also have outlets at Dublin Airport. All advise that you pre-book.

Avis
35-39 Killmainham (1-605 7500/ airport 605 7500/www.avis.com). **Open** 8.30am-5.45pm Mon-Fri, 8.30am-4.30pm Sat, 8.30am-2pm Sun. **Credit** AmEx, DC, MC, V. The airport branch is open 5.30am-11pm daily. Child seats and satellite navigation are available.

Budget
151 Drumcondra Road Lower, Northern suburbs (837 9611/
airport 844 5150/www.budget.ie). **Open** 9am-5pm daily. **Credit** AmEx, DC, MC, V. The airport branch is open 5am-midnight daily.

Hertz
151 South Circular Road, Dublin 8, Southern suburbs (709 3060/ airport 844 5466/www.hertz.com). 9am-4.30pm Sat; 9am-3.30pm Sun. **Credit** AmEx, DC, MC, V. The airport branch is open 6am-midnight daily. Child seats and satellite navigation are available.

National Car Rental
353 Car Rental, The Courtyard, Cranford Centre (near Montrose Hotel), Stillorgan Road, Donnybrook, Dublin 4, Southern suburbs (260 3771/airport 844 4162/www.carhire.ie). **Open** 9am-5.30pm Mon-Sat. **Credit** AmEx, DC, MC, V. The airport branch is open 6am-midnight daily. Satellite navigation costs extra.

Cycling

The biggest problem with cycling in Dublin is not the air pollution, nor avoiding the mad drivers, but rather finding a safe place to keep your bike: Dublin railings are filled with single wheels dangling from locks. If you have to park outdoors, try to use two locks – a strong one for the frame and back wheel and another for the front wheel – and take your lights, saddle and any other detachables with you.

Bicycle hire

For cycle hire you can expect to pay something in the region of €20 per day (based on a 24 hour period), although there are usually weekly rates (€80) and group discounts that will reduce the price somewhat. A refundable deposit of €200 is required.

Cycle Ways Bike Rental
185-186 Parnell Street, Around O'Connell Street (873 4748/ www.cycleways.com). **Open** 9.30am-6pm Mon-Wed, Fri, Sat; 9.30am- 8pm Thur; 11am-5pm Sun. **Credit** AmEx, MC, V. **Map** p251 E1

Directory

Resources A-Z

Addresses

There is no system of postal or zip codes in the Republic of Ireland, and this can make addresses look dangerously vague – this is especially true in rural areas where an address can consist simply of the nearest town or village. Don't worry, though. This is a small country and the system works just fine.

Dublin is slightly different from the rest of the country in that it has a system of postal districts, numbered from 1 to 24. The system is simple: even numbers cover the area south of the River Liffey; odd numbers are north of the river. As a quick guide, locations in the city centre will either have a Dublin 1 (northside) or a Dublin 2 (southside) post code. The area immediately west of Christ Church is Dublin 8; Ballsbridge, Ringsend and Donnybrook, south-east of the centre, are Dublin 4, and the area around the Four Courts and Smithfield is Dublin 7.

Age restrictions

● Entry to pubs: officially 18, although children are tolerated before 9pm (at bar owner's discretion, so this can be earlier; hotels are best)
● Entry to nightclubs: usually 18, although some may have an over-21 or over-23 policy
● Buying alcohol: 18
● Buying and consuming cigarettes: 16
● Driving: 17
● Marriage: 18
● Sex: 17

Business

Couriers & shippers

Call **DHL Worldwide Express** (1-890 725 725, www.dhl.com) or **Federal Express** (1-800 535 800, www.fedex.com).

Consumer

For consumer complaints, contact the **Office of the Director of Consumer Affairs** (4 Harcourt Road, Dublin 2, 402 5500, www.odca.ie), which has the power to prosecute traders; or contact the **European Consumer Centre** (809 0600, www.ecc dublin.ie) for free legal advice. Another option is to check out the Citizens Information website, **www.citizens information.ie**.

Customs

If you're entering Ireland from outside the EU, you're entitled to the following duty-free allowances:
● 200 cigarettes or 100 cigarillos or 50 cigars or 250 grams tobacco
● 2 litres port, sherries or fortified wines or 1 litre spirits or strong liqueurs (over 22 per cent alcohol)
● 2 litres of table wine
● 60 millilitres perfume
● 250 millilitres toilet water
● €184 worth of goods, including gifts and souvenirs.
If you're entering Ireland from inside the EU (excluding new member states), you're entitled to the following duty-free allowances:
● 800 cigarettes or 400 cigarillos or 200 cigars or 1kg tobacco
● 10 litres port, sherries or fortified wines or 10 litre spirits or strong liqueurs (over 22 per cent alcohol)
● 90 litres of table wine
● No limits perfume
● No limit toilet water
● €175 worth of goods, including gifts and souvenirs.

Customs & Excise

Main office *Ship Street Gate, Dublin Castle, around Temple Bar (877 6222/877 6223/www.revenue.ie). All cross-city buses.* **Open** 9am-5pm Mon-Fri. **Map** p251 E3.

Disabled travellers

More and more places provide facilities for disabled people – the easiest way to find out is to call and see if a venue can cater for your needs.

Dublin Bus has a lot of wheelchair-accessible buses, and more are added all the time; contact Dublin Bus for

---

Travel advice

For current information on travel to a specific country – including the latest news on health issues, safety and security, local laws and customs – contact your home country's government department of foreign affairs. Most have websites with useful advice for would-be travellers.

Australia
www.smartraveller.gov.au

Canada
www.voyage.gc.ca

New Zealand
www.safetravel.govt.nz

Republic of Ireland
http://foreignaffairs.gov.ie

UK
www.fco.gov.uk/travel

USA
http://travel.state.gov

details (*see p222*). Few railway or DART stations were built with wheelchair users in mind, but Iarnród Éireann (*see p222*) makes an effort to accommodate those who contact them in advance: staff will meet you at the station, accompany you to the train, arrange a car parking space and set up ramps. All Luas trams have designated spaces for wheelchairs. Wheelchair users should enter through the double doors in the middle of the tram, where information on where and how to position the wheelchair is shown.

For details of access to stations nationwide, call any DART station or train station and ask for the 'InterCity Guide for Mobility Impaired Passengers'. For further information, contact the **Department of Transport** (44 Kildare Street, Southside, 670 7444, www.transport.ie).

Useful organisations

Central Remedial Clinic
01 854 2200/www.crc.ie.
Cystic Fibrosis Association of Ireland *496 2433/ www.cfireland.ie.*
Enable (disability) Ireland *269 5355/www.enableireland.ie.*
Irish Deaf Society *860 1878/www.irishdeafsociety.ie.*
Irish Wheelchair Association *818 6400/www.iwa.ie.*
National Council for the Blind of Ireland *1-850 334 353//from outside Ireland +353 1 830 7033/ www.ncbi.ie.*

Drugs

The official attitude to drug abuse in Ireland remains draconian. Although police attitudes are often relaxed, there are no signs that soft drugs such as cannabis are about to be decriminalised here. Drug problems in some sections of the city remain appalling.

If you get caught with illegal drugs, the result can be an official caution, a night in a cell or much worse.

Drug Treatment Centre

30-31 Pearse Street, around Trinity College (648 8600/www.addiction ireland.ie). All cross-city buses. **Open** 9am-5pm Mon-Fri; 10am-noon Sat, Sun. **Map** p251 G3.

Electricity

Like the rest of Europe, Ireland uses a 220-240V, 50-cycle AC voltage, with three-pin plugs (as in the UK). Adaptors are widely available at airport shops. Note too that Irish and UK VCRs and televisions use a different frequency from those in the USA.

Embassies & consulates

For embassies and consulates not listed below, consult the Golden Pages. Note that many countries (such as New Zealand) do not maintain a full embassy in Dublin. In those cases the embassy in London usually acts as the country's chief representative.
American Embassy *42 Elgin Road, Ballsbridge, Southern suburbs (668 8777/emergency number 668 9612/www.dublin.usembassy.gov). Bus 4, 5, 7, 7A, 8, 45, 63, 84/DART Lansdowne Road.* **Open** 8.30am-5pm Mon-Fri.
Australian Embassy *Fitzwilton House, Wilton Terrace, around St Stephen's Green (664 5300/www.ireland.embassy.gov.au). Bus 10, 11, 13.* **Open** 8.30am-4.30pm Mon-Fri.
British Embassy *29 Merrion Road, Ballsbridge, Southern suburbs (205 3700/emergency number 086 243 4655/www.britishembassy.ie). Bus 5, 7, 45/DART Sandymount.* **Open** 9.30am-5pm Mon-Fri. *Passport enquiries 9am-12.30pm, 2-3.30pm Mon-Fri; visa enquiries (by appointment only) 9am-12.30pm Mon-Fri.*
Canadian Embassy *7-8 Wilton Terrace, around St Stephen's Green (234 4000/www.canada.ie). Bus 10, 18/DART Grand Canal Street.* **Open** 9am-4.30pm Mon-Fri. **Map** p251 H5.
New Zealand Consulate General *46 Upper Mount Street, around St Stephen's Green (all enquiries to New Zealand Embassy in London: 0044 207 9308 422/voice message service in Ireland 660 4233/www.mfat.govt.nz/embassies). Bus 7.* **Map** p251 H5.

South African Embassy
Alexander House, Earlsfort Centre, Earlsfort Terrace, around St Stephen's Green (661 5553). All cross-city buses. **Open** 8.30am-noon Mon-Fri. **Map** p251 H5.

Emergencies

Dial **999** or **112** for Fire, *Garda* (police) and ambulances.

Gay & lesbian

See also pp171-175.

Help & information

Gay Switchboard Dublin
872 1055. **Open** 7.30-9.30pm Mon-Fri; 3.30-6pm Sat. Help and information for the gay community in Dublin.

Lesbian Line
872 9911/www.dublinlesbianline.ie. **Open** 7-9pm Thur. Advice and information.

Other groups

Drugs/HIV Helpline
1-800 459 459. **Open** 9.30am-5pm Mon-Fri. A freephone number for basic health information and advice.

Gay Men's Health Project
19 Haddingdon Road, Ballsbridge, Southern suburbs (600 2189/ www.hse.ie). Bus 10. **Open** 6.30-8pm Tue; 6-7.30pm Wed. Free, confidential drop-in clinic for gay and bisexual men.

Outhouse
105 Capel Street, North Quays (873 4999/www.outhouse.ie). All cross-city buses. **Open** 12.30-5pm Mon; 12.30-9pm Tue-Fri; Sat 1-5pm. **Map** p251 E2. An accessible meeting place for the lesbian and gay community. *See p175.*

Health

The national health service in Ireland is rightly maligned; state investment has risen in recent years, but this follows years of cutbacks. A number of city centre hospitals have moved to the suburbs even as the population in the centre has grown. For details of health insurance, *see p228*.

Complementary medicine

Holistic Healing Centre

38 Dame Street, around Trinity College (671 0813/www.hhc.ie). All cross-city buses. **Open** 10am-7.30pm Mon-Thur; 10am-6pm Fri; 10am-6pm Sat. **Map** p251 E3.

The Inspired Centre

67 Camden Street Lower, around St Stephen's Green (478 5022). All cross-city buses. **Open** 10am-10pm Mon Fri; by appointment only Sat. **Map** p251 E5.

Nelson's Homeopathic Pharmacy

15 Duke Street, around Trinity College (679 0451/ www.nelsons.co.uk). All cross-city buses. **Open** 9.30am-5.45pm Mon-Wed, Fri, Sat; 9.30am-7.30pm Thur. **Map** p251 F3/4.

Contraception & abortion

Abortion is illegal in Ireland, and a highly inflammatory subject. Its prohibition became part of Ireland's constitution in 1983. Irish women generally travel to Britain for terminations.

For women's health matters, visit a **Well Woman Centre**. Services include breast exams, pregnancy counselling, smear tests and the morning-after pill. You don't need an appointment, and staff are friendly.

Condoms are available in pharmacies and in some newsagents, as well as from vending machines in many pubs and from **Condom Power** (57 Dame Street, Around Temple Bar, 677 8963, www.condompower.ie).

Well Woman Centres

35 Liffey Street Lower, around O'Connell Street (872 8051/ www.wellwomancentre.ie). **Open** 9.30am-7.30pm Mon, Thur, Fri; 8am-7.30pm Tue, Wed; 10am-4pm Sat; 1-4pm Sun. **Map** p251 E2. **Other locations**: 67 Pembroke Road, Ballsbridge, Southern suburbs (660 9860); Northside Shopping Centre, Coolock, Northern suburbs (848 4511).

Dentists

Gallagher's Dental Surgery

38 Fenian Street, Dublin 2 (670 3725). All cross-city buses. **Open** 8am-8pm Mon-Wed; 9am-5pm Thur, Fri.

Irish Dental Association

295 0072/www.dentist.ie. A quick and easy online search to find a registered dentist in your area.

Doctors

You must pay for visits to the doctor. This can be quite as expensive, as doctors' charges usually range from around €30 to €50, but can go much higher, depending on the type of consultation. It's always a good idea to check a doctor's fees in advance.

Grafton Medical Practice

34 Grafton Street, around Trinity College (671 2122/www.grafton medical.ie). All cross-city buses. **Open** 8.30am-6.30pm Mon-Thur; 8.30am-6pm Fri. **Map** p251 F4.

Mercer Medical Centre

Stephen Street Lower, around St Stephen's Green (402 2300/ www.rcsi.ie). All cross-city buses. **Open** 9am-6pm Mon-Thur; 9am-5pm Fri. **Map** p251 E4.

Hospitals

In an emergency, call 999/112. The following area hospitals all have 24-hour accident and emergency departments. Note that all casualty patients must pay a flat fee of €66 in order to be treated. EU citizens should *see also right*.

Beaumont Hospital

Beaumont Road, Northern suburbs (809 3000/www.beaumont.ie). Bus 27B.

Mater Hospital

Eccles Street, Dublin 7 (803 2000/www.mater.ie). Bus 13, 13A, 16, 16A.

St James's Hospital

James's Street, Dublin 8 (410 3000/www.stjames.ie). Bus 19, 78A, 123, Luas James's.

Pharmacies

There are branches of the local chain **Hickey's** (www.hickeys pharmacies.ie) and the international brand **Boots** (www.boots.com) at various locations throughout the city.

STDs, HIV & AIDS

Drugs/HIV Helpline *1-800 459 459.* **Open** 9.30am-5pm Mon-Fri; Advice and counselling on HIV- and AIDS-related issues.
Dublin AIDS Alliance *53 Parnell Square West, 873 3799/www.dublin aidsalliance.com.* **Open** 10am-5pm Mon; noon-5pm Fri. A care and education service for drug users and people with HIV and AIDS.

Helplines

For women's support and services *see above*; for gay and lesbian helplines *see p175*; for helplines related to AIDS and HIV *see above*.
Alcoholics Anonymous *842 0700/www.alcoholicsanonymous.ie.*
Asthma Line *1-850 445 464/www.asthmasociety.ie.* **Open** 9am-5pm Mon-Fri. Nurse available for advice 10am-1pm Tue-Thur.
Focus Ireland *881 5900/ www.focusireland.ie.* **Open** 24hrs daily. Emergency accommodation.
Narcotics Anonymous Information line *672 8000/ www.na.ireland.org.* **Open** 24hrs daily.
Samaritans *freephone 1-850 609 090/www.samaritans.org.* **Open** 24hrs daily.

Insurance

If you're an EU citizen, an E111 form will cover you for most medical (though not dental) emergencies. In the UK, get an application form from the post office or apply online (www.ehic.org.uk). It is always advisable to take out medical insurance too: it'll save you the effort of trying to wade through the red tape and ensures more comprehensive coverage.

Non-EU citizens are advised to have travel insurance that covers health, as they will be responsible for any healthcare costs. Organise your travel insurance before you leave your country of origin; it's impossible to sort out once you get to Ireland. Alway read the small print before agreeing to an insurance contract. There's usually an excess or deductible amount.

Internet

Many hotels now offer some kind of internet access: luxury hotels should have broadband internet and wireless connection points in each room and hostels tend to have a clutch of terminals. Look out for the many cafés, bars and restaurants that provide wireless as an added extra to customers. If you want to set up an internet account for your stay, good local ISPs include **Eircom Broadband** (1-800 242 633, www.eircom.ie) and **BT Broadband** (1-800 923 924, www.btireland.ie).

Internet access

If you can't get online in your hotel, you can guarantee that internet access won't be far away; Dublin is positively crawling with cybercafés, most offering a decent number of terminals and other services such as printing, faxing and photocopying.

Central Café Internet
6 Grafton Street (677 8298/ www.centralcafe.ie). **Open** 9am-10pm Mon-Fri; 10am-9pm Sat, Sun. **Rates** varies. **No credit cards.**

Global Café Internet
8 Lower O'Connell Street (878 0295/www.globalcafe.ie). **Open** 8am-11pm Mon-Fri; 9am-11pm Sat; 10am-11pm Sun. **Rates** varies. **No credit cards.**

Language

In the rush towards cultural homogenisation, much has been lost – but the English language as spoken in Dublin is still a breed apart. The real

Dublin accent is rapid and clipped with a dropped 't'. It can be heard to best advantage at the markets on Moore Street and Henry Street.

Entirely different is the 'posh' southside, 'D4' or 'DART' accent (so called because most exponents live near the coastal DART railway line in places like Dalkey and Howth). This accent is nasal and, critics would tell you, rather uptight; most real Dubs don't consider it part of the local vernacular at all.

Left luggage

Busáras
Bus Éireann 703 2434/ www.buseirann.ie. **Open** *Lockers* 7am-11pm daily. **Rates** €6-€10 locker. **No credit cards.** **Map** p251 G2.

Connolly Station
Platform 2 (Iarnód Éireann 703 2358). **Open** 5.30am-12.30am daily. **Rates** *24hrs* €4 small; €6 large. Connolly Station will hold for up to 7 days. **No credit cards.** **Map** p251 H1.

Dublin Airport
Greencaps Left Luggage & Porterage (814 4633). **Open** 6am-11pm daily. **Rates** *24hrs* €4.50 small; €6.50 medium; €9 large. **No credit cards.**

Heuston Station
Next to the ticket office (703 2132). **Open** 7am-9pm Mon-Sat. **Rates** €1.50 small; €3 medium; €5 large. **No credit cards.**

Libraries

There are a number of local city- and state-run libraries in Dublin with ample services including, sometimes, internet access. In addition to those listed below, note that most local universities will allow foreign students a temporary reader's pass for their libraries. For this, you'll need a student ID, and, in some cases, a letter of introduction from your college. For a list of local universities, *see p233.*

Those listed here are Dublin corporation libraries.

Central Library
Ilac Centre, Henry Street, around O'Connell Street (873 4333/ www.dublincity.ie). All cross-city buses. **Open** 10am-8pm Mon-Thur; 10am-5pm Fri, Sat. **Map** p251 F2.

Pearse Street Library
138-144 Pearse Street, around Trinity College (674 4888/ www.dublincity.ie). Bus 3. **Open** 10am-8pm Mon-Thur; 10am-5pm Fri, Sat. **Map** p251 G3.

Lost property

Make sure you always notify the police if you lose anything of value, as you will probably need a reference number from them to validate any subsequent insurance claims. To track down your lost property, call the following:
Bus Éireann *703 2489*
Connolly Station *703 2358*
Dublin Airport *814 5491*
Dublin Bus *703 1321*
Heuston Station *703 2102*
Luas *1-800 300 604*

Media

Newspapers

Dublin is the centre of Ireland's publishing world and all but one of the Republic's national newspapers are based here.

National broadsheets
The *Irish Times* acts as Ireland's serious intellectual broadsheet. The *Times'* main rival, the *Irish Independent*, is tabloid in spirit, although it masquerades as a broadsheet. It's a more actively national paper, and is generally more approachable than the *Times*, as it features less of that paper's metropolitan bias. This said, it is often sensationalist and sometimes could be accused of lacking in objectivity. The third national broadsheet, the Cork-based *Irish Examiner*, is decent reading.

National tabloids
The *Evening Herald*, peddled on the streets and newsstands from lunchtime on, is a tabloid, but is a little loftier in tone than some of the morning rags. In some circles, it's required reading: if you need a flat to rent, then look no further. The *Star* is Ireland's very popular response to Britain's *Sun*, though with a little more conscience and a lot less cleavage. The *Irish Sun*,

meanwhile, is the British *Sun* with a few pages of Irish news inserted to keep the locals happy. When the mother paper has one of its frequent fits of Irish-bashing, its Dublin equivalent quietly pulls the relevant pages.

Sunday papers

Of the many papers you will find lined up in a Dublin newsagent on Sunday morning, few will be Irish. The British press has saturated the Irish market in recent years, offering cheaper cover prices and more pages as a means of boosting circulation figures at home. Most of the papers follow the practice of the *Sun* (*see above*) in modifying their editorial stance, where appropriate, for the Irish market: the *Sunday Times* is a particularly brazen offender. Of the indigenous newspapers, the *Sunday Tribune* and the *Sunday Business Post* both offer good news coverage, comment and columnists. The *Post*, like the *Financial Times*, is good for more than just money talk, and is, at times, the most outspoken of all the papers. The *Sunday Independent* is much like its daily stablemate. Sunday tabloids include the popular *Sunday World*. *Ireland On Sunday* is a new Sunday paper that offers easy reading and current affairs.

Magazines

Listings magazines

Hot Press (www.hotpress.com) is fortnightly. It remains the best guide to the Dublin music scene, with comprehensive listings and reviews, and its debate pages are pretty lively. Alternatives to *Hot Press* include the amiable and very comprehensive *Event Guide*, a handy freesheet available in central cafés and bars. There are also a few websites with listings; *see p238*.

Other magazines

Dublin's shelves are as packed with glossy mags as any city's. All the international mainstays are there, some in special Irish editions. Titles unique to the Irish market include *U*, *Irish Tatler*, *Social & Personal* and *Image*. Good for a horrified laugh is *VIP*, which is modelled on *Hello!* and shares that publication's high-minded ideals.

The *RTÉ Guide* offers the usual celebrity gossip plus full TV and radio listings. For buying and selling stuff, check out the aptly named *Buy and Sell*, or for satire try the *Phoenix*. *Village Magazine*, a new addition to the shelves, is a straight-talking look at Irish politics, current and international affairs. For in-depth comprehensive coverage of Irish

literature and cinema, try *Books Ireland* or *Film Ireland*. The quarterly *Dublin Review* offers excellent, well thought-out essays on literature and the arts. The monthly *Dubliner* is an upmarket glossy carrying comprehensive reviews and news articles. It often has excellent writing, and occasional bouts of solid investigative reporting. *Totally Dublin* is a monthly entertainment and lifestyle mag. Some free magazines can be had at bars, cafés and shops around the city. *Mongrel* has lots of comedy, editorial, fashion, music and more. *Backpacker* is a must for new backpackers arriving in Ireland.

Television

Dublin is one of Europe's more heavily cabled cities, and the full range of UK channels should be available wherever you stay. The national station, RTÉ (Radio Telefís Éireann) runs three national channels: RTÉ1, RTÉ2 and TG4. The station, in spite of a recent licence fee hike, is usually hard-up for money, and its perceived lack of adventurous programming and unflattering comparisons with the BBC make it a prime target for public criticism. Still, it does generally excellent current affairs, creative children's programming and highly regarded sports reporting.

RTÉ1

The daytime diet in Ireland largely consists of soap operas, bland chat shows and DIY programmes. Prime-time programming is better. The most significant programme on Irish TV remains Friday night's *Late Late Show*, formerly hosted by national institution Gay Byrne and now in the hands of Pat Kenny. The *Late Late Show* is the longest-running chat show in the world and countless important events and interviews have taken place on the programme. Today, however, it is a tired shadow of itself, and pressure is building on RTÉ to put it and its unctuous host out of their misery.

RTÉ2

RTÉ's second channel reinvented itself a few years ago, and it did so with largely successful results. At night, music and chat shows aimed at a younger, hip audience come to the fore, and the channel has also

commissioned several new series, such as the well-received comedy drama *Bachelors Walk*. Saturday nights are in the hands of Ryan Tubridy, who hosts *Tubridy Tonight*, the new chat show with little appeal.

Telefis na Gaeilge (TG4)

A predominantly Irish-language station based in Galway, TG4 does imaginative home-grown drama and a few pretty good documentaries, punctuated by smartly selected art-house movies dubbed for those who have not yet fully mastered the native tongue. It's stylish and slick and well worth a look.

TV3

Ireland's newest (and first independent) station was born in 1998, and has used populist scheduling to carve a successful niche for itself. No nonsense about public service broadcasting here, as its schedule is filled with low-budget American TV movies, excitable news broadcasts and low-budget sitcoms. It has also poached many of RTÉ's sporting contracts.

Radio

RTÉ

RTÉ operates four national stations: **RTÉ Radio 1** (88.2-95.2 FM; 567, 729 AM) offers a fairly safe mixture of news, sports programming and phone-in talk shows during the day, and an excellent range of interesting music slots and offbeat docs at night. **RTÉ 2FM** (90.4-97 FM; 612, 1278 AM) is aimed more at the kids with the usual pop and rock shows during the day and the ever-reliable *Hotline* request show at 7pm daily. **RTÉ Lyric FM** (96-99 FM), based in the town of Limerick, is the classical music station. Another option is **RTÉ Raidio Na Gaeltachta** (92.6-94.4 FM), the national Irish-language station, offering news, current affairs, arts, music and talk shows.

Other stations

A number of new licensed stations have challenged the hegemony of RTÉ in the last ten years. After a rocky start, **Today FM** (100-102 FM) has now successfully established itself, offering a broad combination of music shows, news and chat. **Anna Livia FM** (103.2 FM) is Dublin's community station, putting out a good selection of programmes made by people who love radio; while chart enthusiasts prefer the same-old, same-old diet of **98FM** (er, 98 FM), **FM104** (oh, find it yourself) and **Lite FM** (95.8 FM). **NewsTalk 106** (106 FM), which has been climbing up the ratings ladder over the past few years, offers rolling news, debate and occasional documentaries and is well worth a listen.

Pirate radio

The diet of blandness offered by the mainstream music stations, however, has meant that the city's handful of pirate stations have come to fulfil certain music needs in the city. Among the best are **Power FM** (97.2 FM) – a lot of techno and other dance music; **Phantom FM** (91.6 FM) – generally loud indie rock; and **XFM** (107.9 FM) – more loud indie rock. If you want originality, you're most likely to find it here.

Multimedia

Modest success stories abound in the virtual world and include www.ireland.com, linked to the *Irish Times*, as well as a number of other websites; *see p238*.

Money

In February 2002 the euro became Ireland's sole currency. It was officially launched on 1 January 1999, and cash in the form of euros (€) and cents (c) came into circulation on 1 January 2002. The Irish pound was then withdrawn on 9 February 2002, with the euro becoming the sole legal tender. Since then there have been cries of what has become known as 'euro inflation' – meaning that when the currency changed over prices went up across the board. This could go a long way towards explaining how expensive things often seem in Dublin, which was formerly known as one of the world's less expensive tourist towns. Still, the Irish government has not endorsed this theory, and denies there has been any euro inflation at all, and some economists deny that it even exists, although others insist that it is a real situation, or a valid problem in any euro member state.

The euro comes in seven notes – €5 (grey), €10 (red), €20 (blue), €50 (orange), €100 (green), €200 (yellow) and €500 (purple) – and eight coins. One face of each coin features a communal map and flag illustration and the other a country-specific design (all can be used in any EU nation). Irish coins all display the emblem of the harp.

ATMs

Automatic cash machines can be found outside most banks and some building societies and in many shops around the city. Most are linked up to international networks (such as Cirrus), so you should not anticipate any problems withdrawing money directly from your account with your standard cash card, although you should expect a nominal charge for each transaction.

Banks

In general, banking hours in Dublin are 10am to 4pm Monday to Wednesday and Friday, and 10am to 5pm on Thursday (closed on Saturday and Sunday). The main Dublin branches of the major Irish banks are listed below.

AIB (Allied Irish Bank)
AIB Bank Centre, Ballsbridge, Southern suburbs (660 0311/ www.aib.ie). Bus 7. **Open** 10am-4pm Mon-Wed, Fri; 10am-5pm Thur.

Bank of Ireland *Baggot Street Lower, around St Stephen's Green (661 5933/www.boi.ie). Bus 10.* **Open** 10am-4pm Mon-Wed, Fri; 10am-5pm Thur. **Map** p251 G5.

Ulster Bank *33 College Green, around Trinity College (702 8600/ www.ulsterbank.com). All cross-city buses.* **Open** 10am-4pm Mon-Wed, Fri; 10am-5pm Thur. **Map** p251 F3.

Bureaux de change

Nearly all banks, building societies and post offices in Dublin have foreign exchange facilities, so you shouldn't have any trouble finding places across the city to change your currency into euros.

There are desks at the airport and at the main bus station, **Busáras** (*see p220*), so you can stock up on euros as soon as you arrive.

Another option if you need to change once you're in the city itself is the bureau de change inside Clery's department store (*see p139*).

Other useful bureaux de change include:

First Rate Bureau de Change

2 Westmoreland Street, around Trinity College (671 3233/www.boi.ie). **Open** 9am-6pm daily (summer time opening until 8pm Thur-Sat). **Map** p251 F3.

Foreign Exchange Company of Ireland

12 Ely Place, around St Stephen's Green (661 1800/www.fexco.com). All cross-city buses. **Open** 9am-5pm Mon-Sat. **Map** p251 G4.

Joe Walsh Tours (JWT)

69 O'Connell Street Upper (872 5536). All cross-city buses. **Open** 8am-8pm Mon-Sat; 10am-6pm Sun and bank hols. **Map** p251 F1.

Thomas Cook Foreign Exchange

118 Grafton Street, around Trinity College (677 1307). **Open** 9am-5.30pm Mon, Tue, Thur-Sat; 10am-5.30pm Wed. **Map** p251 F4. **Other locations**: *51 Grafton Street (677 7422).* **Open** 9.30am-5.15pm Mon, Tue, Thur-Sat; 10.30am-5.15pm Wed.

Credit cards

Ireland is still a cash culture, but most places will accept MasterCard and Visa, although only a few accept American Express or Diners' Club cards.

If your credit cards are lost or stolen

As you would at home, it's best if you first inform the police and then contact the 24-hour numbers listed below.
American Express Customer Services *1-800 282 728.*
American Express Travellers' Cheques *1-800 626 000.*
Diners' Club *0818 300 026/ authorisation service 1-800 709 944.*
MasterCard *1-800 557 378.*
Visa *1-800 558 002.*

Directory

Tax

Sales tax (VAT) in the Irish Republic is set at 20 per cent. Visitors from outside the European Union can get a refund by filling in a tax-free shopping cheque (available from participating stores) and handing it in to the Refund Desk at Dublin Airport.

Opening hours

General business hours are 9am to 5.30pm Monday to Friday. Banks are open 10am to 4pm Monday to Wednesday and Friday, and from 10am to 5pm on Thursday. Shops in the city centre generally open between 9.30am and 6pm on Monday, Tuesday, Wednesday, Friday and Saturday, and from 2pm to 6pm on Sunday, with late-night opening until 8pm on Thursday and Friday. Hours during which alcohol can be sold have been tightened once more after an experiment in slackness resulted in excessive drinking and late-night violence; pubs are now usually open from 11.30am to 11.30pm Monday to Thursday, and 11.30am to 12.30am Friday and Saturday (though many pubs in Dublin have permission to open until 1.30pm and later) and noon to 11pm on Sunday.

Under new law, children are allowed in pubs, with adults, until 9pm. This is however at the discretion of the pub owner and you may see signs stating earlier times.

Police stations

The emergency telephone number for police (called Garda), fire and ambulance is 999 or 112. City centre Garda stations are located at the following addresses; all are open 24 hours daily. Non-emergency confidential calls to the Garda can also be made on 1-800 666 111.

Garda stations

Pearse Street, around Trinity College (666 9000); Store Street, North Quays (666 8000); Fitzgibbon Street, Northside (666 8400); Metropolitan HQ, Harcourt Square, Southside (666 6666).

Post

Post boxes are green and many have two slots: one for 'Dublin Only' and one for 'All Other Places'. It costs 55c to post a letter, postcard or unsealed card (weighing up to 50g) inside Ireland, 82c to the UK, Europe and all other international destinations. All airmail letters – including those to the UK – should have a blue priority airmail *(aerphost)* label affixed: you can get these free at all post offices. Post is generally delivered in fairly quick order within Ireland itself, and you should expect letters sent from Dublin to reach their destination within a day. International mail varies: it takes several days for letters or parcels to reach Europe and about a week to reach the US, or slightly more than that to reach Australia, South Africa or New Zealand.

Post offices

Generally speaking post offices are open from 9am to 5pm Monday to Friday. Larger branches are also open from 9am to 1pm on Saturday. This rule is not inviolable, as offices have varying opening hours. Note that many smaller post offices still close for lunch from 12.45pm to 2pm.

General Post Office

O'Connell Street, around O'Connell Street (705 7000/www.anpost.ie). All cross-city buses. **Open** 8am-8pm Mon-Sat. **Map** p251 F2.

Religion

There are many churches and places of worship for Muslims and Jews. Check the *Golden Pages* for more listings.

Safety & security

Levels of street crime in Dublin have risen dramatically in the last decade. Pickpockets and bag-snatchers have always been fairly prevalent in the city, but in recent years some assailants have been known to use syringes as weapons – threatening their victims with the possibility that whatever is in them is tainted with HIV. They have even, if rarely, robbed people on city buses, walking the victim off at needle-point to get to a cash machine.

The majority of safety hints amount to little more than simple common sense. If you're worried about travelling on buses, then sit downstairs and in sight of the driver. When wandering around town, avoid wearing ostentatious jewellery that says 'rob me'. Always strap your bag across your chest with the opening facing towards your body. When withdrawing money from cash machines, don't stand around counting your money; put it away quickly, and, if there's a machine inside the bank, use that instead. Never leave your wallet in your back pocket. In bars, don't leave your wallet on a table, and keep your bag with you at all times.

Most of all, safety is about being aware and looking confident. This is especially important at night: if you're on your own, stay in well-lit, populated areas and try to avoid consulting a huge map every couple of streets. Arrange to meet people inside a pub or restaurant rather then waiting outside on your own.

Smoking

In March 2004 a wide-ranging law banning all smoking in the workplace came into effect in Ireland. It is viewed as the most far-reaching anti-smoking legislation in the world and has proved to be a big success. It prohibits smoking in any bar, restaurant or public space in the whole country. The effect has been dramatic: all Dublin pubs, for example, became no-smoking areas overnight. Most pubs and bars have an outdoor, heated and seated area for smokers. However, some pubs don't; get used to seeing small groups of people standing at bar doors having a puff.

Students

Considering the sheer number of language schools, business colleges and universities in Dublin, it's not surprising that the city's student population is considerable. It's also diverse: over summer, thousands of people come to Dublin to study English, and for the rest of the year colleges are filled with academic students from Ireland and abroad.

Citizens of roughly 60 countries (including all EU-member states) do not require visas to study here. However, the law requires long-term visitors to register with the Immigration Department at the Garda National Immigration Bureau, Harcourt Square, Southside (666 9100). For more information consult the website (http://foreign affairs.gov.ie) or get in touch with the Irish Department of Foreign Affairs, 80 St Stephen's Green, Southside (478 0822).

If you do end up going to school here, you'll find that rents in Dublin have risen sharply in the last decade: expect to pay upwards of €100 a week for a reasonable place. The rental market has become much less cut-throat in the last few years, but is still fairly frantic around

September when all the students return to Dublin to sort out lodgings. Summer, therefore, is the best time to look for bargains.

The *Evening Herald* is probably the best paper to check for ads, though you might get lucky at USIT (*see below*). You could also go through your college's accommodation service if it has one, or a letting agency. Best of all, though, is the DAFT website (www.daft.ie) which is excellently designed and easy to use.

Language schools

French

Alliance Française *1 Kildare Street, around St Stephen's Green (676 1732/www.alliance-francaise.ie). All cross-city buses.* **Map** p251 G4.

German

Goethe-Institut *37 Merrion Square, around St Stephen's Green (661 1155/www.goethe.de/dublin). Bus 4, 7, 44, 45.* **Map** p251 H4.

Irish

Gael-linn *35 Dame Street, around Temple Bar (675 1200/www.gael-linn.ie). All cross-city buses.* **Map** p251 E3.

Spanish

Instituto Cervantes *Lincoln House, Lincoln Place, around Trinity College (631 1500/www.dublin.cervantes.es). All cross-city buses.* **Map** p251 G3.

Universities & colleges

The three biggest colleges in the Dublin metropolitan area are as follows:

Dublin City University

Glasnevin, Northern suburbs (student services 700 5000/www.dcu.ie). Bus 11A, 11B, 13A, 19A.

Trinity College Dublin

College Green (896 1000/www.tcd.ie). All cross-city buses. **Map** p251 F3.

University College Dublin

Belfield, Southern suburbs (716 7777/www.ucd.ie/international). Bus 3, 10, 11B, 17.

Other schools & colleges

American College Dublin

2 Merrion Square, around St Stephen's Green (676 8939/www.amcd.ie). All cross-city buses. **Map** p251 G4.

Dublin Business School

13-14 Aungier Street, around St Stephen's Green (417 7500/www.dbs.edu). Bus 16, 16A, 19, 19A, 83. **Map** p251 E4.

Dublin Institute of Technology

Cathal Brugha Street, around O'Connell Street (402 3000/www.dit.ie). All cross-city buses. **Map** p251 F1.
There are six DITs in and around the city, offering a wide range of courses, including in popular areas such as architecture, music, engineering and tourism.

Griffith College Dublin

South Circular Road, Southern suburbs (415 0400/www.gcd.ie). Bus 16, 19, 122.

Useful organisations

Union of Students in Ireland Travel (USIT)

19-21 Aston Quay, around Trinity College (602 1906/www.usit.ie). All cross-city buses.
Open 9am-6pm Mon-Fri; 10am-5pm Sat. **Map** p251 F2.
USIT handles all student travel arrangements, so wherever you're going, it can tell you the cheapest way to get there. It's also very much a meeting of the ways: its noticeboards are filled with details of flatshares, language tuition, jobs and cheap flights. You'll probably have plenty of time to browse through the small ads while you're waiting to be served: you should expect at least 30 minutes' queuing.

Telephones

Dialling & codes

The dialling code for Dublin is 01, although you don't need to use the prefix if you're calling within the Dublin region itself. Local phone numbers in Dublin all consist of seven digits, though you'll notice that

Directory

elsewhere in Ireland phone numbers may be either short§er or longer. As in the US, numbers with the prefix 1-800 are free.

All Dublin numbers listed in this book have been listed without the city code of 01. If you need to dial any of these numbers within Dublin, simply use the numbers as they appear in the listings. If you are dialling from outside Dublin but within Ireland, add 01 to the front of the numbers listed. If you are dialling from outside Ireland, you need to dial the international dialling code + 353, then the Dublin city code 1 (omitting the initial 0), then the number as it appears in the guide.

To make an international call from within Ireland, dial 00, then dial the appropriate international code for the country you're calling (*see below*), and then dial the number itself, omitting the first 0 from the area code where appropriate.

● Australia: 00 61
● United Kingdom: 00 44
● USA &Canada: 00 1
● South Africa: 00 27
● New Zealand: 00 64

Making a call

If you have access to a private telephone, the charges for your calls will be significantly lower than they would be from your hotel or your mobile: for example, a three-minute local call will cost around 24c during the day, and the same amount of money will net you double minutes' chat during off-peak hours at night or on weekends.

Reduced rates are available for calls made between 6pm and 8am from Monday to Friday, and all day Saturday, Sunday and Bank Holidays. If you need to make international calls, try to wait until these off-peak hours, as it is considerably cheaper.

If you can't use a private phone, the next easiest way to make long-distance calls is to buy a phone card, available from most newsagents and post offices, which you can use on public pay phones. The majority of pay phones only accept these cards, not cash. The cards are especially useful outside Dublin, where payphones of all kinds are scarce, and it's best to be prepared.

With hotel phones, check rates in advance. It is unlikely that there will be any off-peak reductions, and prices can be dizzyingly high.

Public phones

Cash- and card-operated pay phones are found in phone boxes across the city. They are not cheap, however, as a local telephone call from a pay phone generally costs 25c a minute; calls to mobiles are 50c a minute. A minimum €1 charge applies.

Operator services

Call 10 to reach the operator for Ireland and the UK, and 114 for international assistance.

Reverse-charge ('collect') calls are available via 1-800 55 88 90 and cost extra.

For directory enquiries, dial 11811 or 11850 for Ireland and Northern Ireland, and 11818 for international numbers, including UK numbers.

UK visitors planning their trip should note that when calling directory enquiries from the UK, Irish numbers are now listed on the myriad UK directory enquiries numbers, not under international directory enquiries.

Telephone directories

The *Golden Pages* is Dublin's equivalent of the *Yellow Pages*. You can search online at www.goldenpages.ie to find

addresses in a given area. The 'Independent Directory', distributed annually, is a smaller version, with the added bonus of fairly good restaurant listings.

Mobile phones

There are several mobile networks in Ireland. Vodafone Ireland, O2, Meteor and Three each have about 98 per cent coverage across the country. Ireland's network uses the 900 and 1800 GSM bands, and a UK handset will therefore work in Ireland as long as you have a roaming agreement with your service provider. Holders of US phones (usually 1900 GSM) should contact their service provider to check compatibility.

If you find you need to buy a mobile phone, or if you need to buy a new handset for your existing service, or if you want to sign up to an Irish mobile phone network, there are plenty of options. If you're here for just a short period of time, contact one of the following companies and get a pay-as-you-go phone that lets you buy talk time in advance.

If you intend to rent a mobile phone to use during a short stay in the country, contact the Dublin Tourist Information office for vendors (*see p235*).

Carphone Warehouse
30 Grafton Street, around Trinity College (1-800 424 800/www.carphonewarehouse.ie). All cross-city buses. **Map** p251 F4.

Vodafone *48 Grafton Street, around Trinity College (673 0120/www.vodafone.ie). All cross-city buses.* **Map** p251 F4.

Time

Ireland is in the same time zone as Britain, so it runs to Greenwich Mean Time. In spring, on a Saturday towards the end of March (exactly as happens in the UK and the US) the clocks go forward one hour for Summer Time. Clocks return to normal towards the end of October – on the same dates as the UK.

If you're not sure what time it is, call the 24-hour speaking clock by dialling 1191.

Tipping

You should tip between 12 and 15 per cent in restaurants. However, if – as is often the case – a service charge is included on your bill, ask waitstaff if they actually receive that money: you have every right to refuse to pay it if they don't. Always pay the tip in cash where you can, to make sure the people it's intended for get it.

Tip hairdressers and beauticians if you feel like it, and don't feel obliged to tip taxi drivers. A lot of city bars and clubs now have attendants in their lavatories, but don't feel that you have to tip them.

Toilets

Clean and safe public toilets are thin on the ground in central Dublin. It's perfectly acceptable to use the toilets in bars and shopping centres. The toilets at Bewley's on Grafton Street (*see p118*), in the Jervis Centre on Henry Street (*see p140*), and at Marks and Spencer on Grafton Street (*see p139*) are all generally clean and pleasant.

Tourist information

Located in a lovely converted church, this almost absurdly helpful centre will do just about everything but your laundry. It has a bureau de change, a car rental agency, a booking service for tickets for tours and travel excursions, a ticket booking desk for concerts, theatre performances and other events, a friendly café and a surprisingly good souvenir shop with fair prices.

You might check out the **Dublin Pass** (www.dublin pass.ie), a 'smart card' which, for a fee, gets you in 'free' to sights across the city. How affordable it is depends on how much you plan to see – prices start at €31 for a one-day card to €89 for a six-day pass.

You can also book hotel rooms here, though you will have to pay a booking fee for each reservation. To make a booking before you arrive, call ResIreland (1-800 668 668; 0800 783 5740 from the UK; 00800 6686 6866 from the rest of Europe; 011-800 6686 6866 from the US and Canada; or 00 353 669 792 082 from all other countries, or try online at www.goireland.com).

Dublin Tourism Centre

St Andrew's Church, Suffolk Street, around Trinity College (1-850 230 330/0800 039 7000 from the UK/ www.visitdublin.com). All cross-city buses. **Open** *Jan-May, Oct-Dec* 9am-5.30pm Mon-Sat; 10.30am-3pm Sun. *June* 9am-7pm Mon-Sat; 10.30am-3pm Sun. *July* 9am-7pm Mon-Sat; 10.30am-5pm Sun. **Map** p251 F3.

Irish Tourist Board

Information 1-850 230 330 from within Ireland; UK office 0800 039 7000/www.Ireland.ie. **Call centre:** 24 hrs daily. **Walk-in centre** Nation House, 103 Wigmore Street, London. Open 9am-5pm Mon-Fri.

Other tourism centres

14 Upper O'Connell Street. **Open** 9am-5pm Mon-Sat. **Map** p251 F1. *Baggot Street Bridge, around St Stephen's Green. Bus 10.* **Open** 9.30am-noon, 12.30-5pm Mon-Fri. **Map** p251 H5. *Dublin Airport. Bus 747, 748.* **Open** 8am-10pm daily. *Dún Laoghaire Ferry Terminal, Dublin Bay. DART Dún Laoghaire.* **Open** 10am-12.45pm, 2-6pm Mon-Sat.

Tours

City Tour Hop On Hop Off

59 Upper O'Connell Street (873 4222/www.dublinsightseeing.ie). Daily Dublin sightseeing bus tours with 23 stops. Tickets are valid for 24 hours and cost €15.

Dublin tasting trail

44 Oakley Road, Ranelagh (497 1245/www.fabfoodtrails.ie).

A tasting and cultural walk around the less well-known streets of Dublin. Tours depart every Friday at 10am, 2.5 hours, €45.

iWalks

Dublin Tourism Centre, Suffolk Street, (605 7700/www.visitdublin. com/iwalks). Free of charge, downloadable podcasts on 11 city themes available from the website.

Viking Splash Tours

64-65 Patrick Street, (707 6000/www.vikingsplash.ie). Take to the river in a DUKW, an amphibious World War II craft on a sightseeing tour with guides dressed as vikings. Note that only part of the tour is in the water. There are 5 departures daily. Tickets cost €20; reductions €10-18.

Visas & immigration

Citizens of the USA, New Zealand, Australia, South Africa and Canada do not require special visas to enter Ireland and are permitted to stay in the country for a maximum of three months. British citizens and members of all EU states have unlimited residency and employment rights in Ireland.

Passport control at Dublin's airport is surprisingly strict and suspicious, even of American visitors. So be prepared for the third-degree.

As with any trip, countries can change their immigration regulations at any time, check visa requirements well before you plan to travel, either at the Irish embassy in your country or on http://foreign affairs.gov.ie.

If you require a visa, you can apply to the Irish embassy or consulate in your own country. It is best to do so months in advance. You can also now apply online (www.inis.gov.ie/en/INIS/ pages/supported_countries). If there is no Irish representative in your country, you can apply to the Foreign Affairs Department in Dublin (*see p235*).

Average temperatures

Month	Maximum	Minimum
January	8°C/46°F	2°C/35°F
February	8°C/46°F	2°C/35°F
March	10°C/51°F	2°C/35°F
April	13°C/55°F	4°C/39°F
May	15°C/60°F	6°C/43°F
June	18°C/65°F	9°C/48°F
July	20°C/68°F	11°C/52°F
August	19°C/67°F	11°C/52°F
September	17°C/63°F	9°C/48°F
October	14°C/57°F	6°C/43°F
November	10°C/51°F	4°C/39°F
December	8°C/46°F	3°C/37°F

Consular Section, Department of Foreign Affairs

69-71 St Stephen's Green (408 2308/foreign affairs.gov.ie). All cross-city buses. **Open** *Office* 10am-12.30pm Mon-Fri. *Phone enquiries* 2.30-4pm Mon-Fri. **Map** p251 F5.

Weights & measures

The Republic of Ireland is now (very nearly) fully metric, although the good old imperial measurements are still readily used and understood – most importantly, pints are still pints at the bar.

When to go

The high tourist season runs from July to August; these are the months when the majority of major festivals and events take place across the country. Accommodation is at its most scarce and expensive during this period, special offers are few and far between, and Dublin and other popular districts are at their most crowded. Prices are lower and the weather is generally better in May, June and September, so these months might be the best time to visit.

In winter, prices are lowest of all, but the weather is rather dismally wet and cold. Note that during the St Patrick's weekend (around 17 March), Dublin is packed to the gills, so you'll need to plan months ahead if you want to come to town for that festival.

Climate

It will come as no surprise to get an Irish weather report that emphasises rain and chill. Winters tend to be very chilly with lots of rain, and a heavy coat will be necessary from about November through February. Throughout the rest of the year the weather is so variable that, even after winter is long gone you would be wise to expect the worst and pack a warm sweater and a raincoat. Do it even in the summer, just in case. If the weather takes a turn for the worse you'll be glad you did.

For an up-to-date weather forecast for Dublin, telephone 1-550 123 854 (calls cost about 75c per minute).

Public holidays

The following public (bank) holidays occur annually:

1 January New Year's Day
17 March St Patrick's Day
Good Friday
Easter Monday
First Mondays in May, June and August
The Monday closest to **Hallowe'en** (31 October)
25 December Christmas Day
26 December St Stephen's Day
29 December

Women

Although Ireland has made impressive economic progress, over the recent years, changes in the still fundamentally patriarchal social structure have been much more gradual, and many women's issues remain, on the whole, largely neglected.

One item of good news is that the number of women in Irish politics is gradually increasing, thanks in part, no doubt, to Mary Robinson's groundbreaking presidency (1990-97). Along with that, there has also been an enormous increase in awareness of women's rights over the last 15-20 years. That said, public funding for women's aid is tragically scarce. Divorce is now legal in Ireland, although it is a much longer process than it is in countries like England or the US, and abortion is illegal.

These organisations offer support and/or information:

Albany Women's Clinic

Clifton Court, Fitzwilliam Street Lower, around St Stephen's Green (661 2222). **Open** 8am-6pm Mon-Fri. **Map** p251 H5.

Rape Crisis Centre

70 Leeson Street Lower, around St Stephen's Green (1-800 778 888/661 4911/www.drcc.ie). **Open** *phone lines* 24hrs daily. **Map** p251 G5.

Women's Aid

1-800 341 900/www.womensaid.ie. **Open** 10am-10pm daily. Offers advice and support.

Women's Refuge & Helpline

496 1002. **Open** 24hrs daily. Offers support and advice.

Further Reference

Books

Drama & poetry

Samuel Beckett *Waiting for Godot* Two blokes hang around for a couple of hours.
Brendan Behan *The Quare Fellow* A shocking drama from the notorious Dublin drinker.
Eavan Boland *In a Time of Violence* Collected poems.
Nuala Ni Dhomhnaill *The Astrakhan Cloak* Well-rated works by the best-known poet writing in Irish today.
Seamus Heaney *Opened Ground: Poems 1966-1996* Good introduction to the Nobel Laureate.
Patrick Kavanagh *The Great Hunger* The Famine as metaphor.
Tom Murphy *The Gigli Concert* Art, addiction and music: a masterful play by Dublin's greatest living dramatist.
Sean O'Casey *Collected Plays* Politics and morality in 1920s Ireland, including *The Plough & the Stars*.
George Bernard Shaw *Selected Plays* 'My Fair Lady' wasn't really his fault. Honest.
JM Synge *The Playboy of the Western World* Championed by Yeats, this play caused riots in the streets, although we fail to see why.
Oscar Wilde *Plays, Prose, Writings and Poems* In which the 19th century's finest wit declares his genius.
WB Yeats *Collected Poems* Dublin's mighty bard.

Fiction

John Banville *Ghosts* A haunting narrative with Beckett-like overtones.
Samuel Beckett *Murphy* A darkly humourous Irish portrayal of London life. *Molloy/Malone Dies/The Unnamable* Compelling, and compellingly odd, fiction.
Brendan Behan *Borstal Boy* Extraordinary autobiographical novel of a Dublin childhood with the IRA.
Dermot Bolger *The Journey Home* A hard-hitting account of life lived on the edge.
Elizabeth Bowen *The Last September* Quintessential Anglo-Irish 'big house' novel.
Emma Donoghue *Stir-fry* A wry lesbian love story.
JP Donleavy *The Ginger Man* The high japes of a drunken Trinity student; banned by the Catholic Church.
Roddy Doyle *The Commitments* Most Dubliners agree that the book was much better than the film.
Anne Enright *The Gathering* A journey through grief for a Dublin family.
Jeffrey Gantz (trans) *Early Irish Myths and Sagas* For those who want to learn more about the country mystical heritage.
Henry Glassie (ed) *Penguin Book of Irish Folktales* Fairies, leprechauns and big potatoes.
Seamus Heaney *Sweeney Astray/Buile Suibhne* The crazy King Sweeney updated.
Jennifer Johnston *How Many Miles to Babylon?* Protestant gentry and Catholic peasant bond.
James Joyce *A Portrait of the Artist as a Young Man* Cuts through superstition like a knife. *Dubliners* Compelling short stories from the master at his most understandable. *Finnegans Wake* defines the phrase 'unreadable genius'. *Ulysses* The most important 24 hours in literary history.
Pat McCabe *The Butcher Boy* A hilariously grotesque tale of an Irish childhood.
Barry McCrea *The First Verse* A gay Irish student becomes entangled in a literary cult on a Dublin campus.

Edna O'Brien *The Country Girls* Bawdy girlish fun that roused clerical ire.
Flann O'Brien *At-Swim-Two-Birds* Hilarious novel about a struggling writer.
Joseph O'Connor *Star of the Sea* Fascinating emigration drama on the high seas.
Liam O'Flaherty *The Informer* Terse social comment from a civil war veteran.
Jamie O'Neill *At Swim Two Boys* A homosexual *bildungsroman* set against the backdrop of the Easter Rising.
Sean O'Reilly *The Swing of Things* Dark comic thriller set in contemporary Dublin.
Stephen Price *Monkey Man* Savage parody of Dublin's media darlings during the boom years of the late 1990s by an ex-producer at Radio Ireland who saw it all.
Bram Stoker *Dracula* The original horror novel.
Jonathan Swift *Gulliver's Travels* The political satire to beat all political satire.
Colm Tóibín *The Heather Blazing* An elderly city judge is forced to confront history.
William Trevor *The Ballroom of Romance* Short stories by the Northern Irish master, set in rural Ireland.

Non-fiction

John Ardagh *Ireland and the Irish* An acute look at present-day Ireland.
Douglas Bennett *Encyclopaedia of Dublin* Just packed with vital information.
RF Foster *Paddy and Mr Punch* A media-savvy study of modern 'Irishness'.
Robert Kee *The Green Flag* A chunky nationalist history. *The Laurel and the Ivy* Parnell, Gladstone and Home Rule.
FS Lyons *Ireland Since the Famine* A definitive text.
Frank MacDonald *The Construction of Dublin*

Directory

Exploration of the city's architectural development during its Celtic Tiger days.

Máire & Conor Cruise O'Brien *A Concise History of Ireland* A thorough overview.

Jacqueline O'Brien & Desmond Guinness *Dublin – A Grand Tour* A useful guide to the Irish capital.

Nuala O'Faolain *Are You Somebody?* Dublin memories from a respected columnist.

Seán O'Faolain *The Great O'Neill* Queen Elizabeth I, Hugh O'Neill and the battle of Kinsale.

Paul Williams *Gangland, The General* Two fine dissections of Dublin's organised crime.

Cecil Woodham-Smith *The Great Hunger* The definitive study of the Great Famine.

Film

About Adam (dir Gerard Stembridge, 2000) Sharp, witty drama about *menage à cinq* of young Dubliners.

Bloom (dir Sean Walsh, 2004) The brave new adaptation of *Ulysses*, starring Stephen Rea.

Breakfast on Pluto (dir Neil Jordan, 2005) The story of Patrick 'Kitten' Braden (Cillian Murphy), who leaves behind small-town Ireland and becomes a transvestite cabaret singer in '70s London.

The Butcher Boy (dir Neil Jordan, 1998) Entertaining version of Pat McCabe's surreal novel.

The Commitments (dir Alan Parker, 1991) Love it or hate it, we can all hum the tunes.

The General (dir John Boorman, 1998) Gritty urban drama about Dublin's most notorious gangster.

Intermission (dir John Crowley, 2003) Colin Farrel goes back to his roots in this lively urban romance.

In The Name of The Father (dir Jim Sheridan, 1993) A man fights for justice to clear his father's name.

Michael Collins (dir Neil Jordan, 1996) A fine bio-pic using lots of Dublin locations.

Nora (dir Pat Murphy, 2000) Superior bio of James Joyce and his highly tempestuous paramour.

Pavee Lackeen (dir Perry Ogden, 2005) Naturalistic drama set in Dublin's traveller community.

Reefer and the Model (dir Joe Comerford, 1987) Quirky psychological thriller that continues to split the critics.

Veronica Guerin (dir Joel Schumacher, 2003) A dark, fact-based film with Cate Blanchett playing the doomed investigative reporter.

When Brendan Met Trudy (dir Kieron J Walsh, 2000) Boy loves girl. Girl nicks stuff. Etc.

Music

Paddy Casey *Living (2004)* Brilliant Dublin singer and writer who recently supported U2 at their home concerts.

Adrian Crowley *When You are Here, You are Family* (2001) The second album from this eclectic singer/songwriter.

Damien Dempsey *Seize the Day* (2003), *Shots* (2005) Dublin singer/songwriter who made his name at home, and is now taking the UK by storm.

Dinah Brand *Pale Monkey Blues* (2003) Melodic country rock in the vein of Big Star from respected Dublin songwriter, Dylan Philips.

The Frames *Set List* (2004), *For the Birds* (2001) This critically accclaimed Dublin band may make it big at last.

Gemma Hayes *The Road Don't Love You* (2006) Second album from Tipperary gal and Mercury Prize nominee.

Barry McCormack *We Drank Our Tears* (2003) Critically-acclaimed acoustic folk music from a fine Dublin songwriter.

Christy Moore *Live at the Point* (1994) An institution in Irish music.

Declan O'Rourke *Since Kyabram* (2005) Sensational debut album.

Planxty *Planxty* (1972) Seminal trad band (newly reformed) that inspired many of today's biggest Irish stars.

Redneck Manifesto *Cut Your Head Off From Your Head* (2002) Second album from instrumental punk band.

Damien Rice *O* (2003) The Kildare man, currently doing great things in the US, still plays regular gigs in Dublin.

Websites

www.abbeytheatre.ie Ireland's national theatre.

www.cluas.com Excellent independent Irish music site.

www.dublinks.com Detailed listings of the best events in town.

www.dublinbus.ie The official Dublin city bus website has a useful bus route search facility.

www.dublinevents.com Online entertainment listings.

www.dublinpubscene.com Invaluable guide to the city's many watering holes.

www.dublintourist.com Tourist guide to the capital.

www.dublinuncovered.net Everything from taxis companies to shopping tips.

www.entertainment.ie Comprehensive event listings.

www.eventguide.ie Dublin's best fortnightly guide.

www.eventsoftheweek.com All major events, and more.

www.gate-theatre.ie Offical website of the Gate Theatre.

www.ireland.com Online version of the *Irish Times*.

www.discoverireland.com The Irish tourist board.

www.local.ie If it's in Ireland, you'll find it here.

www.nch.ie National Concert Hall: classical music aplenty.

www.visitdublin.com Culture, events, getting around and special offers.

www.whelanslive.com A must for live music lovers.

Directory

Index

Note: Page numbers in
bold indicate section(s)
giving key information
on a topic; italics
indicate photographs.

a

Abbey theatre 28,
80, 83, 90,
195, *195*, **197**
abortion 20, 228
**accommodation
36-52**
by price: deluxe 37,
39, 45-47, 48, 51;
expensive 39-42,
47, 48, 49-50, 52;
moderate 43, 47,
48-49, 50-51, 52;
budget 39, 43-45,
49, 51, 52
best hotel breakfasts
51
top ten hotels 37
see also p243
Accommodation index
Act of Union 1801 15
addresses 226
Adebari, Rotimi 23
Adidas Dublin City
Marathon 158
Aer Rianta 220
age restrictions 226
Ahern, Bertie 21, 24
Aircoach 221
Aires Mateus, Manuel 28
airlines 220
Airlink 221
airport 220
transport to &
from 221
All-Ireland Hurling &
Football Finals 157
amphitheatres 183
Anglo-Irish Treaty 18
antiques shops 141
Anúna 183, **184**
architecture 25-28
art deco 80
the best buildings 26
brutalism 57
Ardgillen Castle 96
Ark Children's Cultural
Centre 27, 159,
160-161
Art House 28
Asgard 93
ATMs 231
Aughrim 207, **212**
Avoca 210-211, *211*
Avoca Handweavers
211, *211*, **212**

Avondale House &
Forest Park **210**, **212**

b

babysitting 162
Bachelors Walk 83
Bacon, Francis 81
Balbriggan Beach 160
Ballsbridge
restaurants 116
Ballyhack Castle 215
Ballymascanlon House
Hotel 205
Bank of Ireland 26, 59
banks 231
Banville, John 33
bars *see* pubs & bars
Battle of the Boyne
15, 202
Beckett, Samuel
20, **32**, 57
bridge 28
Behan, Brendan 20,
32-34,123
Benson + Forsyth 27
Beresford Place 14
Berkeley Library
26, 27, 57
Bewley's Café Theatre
196, 197
Bewley's Oriental Café
19, 65, **118**
Bhamjee, Moosajee 23
bicycle hire 225
Bite of Life 64
Black Church Print
Gallery 28
Black Death 13, 14, *14*
Blackhall Place 85
Blessington 207-208
Blessington Lakes 207
Bloody Sunday 20
Bloom Lane 78
Bloomsday Festival
154, **155**, *155*
Boland, Eavan 34
Boland's Mill, 18
Book of Kells 12, **58**, 203
books 237-238
shops 141-143
see also Literary
Dublin
Boomtown Rats 176
Borœ, Brian 12
Bowen, Elizabeth 34
**Boyne Valley, the
201-206**
Bray 97-98, *212*
Brazen Head pub 65, **125**
breakdown services 225
Brown Thomas 65, 138,
138, **139**

Brú na Bóinne Visitor
Centre **201**, **203**
Bucholz McEvoy
Architects 27
Bull Island 95
bureaux de change 231
Burke, Edmund 15, 57
Bus Éireann 200, 220
bus services 200, 220,
222
routes 223
tickets 221
to & from the
airport 221
Busáras 25, 200, **220**
business 226

c

**cafés & coffee shops
117-122**
Calatrava, Santiago
28, 85
camera shops 146
Campanile, Trinity
College 57
Campus Tours **57**, **58**
'Capability' Brown 202
car hire 225
Carlingford 206
Carlton cinema 80
Carr, Marina 33
Casement, Roger 16
Casino garden 26
Cassels, Richard 26
Castle Market 61, 138
Castle, Richard 81
Castlecomer Discovery
Park 217
CD & record shops
143-145
Celtic Tiger 20, 21,
22-24
Central Bank 28, 61
Central Bus Station
(Busáras) 200, **220**
Chambers, William
26, 57
Chancery 83
Chapel, Trinity College
57
Chapter One restaurant
82, **112**
chauffeur services 223
Chester Beatty Library
61, **62**, *62*
Chieftains 176
Childers, Erskin 93
children 159-162
shops 145
Children of Lir statue
81
Chinatown 78

chocolate
cafés **118**, 160
festivals & events 156
choirs 184-185
chq 28
Christ Church Cathedral
26, 64, **66**
Christmas Day 154
Christmas Eve Vigil 154
Church of St Columba,
Kells 203
Church of St Nicholas
of Myra 91
Church of the
Immaculate
Conception **64**, **67**
Churchill, Winston 18
cinemas 163-164
Cineworld cinema 163
City Hall 26, *27*,
61, **62**, 65
Clann na Poblachta 19
Clarence hotel 28, 36,
36, **39**, **41**, *41*, 65
Clarion Quay 26
Clarke, Austin 20
Clery's 80, **139**
climate 236
Clontarf 95
coach services 200,
220 to & from
the airport 221
Cobalt Café & Gallery
82, **122**
Coliemore Harbour 98
colleges 233
Collins Barracks **85**, 86
Collins, Michael 18, 19,
73
complementary
medicine 228
computer shops 146
Congreve, William 15
Connolly Station 221
Connolly, James 16
consulates 227
consumer affairs 226
contraception 228
Convention Centre 28
Convergence Festival
155
Cooley, Thomas 26
County Wexford 213-216
Cow Lane Market 138
craft & gift shops
145-146
Crash Ensemble 183,
184
credit cards 231
Croke Park 18, 177, 191,
192
Cromwell, Oliver *14*, 204
Cross Gallery 167, **170**

Curragh Racecourse 193
Custom House 14, *25*, 26, 83, *87*, 88, 90
Custom House Visitor Centre 88
customs 226
cycling 225

d

Dáil Éireann 18, 19, 24
Dalkey 98
Dame Street 61-63
dance 198
festivals & events 155
Dark/Light Festival 163
DART 222
Davy Byrnes 65, **127**
de Clare, Richard 13
De Valera, Eamon 18, 19
Deane, Thomas 26, 57
dentists 228
department stores 139
Dillon's Park 98
directory 220-238
disabled travellers 226-227
Docklands 87-90
accommodation 49-51
history of 87, 88
sightseeing 87-90
Docklands Maritime Festival 155
doctors 228
Douglas Hyde Gallery 58
Doyle, Roddy 34
driving 221, **225**
Drogheda 14, **204-206**
Drogheda Heritage Centre 204
Drogheda Street 79
Drogheda, Earl of 14, 79
drugs 227
Drury Street 138
Dublin Airport 220
transport to & from 221
Dublin Bay & the Coast 95-98
accommodation 51-52
restaurants 114-116
sightseeing 95-98
Dublin Bus 222
Dublin Castle **61**, **62**
Dublin Circus Festival 156
Dublin City Council 28
Dublin Film Festival 163
Dublin Fringe Festival 158
Dublin Gay and Lesbian Film Festival 163
Dublin Horse Show 157
Dublin Pass 221
Dublin Port 220
Dublin Theatre Festival 158
Dublin Today 22-24

Dublin Tourism Centre 200, **235**
Dublin Writers Festival 154, **155**, 158
Dublin Writers' Museum **81, 82**
Dublin Zoo **86**, 159, 160
Dubliners 176
Dublinia 66, **67**, *67*, 160
Dún Laoghaire **98**, 220
Dunbrody Abbey & Castle 215
Dundrum Town Centre 138, **140**

e

Easter Rising 16, 79, 80, 81
economy 22-24
Eden Quay 83
Electric Picnic 157, *156-157*
electricity 227
electronics shops 146
Elizabeth I of England, Queen 57
embassies 227
emergencies 227
Emmet, Robert 15, *16*, 84
English Privy Council 15
Enlightenment 14
Enniscorthy 213
Enright, Anne 34
Examination Hall, Trinity College 57
Exchange, the 26

f

Fairyhouse Racecourse 193
famine of 1317 13
see also potato famine of 1846-51
fashion shops 146-150
Fenians, the 15
ferry services 220
Festival of World Cultures 157
festivals & events 154-158
chocolate 156
dance 155
film 154, 156
gay & lesbian 156
literary 155
music 154, 156, 157
sport 154, 155, 157, 158
theatre 158
Fianna Fáil 19, 21, 23
film 163-166, 238
festivals & events 154, 156, 163
Fine Gael 19
Fishamble Street 15, 65
fitness centres 194

Fitzwilliam Square 27, **75-76**
Flowing Tide bar 83, **136**
Foley, John Henry 79
food & drink shops 150-151
Forty-Foot bathing spot 98
Foster + Partners 28
Four Courts 14, 19, 26, 83
Four Knocks 202
Free State *see* Irish Free State

g

Gaelic Athletic Association 191, 192
Gaelic football 191, **192**
Gaiety theatre 195, **197**
galleries 167-170
Gallery Number One 167, *169*
Gallery of Photography 27, 168
Gallery of Photography 64, 168
Gandon, James 14, 26
Garda (police) 232
Garden of Remembrance 81
Gardiner Street 14, 79
Gardiner, Luke 14, 79
Gate theatre 80, 158, 195, **197**
gay & lesbian 171-175
bars 172-173
club nights 173-175
festivals & events 156, 171
help & information 227
information & advice 171, **175**
media 171
saunas 175
Geldof, Bob 176
General Post Office **78**, 79, *80*, **81**, 232
George, Lloyd 18
George's Dock *88*, 89
George's Street Arcade 61, 138
Georgian architecture 25, 75-76
gift shops 145-146
Glasnevin pubs & bars 137
Glendalough 200, *200*, 207, **208-210**, *209*
Goldsmith, Oliver 15, 57
golf 194
Gorry Gallery 167, **168**
GPO *see* General Post Office
Grafton Architects 27

Grafton Street 65-66
Grand Canal 77
Grand Canal Dock 28, 90
Grand Canal Square 90
Grand Canal Theatre 28
Grattan, Henry 15, 59
Green Building 28
Green on Red 167, **170**
Gresham Hotel 37, 48, 80
greyhound racing 192-193
Griffith, Arthur 19, 73
Guerin, Veronica 20
Guinness 25, **91**, **92**, 123
Guinness Storehouse 25, **91**, **92**, *93*
Guinness, Arthur 92
gyms 194

h

Ha'penny Bridge 28, 83
hairdressers 152
Hallowe'en 158
Handel, George Frederic 15, 65
Hanover Quay 26
Harris, Richard 123
Haus 28
health & beauty shops 151-152
health 227-228
Helix 177, **181**
helplines 228, 236
Henrietta Street 14
Henry II of England, King 13
Henry Street *79*, 80, 138
Henry VIII of England, King 13
Heraldic Museum 71
Heuston Station 221
Hill of Slane 201, **202**
Hill of Tara 201, **202**, *204, 205*
history 12-21
HIV & AIDS 228
Home Rule 16
horse racing 193
Horslips 176
hospitals 228
House of Commons 59
House of Lords 59
Houses of Parliament 59
Howth 95-96
Hugh Lane Gallery **79**, 81, *81*, **82**, 167, 185
Huguenots 91
hurling 191, **192**

i

Iarnród Éireann 200, 220, 222
ILAC 138, **140**
Imaginosity 159
immigration 20, 23, 34, 235

Inner Dock 89
insurance 228-229
interiors shops 152
International Bar 176,
  179
International Dance
  Festival
Ireland 155
International Financial
  Services Centre 89
internet 229
Irish Architectural
  Archive 27
Irish Ferries 220
Irish Film Institute 27,
  63, 163, **164**
Irish Free State 18, 19,
  73
Irish Museum of Modern
  Art 93
Irish National Heritage
  Park 215
Irish National War
  Memorial Gardens
  28
Irish Parliament *see*
  Dáil Eireann Irish
  Parliamentary Party
  16
Irish Republican Army
  (IRA) 18, 19, 20
Irish Republican
  Brotherhood 18
Irish Tourist Board 200,
  235
Irish Writers' Centre 81
Italian Quarter 78
Iveagh Gardens **70**, *70*,
  72
Iveagh Market 65

James II, King of
  England 15, 202
James Joyce Bridge
  28, 85
James Joyce Centre 82
James Joyce Museum
  31, **98**
Jameson International
  Dublin
Film Festival **154**, 163
Jameson Movies on the
  Square 156
Jeanie Johnston **89**, **90**
Jerpoint Abbey 213,
  217, **218**
Jervis Centre 138, **140**
jewellery shops 149
Jewish Museum *76*,
  77
JJ Smyth's 176, *178*,
  179
John Dillon Street 65
Johnston, Jennifer 34
Johnstown Castle &
  Gardens 215
Jordan, Neil 34

Joyce, James **31-32**
  bridge 28, 85
  museum (Sandycove)
    31, **98**
  statue 80

k

Kart City 161, **162**
Kavanagh, Patrick 34
Kells 201, 203
Kells, Book of 12, 58, 203
Kelly, Oisin 79, 81
Kerlin Gallery 167, **168**
Kildare Street 71-73
Kilkenny 200, 213,
  213-218
Kilkenny Castle 213,
  214, **216**, **218**
Killiney Hill 98
Kilmainham Gaol *12-13*,
  18, **93**, **94**
Kilmainham *see*
  Liberties &
  Kilmainham
King John's Castle,
  Carlingford 206
Kings Inn 14
Knowth 201, *202*
Koreatown 78

o

Lady Gregory 80
language 229
  schools 233
Lansdowne Road
  Stadium 191, **193**
Laragh 207, 209
Larkin, Jim 79
Le Fanu, Joseph
  Sheridan 75
left luggage 229
Leinster House 26, **71**,
  72, 73
Leinster, King of 13
Leisureplex 161, **162**
Lemass, Sean 20
Leopardstown
  Racecourse 193
lesbian *see* gay
  & lesbian
Liberties &
  Kilmainham
  91-94
  galleries 170
  pubs & bars 137
  sightseeing 91-94
Liberty Boys 15
Liberty Hall **87**, **88**, 181
Liberty Hall Centre 87
Libeskind, Daniel 28
libraries 229
  see also individual
  library names
Liffey Swim 157
Light House cinema 163,
  164, **166**, *166*
Lisbon Treaty 21

Literary Dublin
  29-34, 158
  festivals & events 155
Lord Edward pub 66,
  129
lost property 229
Lower Ormond Quay 78
LUAS (trams) 222
  map 256
Lutyens, Edwin 28
Lynott, Phil 65

m

MacBride, Sean 19
MacDermott, Sean 16
MacGowan, Shane 176
MacNeill, Eoin 16
magazines 230
Mahon Tribunal 21
Malahide 96-97
Malahide Castle **96**, *96*,
  160
Malone, Molly 65
markets
  farmers' market 90
Meeting House Square
  160
Marsh's Library 14, 65,
  66, **67**
McCann, Colum 34
McDaid's 65, **123**
McGahern, John 34
media 229
MediaLab Europe 91
Meeting House Square
  27, **63**, 160
Mellifont Abbey 205
Merrion Square 27,
  73-77
Messiah 15, 65
Millennium Footbridge
  28, 83
Mint, Carlingford 206
mobile phones 234
Monasterboice 205
money 231-232
Monster Truck 167,
  170
Moore Street 78
Moore, Christy 176
Moore, Henry *see* Earl
  of Drogheda
Morrison Hotel 37, **48**,
  52, 83
Mosse, Dr Bartholomew
  81
Mount Usher Gardens
  211, **212**
Mountjoy Square 27
Muiredach's Cross 205
multicultural Dublin 23,
  24, 78
multiplexes 164
Municipal Gallery of
  Modern Art *see* Hugh
  Lane Gallery
Museum Building,
  Trinity College 57

museums & galleries
  Douglas Hyde Gallery
    58
  Dublin Writers'
    Museum **81**, **82**
  Hugh Lane Gallery
    79, 81, *81*,
    82, 167, 185
  Irish Museum of
    Modern Art 93
  James Joyce Museum
    31, **98**
  Jewish Museum *76*,
    77
  National Gallery of
    Ireland 27, 69, **73**,
    75, **76**
  National Museum of
    Archaeology &
    History 26, 69, **71**,
    73
  National Museum:
    Decorative Arts
    & History **85**, *85*,
    86, 159
  National Print
    Museum 77
  National Transport
    Museum 95, *95*
  Natural History
    Museum **73**, **77**, 160
  Science Gallery *58-59*,
    59
  Shaw Birthplace 30,
    30, **77**
music 176-185, 238
  classical 183-184
  festivals & events 154,
    156, 157
  opera 184
  orchestras, choirs &
    ensembles 184-185
  venues 177-183, 185
Music in the Park 156
My Bloody Valentine
  176

n

National 1798 Visitor
  Centre **213**, **215**
National Concert Hall 70,
  72, 183, **185**
National Gallery of
  Ireland 27, 69, **73**,
  75, **76**
National Library of
  Ireland 26, *29*, **71**, **73**
National Museum of
  Archaeology &
  History 26, 69, **71**, **73**
National Museum:
  Decorative Arts &
  History **85**, *85*, **86**,
  159
National Photographic
  Archive 27, 64
National Print Museum
  77

National Sealife Centre 161
National Stadium 177, **183**
National Transport Museum 95, *95*
Natural History Museum **73**, **77**, 160
Naul 202
Navan 201, 204
Nelson's Pillar 20
New Model Army 204
Newbridge House & Traditional Farm **96**, *97*, 161
Newgrange 200, 201-206
Newman House 70, *71*
Newman University Church **70**, **71**
newspapers 229-230
Nicholas Street 65
night buses 222
nightlife 186-190
clubs & dance bars 187-190
indie scene 188
North Quays & Around 83-86
accommodation 49-51
galleries 170
pubs & bars 136-137
restaurants 112-114
sightseeing 83-86
Number Twenty-Nine **75**, **77**

O

O'Brien, Edna 20
O'Casey, Sean 90
O'Connell Street & Around 78-82
accommodation 48-49
cafés & coffee shops 122
galleries 169-170
pubs & bars 136
restaurants 112-114
riots (1922) 19
riots (2006) 21
sightseeing 78-82
O'Connell, Daniel 75, 80
statue 79
O'Connor, Sinead 176
O'Dwyer Cottage **207**, **208**
O'Dwyer, Michael 207
O'Higgins, Kevin 73
O'Mahoney Pike 25-26
O'Nolan, Brian 34
O'Reilly, Sean 34
O'Shea brothers 57
O2 venue 90, 176, **183**
Old Jameson Distillery *84*, 85

Old Library, Trinity College 14, **57**, **58**
Oldtown Riding Stables 161
Olympia Theatre 61, 176, **198**
opening hours 232
opera 184
Opera Ireland 184
Opera Theatre Company 184
operator (phone) 234
Opie, Julian 79
opticians 152
orchestras 184-185
Original Print Gallery 65, **168**
Ormond, Duke of 14
Oscar Wilde House **75**, **77**
Oxegen 156

P

P&O Irish Sea 220
Panem coffee shop 83, **122**
Papal Cross 86
Papworth, George 61
parking 225
Parliament complex 59, 75
Parnell Park 191, 192
Parnell Square 81-82
Parnell Street 78
Parnell, Charles Stewart 210
statue 79
Peacock Theatre 80, 96
Pearce, Edward Lovett 26, 59
Pearse, Patrick 16, 18
People's Garden 86
pharmacies 228
Phoenix Park **85-86**, 93, 159, 160
Phoenix Park Visitors' Centre 86
Planxty 176
Plunkett, Oliver 204
Pogues, the 176
police stations 232
Pomodoro 58
Poolbeg Peninsula 98
post 232
potato famine of 1846-51 15
sculpture 89
Powerscourt House & Gardens 210
Powerscourt Townhouse Centre 66, **140**
Pride 156
Project Arts Centre 65, 167, **168**, *170*, 171
property market 22, 24
public holidays 236
public phones 234

public transport **220-223**
see also individual methods of transport
pubs & bars 123-137
authentic Irish 128
the best 124
music venues 177-179
Punchestown Racecourse 177, 193

Q

Queen Victoria's obelisk 98

R

radio 230-231
rail services *see* train services
Rail Travel Centre 222, **223**
Ranelagh restaurants 116
RDS Showgrounds 177, **183**
Redmond, John 16
religion 232
Rennie, John 28
restaurants 100-116
the best **100**, 115
burgers 106
by cuisine
American 108
French 100-101, 108, 116
Haute cuisine 101, 108-109, 112, 114-115
Indian & Nepalese 101
International 102-105, 109-110, 112, 116
Italian 105, 110, 112-114, 116
Japanese 114
Middle Eastern 107
Modern European 107
Modern Irish 110-111, 114, 115, 116
Oriental 107
Polish 114
Seafood 116
Tapas 111
Vegetarian 108
Wine bars 111-112
for children 159-160
see also p244
Restaurants index
Ridgway, Keith 34
Ritchie, Ian 28
Roche, Kevin 28
Rothe House 213, **216**, *217*, **218**
Rotunda Hospital 81

Roundwood 207, **210**
Royal Hibernian Academy 169
Royal Hospital 93
Royal Institute of the Architects of Ireland 27
RTÉ Concert Orchestra 183, **185**
RTÉ National Symphony Orchestra 183, **185**, *185*
Rubicon Gallery 167, **169**
rugby union 193
Ruskin, John 57
Russborough House **207**, **208**
Russell, George (ÆÆ) 75

S

Sackville Street 79
safety & security 232, 236
Sally Gap 207
Samhain Festival (Hallowe'en) 158
Samuel Beckett Bridge 28
Sandycove 31, **98**, 160
Sandymount restaurants 116
Sandymount Strand 98
Savoy cinema 80, 163, **164**, *165*
schools 233
Schrödinger, Erwin 75
Schwartz, Martha 28
Science Gallery *58-59*, 59
Seapoint 98
Sechnaill, Mael 12
Shaw, George Bernard 20, **30**, 195
birthplace/museum 30, *30*, **77**
Sheridan, Richard 15
Shields, Kevin 176
shoe shops 156
shopping centres 140
shops & services 138-152
the best 139
sightseeing 54-98
the best sights 54
itineraries 55
Sinn Féin 18, 19
Six Nations Rugby **154**, 191, 193
Skerries Mill Complex 96
Skycatcher 28
Slane Castle 202, **203**
Smirke, Robert 86
Smithfield 84
Smithfield Chimney 84-85

Index

smoking 232-233
soccer 193-194
Sorrento Terrace 98
South Great George's
 Street 61
spas *see* wellbeing
speed limits 225
Spencer Dock Bridge
 28
Sphere within a Sphere
 58
Spire, the 28, **78**, **79**
sport & fitness
 191-194
 active sports & fitness
 194
 festivals & events 154,
 155, 157, 158
 for children 161-162
 shops **150**, 152
spectator sports 191-194
St Anne's Church 71
St Audeon's Church 65,
 66, **68**
St Canice's Cathedral,
 Kilkenny *213*, **216**,
 218
St James Gate brewery
 92, 123
St Kevin's Park **71**, **72**
St Lawrence,
 Christopher 95
St Mary's Abbey 95
St Mary's Pro-Cathedral
 80
St Michan's Church 84
St Nicholas of Myra 65
St Patrick's Cathedral
 21, 26, 64, **66**, **68**
St Patrick's Church,
 Trim 203, *205*
St Patrick's Day Parade
 & Festival 154
St Patrick's Park 64, **68**,
 68
St Peter's Catholic
 Church, Drogheda 204
St Stephen's Day 154
**St Stephen's Green
 & Around 69-77**
 accommodation 45-48
 cafés & coffee shops
 122
 galleries 168-169
 play area 160
 pubs & bars 133-134
 restaurants 108-112
 sightseeing 69-77
STDs 228
Steele, Richard 15
Stena Line 220
Stephen's Green Centre
 70
Stoker, Bram 57, 84
Stoneybatter 85
Strongbow 13
students 233
Succat, Maewyn 12
Sunlight Chambers 65

Swift, Jonathan 15, **17**,
 17, 29, 57, 68
Synge, JM **31**, 57

Táin Bó Cúailnge 203
Táin Trail 206
Talbot Botanic Gardens
 97
Talbot Castle 203
Tallon, Ronnie 25
tax 232
taxis 223
 to & from the airport
 221
telephones 233-234
television 230
**Temple Bar & the
 Cathedrals
 61-68**, *66*
 accommodation 39, 45
 cafés & coffee shops
 117-121
 galleries 167-168
 pubs & bars 124-133
 restaurants 100-108
 sightseeing 61-68
Temple Bar Gallery
 & Studios 28, 65,
 167, **168**
Temple Bar Music
 Centre 28
Temple Bar Square
 64
Temple Bar's Chocolate
 Festival 156
theatre 195-198
 festivals 158
Thin Lizzy 65, 176
Thomas Street 91
Tickemaster 176
tickets 184
time 234-235
Tintern Abbey 215
tipping 235
Tóibín, Colm 33, 34
toilets 235
Tone, Wolfe 15
tourist information 200,
 235
tours 57, 58, 235
toy shops 145
train services 200,
 220-221, **222-223**
tickets 221
trams 222
transport *see* individual
 methods of transport
travel advice 226
Trim 203, 204
Trim Castle 203
**Trinity College &
 Around** 27, **57-59**
 accommodation
 37-39
 galleries 167
 pubs & bars 123-124
 sightseeing 57-59

**trips out of town
 200-218**
12 Points! Festival of
 Europe's New Jazz 154

U2 176
U2 Tower 28
universities 233
Ussher Library 27, 57

Vale of Avoca 207
Vicar Street music venue
 91, **181**
Vico Road & bathing
 spot 98
Viking Splash Tour 161,
 162, *162*
Vikings 12
Vinegar Hill 213
vintage shopping 147
visas 235

walking 200
walks 64
 Poolbeg Peninsula 98
War Memorial Gardens
 93, **94**, *94*
weather 236
websites 238
wellbeing 194
Wellington Monument
 86, *86*
Wellington, Duke of 75
Wexford Town 14,
 215-216
Whelan's 176, **183**
Whitefriar Street
 Carmelite Church 61,
 63, *63*
Wicklow Gaol **211**, **212**
Wicklow Gap 207
Wicklow Mountains
 200, **207-212**
Wicklow Town
 210-212
Wicklow Way 207
Wilde, Oscar **30**, 57, **75**,
 77, *123*
William of Orange 15,
 202
William Street South
 138
Winding Stair bookshop
 83, 114, 143
women 236
Women's Mini-
 Marathon 155
Woodward, Benjamin 57
World War I 16
World War II 19

Yeats, WB **30-31**, 75, 80

zoo **86**, 159, 160

Accommodation
Abigail's Hostel 43, *45*
Abode Apartments 48
Ashfield House 44
Avalon House 44
Brooks Hotel 39
Buswells Hotel 41, *42-43*
Cassidy's Hotel 48
Central Hotel 43
Clarence hotel 28, 36, *36*,
 39, **41**, *41*, 65
Clarion Dublin IFSC 37,
 49
Clontarf Castle Hotel 37,
 51
Conrad Hotel 45
Days Inn 50
Deer Park Hotel & Golf
 Courses 52
Dylan 36, 45
Eliza Lodge 43
Fitzpatrick Castle
 Dublin 37, 52
Fitzwilliam 37, **39**
Four Courts 44
Gresham Hotel 37, 48, 80
Harrington Hall 47
Hilton Dublin 47
Hotel Isaac's 50
Hotel St George 49
Isaac's Hostel 51
Kilronan House 47, *50*
Kinlay House 44
Marina House 52
Merrion Hotel 45, *48-49*
Molesworth Court Suites
 42
Morgan 42
Morrison 37, **48**, *52*, 83
Mount Eccles Court 49
Number 31 37, 48
O'Callaghan Davenport
 Hotel 47
Paramount 42, *44*
Park Inn 50
Phoenix Park House 51
Portmarnock Hotel &
 Golf Links 52
Shelbourne Hotel 37, **47**,
 69
Temple Bar Hotel 43
Trinity Capital Hotel 39
Trinity College 39
Trinity Lodge 43
Westbury Hotel 39
Westin 37

Pubs & bars
AKA 124
Auld Dubliner 124
Ba Mizu 124
Bailey 124
Bank 125

Bernard Shaw Bar 133
Bleeding Horse 133
Brazen Head 65, **125**
Bruxelles 125
Café en Seine 125
Cobblestone 85, 128, **136**
Cocoon 125
Corner Stone 133
Dakota 127
Davy Byrnes 65, *124-125*, **127**
Dawson Lounge 127
Doheny & Nesbitt 133
Dragon 127
Duke 127
Farrington's 127
Flannery's 133
Floridita 136
Flowing Tide 83, **136**
Foggy Dew 127
Front Lounge 127
4 Dame Lane 127
Ginger Man 123
Gravediggers 128
Gravity Bar 137
Grogan's Castle Lounge 129
Hairy Lemon 129
Hogan's 129
Hughes' Bar 137
International Bar 129
Isaac Butt Café Bar 136
Jack Nealons 137
JJ Smyths 129
Kavanagh's ('The Gravediggers') 137
Kehoe's 128, *128*, 129
Kiely's 136
Long Hall 129
Long Stone 129
Lord Edward 66, **129**
Market Bar 130, *130*
McDaid's 65, **123**
Messrs Maguire 123

Morrison Hotel Bar 137
Mulligan's 123, 128
Neary's 130
O'Donoghue's 134
O'Neill's 124
O'Neill's 130
O'Reilly Bros aka The Chancery 137
O'Shea's Merchant 130
Ocean Bar 133
Octagon Bar 130
Odeon 134
Oliver St John Gogarty 130
Palace 130
Patrick Conway 136
Peter's Pub 130, *132*
Porterhouse 131
Pravda 136
Ron Blacks 131
Samsara 131
Searson's 134
Sheehan's 132
Smyth's 134
Solas 134, *135*
Southwilliam 132
Stag's Head 132
Temple Bar 132
Thomas Read 133
Toner's 128, 134
Traffic 136
Turk's Head 133
Village 134
Voodoo Lounge 85, **137**
Whelan's 134
Woolshed 136
Zanzibar 137

Restaurants
Antica Venezia 116
Aqua 116
Aya 107
Baccaro, Il 105
Bang Café 110

Bar Italia 78, **112**
Bleu Bistro 107
Bôbó's 72,**108**, 159
Bon Appetit 114
Canal Bank Café **109**, 160
Cedar Tree, The 107
Cellar, The 111
Chapter One 82, **112**
Cornucopia 108
Da Vincenzo 110
DAX 111
Diep Le Shaker 111
Dobbins 110
Ecrivain, L' 108
Ely 111
Enoteca delle Langhe 78, **114**
Fallon & Byrne 102
Farm, The **102**, 160
Fitzers 103
French Paradox 116
Frères Jacques, Les 100
Gospoda Polska 114
Gruel *101*, **103**, 160
Gueuleton, L' 100
Havana 111
Hugo's 111
Itsa4 Sandymount 116
Jaipur 101
Jo'Burger *106*, **108**, 159
Larder, The *102*, 103
Mao 107
Mermaid Café 103
Milano (Pizza Express) 160
Mint *115*, 116
Montys of Kathmandu 101
Nosh 115
101 Talbot 112
Pearl 108
Peploe's 112
Posto, Il 110
Restaurant Patrick

Guilbaud 108
Rhodes D7 112
Shanahan's 108, *110*
Sixty6 103, *105*
Tante Zoé's 103
Tea Room, The 107
Thornton's 101
Town Bar and Grill 105, *109*
Wagamama **107**, 160
Winding Stair 83, *113*, **114**
Yamamori Sushi 114

Cafés & coffee shops
Avoca 117
Bald Barista *117*, 118
Bewley's Oriental Café 65, **118**
Bite of Life 64, **118**
Brick Alley Café 118
Butler's Chocolate Café **118**, 160
Café Cagliostro 122
Cake Café 72, **122**, *122*, 160
Carluccio's 119
Cobalt Café & Gallery 82, **122**
Dunne & Crescenzi 119
Gallery Café 122
Govinda's 119
Hugh Lane Café 122
Lemon Crêpe & Coffee Company **119**, 160
Léon 121
Maison des Gourmets, La 121
Nude *119*, 121
Panem 83, **122**
Queen of Tarts 121
Silk Road 121
Simon's Place 121

Advertisers' Index

Covers

CHQ Building   IFC

Where to Stay

Abode Dublin   38
Clarion Hotel IFSC   38

Sightseeing

Diep Shaker   56
Diep Noodle Bar   56
Dublinia & The Viking World   74
National Museum of Ireland   182
Queen of Tarts   60

Viking Splash Tours   74

Eat, Drink, Shop

Anglers Rest   126
Byblos   104
Cedar Tree   104
Counter Burger   120
Eddie Rockets   104
Hard Rock Café   10
Spectacle Parade Opticians   142
The Bloody Stream   120

Getting Around

Norfolkline.com   224

Major sight or landmark	....	
Railway station	....	
Park	....	
Hospital	....	
Neighbourhood	....	RANELAGH
Pedestrian street	....	
Main road	....	
Church	....	✚
Airport	....	✈
Luas	....	Ⓛ
Luas under construction	....	Ⓛ
Hotels	....	❶
Restaurants	....	❶
Bars	....	❶
Cafés	....	❶

Maps

Ireland	246
Dublin Environs	247
Dublin Overview	248
Dublin City	250
Central Dublin	252
Street Index	253
DART & Rail	255
Luas	256

Trips Out of Town

NORTHERN
IRELAND

Rathlin Is.

Dunfanaghy
Glenveagh
National Park
Aran Is.
Letterkenny
Londonderry
Coleraine
ANTRIM
DONEGAL
LONDONDERRY
Larne
Glencolumbcille
Donegal
Omagh
Ballymena
Killybegs
U L S T E R
Belfast
Interl.
Lough
Neagh
BELFAST
Donaghadee
Ballyshannon
Donegal
Bay
L. Lough
Erne
Harbour
Airport
N15
LEITRIM
Enniskillen
FERMANAGH
N2
Armagh
Portadown
Ballina
Sligo
U. Lough
Erne
Monaghan
ARMAGH
DOWN
Lough Conn
Sligo
MONAGHAN
Newry
Achill Is.
MAYO
SLIGO
Lough
Allen
Cavan
Carlingford
Clare Is.
Castlebar
Knock
Carrick-on-
Shannon
CAVAN
Dundalk
Dundalk
Bay
Clew
Bay
Knock
ROSCOMMON
N3
LOUTH
Westport
Longford
Drogheda
(p214)
C O N N A U G H T
Lough Mask
N17
Roscommon
LONGFORD
N4
Kells
(Ceannanas Mór)
MEATH
Navan
Newgrange
(p211)
Clifden
Connemara
Oughterard
Tuam
Lough Ree
Athlone
Trim
N3
Dublin
Galway
GALWAY
Lough Corrib
Ballinasloe
Mullingar
N4
See p247
DUBLIN
Galway Bay
N6
WESTMEATH
L E I N S T E R
Dún Laoghaire
Aran
Islands
I R E L A N D
OFFALY
Tullamore
KILDARE
Bray
Doolin
The
Burren
Birr
Kildare
Wicklow
Mtns
Blessington
(p207)
Glendalough
(p209)
N18
Lough
Derg
Port Laoise
N7
Wicklow
(p211)
CLARE
Roscrea
LAOIS
Athy
WICKLOW
Ennis
N7
Carlow
Avoca
(p210)
Arklow
Shannon
Thurles
N8
Kilkenny
(p210)
CARLOW
Limerick
N11
Limerick
N24
KILKENNY
WEXFORD
I R I S H
S E A
LIMERICK
Tipperary
TIPPERARY
Enniscorthy
(p211)
KERRY
Tralee
M U N S T E R
N25
Wexford
(p211)
Great
Blasket
Is.
Dingle
Killorglin
Kerry County
Mallow
Dungarvan
Rosslare
Dingle Bay
Lough
Leane
Killarney
CORK
WATERFORD
Waterford
Valentia
Is.
Cahirciveen
Kenmare
Macroom
Cork
Youghal
Waterford
Sneem
N22
Cork
Bear Is.
Glengarriff
Kinsale
Dursey Is.
Bantry
Clonakilty
Bantry Bay
Skibbereen
Clear Is.

St George's Channel

0   100 km
0   60 miles

© Copyright Time Out Group 2009

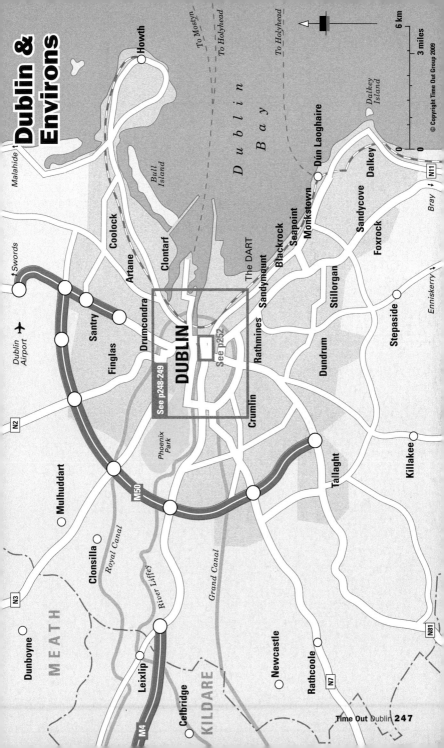

Dublin & Environs

Dublin Bay

To Mostyn
To Holyhead
To Holyhead
To Holyhead

Dalkey Island

© Copyright Time Out Group 2009

6 km
3 miles

Howth

Bull Island

Dún Laoghaire
Dalkey
Sandycove
Foxrock

Bray
N11

Malahide

Coolock
Artane
Clontarf

The DART

Blackrock
Seapoint
Monkstown

Stillorgan

Enniskerry

Stepaside

Swords

Dublin Airport

Santry
Finglas
Drumcondra

DUBLIN

See p248-249
See p252

Rathmines
Sandymount

Dundrum

N2

Crumlin

Killakee

Phoenix Park

M50

Tallaght

Mulhuddart

Royal Canal

Grand Canal

Clonsilla

N81

River Liffey

MEATH

Dunboyne

N3

Newcastle
Rathcoole
N7

Celbridge
Leixlip
M4

KILDARE

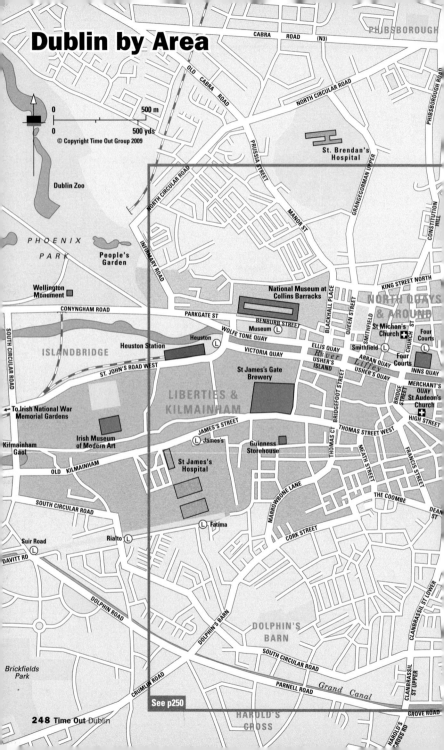

Dublin by Area

CABRA ROAD (N3)

PHIBSBOROUGH

OLD CABRA ROAD

0 ———— 500 m
0 ———— 500 yds
© Copyright Time Out Group 2009

NORTH CIRCULAR ROAD

PHIBSBOROUGH ROAD

PRUSSIA STREET

St. Brendan's Hospital

GRANGEGORMAN UPPER

Dublin Zoo

PHOENIX PARK

People's Garden

Wellington Monument

NORTH CIRCULAR ROAD

INFIRMARY ROAD

MANOR ST

CONSTITUTION MILL

KING STREET NORTH

NORTH QUAYS & AROUND

St Michan's Church

CONYNGHAM ROAD

PARKGATE ST

National Museum at Collins Barracks

BLACKHALL PLACE

QUEEN STREET

Smithfield

CHURCH ST

Four Courts

Four Courts

SOUTH CIRCULAR ROAD

BENBURB STREET

Museum

WOLFE TONE QUAY

Heuston

Smithfield

ARRAN QUAY

INNS QUAY

ISLANDBRIDGE

Heuston Station

VICTORIA QUAY

ELLIS QUAY

USHER'S ISLAND

River Liffey

USHER'S QUAY

MERCHANT'S QUAY

St Audeon's Church

ST. JOHN'S ROAD WEST

St James's Gate Brewery

BRIDGEFOOT STREET

BRIDGE STREET

HIGH STREET

To Irish National War Memorial Gardens

LIBERTIES & KILMAINHAM

Irish Museum of Modern Art

THOMAS CT

THOMAS STREET WEST

MEATH STREET

FRANCIS STREET

Kilmainham Gaol

JAMES'S STREET

James's

Guinness Storehouse

OLD KILMAINHAM

St James's Hospital

THE COOMBE

DEAN ST

SOUTH CIRCULAR ROAD

MARROWBONE LANE

Suir Road

Fatima

Rialto

CORK STREET

DAVITT RD

CLANBRASSIL ST LOWER

DOLPHIN ROAD

Brickfields Park

DOLPHIN'S BARN

DOLPHIN'S BARN

CRUMLIN ROAD

SOUTH CIRCULAR ROAD

Grand Canal

PARNELL ROAD

CLANBRASSIL ST UPPER

See p250

HAROLD'S CROSS RD

GROVE ROAD

HAROLD'S CROSS

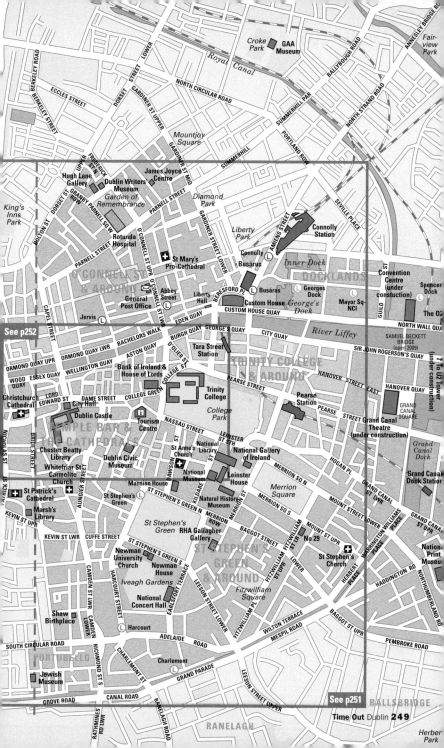

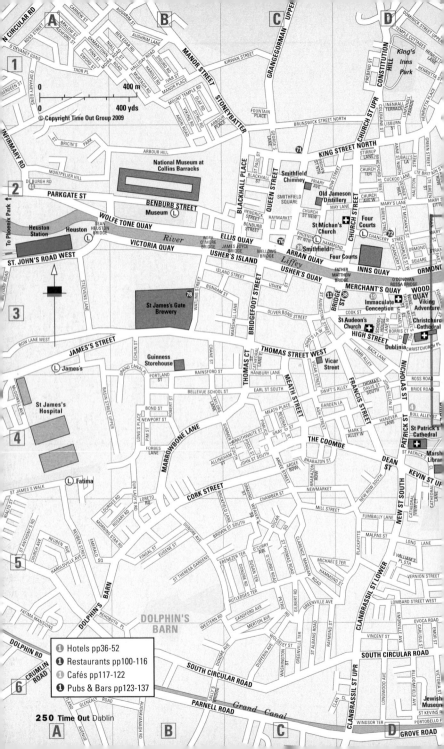

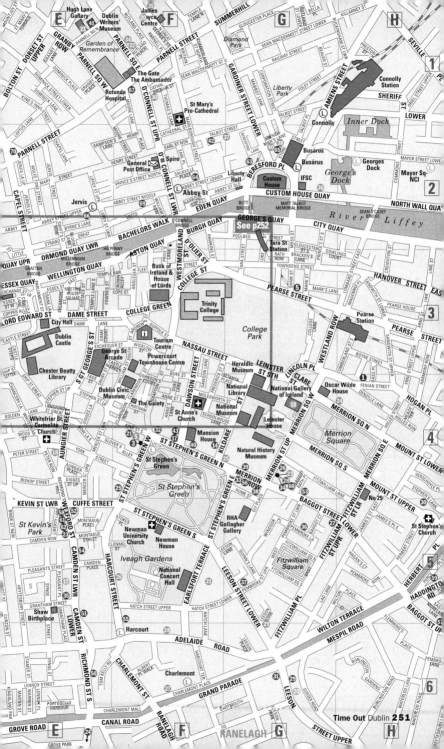

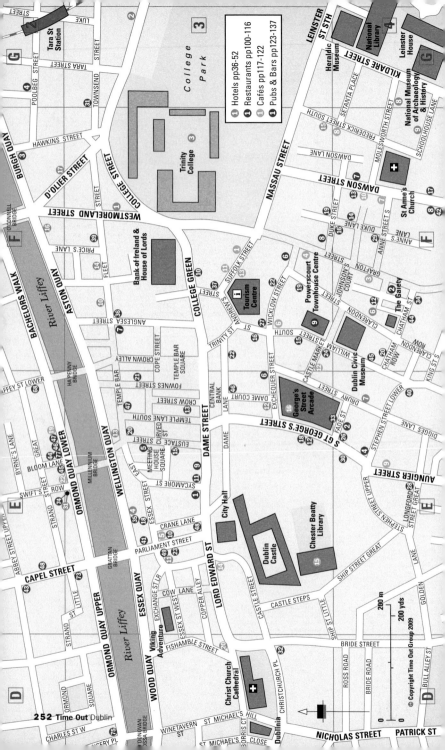

Street Index

Abbey Street Lower - p251 F2/G2
Abbey Street Middle - p251 F2
Abbey Street Old - p251 F2/G2
Abbey Street Upper - p251 E2, p252 E3
Aberdeen Street - p250 A1
Adelaide Road - p251 F6/G6
Albert Place Walk - p251 F6
Allingham Street - p250 D4/C4
Amiens Street - p251 G1/2/H1
Anglesea Row - p250 D2
Anglesea Street - p251 F3, p252 F3
Anne Street North - p250 D2
Anne Street South - p251 F4, p252 F4
Anne's Lane - p251 F4, p252 F4
Arbour Hill - p250 B2
Arbour Place - p250 B1/2
Ardee Row - p250 C4
Ardee Street - p250 C4
Ardri Road - p250 B2
Arklow Street - p250 A1
Arnott Street - p251 E5
Arran Quay - p250 C2/3
Arran Street East - p250 D2/3
Ash Street - p250 C4
Ashford Street - p250 A1
Aston Quay - p251 F2/3, p252 F2/3
Aughavanagh Road - p250 B6
Aughrim Lane - p250 B1
Aughrim Street - p250 B1
Aungier Place - p251 E4
Aungier Street - p251 E4, p252 E4
Bachelors Walk - p251 F2, p252 F2
Back Lane - p250 D3
Baggot Court - p251 G5
Baggot Rath Place - p251 G4
Baggot Street Lower - p251 G4/5/H5
Baggot Street Upper - p251 H5/6
Ball's Lane - p250 D2
Basin Street Upper - p250 A4/B4
Bass Place - p251 H3/4
Beaver Street - p251 G1
Bella Place - p251 G1
Bellevue School Street - p250 B4/C4
Ben Edar Road - p250 B1
Benburb Street - p250 B2/C2
Beresford Lane - p251 G2
Beresford Place - p251 G2
Beresford Street - p250 D2
Bishop Street - p251 E4
Blackhall Place - p250 C2
Blackhall Street - p250 C2
Blackpitts - p250 D5
Blloomfield Avenue - p250 D6
Bloom Lane - p251 E2, p252 E2
Bolton Street - p251 E1
Bond Street - p250 B4
Bonham Street - p250 B3/C3
Borris Court - p250 D3, p252 D3
Bow Lane East - p251 E4
Bow Lane West - p250 A3
Bow Street - p250 C2/D2
Boyne Street - p251 H3
Brabazon Row - p250 C4
Brabazon Street - p250 C4
Bracken's Lane - p251 G3
Braithwaite Street - p250 C4
Brickfield Lane - p250 B4/C5
Bride Road - p250 D4, p252 D4
Bride Street - p250 D4, p252 D4
Bride Street New - p251 E5
Bridge Street - p250 C3/D3
Bridgefoot Street - p250 C3
Britain Place - p251 F2
Brown Street North - p250 C2
Brown Street South - p250 B5/C5

Brunswick Street North - p250 C1/2/D1
Buckingham Street Lower - p251 G1/H1
Bull Alley Street - p250 D4, p252 D4
Burgh Quay - p251 F2, p252 F2
Burlington Gardens - p251 H6
Burlington Road - p251 H6
Butt Bridge - p251 G2
Byrne's Lane - p251 E2, p252 E2
Camden Place - p251 E5
Camden Row - p251 E5
Camden Street Lower - p251 E5/6
Canal Road - p251 E6/F6
Capel Street - p251 E2, p252 E2
Carlisle Street - p250 D6
Carnew Street - p250 A1
Castle Market - p251 F3, p252 F3
Castle Steps - p251 E3, p252 E3
Castle Street - p251 E3, p252 E3
Cathal Brugha Street - p251 F1
Cathedral Lane - p250 D4/5
Cathedral Street - p251 F2
Cathedral View Court - p250 D5
Chamber Street - p250 C4/5
Chancery Lane - p251 E4, p252 E4
Chancery Place - p250 D2/3, p252 D2/3
Chancery Street - p250 D2
Chapel Lane - p251 E2
Charlemont Mall - p251 E6/F6
Charlemont Place - p251 F6
Charlemont Street - p251 F6
Charles Street West - p250 D2/3, p252 D2/3
Chatham Row - p252 F4
Chatham Street - p251 F4, p252 F4
Christchurch Place - p250 D3, p252 D3
Church Avenue - p250 A5
Church Avenue West - p250 D2
Church Street - p250 D2
Church Street New - p250 C2
Church Street Upper - p250 D1/2
Church Terrace - p250 D2
City Quay - p251 G2/H2
Clan Close - p250 C6/D6
Clanbrassil Street Lower - p250 D5/6
Clanbrassil Street Upper - p250 D6
Clare Street - p251 G4
Clarence Mangan Road - p250 C5
Clarendon Row - p251 F4, p252 F4
Clarendon Street - p251 F3/4, p252 F3/4
Clonmel Street - p251 F5
Coleraine Street - p250 D1/2
College Green - p251 F3, p252 F3
College Lane - p251 G3
College Street - p251 F3, p252 F3
Commons Street - p251 H2
Constitution Hill - p250 D1
Cook Street - p250 D3
Cope Street - p251 E3/F3, p252 E3/F3
Copper Alley - p251 E3, p252 E3
Cork Street - p250 B4/5/C4
Corporation Street - p251 G1
Cow Lane - p251 E3, p252 E3
Crane Lane - p251 E3, p252 E3
Crane Street - p250 B3
Creighton Street - p251 H2/3
Crown Alley - p251 F3, p252 F3
Crumlin Road - p250 A6
Cuckoo Lane - p250 D2
Cuffe Street - p251 E5
Cumberland Street North - p251 F1
Cumberland Street South - p251 H3

Curved Street - p252 E3
Curzon Street - p251 E5
Custom House Quay - p251 G2/H2
Dame Court - p251 E3, p252 E3
Dame Lane - p251 E3, p252 E3
Dame Street - p251 E3, p252 E3
Dartmouth Square - p251 F6/G6
Dawson Lane - p251 F3/4, p252 F3/4
Dawson Street - p251 F3/4, p252 F3/4
De Burgh Road - p250 A2
Dean Street - p250 D4
Denzille Lane - p251 H4
Digges Lane - p251 E4, p252 E4
Digges Street Upper - p251 E4
D'Olier Street - p251 F2/3, p252 F2/3
Dolphin Road - p250 A6
Dolphin's Barn - p250 A5/6
Dominick Lane - p251 E1
Dominick Place - p251 E1
Dominick Street Lower - p251 E1
Dominick Street Upper - p250 D1
Donore Avenue - p250 B5/6/C6
Donore Road - p250 C5
Dorset Street Upper - p251 E1
Dowlings Court - p251 G3/H3
Drury Street - p251 E3/4, p252 E3/4
Dufferin Avenue - p250 C6
Duke Lane - p251 F4, p252 F4
Duke Street - p251 F3/4, p252 F3/4
Earl Place - p251 F2
Earl Street North - p251 F2
Earl Street South - p250 C4
Earlsfort Terrace - p251 F5
Eastmoreland Lane - p251 H5
Ebenezer Terrace - p250 C5
Echlin Street - p250 B3
Eden Quay - p251 F2/G2
Ellis Quay - p250 C2
Ely Place - p251 G4/5
Emerald Square - p250 A5
Emor Street - p250 D6
Emorville Avenue - p250 D6
Erne Street Lower - p251 H3
Erne Street Upper - p251 H3/4
Essex Quay - p251 E3, p252 E3
Essex Street East - p251 E3, p252 E3
Essex Street West - p251 E3, p252 E3
Eugene Street - p250 B5
Eustace Street - p251 E3, p252 E3
Exchange Street Lower - p251 E3, p252 E3
Exchequer Street - p251 E3/F3, p252 F3/F3
Fade Street - p251 E4, p252 E4
Father Matthew Bridge - p250 D3
Fatima Mansions - p250 A5/6
Fenian Street - p251 H4
Fingal Street - p250 B5
Finn Street - p250 A1
Fishamble Street - p250 D3, p252 D3
Fitzwilliam Lane - p251 G4/H4
Fitzwilliam Place - p251 G5/6
Fitzwilliam Square North - p251 G5
Fitzwilliam Square South - p251 G5
Fitzwilliam Street Lower - p251 H4/5
Fitzwilliam Street Upper - p251 G5/H5
Fleet Street - p251 F3, p252 F3
Flemming's Place - p251 H5/6
Foley Street - p251 G1
Forbes Lane - p250 B4
Fountain Place - p250 C1

Fownes Street - p251 E3, p252 E3
Francis Street - p250 D3/4
Frederick Street South - p251 F3/4, p252 F3/4
Frenchman's Lane - p251 G2
Friary Avenue - p250 C2
Fumbally Lane - p250 D5
Garden Lane - p250 C4/D4
Gardiner Street Lower - p251 F1/G1/2
George's Hill - p250 D2
George's Lane - p250 C2
George's Quay - p251 G2
Gilbert Road - p250 C5
Glenealy Road - p250 A6/B6
Gloucester Place - p251 G1
Gloucester Street South - p251 G2
Glover's Alley - p251 E4/F4
Golden Lane - p251 E4, p252 E4
Grafton Street - p251 F3/4, p252 F3/4
Granby Lane - p251 E1
Granby Place - p251 E1
Granby Row - p251 E1
Grand Canal Place - p250 B3/4
Grand Parade - p251 F6/G6
Grangegorman Upper - p250 C1
Grantham Place - p251 E5/6
Grantham Street - p251 E5
Grattan Bridge - p251 E3, p252 E3
Gray Street - p250 C4
Greek Street - p250 D2
Green Street - p250 D2
Greenville Avenue - p250 C5
Greenville Terrace - p250 C6
Grove Park - p251 E6
Grove Road - p250 D6, p251 E6
Habcourt Terrace - p251 F6
Haddington Road - p251 H5
Hagan's Court - p251 H5
Halliday Road - p250 B1
Halston Street - p250 D2
Hammond Street - p250 C2
Hammond Street - p250 C5/D5
Hanbury Lane - p250 C3/4
Hanover Lane - p250 D4
Hanover Street East - p251 H3
Ha'penny Bridge - p251 E2/3, p252 E2/3
Harbour Court - p251 F2
Harcourt Street - p251 E5/F5
Harmony Row - p251 H3/4
Harold Road - p250 B1
Haroldville Avenue - p250 A5
Hatch Lane - p251 F5/6
Hatch Street Lower - p251 F5/G5
Hatch Street Upper - p251 F5
Hawkins Street - p251 F2/3, - p252 F2/3
Haymarket - p250 C2
Hendrick Street - p250 C2
Henrietta Lane - p250 D1
Henrietta Place - p250 D1
Henrietta Street - p250 D1
Henry Place - p251 F2
Henry Street - p251 E2/F2
Herbert Place - p251 H5
Herbert Street - p251 H5
Heytesbury Lane - p251 H6
Heytesbury Street - p251 E5/6
High Street - p250 D3
Hogan Place - p251 H4
Holles Row - p251 H4
Holles Street - p251 H4
Hume Street - p251 G4
Infirmary Road - p250 A2
Inns Quay - p250 D3
Island Street - p250 B3/C3
Ivar Street - p250 B1
James's Bare East - p251 H5
James's Street East - p251 H4/5
James's Street - p250 A3/B3

Jervis Lane Lower - p251 E2
Jervis Lane Upper - p251 E2
Jervis Street - p251 E2
John Dillon Street - p250 D4
John Street South - p250 C4
John's Lane West - p250 C3
Johnson's Court - p251 F4, p252 F4
Kevin Street Lower - p251 E5
Kevin Street Upper - p250 D4
Kildare Street - p251 F4/G4, p252 F4/G4
Killarney Street - p251 H1
King Street North - p250 C2/D2
King Street South - p251 F4, p252 F4
King's Inns Street - p251 E1
Kingsland Parade - p251 E6
Kirwan Street - p250 B1/C1
Lad Lane - p251 G5/6/H5
Lamb Alley - p250 D3
Leeson Close - p251 G5
Leeson Lane - p251 F5/G5
Leeson Park - p251 G6
Leeson Place - p251 G6
Leeson Street Lower - p251 F5g/5/6
Leeson Street Upper - p251 G6/H6
Leinster Street South - p251 G3/4, p252 G3/4
Lennox Place - p251 E6
Lennox Street - p251 E6
Liberty Lane - p251 E5
Liffey Street Lower - p251 E2, p252 E2
Liffey Street Upper - p251 E2
Lime Street - p251 H3
Lincoln Place - p251 G3
Linenhall Parade - p250 D1
Linenhall Terrace - p250 D1
Lisburn Street - p250 D1/2
Little Britain Street - p250 D2
Little Green Street - p250 D2
Loftus Lane - p251 E1/2
Lombard Street East - p251 H2/3
Lombard Street West - p250 D5
Long Lane - p250 D5
Longford Street Great - p251 E4, p252 E4
Long's Place - p250 B4
Longwood Avenue - p250 D6
Lord Edward Street - p251 E3, p252 E3
Loreto Road - p250 B4/5
Lotts - p251 F2
Lourdes Road - p250 A5/B4
Luke Street - p251 G2/3, p252 G2/3
Mabbot Lane - p251 G1/2
Magennis Place - p251 H3
Malpas Street - p250 D5
Manor Place - p250 B1
Manor Street - p250 B1
Mark Street - p251 G3
Mark's Alley West - p250 D4
Mark's Lane - p251 G3
Marlborough Street - p251 F1/2
Marrowbone Lane - p250 B4
Marshall Lane - p250 C3
Martin Street - p251 E6
Mary Street - p251 E2
Mary Street Little - p250 D2
Mary's Abbey - p251 E2
Mary's Lane - p250 D2
Mary's Abbey - p250 D2
Matt Talbot Memorial Bridge - p251 G2
May Lane - p250 C2/D2
Mayor Street Lower - p251 H2
McDowell Avenue - p250 A4
Meade's Terrace - p251 H4
Meath Place - p250 C4
Meath Street - p250 C4
Meeting House Square - p251 E3, p252 E3
Mellows Bridge - p250 C2/3
Mercer Street Lower - p251 E4
Mercer Street Upper - p251 E4
Merchant's Quay - p250 D3

Merrion Row - p251 G4
Merrion Square East - p251 H4
Merrion Square North - p251 G4/H4
Merrion Square South - p251 G4/H4
Merrion Street Upper - p251 G4
Merton Avenue - p250 C5/6
Mespil Road - p251 G6/H5/6
Michael's Terrace - p250 C5/D5
Military Road - p250 A3
Mill Street - p250 C5/D5
Millennium Bridge - p251 E3, p252 E3
Moira Road - p250 A1/B1
Molesworth Street - p251 F4, p252 F4
Montague Place - p251 E5
Montague Street - p251 E5
Montpelier Hill - p250 A2
Moore Lane - p251 F1/2
Moore Street - p251 E1/F2
Morning Star Road - p250 A5/B5
Moss Street - p251 G2/3
Mount Street Lower - p251 H4
Mount Street Upper - p251 H4/5
Mount Temple Road - p250 B1
Mountjoy Street - p251 E1
Murtagh Road - p250 B1
Nassau Street - p251 F3/G3, p252 F3/G3
New Great George's St - p251 F1
New Row South - p250 D4/5
New Street South - p250 D4/5
Newmarket - p250 C4
Newport Street - p250 B4
Niall Street - p250 A1/B1
Nicholas Street - p250 D3/4, p252 D3/4
North Circular Road - p250 A1
North Wall Quay - p251 H2
O'Connell Bridge - p251 F2, p252 F2
O'Connell Street Lower - p251 F2
O'Connell Street Upper - p251 F1/2
O'Curry Avenue - p250 C5
O'Curry Road - p250 C5
O'Devaney Gardens - p250 A1
O'Donovan Rossa Bridge - p250 D3, p252 D3
Olaf Road - p250 B1
Oliver Bond Street - p250 C3
Oriel Street Upper - p251 H1
Ormond Quay Lower - p251 E2/3, p252 E2/3
Ormond Quay Upper - p250 D3, p251 E3, p252 E3
Ormond Square - p250 D2/3, p252 D2/3
Ormond Street - p250 C4/5
Oscar Square - p250 C5
Our Lady's Road - p250 B4/5
Ovoca Road - p250 D5/6
Oxmantown Road - p250 A1/B1
Parkgate Street - p250 A2
Parliament Street - p251 E3, p252 E3
Parnell Place - p251 F1
Parnell Road - p250 B6/C6
Parnell Square East - p251 E1/F1
Parnell Square North - p251 E1
Parnell Square West - p251 E1
Parnell Street - p251 E1/2/F1
Patrick Street - p250 D4, p252 D4
Pearse House - p251 H3
Pearse Street - p251 G3/H3
Pembroke Lane - p251 G5/H6
Pembroke Row - p251 H5
Pembroke Street Lower - p251 G5
Pembroke Street Upper - p251 G5
Percy Place - p251 H5
Peter Row - p251 E4
Peter Street - p251 E4
Petrie Road - p250 C5
Phoenix Street Nth - p250 C2
Pim Street - p250 B4
Pimlico - p250 C4
Pleasant Place - p251 E5
Pleasants Street - p251 E5

Poolbeg Street - p251 G2, p252 G2
Poole Street - p250 C4
Portland Street - p250 B3/4
Portobello Harbour - p251 E6
Portobello Road - p250 D6
Prebend Street - p250 D1
Preston Street - p251 H1
Price's Lane - p251 F2/3, p252 F2/3
Prince's Street North - p251 F2
Prince's Street South - p251 G2/3
Queen Street - p250 C2
Quinn's Lane - p251 G5
Railway Street - p251 G1
Rainsford Street - p250 B3
Ranelagh Road - p251 F6
Rath Row - p251 G3
Raymond Street - p250 C5/6
Redmond's Hill - p251 E4
Reginald Street - p250 C4
Rehoboth Place - p250 A5/B6
Reuben Avenue - p250 A5
Reuben Street - p250 A5
Rialto Street - p250 A5
Richmond Street South - p251 E6
Robert Street - p250 B4
Rory O' More Bridge - p250 B2
Rosary Road - p250 B5
Ross Road - p250 D4, p252 D4
Ross Street - p250 A1
Rutland Avenue - p250 A6
Rutland Place - p251 F1
Rutland Street Lower - p251 G1
Rutledges Terrace - p250 C5
Sackville Place - p251 F2
Sally's Bridge - p250 B6
Sampson's Lane - p251 E2
Sandford Avenue - p250 C5
Sandwith Street Lower - p251 H3
Sandwith Street Upper - p251 H3/4
Schoolhouse Lane - p251 F4, p252 F4
Schoolhouse Lane West - p250 D3
Sean Heuston Bridge - p250 A2
Sean MacDermott Street Lower - p251 G1
Sean MacDermott Street Upper - p251 F1
Sean O'Casey Bridge - p252 H2
Setanta Place - p251 F4/G4, p252 F4/G4
Seville Place - p251 H1
Shaw Street - p251 G3
Sheriff Street Lower - p251 H1
Ship Street Great - p251 E4, p252 E4
Ship Street Little - p251 E3, p252 E3
Sigurd Road - p250 B1
Sitric Road - p250 B1/2
South Circular Road - p250 B6/C6/D6
South Great George's Street - p251 E3/4, p252 E3/4
St Albans Road - p250 C5/6
St Andrew's Street - p251 F3, p252 F3
St Anthony's Road - p250 A5
St Augustine Street - p250 C3
St Bricin's Park - p250 A2
St Cathedral Lane East - p250 C3
St James's Walk - p250 A4
St Kevins Road - p250 D6
St Mary's Terrace - p251 E1
St Michael's Close - p250 D3, p252 D3
St Michael's Hill - p250 D3, p252 D3
St Michan's Street - p250 D2
St Patrick's Close - p250 D4
St Paul Street - p250 C2
St Stephen's Green East - p251 F5/G4
St Stephen's Green North - p251 F4
St Stephen's Green South - p251 F5
St Stephen's Green West - p251 F4
St Theresa Gardens - p250 B5

St Thomas Road - p250 C5
St. John's Road West - p250 A3
Stamer Street - p251 E6
Steevens Lane - p250 A3
Stephen Street Lower - p251 E4, p252 E4
Stephen Street Upper - p251 E4, p252 E4
Stephen's Lane - p251 H4/5
Stirrup Lane - p250 D2
Stokes Place - p251 F4
Stoneybatter - p250 B1/C1/2
Store Street - p251 G2
Strand Street Great - p251 E2, p252 E2
Strand Street Little - p250 D3, p251 E3, p252 E3
Suffolk Street - p251 F3, p252 F3
Summer Street South - p250 B4/C4
Summerhill - p251 F1/G1
Susan Terrace - p250 C5
Sussex Road - p251 G6
Swift's Row - p251 E2, p252 E2
Swift's Alley - p250 C4/D4
Sword Street - p250 A1
Sycamore Street - p251 E3, p252 E3
Synge Street - p251 E5/6
Talbot Place - p251 G1/2
Talbot Street - p251 F2/G1/2
Tara Street - p251 G2/3, p252 G2/3
Taylors Lane - p250 B4
Temple Bar - p251 E3/F3, p252 E3/F3
Temple Cottages - p250 D1
Temple Lane North - p251 F1
Temple Lane South - p251 E3, p252 E3
The Coombe - p250 C4/D4
Thomas Court - p250 C3/4
Thomas Davis Street South - p250 D4
Thomas Street West – p250 C3
Thomas's Lane - p251 F1
Thor Place - p250 A1
Tom Kelly Road - p251 E6
Townsend Street - p251 G3, p252 G3
Usher Street - p250 C3
Usher's Island - p250 B3/C3
Usher's Quay - p250 C3
Vernion Street - p250 D5
Verschoyle Place - p251 H4
Vicar Street - p250 C3/4
Victoria Quay - p250 B2/3
Victoria Street - p250 D6
Viking Road - p250 B1/2
Vincent Street - p250 D6
Warren Street - p251 E6
Washington Street - p250 C6
Waterloo Lane - p251 H6
Waterloo Road - p251 H6
Watling Street - p250 B3
Weaver's Square - p250 C5
Wellington Quay - p251 E3, p252 E3
Western Road - p250 B5/6
Westland Row - p251 G3
Westmoreland Street - p251 F2/3, p252 F2/3
Wexford Street - p251 E5
Whitefriar Street - p251 E4
Wicklow Street - p251 F3, p252 F3
William Street South - p251 F3, p252 F3
William's Place South - p250 D5
William's Row - p251 F2
Wilton Place - p251 G5/H5
Wilton Terrace - p251 G6/H5
Windsor Place - p251 G5
Windsor Terrace - p250 D6
Winetavern Street - p250 D3, p252 D3
Wolfe Tone Quay - p250 A2/B2
Wolfe Tone Street - p251 E2
Wolseley Street - p250 C6
Wood Quay - p250 D3, p252 D3
Wood Street - p251 E4
York Street - p251 E4/F4

The DART Network

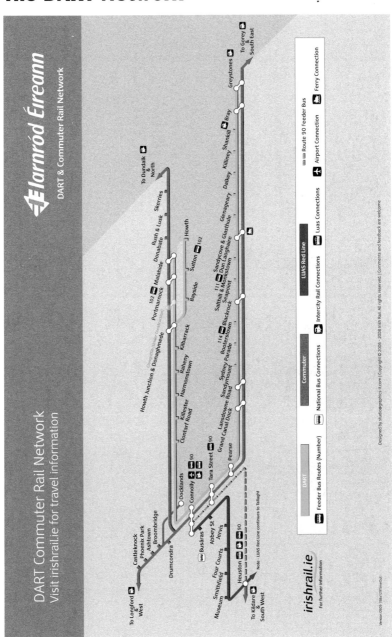

DART Commuter Rail Network
Visit irishrail.ie for travel information

Iarnród Éireann
DART & Commuter Rail Network

To Longford & West
Castleknock
Phoenix Park
Ashtown
Broombridge
Drumcondra
Docklands
Connolly
Tara Street
Busáras
Four Courts
Smithfield
Museum
Heuston
Abbey St
Jervis
Pearse
Grand Canal Dock
Lansdowne Road
Sandymount
Sydney Parade
Booterstown
Blackrock
Seapoint
Salthill & Monkstown
Dun Laoghaire
Sandycove & Glasthule
Glenageary
Dalkey
Killiney
Shankill
Bray
Greystones
To Gorey & South East
To Kildare & South West

note - LUAS Red Line continues to Tallaght

Clontarf Road
Killester
Harmonstown
Raheny
Kilbarrack
Howth Junction & Donaghmede
Donaghmede Station Under Construction
Portmarnock
Malahide
Donabate
Rush & Lusk
Skerries
To Dundalk & North
Bayside
Sutton
Howth

irishrail.ie
For further information

Designed by studioagraphics-it.com | Copyright © 2005 - 2008 Irish Rail. All rights reserved. | Comments and feedback are welcome

| DART | Commuter | LUAS Red Line | Route 90 Feeder Bus |

Feeder Bus Routes (Number)
National Bus Connections
Intercity Rail Connections
Luas Connections
Airport Connection
Ferry Connection

Version 0909 19kn12FlimeOut

The LUAS Network

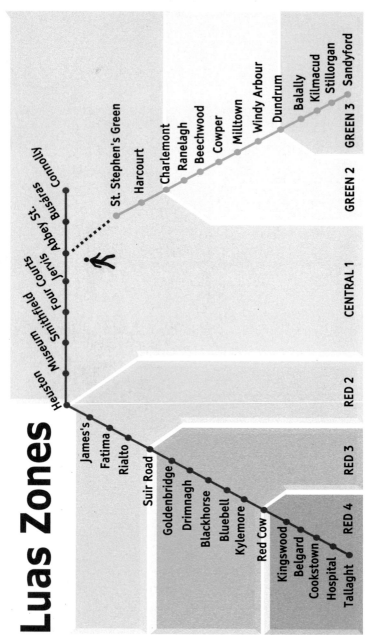

Luas Zones

Connolly
Busáras
Abbey St.
Jervis
Four Courts
Smithfield
Museum
Heuston

St. Stephen's Green
Harcourt
Charlemont
Ranelagh
Beechwood
Cowper
Milltown
Windy Arbour
Dundrum
Balally
Kilmacud
Stillorgan
Sandyford

GREEN 2   GREEN 3

CENTRAL 1

James's
Fatima
Rialto
Suir Road
Goldenbridge
Drimnagh
Blackhorse
Bluebell
Kylemore
Red Cow
Kingswood
Belgard
Cookstown
Hospital
Tallaght

RED 2   RED 3   RED 4